Windows 2000
Server

Published by :

FIREWALL MEDIA

(*An Imprint of Laxmi Publications Pvt. Ltd.*)

113, Golden House, Daryaganj,

New Delhi-110002

Phone : 011-43 53 25 00

Fax : 011-43 53 25 28

www.laxmipublications.com

info@laxmipublications.com

Economy Edition Price : **Rs. 250.00** *Only.* *Edition* : 2008

OFFICES

India

© **Bangalore**	080-26 61 15 61
© **Chennai**	044-24 34 47 26
© **Cochin**	0484-239 70 04
© **Guwahati**	0361-254 36 69, 251 38 81
© **Hyderabad**	040-24 65 23 33
© **Jalandhar**	0181-222 12 72
© **Kolkata**	033-22 27 37 73, 22 27 52 47
© **Lucknow**	0522-220 95 78
© **Mumbai**	022-24 91 54 15, 24 92 78 69
© **Ranchi**	0651-230 77 64

USA

Boston

11, Leavitt Street, Hingham,

MA 02043, USA

FKA-2742-250-KA_WINDOWS 2000 SERVER

ISBN: 81-7008-467-9

C—14389/07/06

Printed at : Sanjeev Offset Press, Delhi.

Introduction Chapter 1

A. Overview of Windows 2000 operating systems . . **8**

B. Windows 2000 Server **11**

Installing Windows 2000 Advanced Server Chapter 2

A. Required configuration **20**

B. Installing **20**

Configuring the system Chapter 3

A. Registry **42**

B. Configuring devices **48**

C. Choosing a protocol **65**

D. Optimizing bindings **73**

DNS Chapter 4

A. TCP/IP and Internet protocols 78

B. Domain Name System 86

Active Directory Chapter 5

A. Overview 108

B. Terminology 109

C. Installing 113

D. Roles of domain controllers 123

E. Replication 128

F. Uninstalling 137

Group policies Chapter 6

A. Overview 142

B. Managing GPOs 142

C. Group policy settings 145

D. User environment 147

E. Applying GPOs 149

User and group management Chapter 7

A. Managing a local computer 154

B. Managing a domain 163

Managing disk resources — Chapter 8

A. File systems 188

B. Sharing folders 190

C. Access security 202

D. DFS 212

E. Managing disk quotas 219

F.

Configuring disks, partitions and volumes — Chapter 9

A. Basic disks 226

B. Dynamic disks 231

C. Fault tolerance 239

Security Chapter 10

A. Encrypting documents 250

B. Security of IP network traffic 255

C. Accounts and password security 257

D. Audit 263

E. User rights 269

F. Security options 270

Network services Chapter 11

A. Dynamic Host Configuration Protocol 272

B. Windows Internet Name Service 289

C. Remote access 299

Backing up, restoring and troubleshooting

Chapter 12

A. Backing up **326**

B. Restoring **331**

C. Troubleshooting **335**

Introduction

A. **Overview of Windows 2000 operating systems** **8**

1. Pre-emptive and co-operative multitasking . . . **8**
2. Multithreading **9**
3. Multiprocessing **9**
4. Microsoft Windows 2000 architecture **10**

B. **Windows 2000 Server** **11**

1. Windows 2000 Professional **12**
2. Windows 2000 Server **15**
3. Windows 2000 Advanced Server **18**
4. Windows 2000 Datacenter Server **18**

A. Overview of Windows 2000 operating systems

Before you start looking at Windows 2000, you must note that this is by no means a completely new operating system. Windows 2000 is an evolved version of the Windows NT 4.0 system that draws on Microsoft's experience in the fields of servers and operating systems. However, Windows 2000 is the biggest server development that Microsoft has undertaken since 1993. This operating system benefits from increased power, increased reliability and increased security. Under Windows 2000, administration is easier. In addition, flexible administration tools that can be fully customized in order to assist you with these tasks.
In order fully to understand the characteristics of Microsoft operating systems, a few concepts must be defined.
First, this chapter will describe multitasking. It will clearly distinguish between co-operative and pre-emptive multitasking. Next, multithreading will be studied, and this will be followed by multiprocessing. When you examine multiprocessing, you will discover how asymmetric multiprocessing can be used in order to improve fault tolerance.

1. Pre-emptive and co-operative multitasking

Multitasking is the ability of an operating system to manage several programs at once. It allocates processor time to each of the programs in turn, so that they can execute. This means that devices and memory must be shared so that the programs can use them. Multitasking can be implemented in two ways: co-operative multitasking and pre-emptive multitasking.
With **co-operative multitasking**, one of the applications that is running on the operating system uses the processor (together with the associated resources). Then, the application frees the processor, and allows the next application in the queue to use it. Each task depends on the others. This means that if a task goes into a loop, or gets blocked, then it will pause all the applications, and it will sometimes even pause the operating system itself. This implementation is used with 16bit Windows systems.
With **pre-emptive multitasking**, each application uses the processor either for a pre-determined time period, or until another application is given a higher priority than that of the current application. Scheduling and allocation of CPU time for current applications is handled by the operating system without consulting applications that have already run.

Consequently, if an application locks up, it loses its initial processor time and is put to one side, without blocking the system or the other applications. The sharing of the processor and resources (such as printer ports and the keyboard) between applications is managed by the operating system.

2. Multithreading

Multithreading is implemented during the development of a software application, and is managed by the operating system. A thread can be an executable unit, or a part of a program. It can even be the entire program if the application does not offer multithreading.
Multithreading means that several tasks can be carried out "simultaneously", within the same application. With Word for example, when you enter text, the characters are displayed with the required formatting, and any spelling mistakes are corrected at the same time. Furthermore, threads in the same process share the same memory space.

3. Multiprocessing

Multiprocessing is the ability of the operating system to use the processors that are present in the workstation, in order to manage the Windows 2000 system and to run the applications. There are two types of multiprocessing:

- Asymmetric multiprocessing (ASMP): one processor is reserved for the system while the others are used for the applications.
- Symmetric multiprocessing (SMP): execution requests that are made by the operating system and by applications are distributed amongst the different processors. In this case, the system will always have a percentage of free processor time.

The multiprocessing facilities in Windows 2000 are vastly superior to those in NT 4.0. Furthermore, you can now use the task manager so as to link a given process to a given processor.

4. Microsoft Windows 2000 architecture

Windows 2000 is a multitask, multithread 32bit operating system with SMP architecture.

Windows 2000 is made up of layered operating systems and micro-kernel based client/server systems. The grouping together of these two technologies has allowed two parts of Windows 2000 to be distinguished: **execute (or kernel) mode**, and **user** (or application) mode.

Kernel mode

Kernel mode groups together the set of system components that run in this mode. These components are called executive services and have priority in the use of the processor. The kernel plays a key role, as it is responsible for providing the applications with memory, for choosing the processes that must be run at a specific time, and for communicating with the peripherals. The applications depend on the kernel for all their needs. This means that they do not come into direct contact with the peripheral devices, which prevents them from provoking system failure. It must be noted that the Windows 2000 kernel is a development of the Windows NT 4.0 kernel and features improvements such as the handling of several user sessions on the same machine (which allows Windows 2000 to act as a terminal server), and the addition of processor quotas in order to meet the needs of Internet Information Server 5 (such as the ability of controlling the amount of processor time that is granted to each Web site, and the logging of the CPU cycles that are used for each Web query).

Unlike that of Windows NT 4.0, the Windows 2000 kernel supports **WDM** (Windows Driver Model) architecture. This is a new driver model that allows you to use the same drivers on Windows 98 and on Windows 2000. Whilst on Windows NT 4.0 the applications run most of their tasks in user mode, WDM architecture allows these jobs to be transposed into kernel mode, thus allowing them to run quicker. However, in order to take advantage of this feature, applications must be specifically written for this purpose.
Windows 2000 supports **EMA** (Enterprise Memory Architecture), which allows applications to use up to 32 GB of memory. This is a very useful feature for database servers that manage large amounts of data. This is because data can be handled much quicker in RAM than on disk.

In order to benefit from this architecture, your hardware must support it. In addition, the applications must be developed in a specific way. SQL Server is an example of an application that can use this feature.

Kernel mode is equipped with a Plug-and-Play module that reduces the time that is required to configure the hardware. In addition, kernel mode offers an energy management module that runs on **OnNow/ACPI technology** and that reduces the energy that is consumed by the users.
The improvements that have been made to the kernel allow Windows 2000 to operate in cluster mode (two machines that can take over from one another in the case of a problem).

Finally, it must be noted that kernel mode has been developed so as to support any application, whatever the language that is used. To this end, Windows 2000 uses UNICODE, which is a standard that defines a correspondence between bytes and characters. Unlike the ANSI standard that requires an operating system to be developed for each language, UNICODE allows you to use a single source, irrespective of the language that is used. This feature means that you can change the language of the interface without restarting the machine.

User mode

Unlike kernel mode, user mode groups together protected subsystems that underlie user applications. User mode processes do not have direct access to the hardware; they are limited to a memory area that is allocated to them, and they are processed with a low priority level. One of the major developments of Windows 2000 user mode is the presence of Active Directory in the security subsystem.

B. Windows 2000 Server

The Windows 2000 range comprises four platforms:
- Windows 2000 Professional,
- Windows 2000 Server,
- Windows 2000 Advanced Server,
- Windows 2000 Datacenter Server.

Windows 2000 Professional is a workstation product, whilst the three other platforms are Windows 2000 server products. This section describes these different versions, and specifies for each of them, their role in a company and the hardware capacities that are required.

1. Windows 2000 Professional

The purpose of this operating system is progressively to replace Windows 98 and Windows NT 4.0. Windows 2000 Professional combines the simplicity of using Windows 98 with the performance reliability of Windows NT 4.0. In addition, it offers new features that allow you to optimize such aspects as resource access and security in a Windows 2000 domain environment. Furthermore, this operating system offers other features such as plug-and-play, energy options, the new WDM drivers, and the recognition of over 6500 hardware devices.

Resource access

Windows 2000 Professional supports the Active Directory client. This provides access to the resources of the directory database (according to the permissions that have been granted). It also provides access to the resources that are contained in a **DFS** (Distributed File System) topology. This allows users to carry out searches in Active Directory, in order to find an item such as a printer, a contact, a person or a shared directory, by knowing only one characteristic of the object concerned (such as the name, the location or the telephone number).
Users of portable computers will find it easier to work on documents that are stored on the network. Thanks to **work offline** technology, users can work transparently on their documents via the network in the same way as they would work with local files. Thereby, it is ensured that they will always have an up-to-date version of the document, thanks to a synchronization mechanism that runs upon opening and closing a session. In addition they can use the Networking Connection Wizard in order to set up a secure connection to their company network easily, using a remote connection, or simply by creating a **VPN** (Virtual Private Network) via the Internet. Also, IPP (*Internet Printing Protocol*) allows mobile users to print documents via the Internet on their printers in their offices.

Simplified installation

When you are implementing a network architecture, one of the longest phases is the installation of the workstations. As network administrator, you will save time when you install Windows 2000. You can install a Windows 2000 Professional workstation without leaving your office, thanks to a remote installation service that is supplied with the server versions of Windows 2000. This service is called RIS (*Remote Installation Service*). Other techniques are also provided in order to reduce the time that you spend in installing workstations. These include the **sysprep.exe** utility, which can be used in order to duplicate the image of a disk on other workstations, using a disk duplication tool from a third-party manufacturer.

Previously, you had to fill in several fields and select several options during the installation process, which meant that you had to stay in front of your computer. The new graphic installation script creation utility allows you to create files that provide responses automatically during the installation process.

File systems

Here again, Windows 2000 is more developed than Windows NT 4.0, as the latter operating system recognizes only FAT16 and NTFS file systems. In addition, Windows 2000 supports the FAT32 file system (which is used by Windows 95 OSR2 and Windows 98 systems).

Furthermore, NTFS has evolved with the version 5.0 that is offered in Windows 2000. The features that are offered with this version include file encryption, disk quota management and distributed link tracking.

Utilities such as Disk Defragmenter, Disk Cleanup and Scandisk allow you to maintain optimal space usage on your disks.

A major development of the backup manager must also be noted. The new backup manager allows you to backup data to different media such as tapes, recordable CD-ROMs, logical disks, ZIP drives and external hard disks. An integrated backup planning utility simplifies the design of a backup plan.

Security

Security is important for all computing networks. Windows 2000 provides a marked improvement in this field. Amongst the numerous security improvements, a major advance concerns file encryption on NTFS 5 volumes. This public key / private key encryption technique means that only the user who encrypted a document will be allowed to read it. This is done transparently (the document is decrypted automatically without any user intervention). This function is added to the NTFS permissions. However, this feature does not allow you to encrypt documents when you transmit them on the network. The **IPSec** protocol allows you to encrypt all IP traffic within the same LAN, as with a non-secure network such as using VPNs on the Internet. It must be noted that the IPSec (IP Security) standard was developed by the IETF (*Internet Engineering Task Force*) and allows any system that uses IPSec to communicate, thereby ensuring secure IP traffic.

Although versions of Windows NT authenticate using the NTLM protocol, Windows 2000 uses the Kerberos v5 protocol in order to authenticate users. Windows 2000 still supports NTLM protocol for backward compatibility reasons. Thus, a Windows 2000 Workstation that is integrated in a Windows NT4 domain will be authenticated by NTLM. The Kerberos authentication method is quicker and more secure than NTLM. In addition, as it is a standard, a UNIX host can be authenticated by a Windows 2000 domain controller by having an account in Active Directory. Kerberos is also used for authentication across inter-domain trust relationships.

For more information, see RFC 1510, which describes the Kerberos protocol.

Minimal configuration

- 166 MHz processor.
- 32 MB of RAM (64 MB is recommended).
- 685 MB of disk space. You should allow 1 GB in order to allow for future system development.

It is very important to know the hardware items that make up your computer. These hardware items must be included in the Hardware Compatibility List (HCL), so as to ensure the correct functioning of your system.

If you intend to upgrade your old system (Windows 95/98 or NT Workstation), you can use the command **winnt32.exe**. **/checkupgradeonly**, so as to make a list of the hardware items on your workstation that will not be supported by Windows 2000.

2. Windows 2000 Server

The Windows 2000 Server version offers all the features of Windows 2000 Professional, uses the strong points of Windows NT 4.0 Server, and provides numerous additional features, all of which makes it a formidable enterprise server.

Characteristics

Adapting to large networks

Windows 2000 was originally designed to manage very big networks. It meets all administration needs by organizing domains into administrative units. Even for very big networks, a single domain is sufficient. This is because the Windows 2000 directory database allows you to store several million objects (such as user accounts and computer accounts).

Active Directory Service

One of the major new features of Windows 2000 Server is that it manages network objects using a directory. Previously, user accounts, computer accounts and groups were stored in a database called SAM. This database resided on the primary domain controller and a copy was kept on the backup domain controllers. When the primary domain controller was unavailable, users could still open a session on the domain, but the SAM could not be modified without promoting a backup domain controller. In addition, administration was limited by the number of objects that could not exceed 40 000.
The Active Directory database is duplicated on all the Windows 2000 domain controllers, each of which has a read/write copy. This feature enhances fault tolerance. This approach simplifies administration and ensures the development capacity of the system. The total cost of ownership (TCO) is very competitive. This is because the group strategies belong to Active Directory, which limits the time that is required in order to configure each client machine concerning distribution of applications and to set up user working environments. An additional strong point of active directory is that it uses a set of standard protocols. This makes it compatible with any other system. These protocols include the Domain Name System (DNS) and the LDAP protocol for database access.

Administrative tools

Although a number of administration tools are provided as standard, Windows 2000 offers Microsoft Management Console (MMC), which allows you to customize and to create several consoles so as to meet your administration needs. Thereby, you have all the tools that you require.

Enhancing network services

Apart from the supplementary services that are available with Windows 2000, such as the index service, the certificate service, the remote installation service (RIS) and the remote storage service, some services have been markedly improved. For example the DDNS (*Dynamic DNS*) that authorizes DNS and DHCP clients to register with a DNS server automatically. Again the TCO is reduced in this case. This is because the administrator no longer need be concerned by the update of the DNS database, as this item develops according to the clients. Integrating DNS zones into Active Directory provides fault tolerance and load sharing.
The DHCP service is also optimized so as to help clients to register with the DNS server. The class extensions allow you to attribute configurations according to criteria such as that of belonging to a class. You can also create super-extensions and multicast extensions.
Internet services have also been improved thanks to the Windows 2000 kernel, which supports processor quotas and the different supplementary features such as IPP (Internet Printing Protocol), which allows you to print via the Internet, and the reservation of bandwidth for Web sites.

Remote network access

Increasingly, companies need to access remote networks via, telephone lines, the Internet, X25 networks, Frame Relay networks, ATM or ISDN. These requirements are met by standard versions of Windows 2000. These provide a very effective, remote access service that allows you act as remote access server and VPN (Virtual Private Network) server. The security is ensured on the IP transit level, in the tunnel that is created by PPTP or L2TP protocols, and on authentication level.

Backup

The backup utility that is supplied with Windows 2000 is now comparable to tools that are supplied by specialists in this field. Using a graphic calendar, you can program all types of backup.

A major advantage of this utility is that it allows you to make a full backup of your system and to restore a server without losing information. Active Directory objects can be restored also.

Network monitor

The network monitor is derived from that which is delivered with SMS. It allows you to capture frames that are being transmitted on the network. You can do this by filtering them, either according to specific protocols, or according to specific machines, or according to specific contents. This is an essential tool that allows you to understand and to analyze your network. It will help you to solve problems in many situations.

Windows 2000 a veritable router

In addition to the implementation of RIP v2, the routing features of Windows 2000 have been enhanced by the use of OSPF (*Open Shortest Path First*), which is a widely used, link state routing protocol. RIP is used with smaller networks. whilst OSPF is more suitable for large networks.

Terminal Services

The features of Windows NT 4 Terminal Edition are offered by the Windows 2000 Server versions in the form of a service. This service provides a Windows 2000 desktop to users who have machines that are not powerful, and that do not support 32bit applications. The desktop along with the applications that are run by the user in the terminal server session, are run entirely on the server. In addition, administrators can install Terminal Server services with the sole objective of remotely administering servers.

Minimal configuration

- 166 MHz processor.
- 64 MB of RAM (128 MB is recommended).
- 685 MB of disk space. You should allow 1 GB in order to allow for future system development.

It is very important to know the hardware items that make up your computer. These hardware items must be included in the Hardware Compatibility List (HCL), so as to ensure the correct functioning of your system.

3. Windows 2000 Advanced Server

The Windows 2000 Advanced Server version offers the same features as the Server version. In addition, Advanced Server allows you to organize several servers into a cluster configuration. The advantage of this feature is that users can access services 24 hours a day, as, if one server fails, the other server in the cluster will take over automatically. Similarly, if an application fails, you can start it on the other server. In addition to fault tolerance features, organizing machines into a cluster configuration allows you to spread the workload for network services such as Web services.

This Windows 2000 version is more suitable than the Server version, for the processing of large volumes of information (for example, for databases, transactions or for decision aids). This capacity is provided by the EMA (Enterprise Memory Architecture), which allows Windows 2000 to manage up to 8 GB of RAM on Intel.
SMP features allow Windows 2000 Advanced Server to run on 8 processors.

4. Windows 2000 Datacenter Server

Windows 2000 Datacenter Server is characterized by the SMP, which can be configured so as to allow a Windows 2000 server to manage up to 32 processors. This version can manage up to 64 GB of RAM on Intel systems.
Of course, the Datacenter Server version offers all the features that are supported by Windows 2000 Server, along with the cluster configuration and the workload distribution features.

Installing Windows 2000 Advanced Server

A. **Required configuration** **20**

B. **Installing** **20**

1. Disk partitioning scheme **21**
2. Choosing a file system **22**
3. Licensing mode **23**
4. Domain planning **24**
5. Installing using a CD-ROM **25**
6. Installing from the network **28**
7. Using disk duplication **36**
8. Promoting a stand-alone server to member server **39**

A. Required configuration

You can install Microsoft Windows 2000 Advanced Server in different ways. Whichever method you choose, you must carry out a series of tasks that is called the "pre-installation". If you carry out these tasks you will save a lot of time.

First you must check that the hardware that will be used is referenced in the hardware compatibility list (HCL) that is supplied by Microsoft. In fact, a hardware item that in not included in this list could make the operating system malfunction, and cause you to lose time in diagnosing the problem. You can find a copy of this HCL (**HCL.txt**) on the Windows 2000 CD-ROM, in the **support** directory. Alternatively, it is available on the Internet at the address http://www.microsoft.com/hwtest/hcl.

Amongst the pre-installation tasks, it is useful to list certain information such as the choice of licensing mode, how your disks are partitioned, the choice of file systems and the role that your server plays (stand-alone or member server).

Minimal configuration required for the installation of Microsoft Windows 2000 - Server versions:

- Processor: Pentium 166 MHZ.
- 64 MB of RAM (128 MB is recommended) for Intel type computers.
- 1.2 GB of disk space for the system partition (2 GB is recommended so as to accommodate future system evolution).
- Standard VGA graphic card
- Network adapter.
- Keyboard, mouse or other pointer peripheral.
- CD-ROM drive, floppydisk drive (optional). Here is the list of input/output ports that are most commonly used.

B. Installing

During the installation phase, you can modify your partitioning scheme and carry out certain operations on your disks (delete and create partitions). Use this feature simply to configure the partition on which you want to install the system. Subsequently, you can use the **Disk Manager** utility that is supplied with Windows 2000 in order to configure your other partitions or disks.

It is strongly recommended that you install your system on a 2GB partition in order to allow for the future development of your system. If you do not allow enough space for the system partition, you might have to reinstall your server because you lack space (possible causes include evolution of the swap file and the installation of applications that store information on the system partition).

1. Disk partitioning scheme

During the installation phase, you can modify your partitioning scheme and carry out certain operations on your hard disks. This is necessary in order to specify the partitions on which Windows 2000 must be installed.

You can install the preloader, (Windows 2000 boot sector) and the loader, **NTLDR**, on the first partition (the **system partition**), and you can install the rest of the files on a separate partition (the **boot partition**).

On an Intel platform, the system partition is the primary (active) partition.

The system partition does not need a great deal of space. In most cases, 10 MB is ample.

The essential files that are contained on this partition can be duplicated onto a boot diskette. This will provide not only a copy of these files, but also a backup diskette that you can use in the event of a simple system boot problem.

In the most critical cases, the full set of four backup diskettes provide access to the Windows 2000 system in order to allow you to carry out repair work, for instance.
The boot partition, which contains system files such as the Windows 2000 kernel, must have at least 1.2 GB of space This will allow for future system developments such as the inclusion of numerous highvolume DLLs into the system32 subdirectory of the installation directory. In addition, you must not forget to allow space for the swap file and a possible spool file.
This partition will be converted to NTFS for security reasons.

Alternatively, you can install Windows 2000 completely on a single partition. In this case the system partition and the boot partition will be the same.

2. Choosing a file system

Windows 2000 supports FAT, FAT32 and NTFS file systems.

NTFS file system

NTFS (*NT File system*) 5.0 is the recommended file system for Windows 2000. It enhances security by allowing security control at directory and file level. It manages disk and file compression. In addition, it allows users to control the disks by applying quotas and providing data encryption.
If you wish to configure your server as domain controller, you must have at least one partition that is formatted in NTFS in order to store the shared system volume.

FAT/FAT32 file system

If you want still to be able to start up your old operating system, such as MS-DOS, Windows 95 or Windows 98, then you must keep a file system that is recognized by the systems that make up the multiple boot. FAT and FAT32 do not provide security control at file and directory level. The FAT file system does not support partitions larger than 2 GB. FAT32 is a development of FAT that overcomes this limitation.

You can convert a disk from FAT/FAT32 format to NTFS format without losing data. However, it must be noted that this operation is irreversible. You can make this conversion using the following command:
CONVERT 'drive': /FS:NTFS

If you wish to convert from NTFS to another file system, you must back up your data and format the partition for the desired file system. You can then restore your data.

With Windows 2000 you must choose NTFS in the following circumstances:

- Windows 2000 is the only operating system that is installed.
- You wish to install file and print services for Macintosh.
- You would like to have local security control (this is strongly recommended!).
- You would like efficiently to manage large partitions (of over 500 MB).
- An audit of the file system is required.
- You want to manage compression individually.
- You want to keep permission equivalences when you migrate Novell files to Windows.

- You wish to manage disk quotas.
- You wish to encrypt your data (EFS).
- You wish to mount volumes in empty directories.
- You wish to implement remote storage.
- You wish to install Active Directory.

If you decide to use NTFS 5.0, it is advisable to convert your file system during the installation process. This is because permissions are applied for certain specific groups in specific directories in the file system tree. If you convert later using the **convert** command, then irreversible local **Full Control** permissions will be granted to the **Everyone** group.

3. Licensing mode

During the installation phase, you will be asked to choose the licensing mode. You can choose between the **per server licensing mode** and the **per seat licensing mode.**

Per server licensing

The **SMB** (*Server Message Block*) server service, which is based on the NetBIOS protocol, introduces this idea of Microsoft license. The license applies to a given computer that sets up one or more simultaneous connections. Thus, one computer counts as one license, even if several connections are set up on the server.
Consequently, the number of **per server licenses** that is required for a specific server corresponds to the **maximum number of different clients** that could connect to this server at the same time.

When the maximum number of connections is reached, an error message appears and new connections are refused. In this case a message is recoded in the ***Event Viewer.***

You can alter the number of per server licenses using the ***Control panel - Licensing*** *icon.*

Per seat licensing

In this licensing mode, the seat, or the specific client is subject to a license. This license corresponds to a **right of connection**, it does not correspond to the right to add specific software in order to allow system interconnection. In this case, the servers have no particular restriction concerning the maximum number of concurrent connections, provided that each client has a recognized seat.

You can convert from per server licensing mode to per seat licensing mode at any time using the ***Control Panel - Licensing****. However, this action is irreversible.*

4. Domain planning

During the installation, you must choose whether your Windows 2000 server will be integrated into a domain or into a workgroup. A domain is a logical configuration in which all the network resources are administered by domain controllers. Sharing, resource security and configuration of the workstations are centralized; the administrator manages security, resources and network user accounts.

The workgroup, or peer-to-peer network, logically groups together a few users. Its application implies that each user of a computer that is situated in the workgroup is responsible for his/her own data (including sharing, backup, and access restrictions). This also means that each user manages his/her own user account database. Consequently, each user that wants to access each of the machines in the workgroup must be declared in each of the account databases. In summary, the workgroup model is applicable in a network that contains a small number of users and for which security is not a major concern.
A computer that belongs to a peer-to-peer network can join a domain, and a computer that belongs to a domain can join a peer-to-peer network.
If you want to join a domain during the installation, you must know a certain number of parameters:
– The name of the domain (DNS) you wish to join.

– In order to join a domain, a computer must have a unique computer account on the domain. If this computer account was not created before installing Windows 2000, you can create it during the installation. In order to be able to do this, you must know the account name and password, for an account that has enough rights so as to be able to include a computer in the domain.
– A server that acts as domain controller and a server on which the DNS service is installed and configured.

In order to join a workgroup, you need enter only the name of the workgroup you wish to join.

*If you include your Windows 2000 server in a domain, it will become a **member** server. If you include your Windows 2000 server in a workgroup, it will become a **stand-alone** server.*

During the installation of Windows 2000 Server, you can make your server a member server or a stand-alone server. If you want your server to act as domain controller, then you must install Active Directory after you have installed Windows 2000 Server.

5. Installing using a CD-ROM

You can run the Windows 2000 installation program on a CD-ROM in several ways:
– Either, you have a Microsoft operating system; in which case you need only insert the CD-ROM in the CD-ROM drive and then run the installation program, **setup.exe**.
– Or, your BIOS will start up on the CD-ROM, which will start the Windows 2000 installation program, automatically.
– Or, you create a set of installation diskettes. You can do this by running the Makeboot.exe program using the command **makeboot a**. This command is situated in the bootdisk directory of the CD-ROM. Then, start up the computer using these diskettes.

If you run the setup.exe program using an operating system, here are the steps that you must follow:
– Click **Install Windows 2000**.
You then have the choice of upgrading your current system, or of installing a new copy of Windows 2000. Select Install a new copy of Windows 2000 (Clean Install).

- Following this screen, you can select a number of options such as the language that you want to use, whether you wish to use accessibility options, and even the location of the Windows 2000 files and the name of the installation folder (**winnt** by default). In order to access these last two options, click **Advanced Options**.
- Then, you will be able to upgrade your file system to NTFS 5.0. You are strongly advised to do this during the installation of Windows 2000 for security reasons, and also so as to optimize the file system (unless you would like a multiple boot involving another operating system that does not support NTFS, such as Windows 95/98 or MS-DOS).
- Click the **Next** button twice after you have made your choice.
- The installation program then copies the installation files onto your computer before it reboots in order to continue the installation in text mode.

In text mode

Here are the different steps in the text mode:
- The setup program copies a minimal version of Windows 2000 into memory.
- If you have SCSI (Small Computer System Interface) or RAID (Redundant Array of Independent Disks) peripherals that are not listed in the HCL, then press the F6 key at the beginning of text mode so as to load their drivers.
- Then, either choose the installation partition, or possibly create it.
- At this stage, you must select the file system onto which the operating system will be installed.
- Then indicate the name of the installation directory (this is **\WINNT** by default).

*If you are installing by running the **setup.exe** program from the operating system, then the text mode part will not ask you to select the file system and the installation directory. This is because these two steps will already have been carried out.*

At this stage your computer will reboot for the second time.

In graphic mode

Collecting information

During the graphic part of the installation you must specify the following items:

- Regional settings.
- Name and the organization that holds the license.
- Licensing mode (per seat or per server).
- Computer name (which must be unique on the network) along with the password of the local administrator account.

In addition, you must indicate the components that you want to install:

- Certificate Services that allow you to create security authentication certificates using public keys.
- Cluster Service that allows servers to run in clusters.
- Internet Information Service (IIS).
- Management and Monitoring Tools.
- Message Queuing Services.
- Indexing Service, which allows you to find text that is contained in files.
- Script Debugger.
- Networking Service (DHCP-WINS-DNS...).
- Other Network File and Print Services that group together file services for Macintosh, and print services for Macintosh and Unix.
- Remote Installation Service, which allows you remotely to implement Windows 2000 Professional workstations.
- Remote Storage, which allows you to store to magnetic tape, data that is seldom used.
- Terminal Services for terminal emulation.

It must be noted that IIS and the Script Debugger are installed by default.

After you have selected the services, you are asked to adjust the date and time before installation of the network management.

Installing the network management

This essential part of the Windows 2000 installation begins with the detection of the network interface card. When you have configured your network driver, Windows 2000 tries to find a DHCP (*Dynamic Host Configuration Protocol*) server on your network in order automatically to provide you with an IP address. If no DHCP server is available, an IP address that is situated in the network range 169.254.0.0/16 is automatically attributed. This is done so that you will be able to boot your computer without an error message appearing, and so that you will be able to communicate with the hosts that have an address in the same range.
The installation program then asks you whether you wish to install network components automatically or whether you wish to customize their installation. If you choose a typical installation then the following components will be installed:

- Client for Microsoft networks; which allows your computer to access network resources.
- File and Printer sharing for Microsoft networks; which allows other computers to access your computer.
- TCP/IP as DHCP client.

If you choose a custom installation then you can choose other components. For example, you can specify a static IP configuration, or you can add new communications protocols or other services.
The following step allows you to choose whether you want to join a workgroup or a domain.
The components that you have chosen are then installed.
When this step is finished, the installation program copies bitmap type files, applies the configuration that you defined previously, and saves the configuration onto the local hard disk. Then any temporary files that were used during the Windows 2000 installation are deleted before the computer is restarted one last time in order to complete the installation.

6. Installing from the network

This method is more efficient if you want to install Windows 2000 on several computers. In order to start this method you need to copy the contents of the **i386** directory from the CD-ROM to a network share.

Then, you need install only a minimum network management version on the destination machine (for example, network client 3.0 on MSDOS) so that you will be able to connect to this resource and start the installation using the **WINNT.EXE** command. In addition, you can use the **WINNT32.EXE** command if you are installing Windows 2000 from a 32-bit Microsoft operating system. These commands will create a temporary directory called **Win_nt.~ls** and will copy the Windows 2000 installation files into this temporary directory.

If you are installing from an MSDOS client, run the smartdrv program before running the winnt.exe command in order to accelerate the installation process.

Installation-program switches

The programs **WINNT** and **WINNT32** provide command line parameters that allow you to customize Windows 2000 installation:

```
WINNT [/s[:sourcepath]] [/t[:temporary_drive]]
[/u[:answer_file]] [/udf:id[,UDF_file]]
[/r:folder] [/r[x]:folder] [/e:command] [/a]
```

`/s[: sourcepath]`	Specifies the location of the Windows 2000 source files. This must be a full path in the format x:\[path] or \\server\share [\path].
`/t[:] temporary _drive`	Specifies the drive that must contain the temporary installation files, and installs Windows 2000 on this drive. If you do not specify a drive, the installation program will choose the partition that has the most free space.
`/u[:answer_ file]`	Automatic operation that uses an optional script. This type of installation requires the switch */s*.
`/r:folder`	Allows you to install an additional directory.
`/rx:folder`	Allows you to copy an additional directory.
`/e:command`	Runs a command before the final phase of program installation.
`/a`	Installs accessibility options.

Here are the switches for the **winnt32.exe** command:

`/copydir: directory`	Creates an additional directory.
`/cmd: com-mand`	Runs a command before the final phase of program installation.

/debug [level] [:file]	Creates a debugging file. By default the file c:\winnt32.log is created at level 2.
/s: sourcepath	Specifies the location of the Windows 2000 installation source files. In order to copy these files simultaneously from different sources, use the switch */s* for each source.
/syspart: disk	Copies the startup files on a hard disk and marks it as active. When you have run this command you can install the disk on another computer, for example. When you start up this computer, the program will start at the next step. You must use the switch */temp-drive with /syspart*.
/tempdrive	Specifies a drive for installation.
/unattended [number of seconds] [:answer file]	Carries out automatic installation. The answer file supplies the information that you must provide during the installation. You can specify the number of seconds that must elapse between the moment when the system finishes copying the files and system reboot. You can set this number of seconds simply, if you are upgrading to Windows 2000.
/udfid, udf_file	The contents of the udf file replace the values that the answer file supplies, and the identifier defines the values that the system must replace. For example, suppose that you do not want your RAS users to wait longer than the other users during the installation. To this end, you can create a UDF file that will replace the information that concerns the RAS, in the `unattended` file. Example: **/udf:RAS_user, mycompany.udf**. In this example, the **/udf:RAS_user, mycompany.udf.** information that the `udf` file contains under the **RAS_user** will replace the values of the `unattended` file.

*Use the **/makelocalsource** switch if you are installing from a CD-ROM, so as to make a local copy of the installation files. This is particularly useful if you need to add components that are required by the source files. Then, you no longer need the CD-ROM.*

Creating an answer file

You can automate the installation of Windows 2000 so that you will not have to respond to all the steps of the installation sequences that are in text and in graphic mode. In order to do this, you must create an answer file (or unattended file), which is a file that provides responses to the installation program.
Setup Manager is a graphic utility that allows you to create answer files and UDF files. This utility is part of the Windows 2000 Resource Kit.
When you have installed the Resource Kit, start the **Setup Manager** Wizard.

☞ Then, click **Next**.

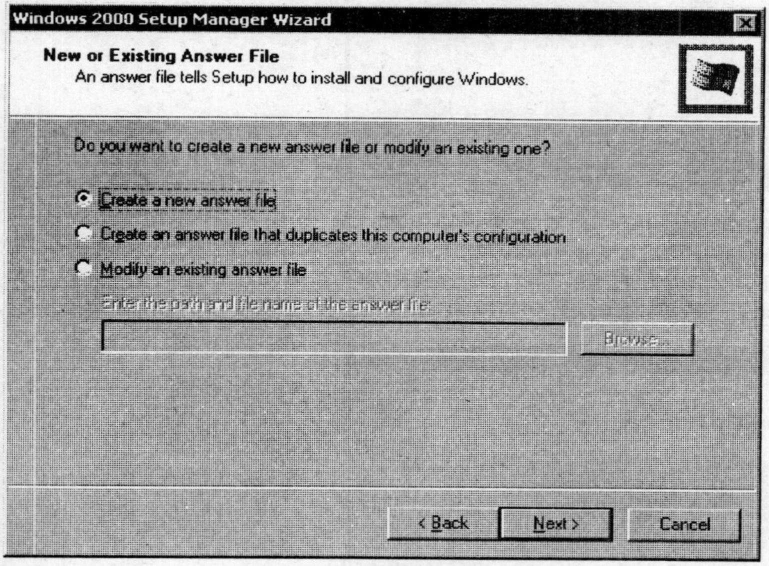

The first option **Create a new answer file**, allows you to create an **unattended** answer file.

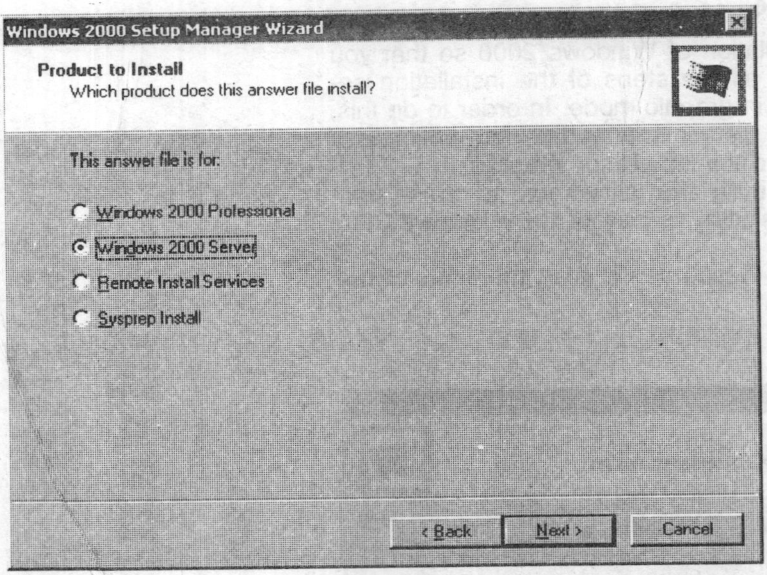

You must select the destination system for this answer file. It must be noted that you can create an answer file for RIS types of installation (remote installation of Windows 2000 Professional), and for Sysprep, which will be covered later on in this chapter.

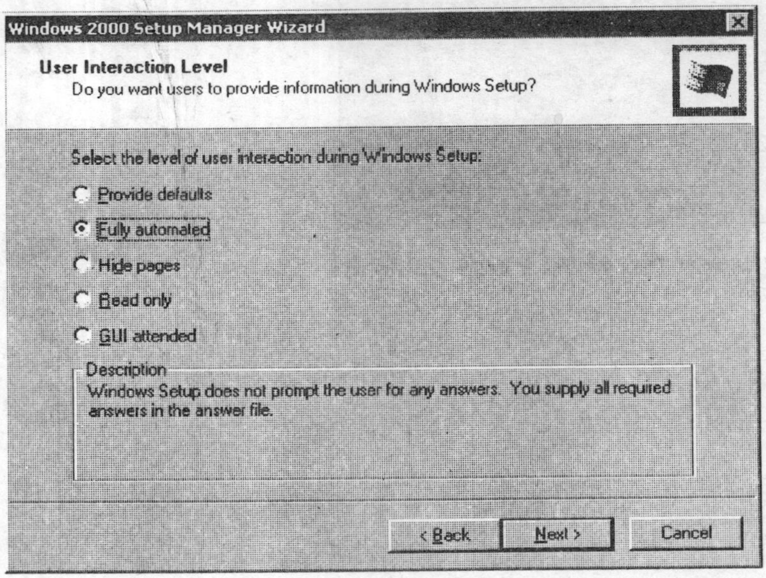

The Setup Manager Wizard offers various options that differ in their levels of interactivity with the installation program. For example, the last option, **GUI attended**, allows you to create an answer file for the text mode part.
Then, enter the name of your company.
The next step asks you to enter the license number of your server product, followed by your chosen licensing mode (per seat or per server).

☛ Then you must specify the names of the destination computers. If you have a text file that contains this list of names, you can import it by clicking the **Import** button. Your file must list one name per line (otherwise, incorrect lines will be omitted).

If you prefer that the system generates names for your computers automatically, then you must activate the **Automatically generate computer names based on organization name** check box.

☛ Then, specify the password of the computer's local administrator. For security reasons, you should never enter an empty password. The longer you make your password, the more difficult it will be to guess. In addition, if you combine uppercase and lowercase letters and numbers, it will be that much more difficult to "crack".

The Setup Manager Wizard then takes you step by step through graphic windows that are similar to those shown above, in order to allow you to specify all the fields that will be required during the installation process (such as display resolutions, settings of network components, whether you want to join a domain or a workgroup and the time zone). When you have completed these steps the following screen will appear, which indicates that you have now created a basic unattended file. If you wish to include specific options in this file, then select **Yes, edit the additional settings.**

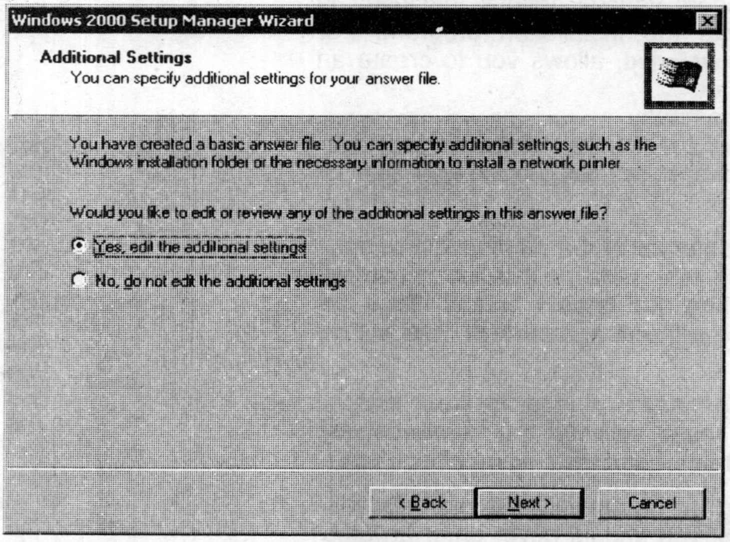

You will then be able to specify telephony options, the different languages you wish to install, the name of the destination directory (**winnt** by default), connection to network printers and a command that must be run upon opening the first session.
When you have specified all the options, you must indicate the method with which you want to use this **unattended** file.

If you select the **No, this answer file will be used to install from a CD** option, then the following step will allow you to specify the location and the name of the file. If you will be installing, by booting on the CD-ROM, place this file on a floppy disk and call it **winnt.sif**. The **winnt.exe** program will search automatically for this file on the floppy-disk when you start from the CD-ROM.

On the other hand, if you select **Yes, create or modify a distribution folder**, then not only will you be able to do as this option suggests, but also you will be able:

- to add mass storage devices to your automatic installation.
- possibly to replace the Hardware Abstraction Layer (HAL) so as to improve the portability of the system by isolating the hardware differences.
- to run a command at the end of the **unattended** installation.
- to change the logos that appear during the installation program.
- to copy additional files or directories to the destination computer.

– copy the distribution files (in the case of the creation of a new distribution directory), either from the CD-ROM or via another path.

The result may be as follows:

```
;SetupMgrTag
[Unattended]
    UnattendMode=FullUnattended
    OemPreinstall=No

[GuiUnattended]
    AdminPassword=PassWord123
    TimeZone=110

[UserData]
    ProductID=000000-000000-000000-000000-000001
    FullName="ENI "
    OrgName=Service

[Display]
    BitsPerPel=32
    Xresolution=800
    YResolution=600
    Vrefresh=72

[LicenseFilePrintData]
    AutoMode=PerSeat

[TapiLocation]

[RegionalSettings]

[MassStorageDrivers]

[OEMBootFiles]

[OEM_Ads]

[SetupMgr]
    ComputerName0=galahad
    ComputerName1=lancelot

[Identification]
    JoinWorkgroup=WORKGROUP
[Networking]
    InstallDefaultComponents=Yes
```

*You can use an answer file so as to promote your member, or stand-alone server to domain controller, after the server has been installed. so as to do this you must indicate the command **dcpromo /answer: answer_file** just after the installation. The **dcpromo** answer file must contain all the information that is required in order to install Active Directory.*

Some parameters must be unique on the network, such as the name of the computer. In order to accommodate this constraint, when you create an **unattend.txt** file, you can create also, a **udf** file so as to specify the parameters that must change from one computer to another. When you use Setup Manager, it will automatically, create this **udf** file, associate it with the **unattend.txt** file, and include in it all the parameters that must be unique. In addition, Setup Manager will create a **.bat** file and include the command line that will be required in order to start these custom installations. Here is an example of the **unattend.udf** file:

```
;SetupMgrTag
[UniqueIds]
    lancelot=UserData
    galahad=UserData

[lancelot:UserData]
   ComputerName=lancelot

[galahad:UserData]
    ComputerName=galahad
```

Here is the syntax that is required in order to run this type of custom installation:

```
Winnt32.exe /u:unattend.txt /
udf:galahad,unattend.udf
```

7. Using disk duplication

In order to install Windows 2000 on a large number of machines, the most efficient technique would be that of disk duplication. This method consists of creating a disk image of a computer on which Windows 2000 has been installed and configured, and then restoring it onto the destination machines. The utility that is used to implement this disk duplication is called **sysprep.exe**.

The following sequence must be followed:

- Install and configure Windows 2000 on a computer that is called the reference computer.
- Install the applications on this computer. Do not forget to copy the custom user parameters in the default user profile. In order to do this, right-click **My Computer** and then select **Properties**. Under the **User Profiles** tab, select the profile that you want to use for the software installation and then click the **Copy To** button.

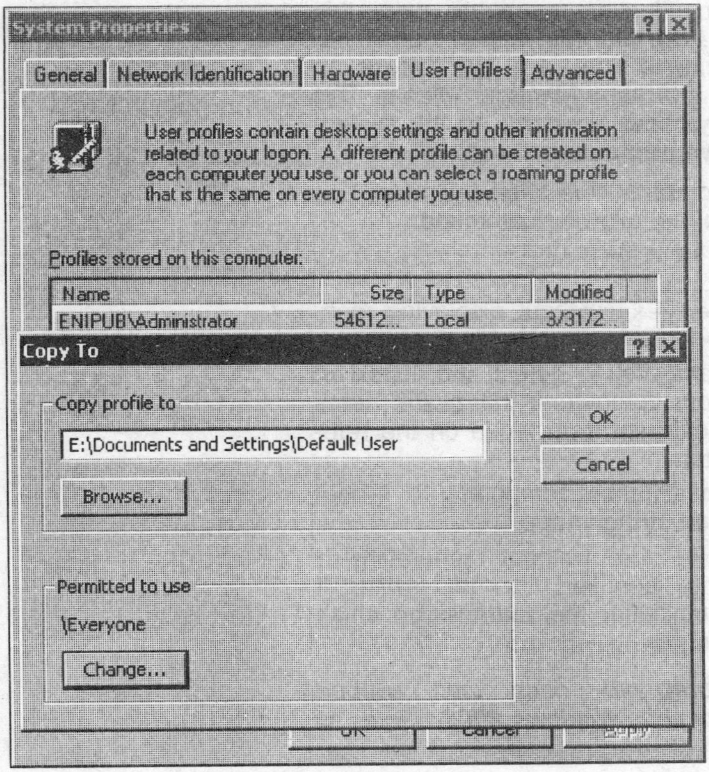

Under **Copy profile to**, enter **%Systemdrive%:\Documents and Settings\Default User**.
Under **Permitted to use**, select the **Everyone** group.

– Run the **sysprep.exe** utility in order to delete all the configuration settings that are specific to a given computer (computer name that must be unique on the network and SID the unique security identifier). In addition, **sysprep.exe** will install the part of the installation program that asks the user to enter a new computer name. This will be done after the image has been restored on the destination computer, once this computer has been restarted. So that this will be carried out automatically without user intervention, you can create an answer file **sysprep.inf** using the Setup Manager Wizard. This file must be located in the **sysprep** directory, on the system partition along with the files **sysprep.exe** and **setupcl.exe**.

Sysprep will be run after your computer has been restarted. Log on as administrator and then run the following command:

```
Drive:\sysprep\sysprep.exe -switches
```

The switches are as follows:

`-quiet` Runs `sysprep.exe` without displaying messages on the screen.

`-pnp` Forces *plug-and-play* to detect and install on the destination computers, hardware items that may be different from those on the reference computer.

`-reboot` Forces the destination computers to reboot after installation of the image.

`-nosidgen` Runs `sysprep.exe` without generating a unique security identifier. Use this switch if you are not duplicating the hard disk on which you are running `sysprep.exe`.

Important note: ***sysprep.exe*** *does not support Windows 2000 Professional or Windows 2000 Server as stand-alone server.*

Important note: you can install the images only on computers that have the same mass storage device driver and the same hardware abstraction layer (HCL) as the reference computer.

Once the disk has been prepared, the image is ready to be created using a disk duplication utility of a third-party vendor.

8. Promoting a stand-alone server to member server

At any time, you can **migrate** your stand-alone server from the workgroup to which it belongs, to a domain so that it will become a member server.
In order to do this right-click the **My Computer** icon and select the **Properties** option.
Under the **Network Identification** tab, click the **Properties** button.

Select **Domain** and then enter the name of the domain that you wish to join.
In order to include a stand-alone server in a Windows 2000 domain, you must create a computer account in the domain concerned. There are two ways of doing this:

– From the server, by specifying a domain user account of a domain into which a computer account can be created.

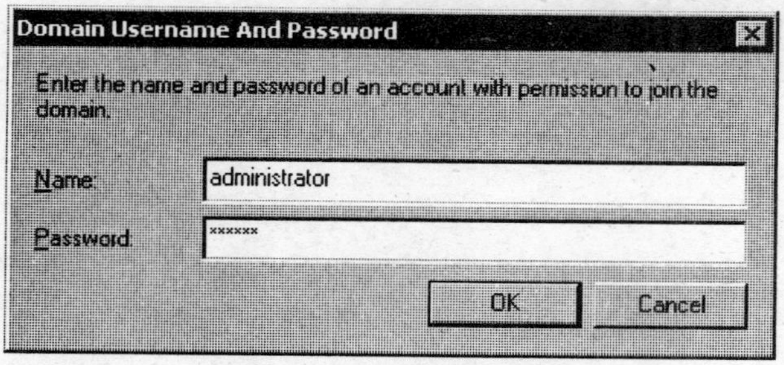

– From a domain controller using the **Active Directory Users and Computers** utility.

The 'Welcome to the domain' window then appears:

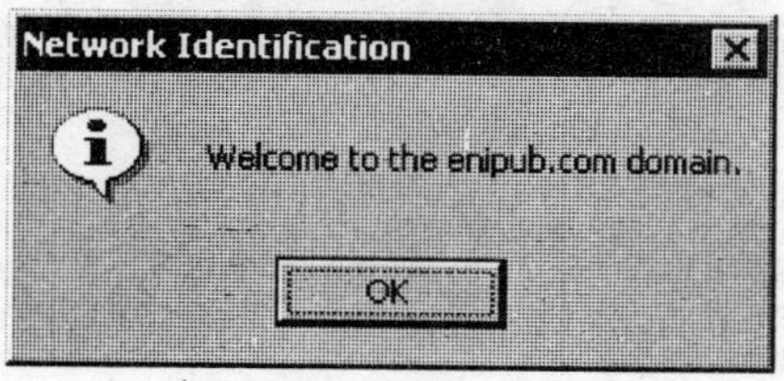

The next time that you log on, you will be able to choose between using a user account that is declared in the domain and using an account that is local to your computer.

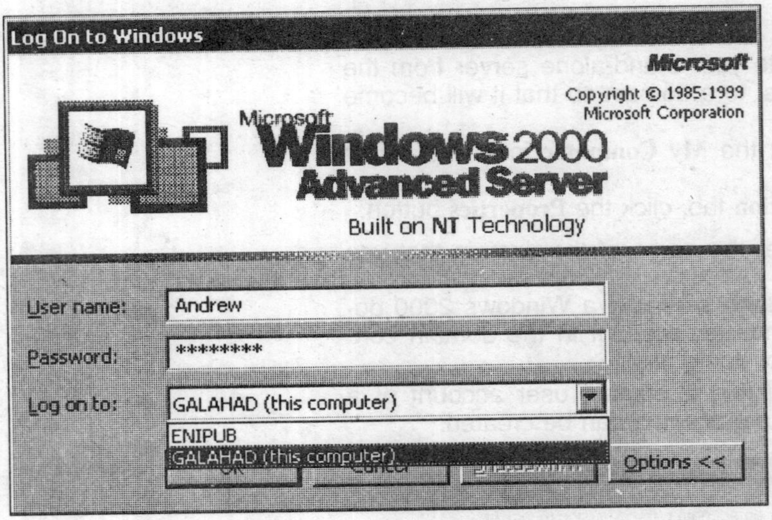

Configuring the system

A. Registry **42**

1. Overview **42**
2. Registry Editors of Windows 95 and of Windows 2000/NT **46**

B. Configuring devices **48**

1. Add/remove Programs **48**
2. Add/remove Hardware **49**
3. System **50**
4. Services **59**
5. Configuring network interface cards **62**

C. Choosing a protocol **65**

1. Internet addressing **66**
2. IP configuration **69**
3. Automatic configuration **70**
4. Manual configuration **71**

D. Optimizing bindings **73**

You can access most of the Windows 2000 settings using the **Control Panel**. You can access other settings in the registry.

You can access **Control Panel** either via **My Computer** or using the **Start** menu. The Control Panel is represented by the  Control Panel icon, and contains a set of modules that concern the different parts of the operating system.

You can access some of these modules by other shortcuts (for example, you can access the **Display** module by right-clicking the desktop, and then selecting the **Properties** option).

All the **Control Panel** modules provide a secure, user-friendly graphic interface. On the other hand, handling settings via the registry is very basic; one erroneous operation can put the operating system out of action. The tool that you can use in order to edit the Windows 2000 configuration registry is described below.

A. Registry

1. Overview

The registry files are the equivalents of the configuration files that were used with Windows 3.x, such as WIN.INI and SYSTEM.INI. As from Windows 95/98, Windows NT 4.00 and Windows 2000, the configuration of the system, the programs and the user's environment is recorded in the registry. In order to edit this registry, you must use the standard tool that is delivered with Windows 2000: the **Registry Editor**.

This tool is not provided in the form of an icon in the **Administrative Tools** group. In order to start it, you must run the **REGEDT32.EXE** program.

In most cases however, you can modify the registry without using the Registry Editor. You can configure the system via the user interface. In particular, you can use Control Panel.

However, some configuration settings can be modified only using the Registry Editor. These include the following operations:

- Locking the numeric keyboard before logon (so as to enter the password),
- Customizing the desktop before logon (so as to display the logo of the company, for example),

— Configuring TCP protocol (size of emission/reception windows),
— Activating the WINS proxy agent,
— Generating an error log for the PPP protocol.

Group policies provide another means of modifying a machine's registry. This registry contains the configuration of the local machine (software and hardware) along with the profile that is implemented by the user upon logon.
The Registry Editor provides a structured view of the complete configuration of a machine. Consequently, there is a separate registry for each computer that is installed.

This registry contains all the system parameters:
— Kernel components,
— Device drivers,
— Installed applications,
— User profiles,
— Profiles of available hardware,
— Database of system users (local to a workstation or to a member/stand-alone server).

The registry has a tree structure. There are **trees** and **subtrees**.

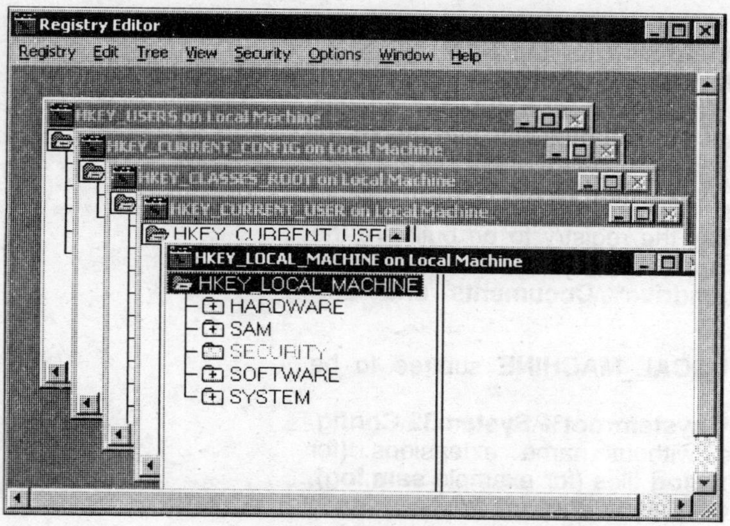

- **HKEY_CLASSES_ROOT**
  is the subtree that is located in HKEY_LOCAL_MACHINE\Software\Classes. This subtree manages file-class association data and OLE (*Object Linking and Embedding*).
- **HKEY_CURRENT_CONFIG**
  is part of the HKEY_LOCAL_MACHINE subtree: HKEY_LOCAL_MACHINE\System\CurrentControlSet\Hardware Profiles\xxx\. This subtree contains settings that are specific to the current hardware profile.
- **HKEY_CURRENT_USER**
  points to HKEY_USERS/SID (*Security IDentifier*).
- **HKEY_LOCAL_MACHINE.**
- **HKEY_USERS.**

The **HKEY_USERS** subtree corresponds to the two previous subtrees, **HKEY_LOCAL_MACHINE** and **HKEY_USERS**. These subtrees will now be described. As its name suggests, **HKEY_USERS** contains configuration settings that relate to the user environment, whilst **HKEY_LOCAL_MACHINE** contains configuration data that relate to, devices, the operating system, system security and the accounts database.

Each subtree is made up of a set of **hives** (for example: the **HKEY_LOCAL_MACHINE** subtree contains the **SAM**, **SECURITY**, **SOFTWARE** and **SYSTEM** hives). Each hive is made up of a set of **keys** and **subkeys**. These keys and subkeys contain **value entries** that accomodate the intermediate information of the structure.

The registry then, is made up of a set of files, which include hives. The other items that allow the registry to be built are the user profiles that are stored in the **NTUSER.DAT** files. These files are located in **\%systemdrive%\Documents and Settings\user_name**.

The hives allow the **HKEY_LOCAL_MACHINE** subtree to be built.
These files are stored in **\%systemroot%\System32\Config**. This directory contains files without name extensions (for example **sam.**). It also contains **.log** files (for example **sam.log**), which allow logging of the modifications that are made to each hive.

These hives are as follows:

SAM

This hive contains the computer's accounts database: *Security Account Manager*.
In the case of a Windows 2000 Professional workstation and a member server, this database is local to the machine.
Associated files: **sam., sam.log**

Security

This hive is extremely important as it contains the Local Security Authority, or LSA. The LSA authorizes, or forbids, a user to **Log on locally** or to **Access this computer from the network**.
Associated files: **security., security.log**

Software

Associated files: **software., software.log**

System

The **system** hive contains information on the devices and the services that are installed. This is the only hive that is duplicated in **system.alt** (backup file).
Associated files: **system., system.alt, system.log**

It must be noted that the HARDWARE subkey is not a hive! It is a volatile key (a key that is stored in volatile memory). It is made up from hardware information that is detected upon system boot by NTDETECT.COM.

The value entries can have different data types:

REG_DWORD
: a numeric value on four bytes.

REG_SZ
: a text string, REGister String Zero (a string of characters that is terminated with a 0 in C language).

REG_MULTI_SZ
: a set of text strings.

REG_BINARY
: binary data.

REG_EXPAND_SZ
: similar to REG_SZ except that you can include variables such as %SYSTEMROOT% and %USERNAME%.

2. Registry Editors of Windows 95 and of Windows 2000/NT

There are two Registry Editors on Windows 2000. **Regedt32.exe** is the registry editor for Windows NT and for Windows 2000, and **regedit.exe**, the registry editor for Windows 95, is also supplied with Windows 2000. The advantages of **regedit.exe** will be discussed later on in this chapter.

*It must be noted that, although the Windows 95 and the Windows NT/2000 registries are not 100 % compatible, it useful to use **regedit.exe** in certain cases. These cases will be discussed later on in this chapter.*

***Regedit.exe** of Windows 95 must not be confused with **regedit.exe** of Windows 3.11! This can easily be done, especially as they have the same name and use the same icon! However, they do not offer the same features. The utility that was supplied with Windows 3.11 was the OLE (Object Linking and Embedding) registration editor. It functioned with **WIN.INI**, and with the **REG.DAT** files for each application that concerned OLE.*

Registry editor for Windows 2000: regedt32.exe

Regedt32 features are suited to Windows 2000. It allows remote administration.

In the menu bar:

– The **Registry** menu provides access to the local register (**Open Local**) and to a remote computer (**Select Computer**). In addition, this menu allows you to print a subtree, and to save it as a text file.

– You can use the **Edit** menu in order to add a key or a value. You can display the value of each key according to its format, for example: binary, decimal or string.

– The **Security** menu allows you to apply permissions on keys and hives. It also allows you to audit the access to the different parts of the registry and to define the ownership of these various parts.

– The **Options** menu allows you to access the registry in **Read Only Mode** so that you can go through the registry without making any changes. It must be noted that this mode does not apply to the administrator, who can modify the registry even in read only mode!

Never change the access permissions for the registry unless you are sure that you know what you are doing! You might prevent certain services from accessing certain keys, and thereby create a problem that is difficult to identify.

Modifying a registry using the Windows 2000 registry editor

In order to modify a value in the registry:

- Select the subtree, followed by the key that contains the value you wish to modify.
- Double-click the value in the right-hand pane and then modify it.

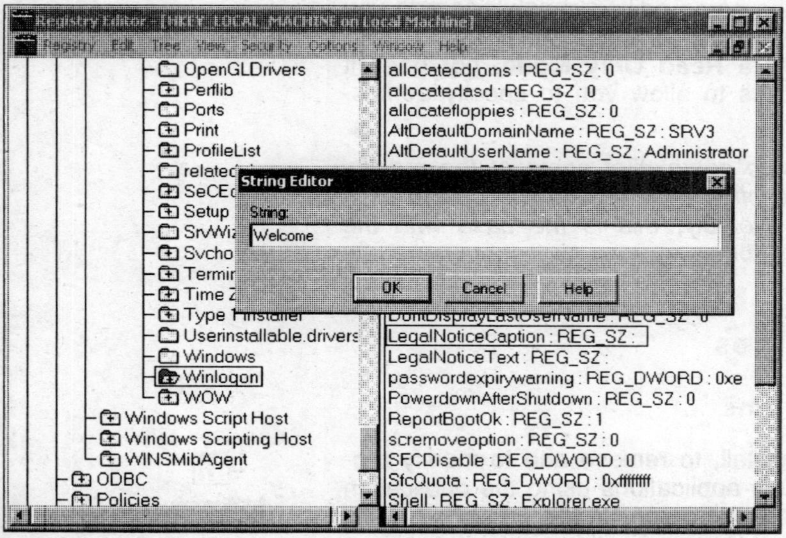

In order to add a value:

- Select the appropriate key and choose the **Add Value** option from the **Edit** menu.
- Specify the name of the value, respecting the case, and then indicate the data type that must be associated with it.
- Enter the data.

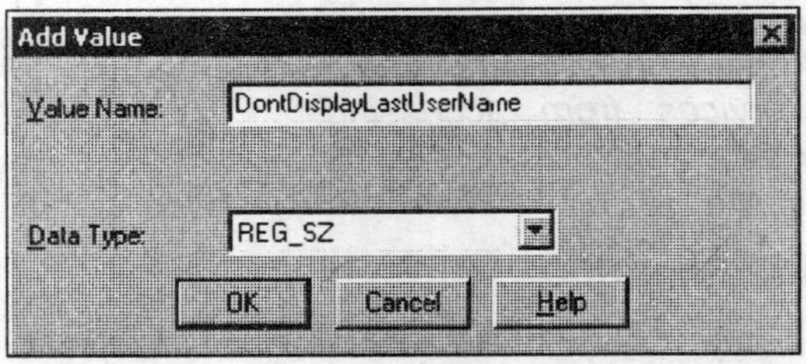

Registry editor for Windows 95: regedit.exe

This registry editor is often used on Windows 2000 because it offers advanced search features. Unlike **regedt32**, which allows you to search only on keys and subkeys, the Windows 95 editor allows you to search at the level of values and their contents.
However, it does not have the same editing capabilities and you are even recommended not to use it for these purposes.
In addition, it does not offer a **Read Only Mode**, nor does it provide a **Security** menu so as to allow you to specify permissions.

*It must be noted once again, that some of the registry components that are offered by regedit.exe do not exist on Windows 2000: Notably, this is the case with the **HKEY_DYN_DATA** subtree.*

B. Configuring devices

1. Add/remove Programs

This module allows you to install, to remove and to modify programs. If you decide to diffuse applications using the publication technique, then users will be able to consult the published applications with a view to installing them using this module.

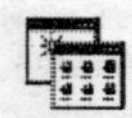
Add/Remove Programs

After you have installed Windows, you can install further services such as DHCP server service, DNS server service, network analysis tools, print services for UNIX, games and accessories. In order to install such services click the **Add/Remove Windows Components** button.

2. Add/remove Hardware

Add/Remove Hardware

Windows 2000 supports the Plug-and-Play feature by automatically installing the drivers of devices that offer the Plug-and-Play feature. This feature means that you can physically connect a new device and then let Windows automatically sort out its configuration (IRQ...). The advantage of this feature is that you no longer have to worry about this set up, which allows you to avoid all sorts of conflict problems.

If you have devices that are not Plug-and-Play, use the **Add/Remove Hardware** program so as to install, remove, disconnect or troubleshoot these devices.

If you select **Add/Troubleshoot a device**, Windows 2000 looks for new Plug-and-Play devices. If no Plug-and-Play device is detected then you can install one by selecting **Add a new device**.

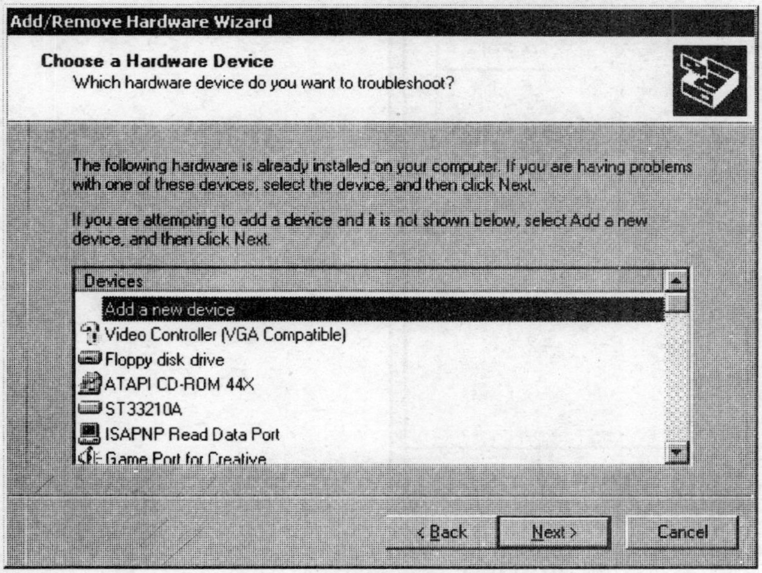

If you select a device that is listed in the pane that appears under **Devices**, and then click **Next**, Windows 2000 will indicate the status of this device.

3. System

This module allows you to access a certain number of tabs that concern system properties.

System

Network Identification tab

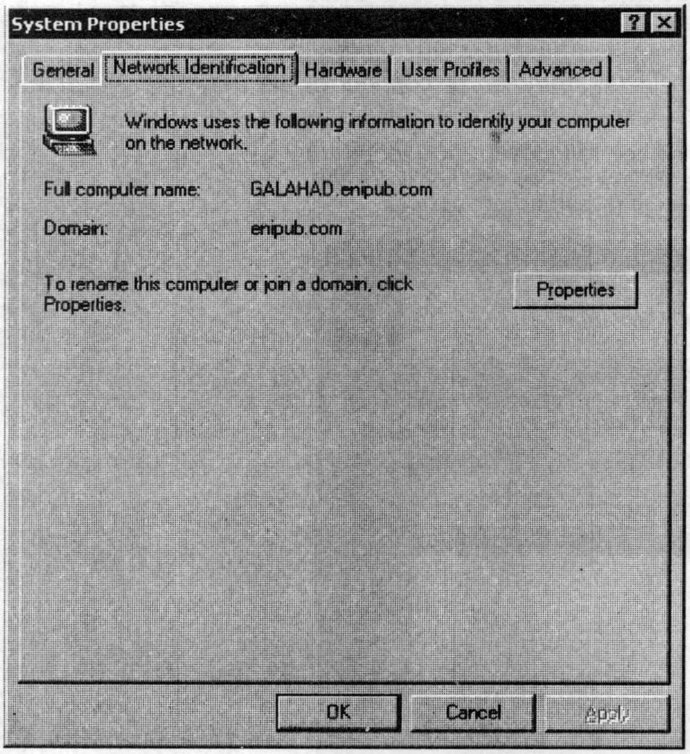

Under this tab you can join a domain or a workgroup. You can even change the name of your computer provided that your computer is not a domain controller.

Hardware tab

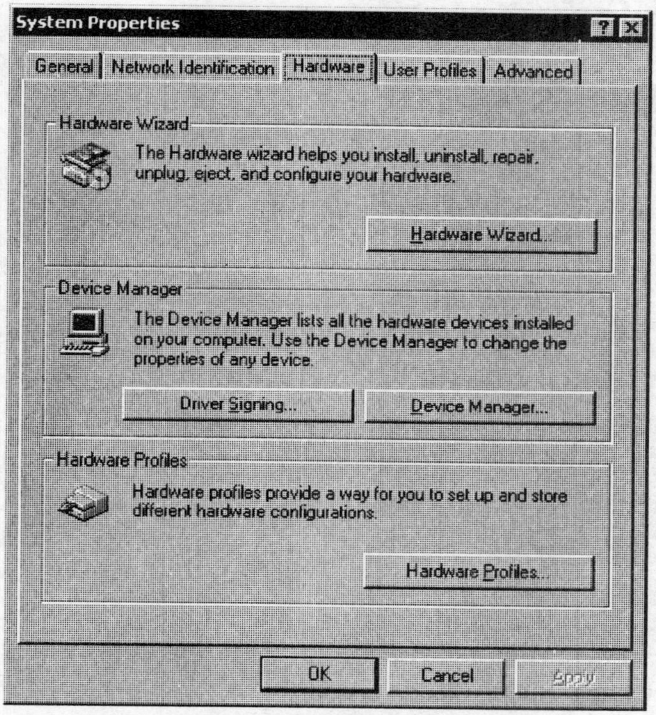

The **Hardware Wizard** allows you to start up the **Add/Remove Hardware module.**

Under **Device Manager**, the **Driver Signing** button allows you to specify a security level that must be met when new drivers are installed.

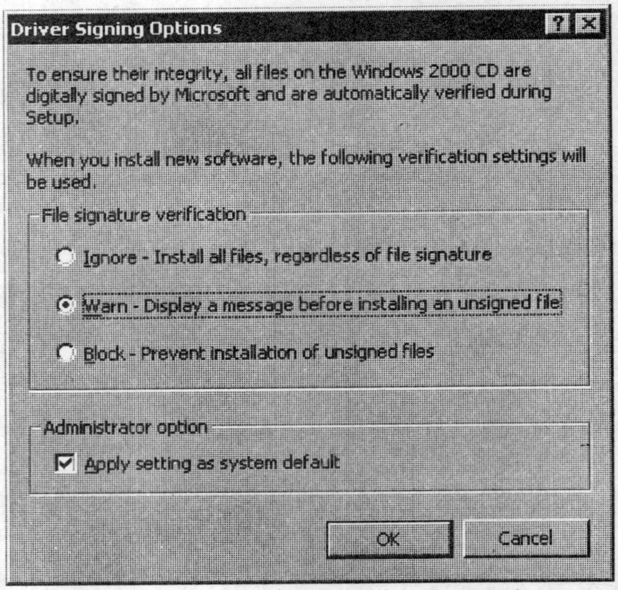

Most system failures are caused by badly written device drivers. Microsoft guarantees that all drivers that are signed by them are compatible with the Windows 2000 environment. However, some drivers have not received this signature because their manufacturers decided that this was not necessary. In order to promote the stability of your system, you can forbid the installation of drivers that have not been signed.

Windows 2000 Datacenter version does not authorize the installation of drivers that have not been signed.

The **Device Manager** allows you to view the status of your devices. It also allows you to uninstall them, to disable them and to view their properties. An alternative way of accessing **Device Manager** is to right-click **My Computer** and then to select **Manage**.

The **Hardware Profiles** button allows you to create different startup configurations. For example, if you use a portable computer, you could create two hardware profiles: one in which the network adapter is disabled, and the other in which the network interface card is enabled.

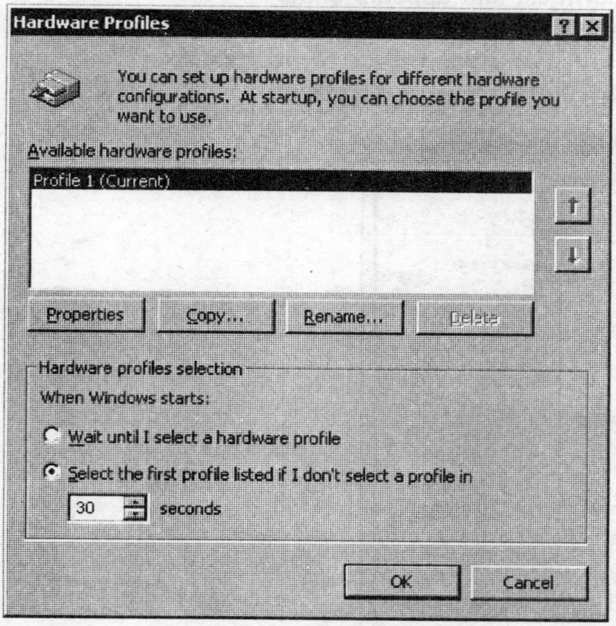

By default, only one hardware profile is created. This hardware profile is called **Profile 1**, and it contains the current hardware configuration. In order to create a second hardware profile, click **Copy**.

A configuration name cannot contain extended characters.

When you have created your alternative hardware profile, all you need do is to start up your machine on the profile that you wish to configure and then start up **Device Manager**.

Select the device that you want to deactivate for the current hardware profile. Then, in the drop-down list that appears under **Device usage**, select **Do not use this device in the current hardware profile (disable)**.

Advanced tab - Performance Options

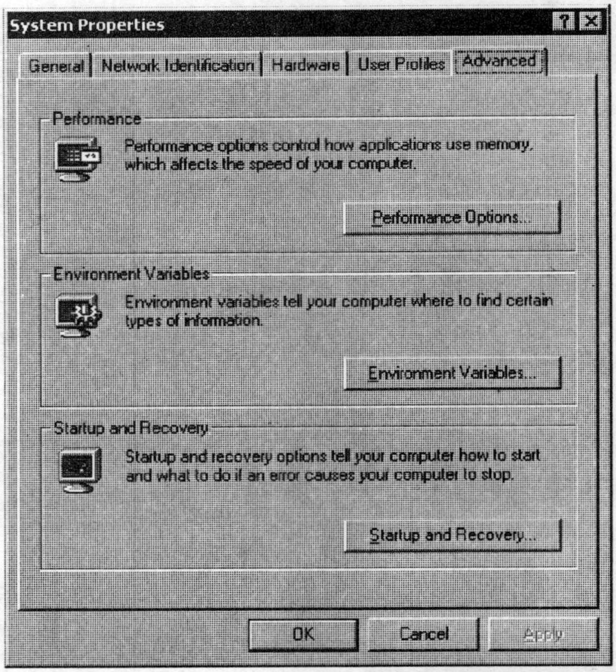

Performance Options allow you to optimize execution priority for applications and services that run in the background.

The application that is running on the foreground is that for which the title bar appears in dark blue (if you are using standard colors). This is the application with which the user is currently working. Select **Applications** in order to define a priority level that is higher than that of the background application. If you select **Background services**, then all the applications will have the same priority.

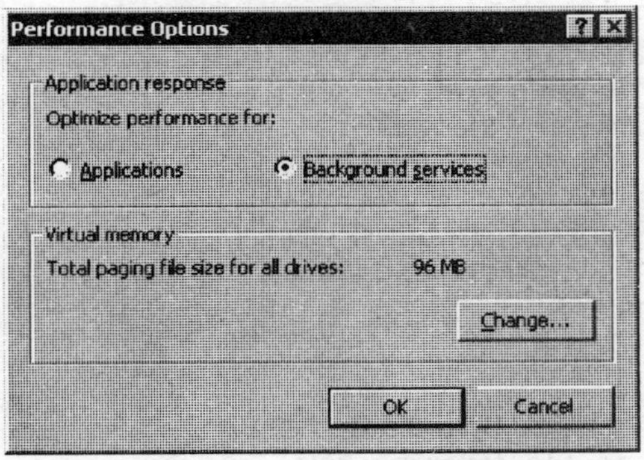

By default, Windows 2000 Server privileges the applications that run in the background (this improves the performance of network services). On the other hand, Windows 2000 Professional privileges the applications that run in the foreground.

Configuring the paging file

In order to modify the size or the location of the paging (swap) file, click the **Change** button in the **Performance Options** dialog box.

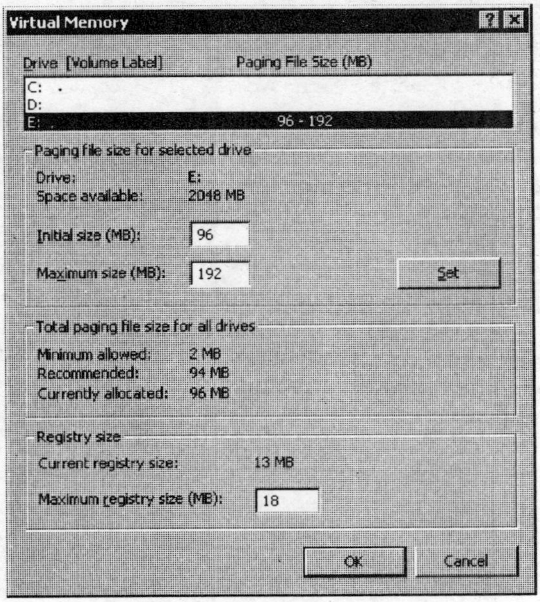

By default, the paging file is located in the root of the partition that contains system files. Its name is **pagefile.sys**. You can resize this file so as to optimize the functioning of the system. In addition, you can move the file so as to optimize read/write access to the disk. In order to do this, select the drive on which you wish to place your paging file, and define the **Initial size (MB)** and the **Maximum size (MB)** in the corresponding text boxes. Then click **Set** so as to fix these values.

Sizing the paging file

For both Windows 2000 Server and Professional, by default, the initial size of the paging file is based on the following relationship:
Size of **Pagefile.sys** = size of the computer's RAM + 50%

If there is not enough free disk space on the system partition, then the partition that contains the most free disk space is used.

The size of the paging file will never fall below its initial size. It will increase according to its needs but it will never exceed its maximum size. The performance of your system will deteriorate if certain applications need to swap to disk.
The minimum size of a paging file is 2 MB.

When you restart your computer, Windows 2000 resizes your paging file to its initial size.

*In order to view information concerning the paging file, select **Folder - Options** in the **Tools** menu of Windows Explorer. Then click the **View** tab and deactivate the **Hide protected operating system file** option.*

Optimizing the paging file

If your system has several hard disks, it might be a good idea to place a paging file on each of them. This can be particularly useful if your disk controller handles simultaneous read/writes. When there are several paging files, the virtual memory manager balances the load between these different files.

As part of the optimization process, it is helpful to separate the hard disks according to types of activity. For example, it is useful to create a paging file on a different partition from that which contains the system files. However, if the size of your paging file on the system partition is less than that of the RAM on your system, then Windows 2000 will not be able to create a debugging information file in the event of an error.

In any case, in order to avoid slowing down the system, you must ensure that the minimum size of the paging file is always adequate. If this is not the case then the paging file will grow up to the maximum size that was specified, to the detriment of the overall performance of the machine.

In addition, it must be noted that you can define the size of the registry. As soon as the size of the registry comes close to the maximum size, you must increase this maximum size. Otherwise, you might lose configuration information.

Advanced tab - Environment Variables

Environment variables contain information that is used by the system, for example the **TEMP** variable, which specifies where temporary files are stored.

There are two types of environment variable:
– user variables,
– system variables.

The user variables that are defined vary according to the user concerned. Users can add, modify and delete user environment variables.

System variables do not apply to an individual user, they apply to the whole system. Consequently, they apply irrespective of the user who is logged on. Only administrators can modify system variables.

Advanced tab - Startup and Recovery

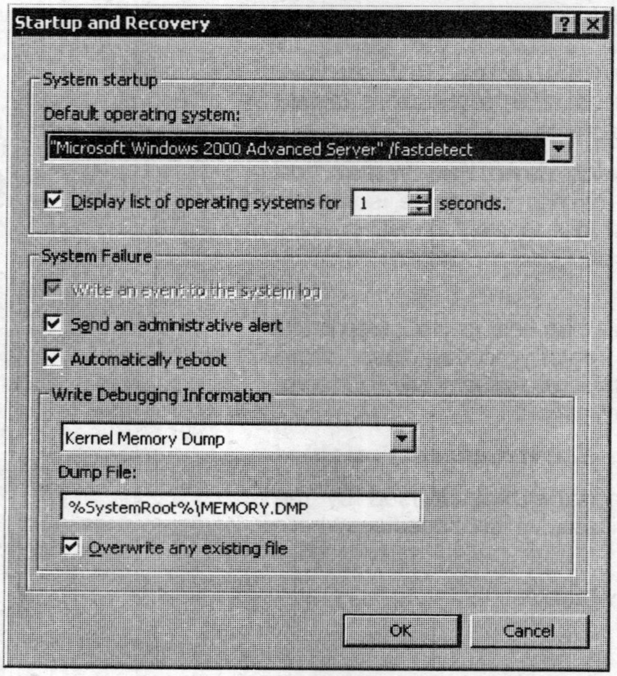

This dialog box allows you to specify the default options that must be configured upon startup. It also allows you to specify what the system must do in the event of a fatal error.

Under **System startup** you can specify the system that must be booted by default (this is the option that is highlighted in the startup menu). In addition, you can indicate for how long the startup menu must be displayed.

In reality, this graphic tool modifies the **boot.ini** file, which contains startup options.

The following options are used in order to define the actions of the system in the event of a fatal error:

– Write an event to the system log.
– Send an administrative alert so that a recipient will receive a message concerning the problem.

– Reboot, copying the contents of volatile memory to a file, which is called **memory.dmp** by default. This file will help the Microsoft technical support to diagnose the causes of this error. In fact, when a failure occurs, the contents of volatile memory are written to the paging file, which is then copied to the memory.dmp file upon the next startup. A new paging file is then created.

4. Services

Users of **Windows NT 4.0** will be used to carrying out operations on services via the **Services** icon of the **Control Panel**.

With Windows 2000, in order to access the services you must select **Administrative Tools** followed by **Computer Management** (alternatively you can right-click **My Computer** and then select **Manage**).

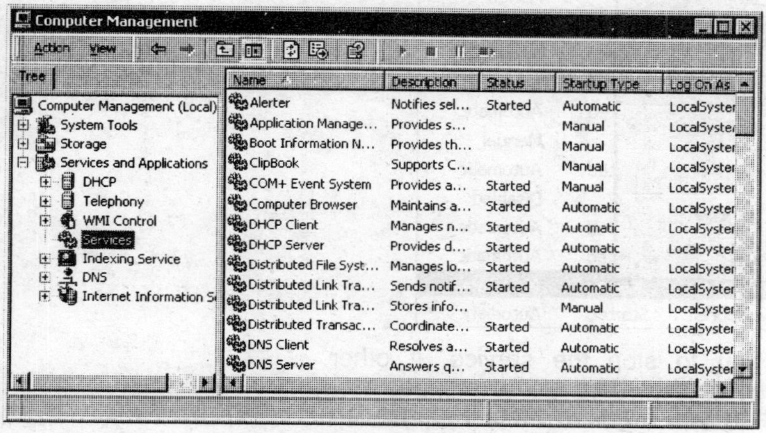

The **Computer Management** console allows you to handle the services of any computer on the network. For this purpose, select **Computer Management (Local)** and then click **Action - Connect to another computer**.

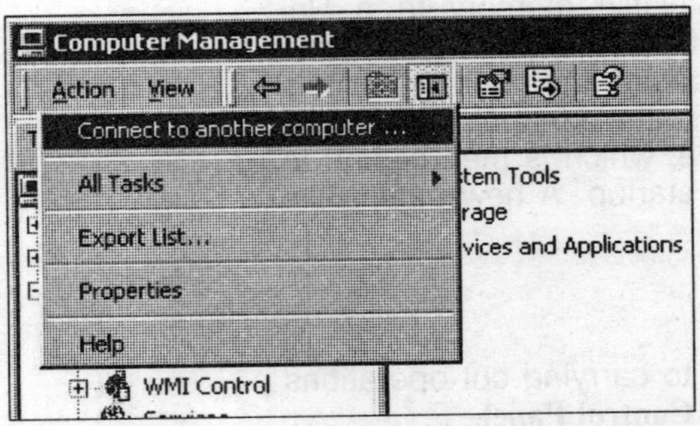

You can carry out different tasks on a service by right-clicking it.

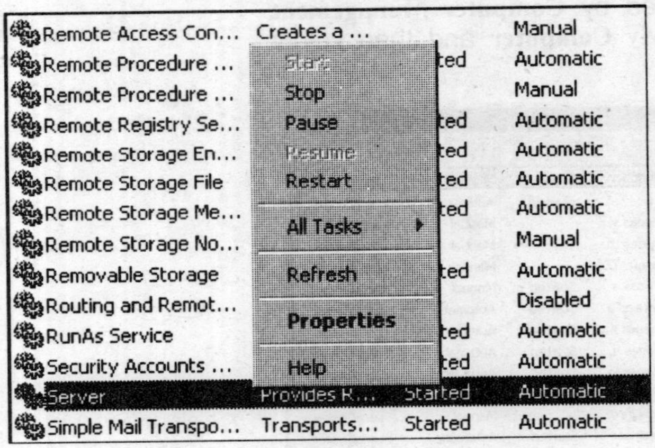

- The **Stop** option allows you to stop the service. If other services depend on this service then they will be stopped too. However, if the service that you want to stop depends on other services, then these other services will not be stopped.
- The **Pause** option stops the service without stopping any of the services that depend on it.
- The **Restart** option allows you to restart the service along with all its dependencies.

In order to view the dependencies of a particular service, right-click the service concerned and select **Properties**. Then, select the **Dependencies** tab.

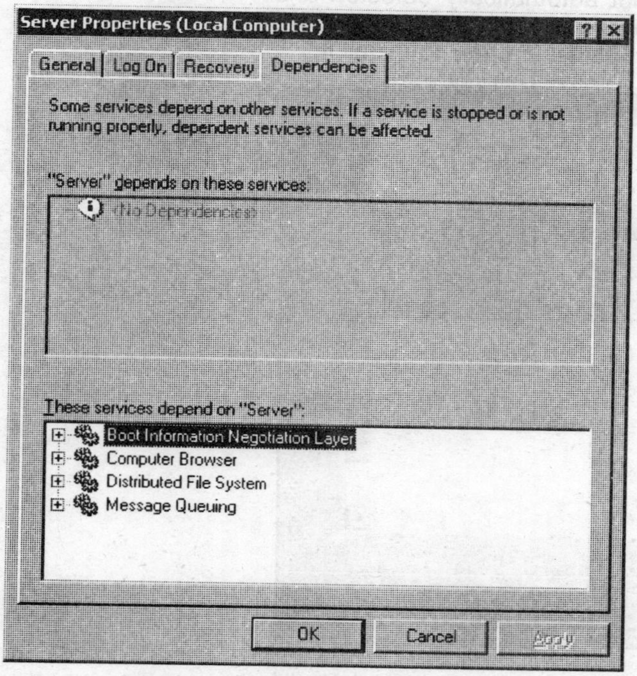

- The **General** tab allows you to change the name and the description that is displayed in the **Computer Management** program. It also allows you to select the type of startup (automatic, manual or disabled). In addition it allows you to start, stop, pause or resume the service.
- The **Log On** tab allows you to specify the user account with which the server must start up. In addition, you can enable or disable the service for specific hardware profiles.
- The **Recovery** tab allows you to define the action that must be taken if the service fails. You can choose from the options: **Take No Action, Restart the Service, Run a File** and **Reboot the Computer**. You can define different actions according to whether it is the first failure, the second failure, or a subsequent failure of the service. A fail count is provided that you can re-initialize automatically after a specified number of days.

5. Configuring network interface cards

If your network interface card is not automatically detected and installed by Windows 2000, then you must use the **Add/Remove Hardware** program from the **Control Panel** in order to install it.

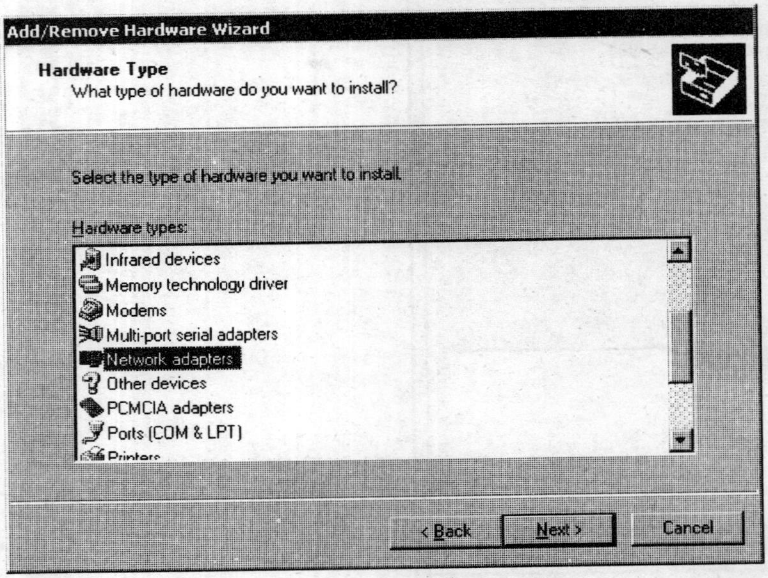

Windows 2000 will then automatically configure your network card.

There are two ways of viewing the properties of your card:

– Right-click **My Network Places** and select **Properties**. Then, right-click **Local Area Connection** and again select **Properties**.

– Alternatively, go into Control Panel and double-click the **Network and Dial-up Connections** icon. Then, right-click **Local Area Connection** and select **Properties**.

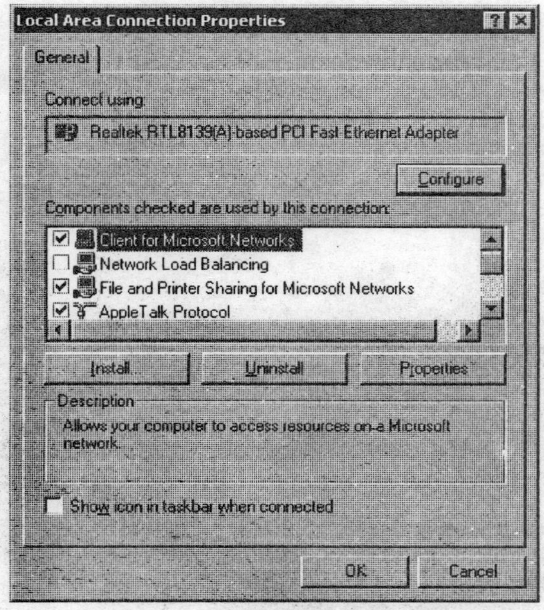

If you activate the **Show icon in taskbar when connected** check box, then you will be able to double-click the  icon in order to display the connection status of your local area network.

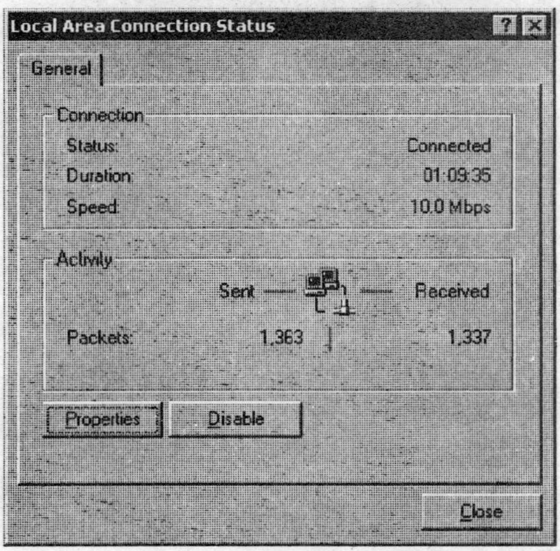

If you click the **Disable** button, then you will disable your network interface card. In order to re-activate the network connection back, select the properties of **My Network Places** and double-click the grayed-out **Local Area Connection** icon. Alternatively, you can right-click this grayed-out icon and then select **Enable**.

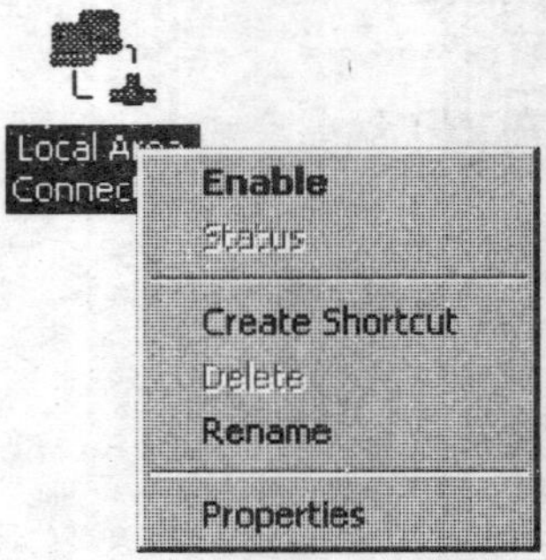

Coming back to the **Local Area Connection Properties** dialog box, the **General** tab shows the card by which the network connection has been made, along with all the items that this connection uses. These items must include a communications protocol. By clicking the **Configure** button, you can view the properties of your network interface card.

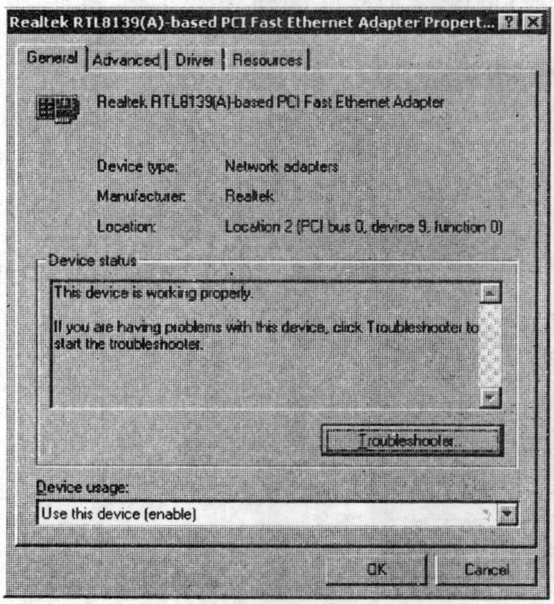

- The **General** tab allows you to enable or to disable this device with respect to the different hardware profiles. It also allows you to run the **Troubleshooter** program, which is useful if you have a problem with your network interface card.
- The **Advanced** tab provides access to settings that you can configure for the card. The settings that are proposed will depend on the card concerned.
- The **Driver** tab provides information on the driver that the card uses (concerning the files that correspond to the driver). This tab also allows you to uninstall or to update this driver.
- The **Resources** tab allows you to view the resource settings that your card uses (such as the IRQ and input/output address).

C. Choosing a protocol

Windows 2000 manages several protocols. Each of them has its peculiarities and its fields of application.

This section will describe the cases in which you must use one protocol rather than another.

TCP/IP (Transmission Control Protocol/Internet Protocol)

The Internet is based on this protocol. It is a routable protocol and handles extended networks. It requires an explicit addressing scheme.

Transport compatible Nwlink IPX/SPX/NetBIOS

This is an NDIS 5.0 version of the Novell IPX/SPX (Internetwork Packet eXchange/Sequenced Packet eXchange) protocol.

NWLink allows communication between MS-DOS, OS/2, Windows and Windows 2000 computers, by means of RPCs (Remote Procedure Calls), of Windows sockets or by Novell NetBIOS IPX/SPX. IPX is a routable protocol. IPX addressing is implemented dynamically on the clients.

NetBEUI (NetBIOS Extended User Interface)

This protocol is used on Lan Manager, Lan Server, Windows 95 and Windows for Workgroups systems. This is a fast and efficient protocol that is usable only on small LANs. It is not a routable protocol and is based on broadcasting. However, it has the advantage that it does not need configuring.

DLC (Data Link Control)

This protocol provides access to SNA systems and to certain network print devices.

AppleTalk

This protocol allows a Windows 2000 server that runs services for Macintosh, to communicate with Macintosh clients. This is also a routable protocol.

1. Internet addressing

An Internet address is called an *IP address*. It uniquely identifies the machine, and also the network in which the machine is situated. This feature allows efficient routing of information. This address is encoded on 32 bits, and is used for all communications with the machine.

Each address is made up of a network identifier and a machine identifier. A first set of bits corresponds to the network, and a second set of bits corresponds to the machine. Under no circumstances, must the bits in either the machine part, or the bits in the network part, be either all set to one, or all set to zero.

IP address classes

The IP address class of an address can be determined from the most significant bits in the address. Only the first three address classes can be used for machine addresses.

Class A

7 bits are used for the address of the network, and 24 bits are used for the address of the machine.

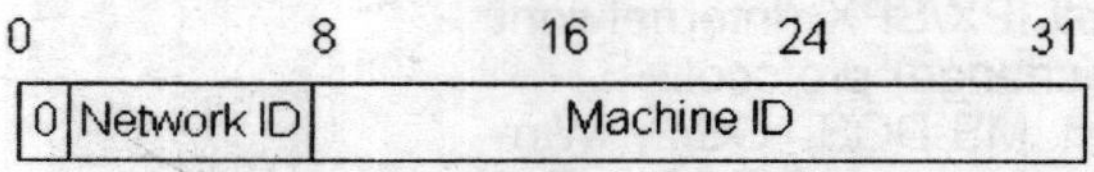

The first-byte value is between 1 and 126 (inclusive).

Class B

This class corresponds to networks in which the number of machines varies from 2 to 2^{16}-2. 16 bits are available for the number of the machine, and 14 bits are available for the number of the network.

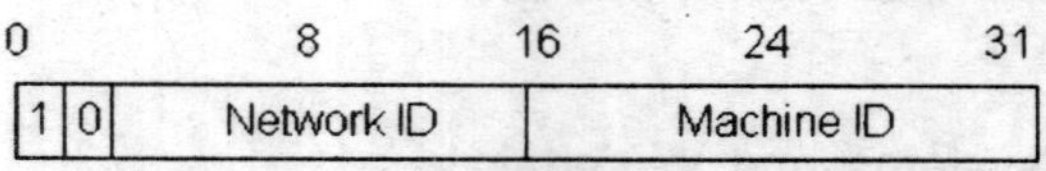

The first-byte value is between 128 and 191 inclusive.

Class C

21 bits are used for the number of the network, and 8 bits are used for the number of the machine. Consequently, you can use this class for small networks that contain from 1 to 2^8-2 (254) machines.

The first-byte value is between 192 and 223 (inclusive).

A router is a machine that has several addresses. Therefore it cannot have a unique address, as it must have as many addresses as it has accesses to different networks. One IP address identifies one access to the network, and not one machine on the network.

Class D

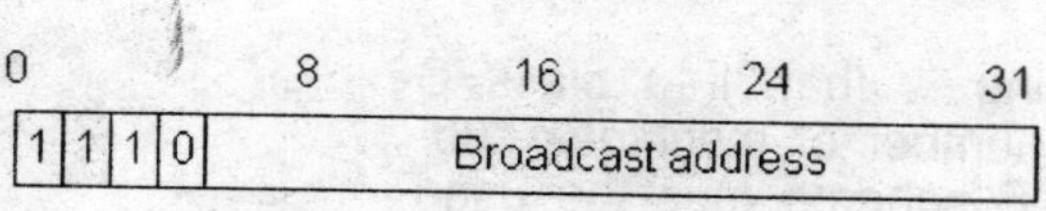

A multicast address can be attributed to a host, in addition to its unique address. This technique allows several peripherals to be identified simultaneously (so that they can receive a multimedia emission, for example).

The first-byte value is between 224 and 239 (inclusive).

Network address and broadcast address

An address in which the machine number is equal to zero is used to refer to the network itself. Consequently, a machine cannot have an address in which all the bits of the machine number are reset to zero.

If all the bits of an address that correspond to the machine number are set to one, then it is a broadcast address. A broadcast address references all the machines in the network.

On some UNIX systems, an address with all its bits reset to zero is used in order to signify a broadcast from the host.

Local broadcast address

An address in which all the bits are set to one, corresponds to a local broadcast address that is intended for all the machines in the network in which the machine that is emitting the address is located. In this case, the emitting machine does not need to know its own network address.

Network address that is completely reset to zero

If a machine does not yet know its network number, it can send a message in which the network number is zero. In this case the destination of the message will be interpreted as being the current network. The workstations that respond to the request will return a network address that is completely formed. This will allow the emitter to know the address of its network.

Drawbacks of Internet addressing

One drawback of Internet addressing is that if a machine is moved from one network to another then its address must be modified accordingly.

Another difficulty of Internet addressing is that, if a class C addressing scheme is used, and the number of machines subsequently exceeds 254, then a class B scheme must be used and the network address must be modified accordingly.

In the event of failure of one of the networks, a machine that has several addresses might be accessible through one address, and not through another.

Dotted decimal notation

IP addresses are composed of four decimal integers that are separated by dots.

Local loopback address

The local loopback address is equal to 127.0.0.1. This address is used for inter-process communications on the local machine. A local broadcast address in which the network number is equal to 127 is never emitted on the network.

NIC (Network Information Center)

All the IP addresses are allocated by a central organization that is called the NIC. This is done in order to guarantee the uniqueness of the network part. However, an organization that is assigned a network number can choose its own machine numbers.

A network number is assigned only when an organization wishes to connect to the Internet. On the other hand, if an organization decides to operate autonomously, it is free to choose whatever network number it considers to be appropriate.

2. IP configuration

IP Address

It is essential that you do not choose the IP address of a LAN arbitrarily. Such an approach could have undesirable effects for you, and for others, and in any case would not allow you to work on the network.

Subnet mask

In order to understand the role of the subnet mask, you must write it in binary (for this purpose you can use the Windows 2000 Calculator in scientific view!). The purpose is precisely to identify the bits that encode the IP network number, from amongst the bits that are used to encode the host number. A bit that is set to '1' in the subnet mask signifies that the corresponding bit in the IP address is part of the network number. On the other hand, a '0' in the subnet mask designates a bit that is used in the IP address so as to encode part of a host number.

For example, suppose you have an IP address of 192.142.1.15 that is associated with a subnet mask of 255.255.255.0. In binary, this IP address is 11000000.10001110.00000001.00001111 whilst the subnet mask in binary is: 11111111.11111111.11111111. 00000000. By carrying out a LOGICAL AND between the address and the subnet mask you determine the IP address of the network. With a LOGICAL AND, the association of two 1s produces 1, and the association of two 0s, or of one 1 and one 0, produces 0. The result in binary is 11000000.10001110.00000001.00000000, which equals 192.142.1.0 in decimal.

Default gateway

The default gateway is the IP address of the router interface that allows you to leave the LAN. Without this indication, a network peripheral cannot communicate beyond a router, and the information could not leave the LAN.

A Windows 2000 computer that has two network interface cards can act as a router for a given protocol.

3. Automatic configuration

For the automatic configuration of TCP/IP protocol, the network must contain a server that will distribute IP configurations to clients that request them. This type of server is called a DHCP (*Dynamic Hosts Configuration Protocol*) server. A DHCP server must have a static IP configuration. Windows 2000 Server can perform this function.

In order to transform your computers into DHCP clients you must:

– Right-click **My Network Places** and then select **Properties**.
– Right-click **Local Area Connection** and then select **Properties**.
– Under the **General** tab, select **Internet Protocol (TCP/IP)** and then click the **Properties** button.

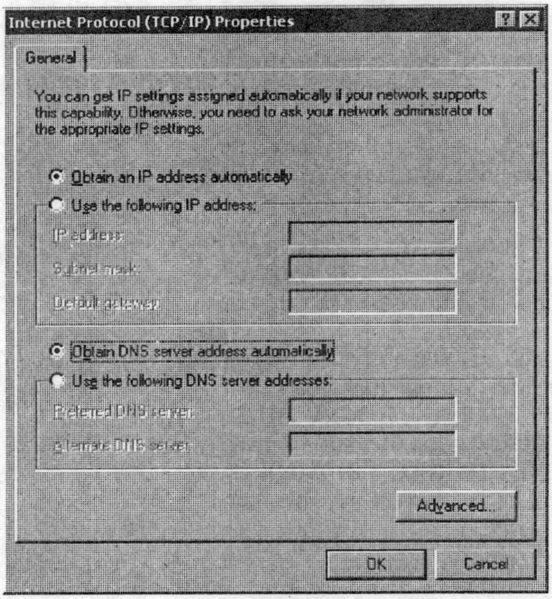

– Select **Obtain an IP address automatically**.
Then, you can choose automatically to obtain the address of the DNS server for which your machine is a client via the DHCP server. Alternatively, you can choose to enter this address manually.

The DHCP server can supply many items of information, including the following:

– IP address (compulsory).

- Subnet mask (compulsory).
- Default gateway(s).
- The IP address of one or more DNS servers.
- The IP address of one or more WINS servers.
- Node type (the resolution mode of netBIOS names).
- Domain name.

4. Manual configuration

For the client computers in your network, it is useful to use DHCP protocol in order to distribute IP configurations. This technique avoids any duplication of addresses. In addition, this approach simplifies and speeds up the administration.

However, your servers require a fixed addressing scheme. This is particularly important if services such as DNS, DHCP and WINS run on these servers.

In order to configure the IP addresses of your servers manually, check to ensure that the addresses that are used by your servers do not correspond to addresses that could be allocated by a DHCP server.

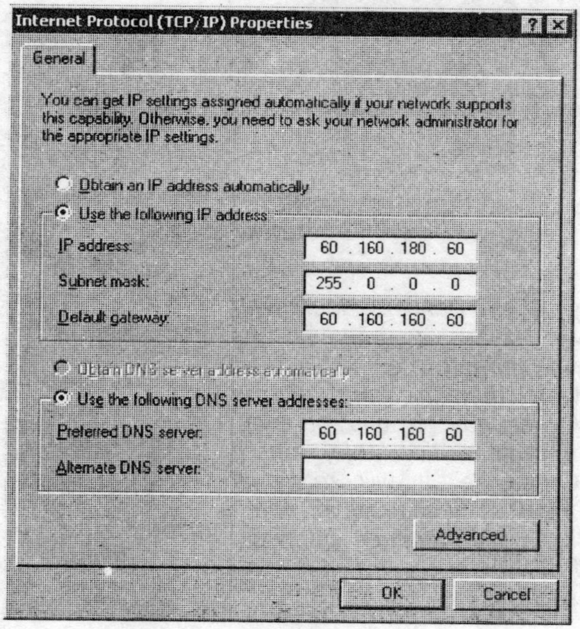

The **Advanced** button allows you to complete this IP configuration.

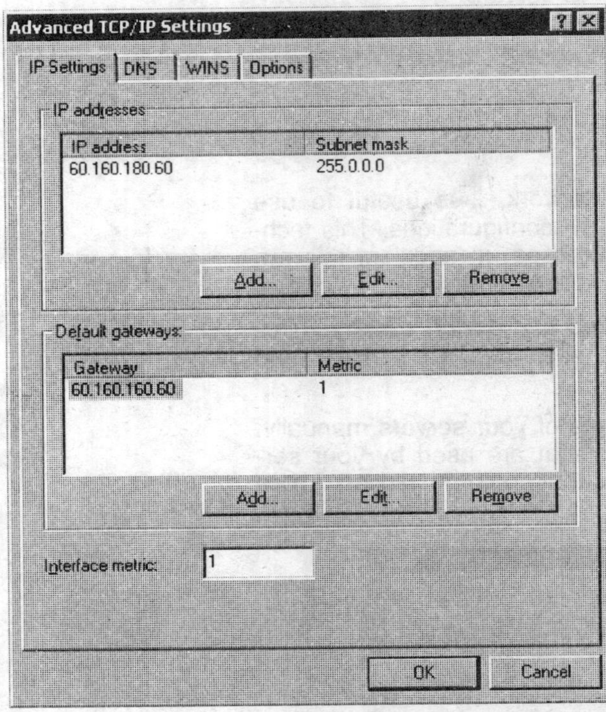

– The **IP Settings** tab allows you to add one or more IP addresses for the same interface, along with several gateway addresses.

Important note: if you specify several gateway addresses for an interface, the first will always be used if it is accessible. For example, if you attempt to contact a host that is not on your sub-network, then the query will be directed to the first default gateway. If this gateway knows the destination host (from its routing table), then it will forward the packet. Otherwise, it will return a message stating that the host is inaccessible, even though it might be accessible via another gateway. These other gateways will be used only if the first gateway is physically inaccessible.

A metric is associated with each network interface. This value is integrated into the routing table of the computer. It indicates the cost of reaching a given network. If, in a routing table, a network is accessible via two separate interfaces, then the interface that has the smaller metric will be used.

- The **DNS** tab allows you to specify the IP addresses for supplementary DNS servers, with a view to providing fault tolerance. A DNS name server allows you to resolve host names into IP addresses (for example: **ping merlin**, or **ping merlin.enipub.com**)
- The **WINS** tab allows you to specify a list of the WINS servers that will be used for resolving NetBIOS names (for example: **net view \\merlin**). This tab also allows you to disable NetBIOS. By default, NetBIOS is enabled on TCP/IP. If you disable NetBIOS, you will no longer be able to use **My Network Places** in order to display the list of servers that are available on your network.
- The **Options** tab allows you to filter IP packets. It also allows you to secure the IP traffic using IPSec.

D. Optimizing bindings

When you install several protocols on a computer that is equipped with one or more network interface cards, then bindings are set up between the protocols, the services and the network adapters. On the same network interface card, several communications protocols can be bound together (for example, TCP, NetBEUI and NWlink), and these protocols can be bound to several services.

The order of these bindings affects the performance of your servers. For example, if you install NetBEUI and TCP/IP on a Windows 2000 server that uses two network adapters, then you might want one of your network segments to run only TCP/IP, whilst another segment runs only NetBEUI. It may be useful to change the order of these bindings.

This is because, when you initialize a communication, the system tries first to communicate using the protocol that is positioned at the top of the bindings list. If this protocol proves to be unsuitable, then it will silently use the second protocol on the list, and so forth. In this case, it might be useful to delete a protocol binding on a card (for example, on a segment that uses TCP/IP, you could disable NetBEUI).

Similarly, if your server needs several communication protocols, then you should position at the top of the list, the protocol that the applications use most frequently. This will improve the performance of your server.

If you need only one protocol, do not install all the protocols on the basis that you may need them at some time in the future. By limiting yourself to those protocols that you really need, you will improve the performance of your machine. You can always install other protocols later, as and when you need them.

You can modify the status of your bindings as follows:

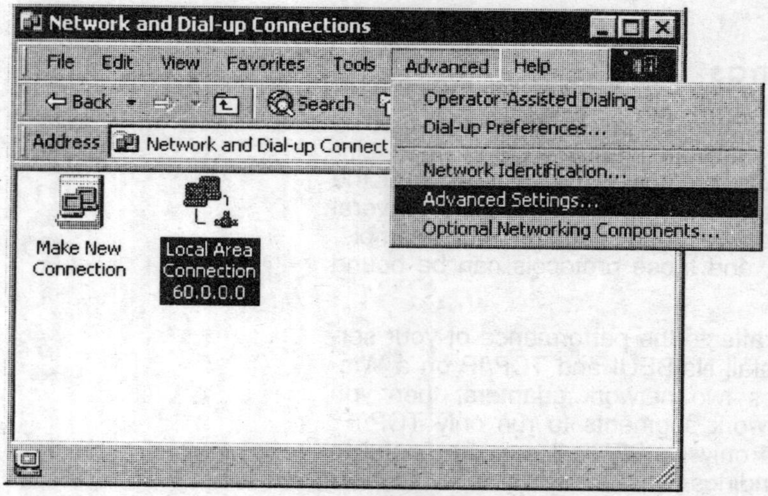

Select **Advanced Settings.**

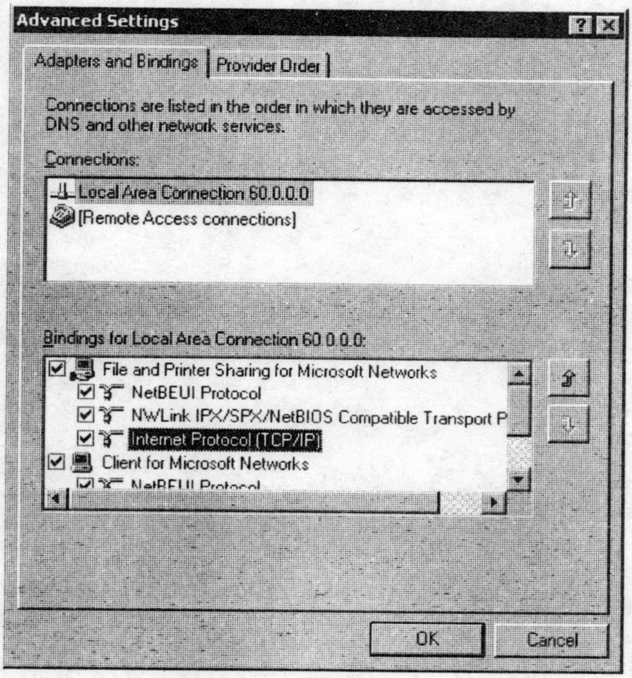

In order to change the order of your bindings, click the protocol concerned and then use the buttons ⇧ and ⇩.

In order to disable a protocol, deactivate the check box for the protocol that you do not want to use on the connection.

↓ personal notes ↓

A. TCP/IP and Internet protocols 78

1. Introduction **78**
2. History **79**
3. The Internet protocol suite and the OSI model . . **79**
4. Resolving names **83**

B. Domain Name System 86

1. General definition **86**
2. Windows 2000 and the DNS **88**
3. Implementing a DNS server **88**
4. Configuring DNS zones **92**
5. Creating records manually **99**
6. Creating subdomains **100**
7. Configuring the clients **103**

DNS

A. TCP/IP and Internet protocols

1. Introduction

The TCP/IP family was developed by an American state organization, the DoD (*Department of Defense*). It comprises around a hundred protocols, and defines a model with four network layers. TCP/IP appeared in the early 70s, ten years before the OSI model.

This is one of the most popular communication and application protocols. It is used to connect together heterogeneous systems, independently of the physical layer.

TCP (*Transfer Control Protocol)* is a transport protocol. It ensures a reliable service, which is connection oriented for a stream of bytes.

In contrast to TCP, **UDP** (*User Datagram Protocol*) is a connectionless transport protocol. It is very fast, but it is not very reliable.

UDP is used on the Internet in order to transport live sound on certain radio sites. In these cases, the data that is transferred does not require the transmission to be perfect.

IP (*Internet Protocol*), provides a packet delivery system that is connectionless and unreliable. It manages logical addresses that decompose the identifier of each node into a logical network number, and a peripheral number. This logical address has a length of 4 bytes (with IP version 4).

IP v.6 protocol, or IP Next Generation, is currently being developed. It will be compatible with IP v.4, but it will require that all the TCP/IP protocols are rewritten. The IP address will be extended to 16 bytes. The Windows 2000, DNS server service allows you to add IPv6 hosts.

One of the keys to the success of the Internet protocols is that the model proposed is independent of the physical layer.

2. History

In 1970, Stanford University developed ARPANET (*Advanced Research Project Agency NETWork*) and the TCP/IP architecture. The DoD financed this work, and the physical media were based essentially on packet communication.

In 1993, the DARPA (*Defense Advanced Research Project Agency*), who had standardized the principal TCP/IP modules, made the use of TCP/IP obligatory for all the machines that were connected to ARPANET.

ARPANET developed from a small packet switching network on point-to-point telephone links, into an immense hybrid network called the **Internet**.

Today, ARPANET is the part of the Internet that is used by the DoD for research and development.

The integration of Internet protocols into BSD (*Berkeley Software Distribution*) Unix, and the free diffusion of this operating system to universities, largely contributed to the success of this protocol suite.

The protocols continue to evolve thanks to the *Internet Activity Board*, and to the readily accessible RFC (*Request For Comment*) standardization documents.

3. The Internet protocol suite and the OSI model

It must be remembered that the TCP/IP model appeared ten years before the OSI model, which was heavily inspired by certain TCP/IP protocols. However, it is useful to compare the OSI model, which has seven layers, with the Internet protocols, which operate on four layers:

OSI model	*TCP/IP model*				
5-6-7	Application	Telnet	ftp	dns	snmp
4	Transport	TCP		UDP	
3	Internet	ARP	IP	ICMP	
1-2	Network Interface	Ethernet	Token Ring	Others	

User application services

A certain number of services and applications are based on the TCP/IP protocol stack.

TELNET is a terminal emulation protocol. A session is set up between a workstation (telnet client) and a remote machine (telnet server). All communication that is entered on the client is transmitted to the telnet server, where it is executed. The echo of the remote process is returned to the work- station, which reads the command report. Consequently, telnet must know the commands of the remote operating system.

FTP *(File Transfer Protocol)* uses a reliable mode and runs on TCP. The big advantage of FTP is that you can use it between different operating systems that are based on heterogeneous file systems. After the connection has been set up (when the name and the password have been accepted), the ftp client sees the directory of the user who logged onto the ftp server, in addition to the client's own local working directory.

On the Internet, there are many ftp sites that allow anyone to download files (this is done using the ftp guest user, which is called anonymous, and which has no password).

Using the special FTP commands, you can copy files from one directory to another (according to the permissions that you have on each system).

Internet operators now offer connections to ftp sites in graphic mode. Such interfaces allow you to download files by a simple click, without knowing any special commands.

TFTP or *Trivial FTP*, allows you to download information rapidly, but it does not guarantee its integrity. It is unreliable because it uses UDP protocol, rather than TCP.

RIP (*Routing Internet Protocol*) is a dynamic routing protocol. One of its fundamental roles concerns the exchange of routing information between routers, so that each of them is able to use the network list in order to propose a *better* route (in this context, a "better" route is one that crosses fewer routers).

***Routed** is a version of RIP that is implemented on UNIX 4.2 BSD.*

SMTP is a simple transfer protocol that is used for electronic mail (*Simple Mail Transfer Protocol*). It uses UDP and IP. It does not provide a user interface.

NFS or *Network File System* was developed by SUN around 1985. It is a distributed file system that runs in a heterogeneous environment (application layer). It allows users of different computers and operating systems to access a remote file system without the need to learn any specific new commands.

DNS is short for *Domain Name System*. Rather than trying to remember the IP address of a machine, it is simpler to work with names. At first, these names were aliases that were stored locally. Then, they were available to everyone from a centralized file (**/etc/hosts** on Unix). Progressively, a distributed hierarchical database management system was set up that associates each IP address with one or more names. Today, the Internet uses such a database. At the root of this world-level domain tree, there are 13 DNS servers. These servers are strategically placed and they know the DNS servers that are situated on the next level down, which manage all types of organization along with the country suffixes. This approach allows you to define DNS servers at different levels of the domain tree.
For example, ***www.dev.microsoft.com*** corresponds to a machine, which is called **www**, and which is in the ***dev*** (development) subdomain, of the ***microsoft*** domain, of the ***com*** (commercial) type of organization.

There is nothing to stop Microsoft from managing one DNS server in the ***microsoft.com*** domain, and another in the ***dev.microsoft.com*** subdomain.

WINS, or *Windows Internet Name Service*, is a (NetBIOS) windows name service that runs in internetwork (internetwork must not be confused with the Internet, and similarly, WINS must not be confused with DNS). The products that are based on the NetBIOS layer (including those of Microsoft) handle high-level identifiers that are called **NetBIOS names** (for example, workstation names). These names must be short (from 8 to 15 characters), and they must be unique on the internetwork concerned. The major drawback with this approach is that it does not allow a hierarchical structure. Internetwork functioning is possible because NetBIOS uses IP, which is a routable protocol.

In fact, NetBIOS was originally intended for LANs. It found a specific machine by sending a broadcast packet to all the workstations (in order to find out the physical address that is associated with a name). The problem with this approach is that, generally, a broadcast does not cross a router.

The purpose of WINS therefore, is to **manage a centralized database** on a WINS server that **associates a NetBIOS name with an IP address**. This **dynamic** database is built up by all the name registration requests that are made by the (WINS) clients. First, these clients register their names and addresses with the server. Then, the other clients query the server.

A client communicates with its server by specifying the server's IP address. The client can either register itself, or it can request the resolution of a name into an IP address.

DHCP or *Dynamic Host Configuration Protocol* is a protocol that automatically configures TCP/IP options for clients, in a NetBIOS environment.

This protocol allows you dynamically to attribute, an IP address, and a subnet mask. In addition, it even allows you to attribute such items as the IP address of a DNS server, and a default gateway IP address (the IP address of a router that allows you to go out of your LAN).

This protocol is very useful, especially for portable machines that must change the network in which they run, and consequently their IP network number.

SNMP or *Simple Network Management Protocol*, uses UDP and allows you remotely to administer both hardware and software. On the one hand, the SNMP agents must provide information, or respond to queries from an administration manager or platform (for example, HPOV, HP Open View on HP-UX). In this way, the SNMP manager collects large amounts of information from routers, switches, bridges and specific applications. In addition, it provides statistical information and sends commands to devices in order to manage events remotely.

Locally, the SNMP agents run on certain, selected layers of the OSI model, and store the information in databases that are called **MIB** (*Management Information Base*).

4. Resolving names

Applications that are developed on Windows 2000 can work directly with TCP/IP sockets, in the same way as Telnet and FTP applications do. Other applications use communications that are based on NetBIOS. This technique frees these applications from the underlying protocol:

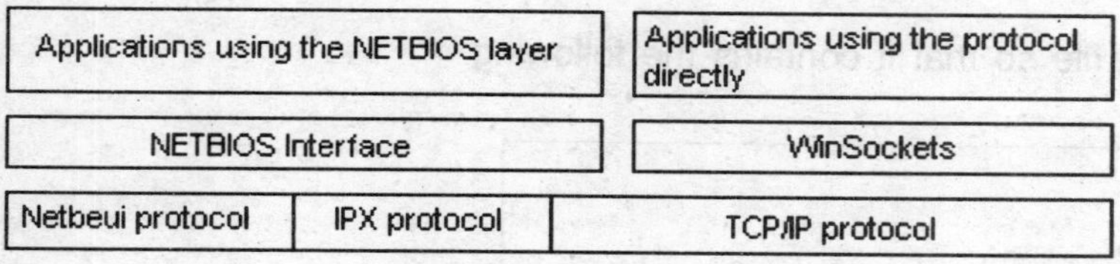

Applications that are based on NetBIOS communicate using machine names such as GALAHAD, MERLIN and EXCALIBUR, for example.

On the other hand, Windows Sockets applications use Internet names or host names. In both cases, the objective is to use convivial names that are easy to remember, in an environment where only IP addresses can be used to identify the computers!

NetBIOS names

Resolution methods

Suppose that you want to access a computer that is located on the other side of a router, by specifying its NetBIOS name. For this purpose, you may wish to use the command **net view\\computer**, for example.
By default, a broadcast will be used in order to resolve a NetBIOS name into an IP address. Consequently, as the broadcast will not get past the router, the **net view** command will generate **Error 53**, so as to indicate that the name was not found.

In order to solve this problem, you can use an LMHOSTS (Lan Manager HOSTS) static mapping file. Alternatively, you can use a service that implements registration requests, in addition to name resolution requests: Windows Internet Name Services (WINS).

Using LMHOSTS

First you must rename the **LMHOSTS.SAM** (sample) file, in order to remove the name extension.
(Remember that on Windows NT and Windows 2000 machines, this file is located, in the **\winnt\system32\drivers\etc** directory, and that on Windows 95 machines it is situated in the **\win95** directory).

Your next step is to edit this file so that it contains the following information:

```
# start of LMHOST file
#
10.0.0.1            merlin

# do not forget at least one new line
# after the line: 10.0.0.1            merlin
```

You will now be able to use commands that call NetBIOS:

```
Microsoft Windows 2000 [Version 5.00.2195]
(C) Copyright 1985-1999 Microsoft Corp.

E:\>net view \\merlin
Shared resources at \\merlin


Share name   Type        Used as  Comment

-------------------------------------------------------------------------------
Domain DFS   Disk
NETLOGON     Disk                 Logon server share
SYSVOL       Disk                 Logon server share
The command completed successfully.


E:\>
```

If you know that an entry in the LMHOSTS file will be used frequently then you can add the **#PRE** command (in uppercase characters) at the end of the line. This will cause this entry to be placed in the memory cache. In this way, not only will you avoid failure of the broadcast, but you will also avoid needless analysis of the LMHOSTS file. The entry will be loaded into the memory cache, either upon initialization, or following the command **nbtstat -R**.

The LMHOSTS file will then look like this:

```
# start of LMHOST file
#
10.0.0.1            merlin   #PRE

# do not forget at least one new line
# after the line: 10.0.0.1          merlin
```

Internet names

Here again you have the problem of resolving host names into IP addresses. Whilst the NetBIOS world offers the WINS and the LMHOSTS solutions, Internet offers two similar solutions: use of the HOSTS file, or use of a DNS server.

Using the HOSTS file

This file is located in the **\WINNT\system32\drivers\etc** directory on Windows NT and Windows 2000 machines, and in the **\WINDOWS** directory on Windows 95 machines. It is compatible with the UNIX format, and is made up of a series of lines that have the following structure:

```
IP_address Host_name alias
```

Here is an example of the HOSTS file on the GALAHAD machine. This file allows you to contact the MERLIN machine that is located on another network:

```
# start of the HOSTS file on the GALLAHAD machine
#
127.0.0.1           localhost
10.0.0.1            merlin  merlin.ediENI.com
#
# end of HOSTS file
```

DNS

You can now use the **PING** command, or the **TELNET** command using, either the simple name, or the FQDN *(Fully Qualified Domain Name)*, rather than the IP address:

```
E:\>ping merlin

Pinging merlin.enipub.com [10.10.2.1] with 32 bytes of data:

Reply from 10.10.2.1: bytes=32 time<10ms TTL=128
Reply from 10.10.2.1: bytes=32 time<10ms TTL=128
Reply from 10.10.2.1: bytes=32 time<10ms TTL=128
Reply from 10.10.2.1: bytes=32 time<10ms TTL=128

Ping statistics for 10.10.2.1:
    Packets: Sent = 4, Received = 4, Lost = 0 (0% loss),
Approximate round trip times in milli-seconds:
    Minimum = 0ms, Maximum =  0ms, Average =  0ms

E:\>ping merlin.enipub.com

Pinging merlin.enipub.com [10.10.2.1] with 32 bytes of data:

Reply from 10.10.2.1: bytes=32 time<10ms TTL=128
Reply from 10.10.2.1: bytes=32 time<10ms TTL=128
Reply from 10.10.2.1: bytes=32 time<10ms TTL=128
Reply from 10.10.2.1: bytes=32 time<10ms TTL=128

Ping statistics for 10.10.2.1:
    Packets: Sent = 4, Received = 4, Lost = 0 (0% loss),
Approximate round trip times in milli-seconds:
    Minimum = 0ms, Maximum =  0ms, Average =  0ms

E:\>
```

B. Domain Name System

1. General definition

TCP/IP utilities, such as Telnet or FTP, can communicate using the IP address of the remote machine. Alternatively, they can use the name of the remote machine, which is different from the NetBIOS name that is used on Windows hosts. It is easier for a user to refer to the "MERLIN" machine, rather than to the 132.147.160.1 IP address!

Because of its size, the Internet network cannot use only simple names in order to refer to all the machines that it contains. As with all big organizations, it was decided to divide the network into different areas, each of which corresponds either to a geographical entity, or to a function, or to a type of activity. Each "department" can then be subdivided itself, so as to form a tree structure, with a manager that is responsible for managing the set of names that are used within the structure.

In the context of TCP/IP interconnections, the mechanism that is used to manage these sets of names is called **Domain Name System** or **DNS**.

The TCP/IP DNS system uses the following domains:

Name	Signification
COM	Commercial enterprise
EDU	Educational establishments
GOV	Government establishments
MIL	Military organizations
NET	Major network sites
ORG	Other organizations
ARPA	Arpanet domains
INT	International organizations
Country Code	Each country

Originally, the Internet existed only in the USA and the domain names had suffixes that indicated the type of organization. The network has since been extended to all countries, and there is now a domain per country. Consequently, the sites with name suffixes that indicate a type of organization are principally located in the USA; whilst for sites outside of the USA with a country suffix, the type of organization is not repeated. Thus, the tree structure is based on the type of organization and on the geographical location.

Examples:

The ANDROMEDA server in the training department of the ENI commercial organization in the UK could have the following name:

`andromeda.training.eni.uk`

For a server called SUPPORT that is situated in the Microsoft organization in the USA, the DNS name would be:

`Support.Microsoft.com`

The DNS is case insensitive.

Here is an example tree structure:

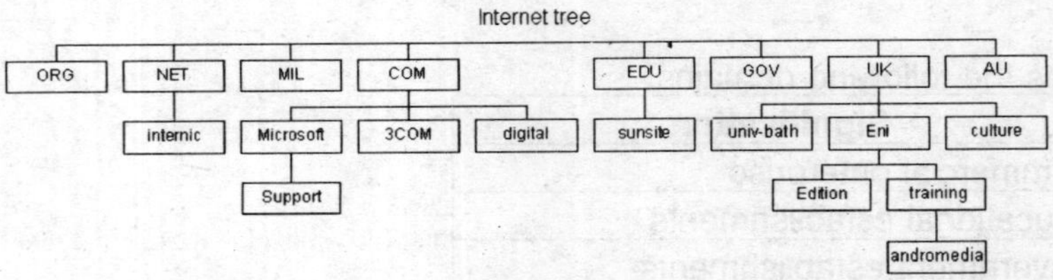

In practice, however, this tree structure is very simplified and there is an extremely large number of domains, already on the third level!

When you access a machine, you can use a relative name, as in the following command:

```
FTP andromeda
```

Alternatively, you can use the FQDN (*Fully Qualified Domain Name*), which is an absolute reference:

```
FTP andromeda.training.eni.uk
```

2. Windows 2000 and the DNS

Windows 2000 uses the DNS standard for its domain names. For example, your Windows 2000 domain could be called ENI.UK.

Consequently, you must use the DNS service in a network that contains Windows 2000 domains. In addition, the DNS system is used in order to resolve host names into IP addresses, and to locate network services that run in the domain. For example, when you open a session on a Windows 2000 domain, you query your DNS server in order to obtain the list of domain controllers that can authenticate your logon.

Before you can promote a member or stand-alone server to a domain controller (by installing Active Directory), you must have access to a DNS server.

3. Implementing a DNS server

The version of the DNS service that is provided by Microsoft for Windows 2000 offers a number of advantages over the versions of this service that can be found on a UNIX system, or even on a Windows NT 4 server.

A DNS server has a database that associates host names with IP addresses. With most DNS servers, this association is done manually. Windows 2000 DNS allows registrations to be made automatically, either by the client itself, or by a DHCP server in the case where the client receives its IP configuration via such a server. In addition to saving administration time, the huge advantage that is offered by this approach is that the DNS database is always up-to-date.

Windows 2000 DNS supports **SRV** type records. These records are used when a client needs to find a server that plays a specific role. Consequently, in addition to its host name, each machine registers the list of roles that it plays. For example, a client that wishes to search in Active Directory must first locate an LDAP server via the DNS server.

The DNS service has also been improved with respect to its zone transfer method. This will be covered later on in this chapter. In addition, the DNS service can be integrated into Active Directory.

You can install the DNS service as follows:

☞ Open **Control Panel**, and double-click the **Add/Remove Programs** icon.

☞ Click the **Add/Remove Windows Components** button, followed by the **Components** button. Then select the **Networking Services** component, and click the **Details** button.

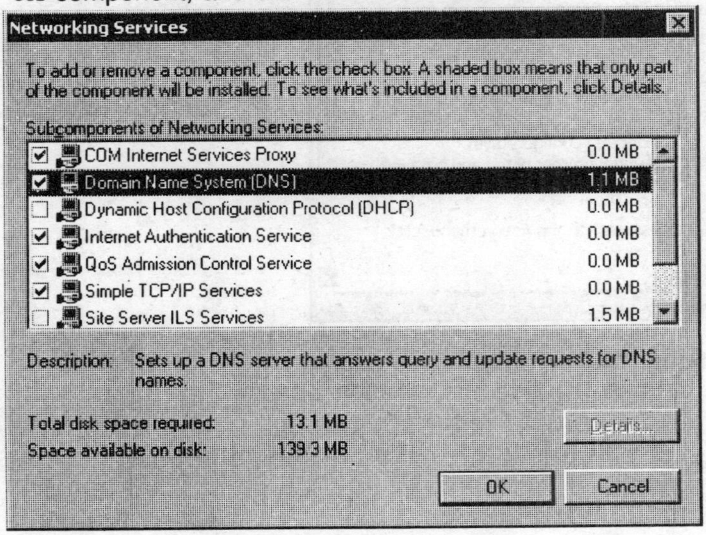

☞ Activate the **Domain Name System (DNS)** check box, and then click the **OK** button.

☞ Click the **Next** button in order to start installing the service (you must provide the Windows 2000 installation source files).

When the DNS service is installed, a registry key is added under HKLM\System\CurrentControlSet\Services\DNS. In addition, a DNS directory, which contains the DNS database, is added under %systemroot%system32.

When you have installed DNS, the first thing you must do is to create a zone over which the server will have authority. In order to do this, start the DNS utility from the Administrative Tools menu, and then right-click the server name.

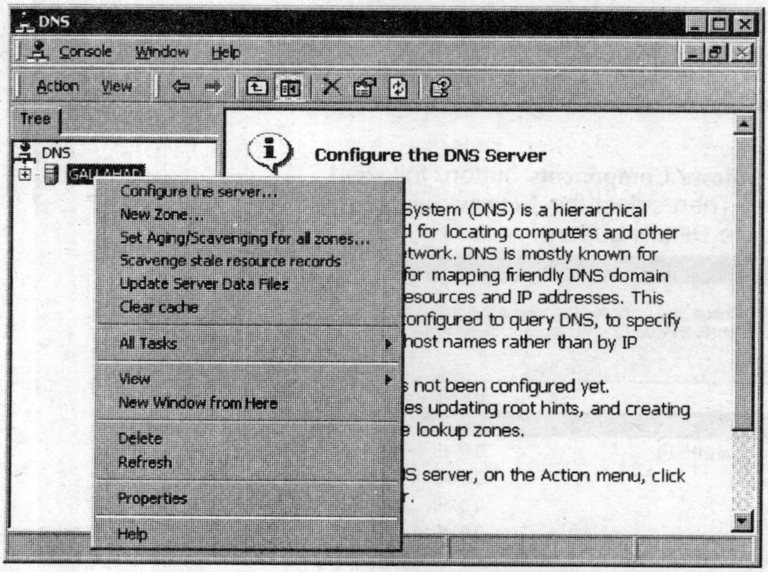

☞ Either, you can select **Configure the server**, in which case a wizard will guide you step by step, through the creation of your zones.

☞ Or, you can select **New Zone**.

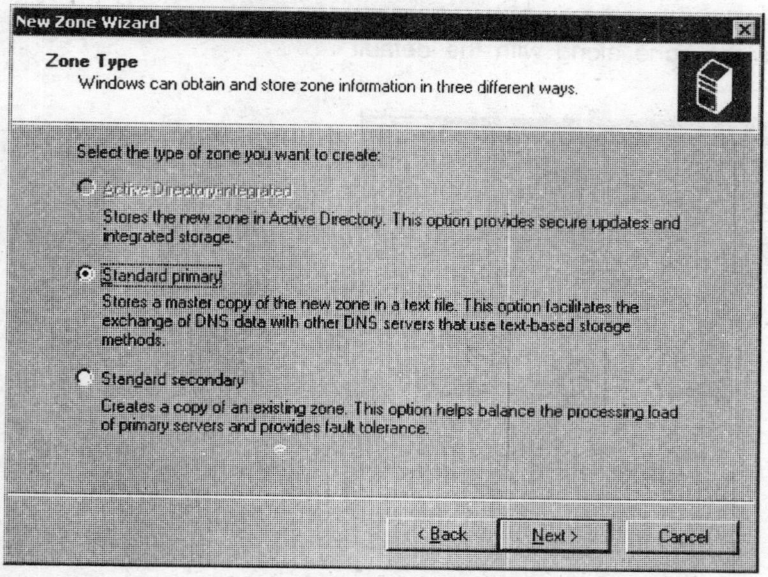

- First, you must create the primary zone. A secondary zone supplies the server with a copy of the primary zone. It provides fault tolerance, and it allows you to spread the workload.
- Select **Standard primary**, and then click **Next**.
- You must select the type of zone that you wish to create: You can choose a forward lookup zone, which allows you to resolve host names into IP addresses. Alternatively, you can choose a reverse lookup zone, which is used in certain applications in order to resolve IP addresses into host names (for example, **NFS** and **Nslookup** use this technique).
- Select **Forward lookup zone**, and then click the **Next** button.
- Enter the name you want to give to the zone that you wish to manage, and then click **Next**.
- The system automatically creates a zone file with a name that is based on that of the zone, as follows: ***zone_name.dns***. You can either modify this name, or you can click **Next** so as to accept it.
- Click **Finish** in order to validate the creation of your zone.

↓ personal notes ↓

The DNS window then shows the zone along with the default records:

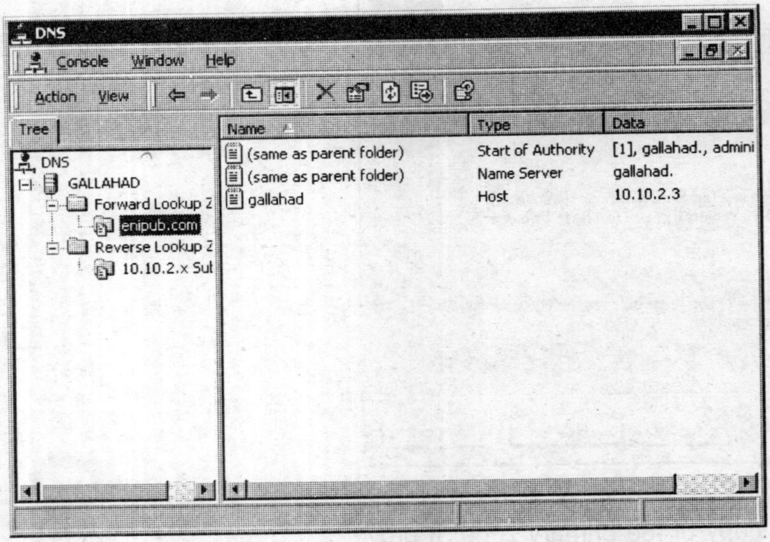

When you have created the forward lookup zone, you can also create the reverse lookup zone. In order to do this, right-click **Reverse Lookup Zone** in the DNS window, and then select **New Zone.**

- Select **Standard primary** and then click **Next.**
- Enter the network address that corresponds to the reverse lookup zone. Windows 2000 then automatically creates the corresponding zone file with the name: ***network_address_in_reverse_order.in-addr.arpa***
- Click **Next**, twice, and then click **Finish** in order to complete the operation.

4. Configuring DNS zones

Zone types

When you configure your DNS server, you can choose from three types of zone:
– Standard primary,
– Standard secondary,
– Active Directory-integrated.

These zones contain records that are associated with the namespace of the zone, in order to resolve the queries that come from the DNS clients.

Standard primary

The server that is configured as the primary server must have this type of zone. This is the primary copy of the zone database (which, in fact, is a text file). The zone can be administered from the server on which this zone file resides.

Standard secondary

This is a copy of the standard primary zone. This copy is in read-only mode. The purpose of such a zone is to provide fault tolerance with respect to the standard primary zone. If clients can no longer access the standard primary zone, then the standard secondary zone can be used. In addition, this type of zone allows you to spread the workload. Clients that send queries to a name server have the IP addresses of the servers to which they can make such requests. You can stipulate that certain users must first send their requests to the server that manages the secondary zone, and that other servers must first query the server that manages the primary zone. You can apply this technique because the secondary zone is a copy of the primary zone, and therefore both of these zone files contain the same information. However, any modifications must always be made to the primary zone.

Active Directory-integrated

This zone file is stored in the Active Directory.

The standard primary zone files and the standard secondary zone files are stored on the servers that accommodate them, in the tree ***%systemroot%\system32\dns****. With an Active Directory-integrated zone, there is no zone file on the server. The zone file is located in the Active Directory.*

You can change the type of zone at any time. This can be useful if you manage a primary zone and a secondary zone, for example. If the primary zone server breaks down, then the secondary zone can respond to client queries. However, no modification can be made to the zone file because it is in read-only mode. In this case, it might be useful to convert the secondary zone into a primary zone.

In order to do this, right-click the zone that you want to convert, and then select **Properties**.

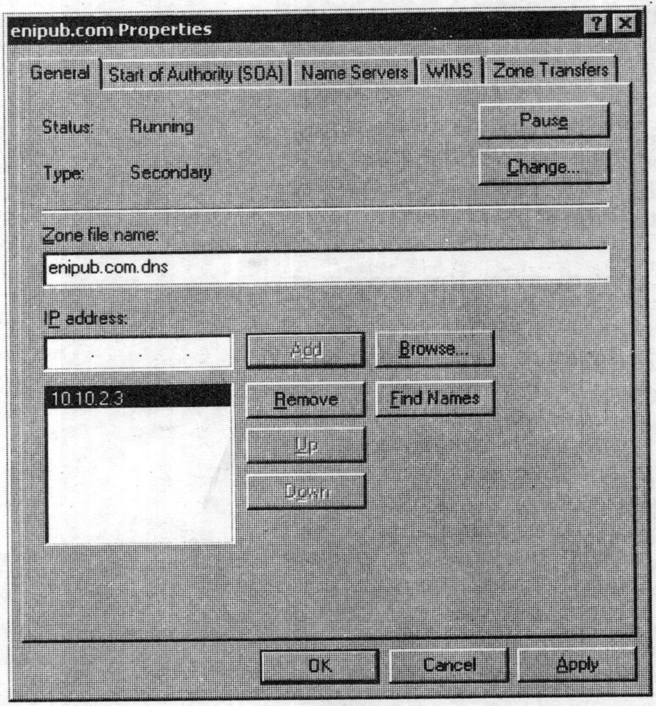

Click the **Change** button in order to display the following dialog box:

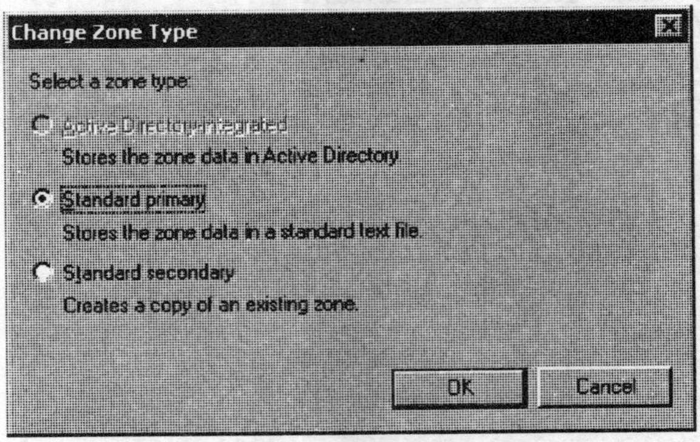

The **Active Directory-integrated** option appears grayed-out in this dialog box unless the zone that you wish to convert is located on a domain controller.

If you change a primary zone into an Active Directory-integrated zone, then the file that is located under **%systemroot%\system32\dns** is copied into the Active Directory before it is deleted from the disk. Following this operation, this zone file is considered as an Active Directory object. The zone information is then duplicated onto all the domain controllers, in the same way as user accounts are copied. In this case, all the domain controllers on which the DNS service has been installed can act as DNS servers. In addition, all the DNS servers are primary servers, and zone modifications can be carried out on any of them.

Dynamic updating

The Windows 2000 DNS service offers a dynamic update feature that automatically modifies zone files. This feature reduces the administrator's maintenance workload.

The implementation of Dynamic DNS is defined in RFC 2136. Secure dynamic update is defined in RFC 2137.

☞ Open the **DNS** console, right-click the zone name and then click **Properties**.

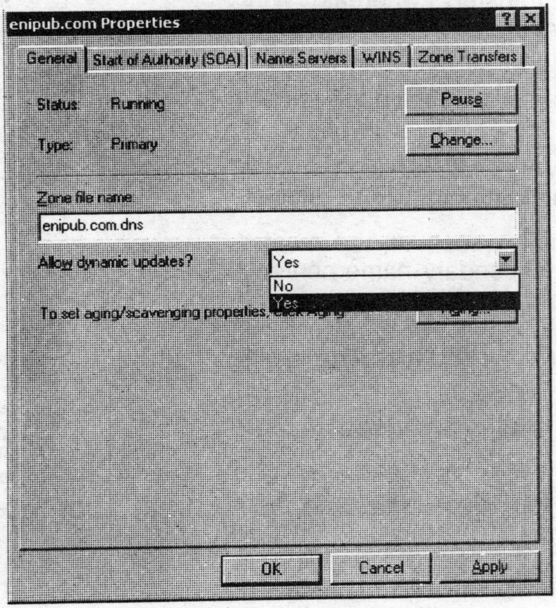

☞ Open the **Allow dynamic updates?** drop down list and then select **Yes**.

If you are managing an Active Directory-integrated zone, then you will also have the **Only secure updates** option. This option allows the DNS server to accept dynamic updates only from servers and clients who are authorized to send dynamic updates. The objective of this option is to prevent non-authorized users from modifying a zone. This feature also allows you to specify the users who are authorized to modify the zones.

During IP configuration of DHCP clients, the Windows 2000 DHCP server service can automatically supply the DNS with the necessary information so that it can update its zone. Chapter 11 of this book, which covers the DHCP, describes how you can implement this technique.

Zone Transfer

When a network contains a master name server (which provides the source of primary zone information) and one or more secondary name servers (each of which has a copy of the primary zone), then a process that is called zone transfer takes place between these servers. Most DNS servers, including that of Windows NT 4, support **AXFR** zone transfer, whereas Windows 2000 supports **AXFR** or **IXFR** zone transfer.

AXFR is also known as full zone transfer. All the zone information is duplicated from the master name sever onto all the secondary name servers.

On the other hand, IXFR transfers only that information that has been modified. IXFR is also known as incremental zone transfer.

This zone transfer process takes place as soon as the master name server sends a notification to its secondary name servers. Zone transfer also occurs, upon startup of a secondary server, or upon startup of the DNS server service, or when the refresh interval expires, or when the SOA *(Start Of Authority)* serial number is incremented.

You can modify some of the settings that define when a zone transfer must take place.

- Open the **DNS** console, right-click the zone name, and then select **Properties**.
- Select the **Start of Authority (SOA)** tab.

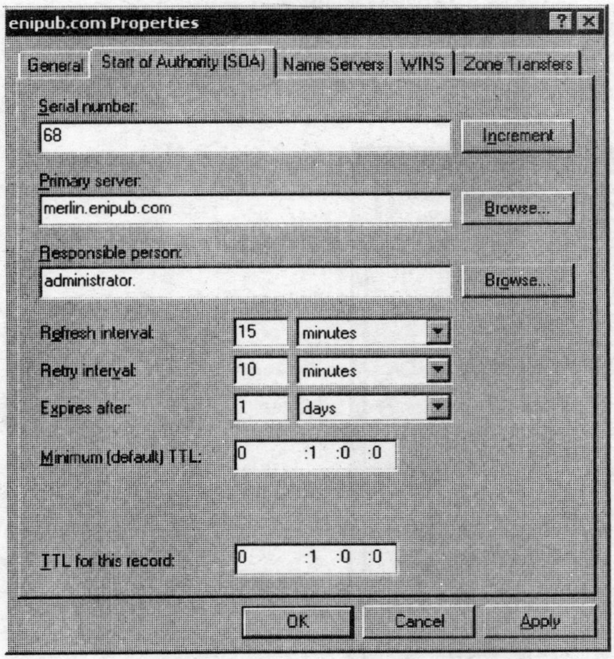

Serial number

This number indicates whether any zone modifications have taken place. It is incremented automatically when a modification is made.

Refresh interval

This item allows you to define the time interval between successive requests for zone transfers that are made from a secondary name server to its primary name server.

Retry interval

This item allows you to define the time that must elapse before a secondary name server that was not able to contact its master name server, tries again to contact its master name server in order to obtain a zone transfer.

Expires after

If this time interval elapses before the secondary name server manages to contact its master name server, then the secondary name server will stop responding to client queries.

In order to force a zone transfer, right-click the secondary zone and then select **Transfer from master**.

In order to adjust the zone transfer settings, right-click the primary zone, and then select **Properties**. Select the **Zone Transfers** tab.

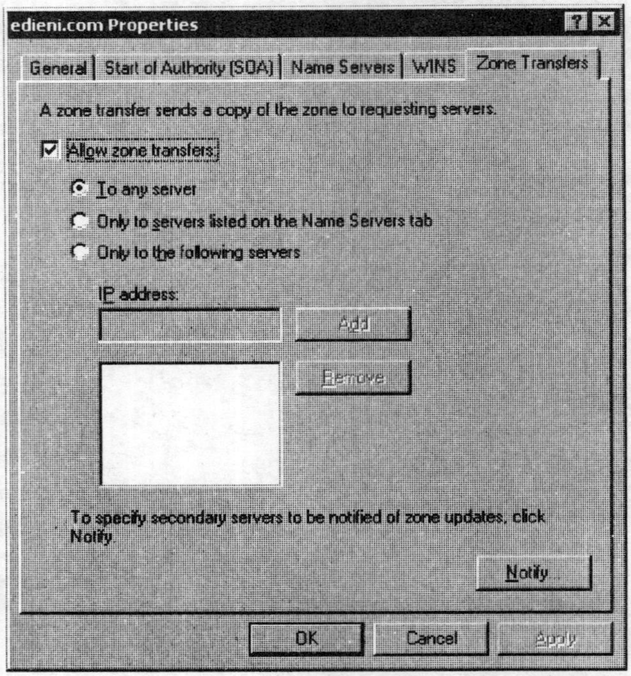

Activate the **Allow zone transfers** option box and then select the option that indicates where you want to transfer this zone.

5. Creating records manually

In addition to supporting dynamic updates, the Windows 2000 DNS server allows you to create new records manually.

In order to create a new record, right-click the zone concerned. From amongst all the available records, you can then choose, a new host, or a new alias.

– New Host: this type of record allows you to map a host name to an IP address for clients that cannot register automatically.

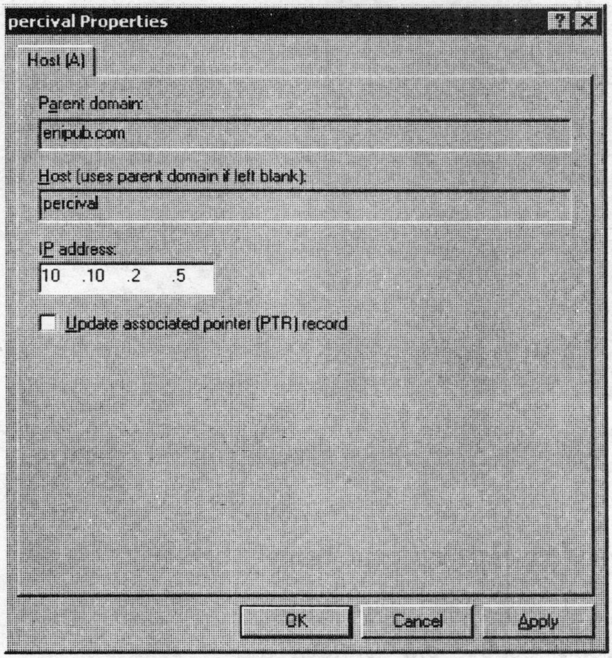

☛ Enter the host name of the client, along with its IP address. Note the **Update associated pointer (PTR) record** option. If you create a reverse lookup zone, this option allows you to record the client in it.

– New Alias: this type of record allows you to create an alias for a host name.

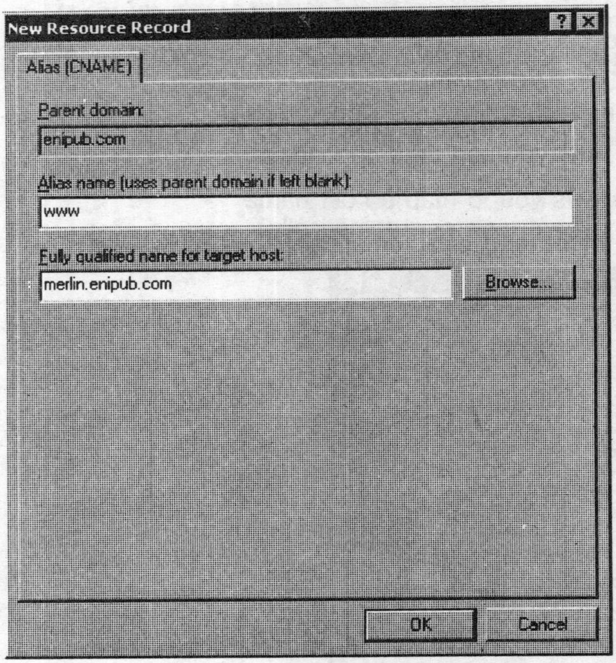

The example that is given above will allow you to use **http://www.enipub.com** instead of **http://merlin.enipub.com**.

6. Creating subdomains

You can create subdomains in order to organize your namespace. If you wish to include several domains in your Windows 2000 network, then you must create several DNS zones. These zones can belong to a contiguous namespace. For example, the **enipub.com** zone can contain a subdomain that is called **training.enipub.com**. The objective of organizing the zone in this way is to allow the administrators of the training service to manage their own zones.

In order to do this, you must create the primary **enipub.com** zone on one server, and the primary **training.enipub.com** zone on another server.

If you do not carry out any further actions, then the DNS client users of the **enipub.com** server will be able to resolve all the names of the **enipub.com** zone, but they will not be able to resolve the names of the **training.enipub.com** zone. Similarly, client users of the DNS server that manage the DNS **training.enipub.com zone**, will be able to resolve the names of this zone, but will not be able to resolve the names of the **enipub.com** zone. However, you may want everyone to be able to resolve all the names, irrespective of the zone to which they belong.

Here are the actions that you must carry out on the DNS server that manages the **enipub.com** zone, so as to implement two-way communication between both DNS domains:

- Right-click the zone name, and then click **New Delegation**.

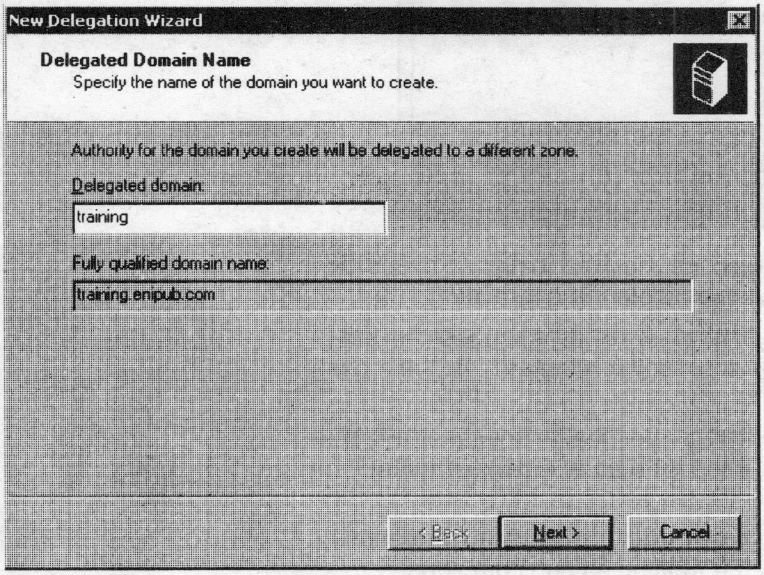

- Enter the name of a delegated domain, and then click **Next**.
- Click the **Add** button in order to indicate the server to which must be sent the queries that refer to the **training.enipub.com** zone.

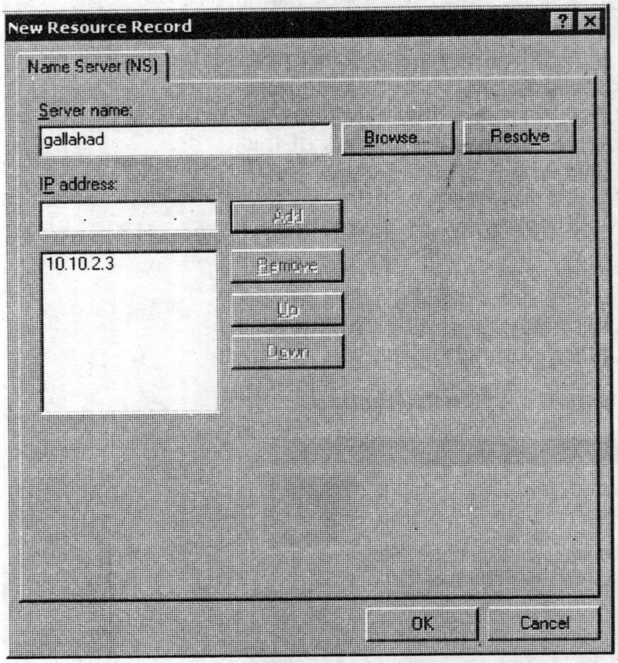

☛ Click the **OK** button followed by the **Next** button. Then click the **Finish** button in order to complete the operation.

At this stage, clients of the DNS server that manages the **enipub.com** zone will be able to resolve queries for the **training.enipub.com** zone.

However, the clients of the DNS server that manages the **training.enipub.com** zone will still not be able to resolve queries for the **enipub.com** domain.

In order to allow them to do so, carry out the following operations on the server that manages the training.enipub.com zone:

☛ Open the **DNS** console. Right-click the server name and then select **Properties**. Then, select the **Forwarders** tab.

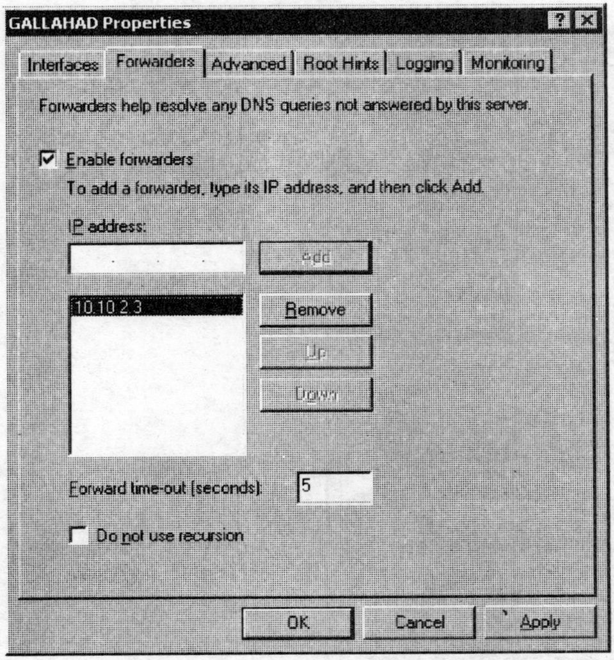

- Activate the **Enable forwarders** check box, and then enter the IP address of the parent server (in the example above, this is the IP address of the server that manages the **eni-pub.com** zone). The objective of this operation is to forward all the queries that cannot be resolved by the server that manages the **training.enipub.com** zone, to the server for which the IP address is indicated as the redirector (in the example above, this is the server that manages the **eni-pub.com** zone).

7. Configuring the clients

In order to be able to use the services that are offered by a DNS server, a machine must be a client of the DNS server.

Configuring the Windows 2000 DNS client

- Right-click **My Network Places**, then click **Properties**.
- Right-click **Local Area Connection**, then click **Properties**.
- Display the TCP/IP properties.

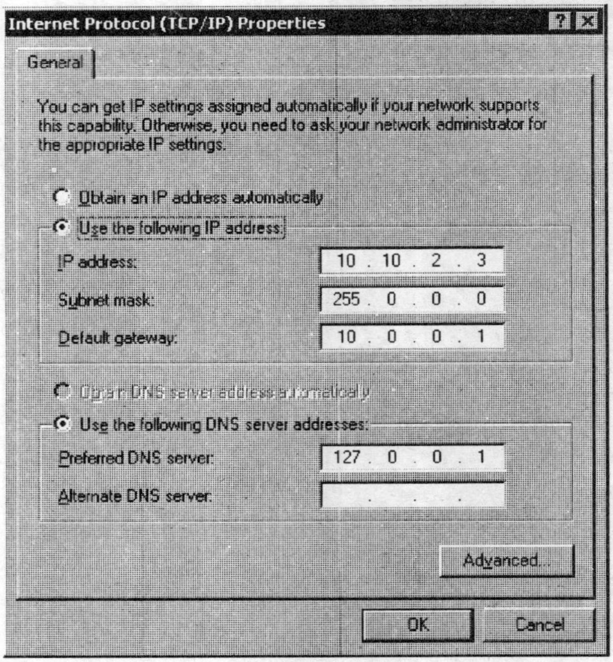

Enter the IP address of your DNS server. If you have a secondary DNS server, then you can add its address in order to provide fault tolerance.

There is no correlation between the concept of master and secondary DNS servers, and that of preferred and alternate DNS servers. In order to spread the workload, you might find it useful to define the master DNS server as the preferred DNS server for one set of users, and then to reverse the roles for a second set of users.

You can define more than two DNS servers using the **Advanced** button.

Configuring the Windows NT DNS client

- Display **Network Neighborhood - Properties**.
- Select the **Protocols** tab and display the **Properties** of the **TCP/IP Protocol**.
- Select the **DNS** tab and click the **Add** button so as to enter the address(es) of the DNS server(s) that you wish to use.

As with all TCP/IP parameters (such as WINS addresses), the DNS servers that are indicated statically have priority over those that are provided by DHCP.

Configuring the Windows 98 DNS client

- Display **Network Neighborhood - Properties**.
- Double-click the TCP/IP protocol that corresponds to the network adapter. Then, select the **DNS Configuration** tab, enter the server address, and click **Add**.

Active Directory

A. Overview **108**

B. Terminology **109**

1. Logical structure **109**
2. Objects **111**

C. Installing **113**

1. Creating a new, or root, domain **116**
2. Adding a domain controller to an existing domain **119**
3. Adding a child domain **120**
4. Adding a tree into an existing forest **120**
5. Choosing a domain mode **121**

D. Roles of domain controllers **123**

1. Operations masters **123**
2. Global catalog server **126**

E. Replication **128**

1. Overview **128**
2. Creating sites and subnets **129**
3. Intra-site and inter-site transport **131**

F. Uninstalling **136**

A. Overview

Active Directory is probably the biggest advance that Microsoft has made since the first server versions. It is a directory database that groups together all the database objects. As soon as you have a domain that is running on Windows 2000, Active Directory is your working tool. This directory database simplifies the administration of your system, and it offers a high fault tolerance as it is a distributed database.

Active Directory uses a set of standard protocols, which makes this database a network component that all applications can use. For example, Exchange 2000 can use distribution groups that are created in Active Directory so as to send messages to the users of these groups. Provided that they written for the purpose, all applications can benefit from the advantages that Active Directory offers.

Active Directory supports the following standard protocols:

- **TCP/IP**: network protocol.
- **DNS**: the Windows 2000 domain namespace is based on this service.
- **DHCP**: this IP configuration distribution protocol allows you to provide IP addressing to clients who request it. In addition it allows you to provide the DNS with information concerning distributed addresses.
- **NTP**: Network Time Protocol. All Windows 2000 machines must be synchronized because the Kerberos authentication message is based on a time-stamped access ticket.
- **LDAP**: this protocol provides access to Active Directory. When you search in Active Directory, you use an LDAP server first.
- **LDIF**: allows you to synchronize Active Directory (*Ldap Data Interchange Format*).
- **Kerberos version 5**: allows logon authentication.
- **X509 v3 certificates**: allows certificate authentication (this is used with EFS in order to encrypt folders or files, for example).

Whereas the Windows NT 4 accounts database can contain 40 000 objects per domain, the Windows 2000 directory database can contain several million objects. This provides a development potential to meet all requirements. Fault tolerance is ensured provided that you have at least two domain controllers in your domain. In fact, as Active Directory is a distributed directory database, all the domain controllers have the same information. This is made possible by a replication technique that is known as Multi-master. It means that a client can consult any domain controller in order to carry out a search in Active Directory. This ensures spreading of the workload.

B. Terminology

1. Logical structure

The logical structure of the Active Directory database is made up of **forests**, of **trees**, of **domains**, and also of **organizational units**.

Here is an example of a forest in which there are two trees, each of which is composed of three domains.

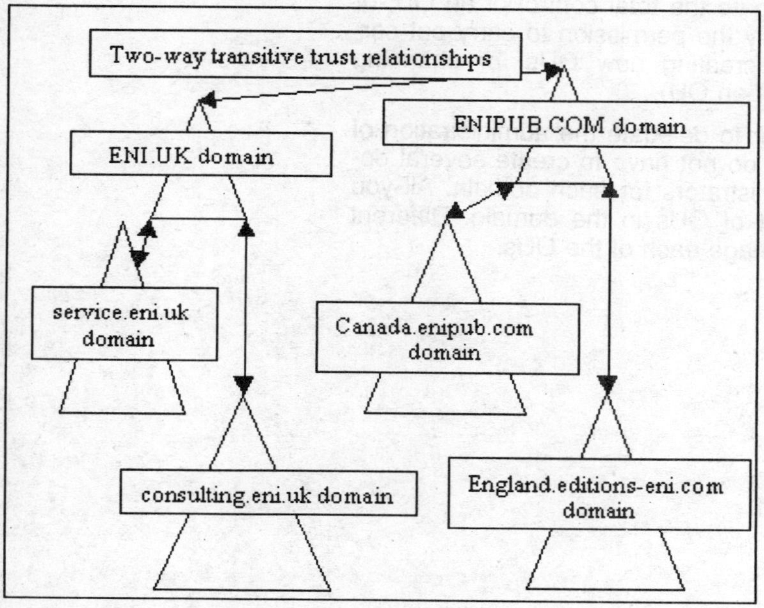

The first tree is composed of the domains **eni.uk**, **service.eni.uk** and **consulting.eni.uk**. The second tree is composed of the domains **enipub.com**, **Canada.enipub.com** and **England.enipub.com**.

This set of two trees makes up a forest.
The domains in a forest are linked together by two-way transitive trust relationships. In the example above, the **consulting.eni.uk** domain trusts the **eni.uk** domain, which in turn trusts the **enipub.com** domain. Therefore, the **consulting.eni.uk** domain trusts the **enipub.com** domain. These relationships are created automatically when the forest is confugured.
Thus, a tree is a set of domains that share a contiguous namespace.
In each domain, the network objects are organized into *organizational units* (a network object can be an item such as a user account, a computer account or a printer). The organizational units (OUs) make up a logical hierachical structure that meets an administrative need. Network objects that are included in the OUs will be subject to the rules that are defined in these OUs.

You can delegate the administration of each OU. In this way, you can spread the administrative tasks amongst several administrators. Thus, you can delegate the total control of an OU, or alternatively, you can grant only the permission to carry out certain specific tasks (such as creating new OUs, or changing account passwords for users of an OU).

Thanks to this feature, in order to delegate the administration of a Windows 2000 domain, you do not have to create several domains and then appoint administrators for each domain. All you have to do is to create a set of OUs in the domain. Different people will then be able to manage each of the OUs.

2. Objects

In the Active Directory, an object can be an item such as a user account, a printer, a computer account, a published shared folder or a group.

Each object is made up of a set of attributes that represent the object. For example, the attributes of the user object could include a first-name, a surname, a login name, a telephone and a web page, whilst those of a printer could include a name, a location and a description.

Some of the attributes of an object are obligatory (for example, a user surname), whilst others are optional (for example a user's telephone number).

All these attributes are defined in the schema. You can modify the schema yourself, so as to add new attributes for the objects. Applications can also modify the schema. For example, you may wish to add to the user object, an attribute that contains the badge number. The schema is present on all domain controllers and it is treated as an object of the Active Directory.

All the objects that have the same type have the same attributes. However, each of these objects must have different attribute values.

A set of objects that have the same attributes is called a class. For example, when you create a user, you create an object in the **User** class. When you create this object you will not modify the schema. You will modify the schema, only when you create, either new classes, or new attributes.

In order to modify the schema, you must use the **Active Directory Schema** snap-in.

You must remember that when you modify the schema, you can affect the state of your network. You must have a thorough understanding of the schema before you modify it.

Adding attributes to the schema is irreversible. You cannot remove an attribute from a schema, once you have created it.

The Directory Service uses several naming conventions.

– **Relative Distinguished Name**: this is the full name of an attribute of an object.

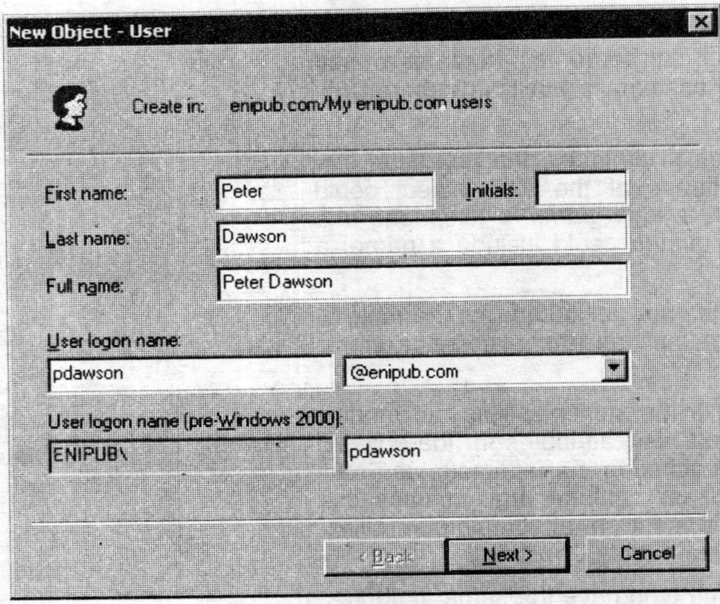

In the example above, the relative distinguished name is Peter Dawson.

- **User Principal Name**: this is a user's login name followed by the name of the domain in which the object is located. In the example above, this name could be **pdawson@enipub.com**.
- **Distinguished Name**: every Active Directory object has a distinguished name that allows you to locate it within a domain or within an OU. In the example above, the distinguished name of the user Peter Dawson is as follows: DC=com, DC=enipub, OU=my users of enipub.com, CN=Peter Dawson. This means that the user for whom the relative distinguished name is Peter Dawson is located in the "**my users of enipub.com**" OU, which is in the **enipub.com** domain (CN stands for *Common Name*, DC stands for *Domain Component*, and OU stands for *Organizational Unit*).

Each object has a unique number called the **GUID** (*Globally Unique IDentifier*). This number never changes, even if you rename the object (if you change its relative distinguished name), or if you change the location of the object (if you change its distinguished name).

As you cannot have two objects in the same OU that have the same relative distinguished name, you cannot have two objects that have the same distinguished name.

C. Installing

You can install Active Directory on a Windows 2000 member or stand-alone server. When the directory database has been installed, your server will become a domain controller.
Active Directory will be a database file called **NTDS.DIT** that is located under **%systemroot%\ntds**, by default. You can choose another path when you install Active Directory.

In order to install Active Directory you need an NTFS partition so as to store the shared system directory (SYSVOL). This is because the replication of directory database modifications is managed according to sequential version numbers that the NTFS system supports.

Active Directory is a Jet Blue aka ESE database.

In order to install Active Directory, you must run the **DCPROMO.EXE** command. The accounts database (SAM) that is on your server will be copied into the directory database before it is removed from your computer. Consequently, you will not lose accounts information when you migrate your Windows NT domain controllers to Windows 2000. If you run the **dcpromo** command on a Windows 2000 domain controller, then you will downgrade your controller to a member or stand-alone server. In this case you will obtain a clean SAM database.

In order to install Active Directory, you need a computer that is running one of the three server versions of Windows 2000 (Server, Advanced Server or Datacenter Server), a partition that is formatted in NTFS, the TCP/IP protocol, and a DNS that has been installed and configured.

If the DNS service is not installed when you run ***dcpromo****, then the Active Directory installation process will offer to install and configure it. You must have a DNS service that supports dynamic records and resource (SRV) type records.*

Before you start installing Active Directory, you must understand exactly the role of your server in the Active Directory logical structure. When you install the Windows 2000 directory database, the system will ask you whether your server must be included into an existing domain, or whether you wish to create a new domain. If you wish to create a new domain then you must know whether your new domain must be included in an existing domain tree, or whether you wish to create a new domain tree. Finally, if you wish to create a new domain tree, then you must know whether your new tree must be included in an existing forest, or whether you wish to create a new forest.

The flow chart below summarizes this decision chain:

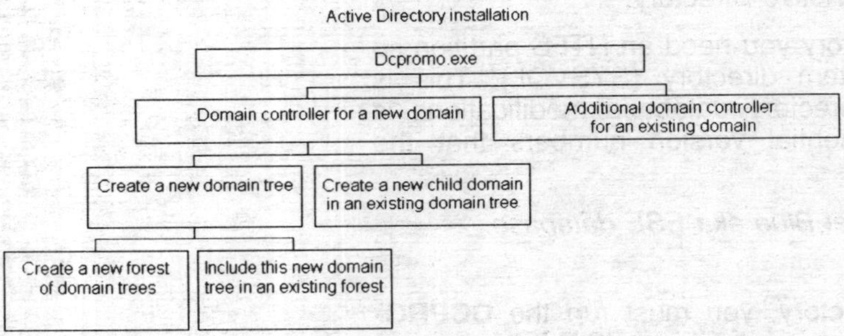

Here are the steps that you must follow in order to install Active Directory:

☛ Open, either a command prompt, or the **Run** menu.

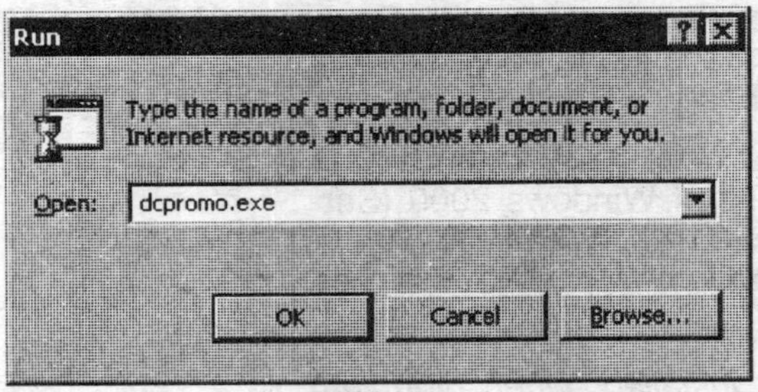

☛ Enter **dcpromo.exe** so as to start the Active Directory Installation Wizard.

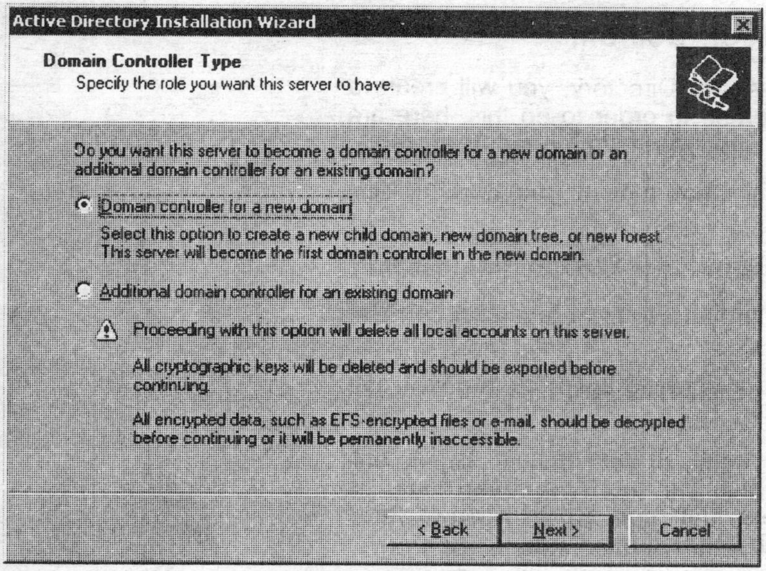

In most cases, you are strongly advised to have a single domain. Before Windows 2000, it was useful to create several domains, either for administrative reasons, or when the limit of 40 000 objects was reached. With Windows 2000, as you can delegate administration, and create several million objects, it may well be preferable to work with a single domain.

However, it may be useful to create several domains in the following cases:

- You wish to reduce replication traffic. The Active Directory information that circulates between domains is that which is brought to the global catalog server.
- You wish to apply different policies in different domains.
- You company is merging with another company and you want to maintain a separation between the data of the two companies.
- You wish to update several Windows NT domains: although several Windows NT domains can be merged into one, you consider it to be useful to carry on working with several domains.

1. Creating a new, or root, domain

The first time that you install Active Directory, you will create a new (root) domain in a new forest. In order to do this, here are the steps that you must follow after you have started **dcpromo**:

- Select **Domain controler for a new domain**, and click the **Next** button.
- Select **Create a new domain tree**, and click the **Next** button.
- Select **Create a new forest of domain trees**, and click the **Next** button.
- Enter the DNS name of your domain, and click the **Next** button.
- Then, enter the NetBIOS name of your domain. By default, Windows 2000 suggests that you keep the same name as the DNS name. Computers that runs a pre-Windows 2000 operating system will be able to use this name.
- Click the **Next** button.
- Indicate the path in which you want to store Active Directory information. By default, the directory **%systemroot%\NTDS** is suggested so as to store the database and the log. These items can be stored on a FAT partition or on an NTFS partition.

In order to optimize the performance of your server, you may wish to place the database and the log on separate disks.

- Click the **Next** button.
- Enter the path for the **Shared System Volume** (**Sysvol**). This folder must be located on an NTFS partition. It includes group policy definitions, scripts, and replication information.
- Click the **Next** button.

Windows 2000 tries to detect a DNS server that has the domain name that you have just indicated. This DNS must support dynamic updates. If there is no DNS server that is configured in order to manage your zone, then the Active Directory Installation Wizard offers to install and to configure the DNS service.

- Select **Permissions compatible only with Windows 2000 servers.**

If you select the **Permissions compatible with pre-Windows 2000** servers option, then the Everyone group will have permission to read all the attributes of all the Active Directory objects. This option is used in the case where you have upgraded a Windows NT 4 server to Windows 2000, with the RAS service installed. When you promote your server to Windows 2000 domain controller, you must choose this option so that you can continue to use the RAS service.
In order to run, the Windows NT 4 RAS service uses a system logon account with a logon name and an empty password. Windows 2000 does not allow NULL sessions to read Active Directory attributes.

- Click the **Next** button.
- Enter a password for the directory services restore mode Administrator, and then confirm it. When you start the system in Active Directory restore mode, you start Windows 2000 without loading the directory database so that you can restore it from a backup copy. In order to do this, you must log on as the Administrator with the password that you indicate in the dialog box below.

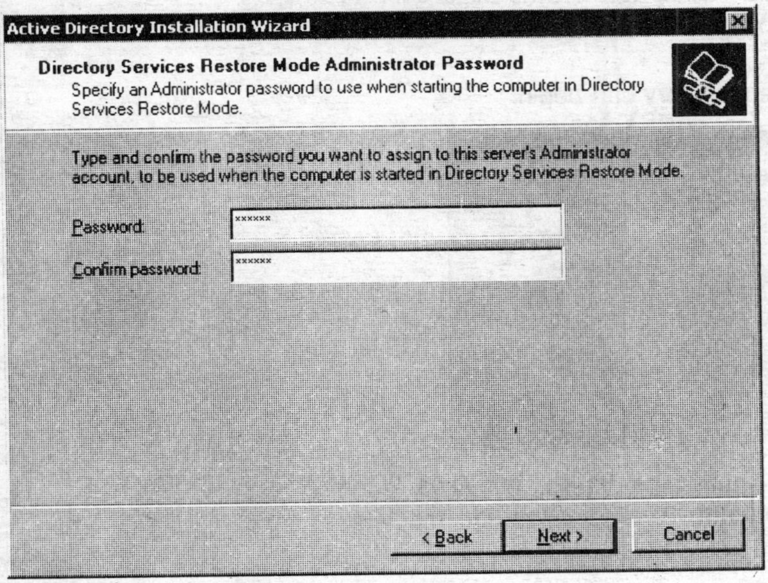

- Click the **Next** button.

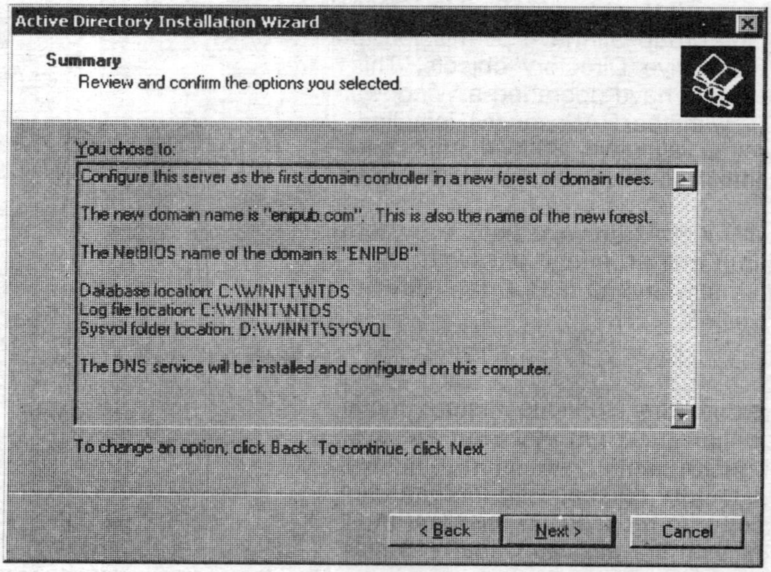

Before you click the **Next** button so as to start the installation of Active Directory, check that you agree with all the actions that will be carried out.

Then, the installation of Active Directory can begin:

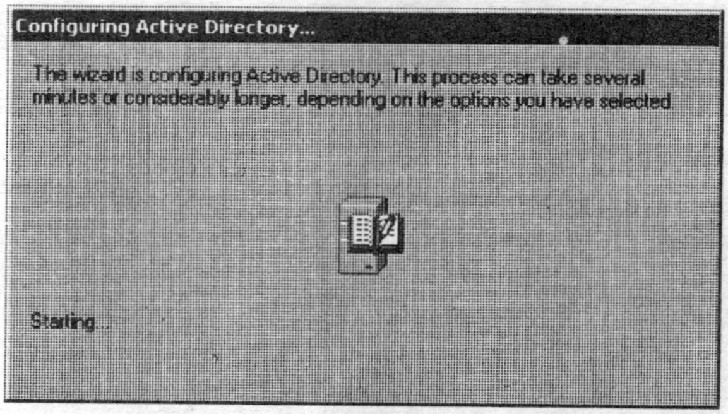

When the installation has finished, click **Finish**. Windows 2000 then offers to restart the computer in order allow the modifications to take effect.

☞ Click the **Restart Now** button.

When you have restarted your computer, you will be able to log on to your domain.

2. Adding a domain controller to an existing domain

Once you have created a domain, you can add new domain controllers to it. You are strongly recommended to have at least two domain controllers in order to ensure fault tolerance and so as to spread the workload.

Here are the steps that you must follow in order to add a new domain controller:

- Run **dcpromo.exe**.
- Select **Additional domain controller for an existing domain.**
- Indicate the domain, and the user name and password of an account that has enough rights in order to add a domain controller.
- Then, indicate the DNS name of the domain for which your server must be a controller.
- Enter the path for the directory database and for the log.
- Enter the path for the shared system volume.
- Indicate the password for the administrator account in order to carry out a possible future restart in restore mode.
- The replication of the Active Directory database then begins:

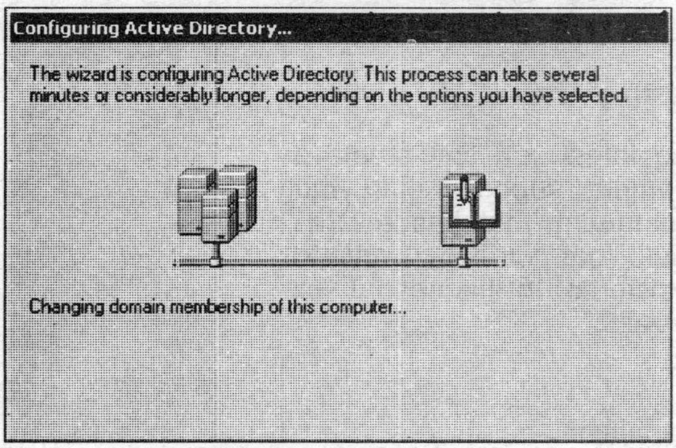

- Restart your computer when the operation is completed.

3. Adding a child domain

You can create a child domain, once you have created a root domain.
For example, if you have a domain that is called **enipub.com**, then you can create a child domain that is called **service.eni.com**. These two domains will make up a tree.

- Run **dcpromo.exe**.
- Select **Domain controller for a new domain.**
- Select **Create a new child domain in an existing domain tree.**
- Indicate the user name, password and domain for an account that is a member of the company's administrators group. This group is situated in the root domain and it grants its members the right to modify the forest.
- Then indicate the DNS name of the parent domain for which your domain will be a child domain, along with the name of your child domain.
- Indicate the NetBIOS name of your new subdomain.
- Enter the path for the directory database and for the log.
- Enter the path for the shared system volume.
- Specify whether on not you use services that run on Windows NT systems.

4. Adding a tree into an existing forest

When you add a tree into an existing forest you can create a new contiguous namespace. For example, suppose that your company has merged with another company that has a DNS domain that is registered on the Internet. Your company wants to keep its namespace, which is also registered. In this case it will be useful to create a new tree in the forest.

- Run **dcpromo.exe**.
- Select **Domain controller for a new domain.**
- Select **Create a new domain tree.**
- Select **Place this new domain tree in an existing forest.**

- Indicate the user name, password and domain for an account that is a member of the company's administrators group that exists in the root domain.
- Indicate the DNS name for the new domain.
- Indicate the NetBIOS name for your new domain.
- Enter the path for the directory database and for the log.
- Enter the path for the shared system volume.
- Specify whether on not you use services that run on Windows NT systems.

5. Choosing a domain mode

When you install a domain, it is configured in **mixed mode** by default. This mode allows both domain controllers that run on Windows 2000 and those that run on Windows NT, to operate together in a Windows 2000 domain. This is very useful when you are upgrading your servers to Windows 2000. Once the migration has been successfully completed (after you have checked that you still have all items such as your user accounts and your groups), you can convert your domain to **native mode**. Some Active Directory features are exclusive to this mode. Native mode allows you to nest groups within other groups, and it allows you to create universal groups.

In order to switch to native mode, open the **Active Directory Users and Computers** console. Right-click the name of your domain and then select **Properties**.

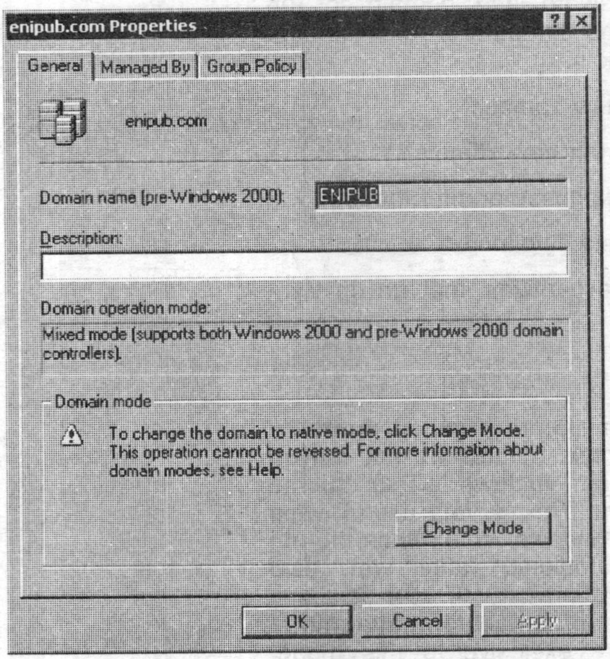

☛ Click the **Change Mode** button. The dialog box then appears as follows:

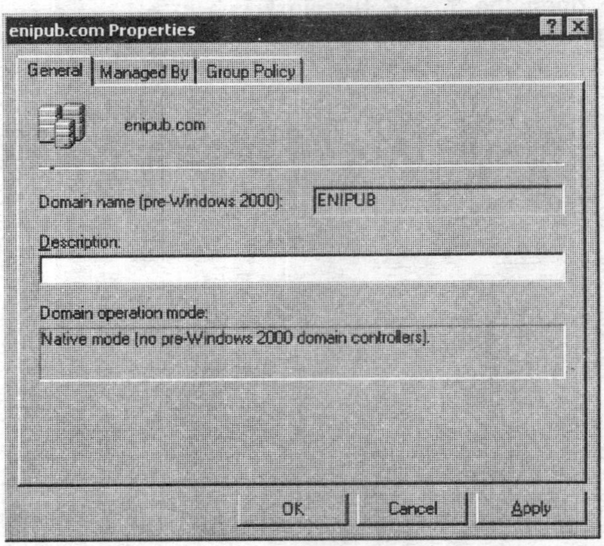

Converting from mixed mode to native mode is irreversible. When you have done this you can no longer return to mixed mode.

D. Roles of domain controllers

1. Operations masters

In a Windows 2000 domain, all the domain controllers are identical. The directory database is duplicated and distributed on each domain controller. This is therefore a multiple master replication. However, certain actions cannot be carried out in multiple master mode. Because of this certain domain controllers play very specific roles. These domain controllers are known as operations masters and they run in *Flexible Single Master Operation (FSMO*) mode.

There are five FSMO roles:
- Schema master,
- Infrastructure master,
- Principal Domain Controller (PDC) emulator,
- Domain naming master,
- Relative Identifier (RID) master.

Some of these roles must be unique in the forest, such as the schema master and the domain naming master.

In each domain of a forest, there can be only one RID master, and there can be only one PDC emulator.
In addition, each domain must have an infrastructure master.
The schema master implements the modifications that are made to the directory schema.
The domain naming master controls the addition and the removal of domains in the forest.
The first domain controller that is installed in the forest plays these two roles.

The RID master is responsible for distributing RID pools to all the domain controllers that request them (domain controllers request new RID pools when they have used up their stock of RID pools). When a domain controller creates an object, it assigns a unique security identifier (SID) to this object. This SID is composed of a unique domain SID, followed by a RID that is unique for each object in the domain.

The PDC emulator is unique in a domain. It acts as PDC for Windows NT clients. This FSMO manages password changes and replicates updates to secondary domain controllers in the case where the Windows 2000 domain is in mixed mode, where both Windows 2000 domain controllers and Windows NT secondary domain controllers are present in the domain.

In native mode, when a domain controller changes a password, it sends the information immediately to the domain controller that is acting as PDC emulator. When a logon fails because of an incorrect password, the domain controller that tried to validate the logon will send the request to the PDC emulator before it refuses the logon.

The infrastructure master is responsible for the consistency of information concerning Active Directory object names with respect to their SIDs. When an account is renamed, a certain amount of time may elapse before the information is updated in all the domains in the forest. The infrastructure master then, maintains the relationship between the names of users, or of groups, and their membership of the groups to which they belong.

You can find out which roles are played by a domain controller.

☛ In order to find out which domain controller plays the domain naming master role, open the **Active Directory Domains and Trusts** console. Then right-click **Active Directory Domains and Trusts** within this console, and select **Operations Master**.

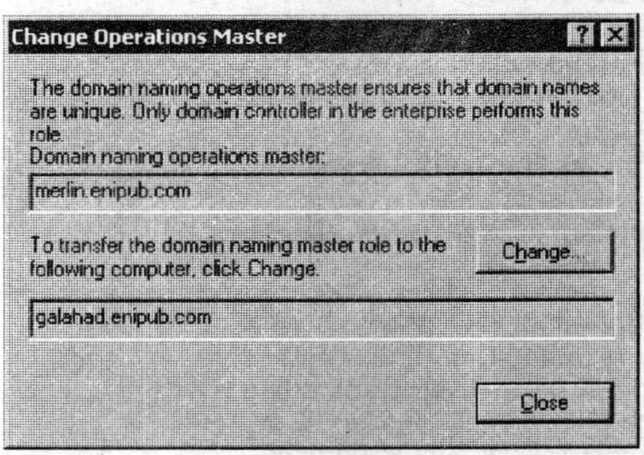

In order to transfer this role to another server, carry out the operation shown above on the domain controller that must become the domain naming master, and then click the **Change** button.

☞ In order to find out which domain controller is playing the role of an operations master that is specific to a domain, open the **Active Directory Users and Computers** console. Then right-click **Active Directory Users and Computers** within this console, and select **Operations Master**.

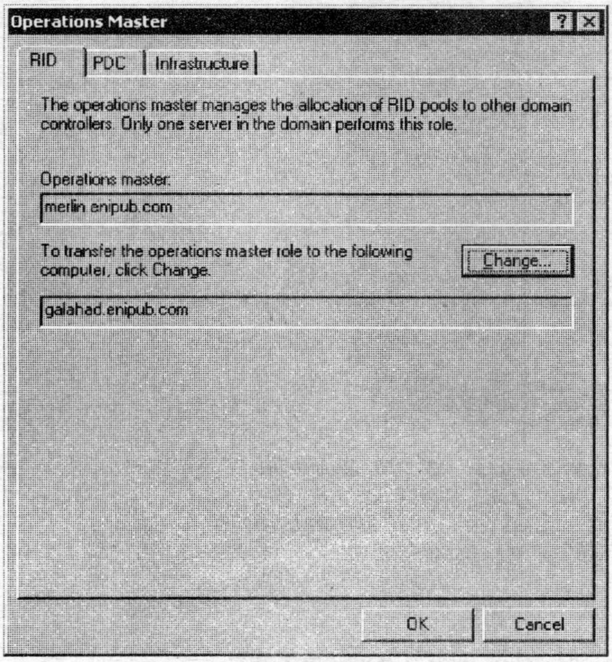

In order to transfer to another server, the role of PDC emulator, that of RID master, or that of infrastructure master display the dialog box shown above on the server that must play the role concerned. Then click the **Change** button.

☞ Finally, in order to find out which server is acting as schema manager, or to transfer it to another server, open an MMC and add the **Active Directory Schema** snap-in. Then, right-click **Active Directory Schema** and select **Operations Master**.

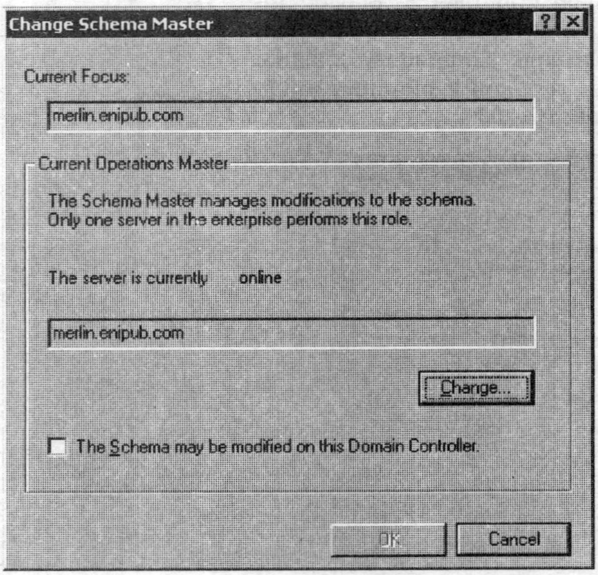

*If the **Active Directory Schema** snap-in is not available when you try to add it, then you must install the adminpack. msi administration tools that are situated in the **i386** directory of the CD-ROM Windows 2000.*

2. Global catalog server

A global catalog server is a domain controller with a catalog that references the attributes that are used most by all the Active Directory objects.

The Active Directory database is divided into three partitions, or naming contexts: the schema naming context, the configuration naming context and the domain naming context. Only schema and configuration information can be replicated between domains. As the information that concerns the objects of a domain are not replicated to the other domains in the forest, then the global catalog server is used for searching at forest level. If you are looking for an object in the forest, you can ask a global catalog server that will be able to answer your query.

The global catalog is the only source of information on the objects that are replicated between domains. Because of this, it is useful to have at least one global server catalog per domain. The global catalog servers keep a copy of the catalog of each of the other domains. By default, only one global catalog server is created on the first server in the forest in which Active Directory was installed. You can add new global catalog servers as follows:

- Open the **Active Directory Sites and Services** console.
- Expand **Sites**, followed by the name of the site containing the server that must become the global catalog server. By default, there is only one site, which is called **Default-First-Site-Name**.
- Then, expand the **Servers** folder, followed by the server concerned. Right-click the **NTDS Settings** icon and select **Properties**.

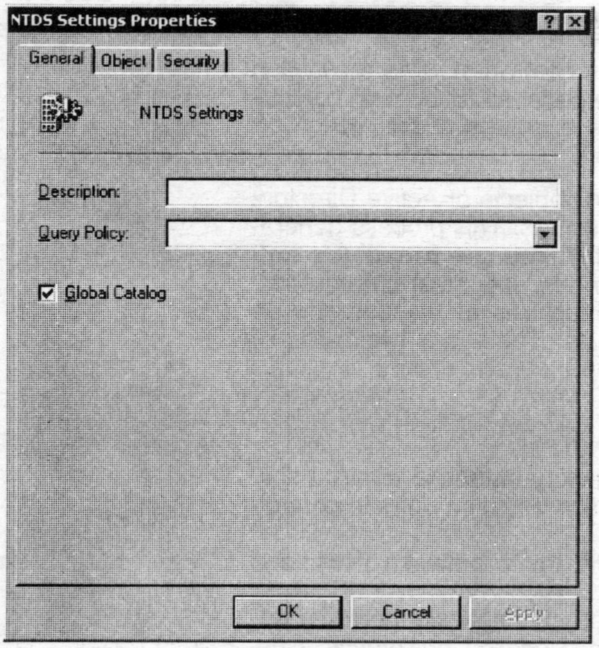

- Activate the **Global Catalog** check box.

In addition to allowing you to search in a forest, global catalog servers are useful during the logon process. When a logon is made, the server that receives the request consults a global catalog server in order to obtain information concerning membership of universal groups so that it can create an access token. If the global catalog server is not available, then the user will not be able to logon locally. However, members of the administrators group will still be able to log on to the domain.

It is advisable to have a global catalog server on either end of slow links.

E. Replication

1. Overview

The replication process provides all domain controllers with an up-to-date directory database. When an administrator or a user alters the Active Directory, then the modified Active Directory must be replicated on all the domain controllers. This replication takes place in multiple master mode because all domain controllers have equal status. No master is in charge of the replication process.

Within a domain, all the attributes and objects of Active Directory are replicated on all the domain controllers. This process generates a certain amount of network traffic. You can control this traffic across slow links. In order to do this, you must create sites, which are independent of logical structures of the domains. A site is a set of one or more subnets. There are two types of replication:
– intra-site replication,
– inter-site replication.

Intra-site replication updates the directory database within a site. Consequently, this process takes place between domain controllers over fast links.
Inter-site replication involves network traffic between sites, and consequently, over slow links.
Within a site, replication is generated automatically between domain controllers using KCCs (*Knowledge Consistency Checkers*). On the other hand, you must set up inter-site replication manually.

When you install the first domain controller in a forest, then a site that is called Default-First-Site-Name is created automatically, by default. This site contains all the subnets, and when you create a domain controller, it will also belong to this site.

You can rename the Default-First-Site-Name site.

2. Creating sites and subnets

You can create sites and subnets using the **Active Directory Sites and Services** console.

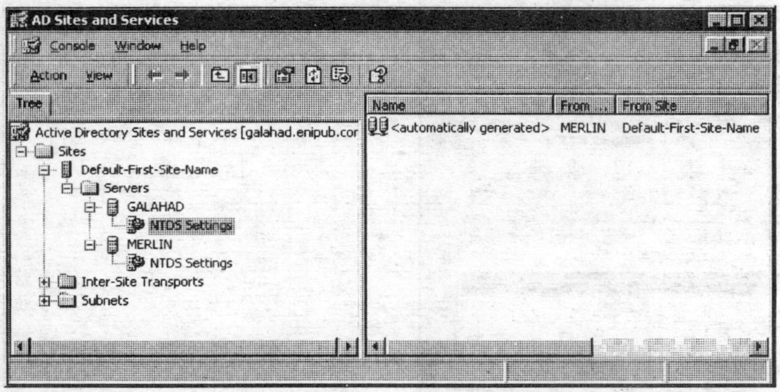

☞ Right-click the **Sites** folder, and then select **New Site.**

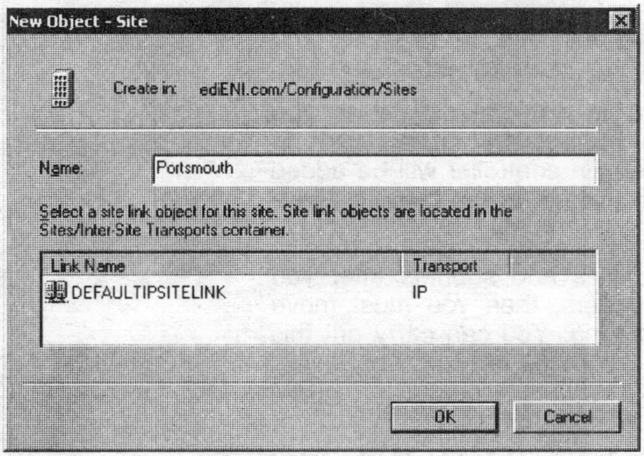

☛ Enter the name that you want to give to your site, and select the link that you wish to use in order to replicate. Then click the **OK** button.

Your next step is to associate this site with one or more subnets.

☛ Right-click the **Subnets** folder and then select **New Subnet**.

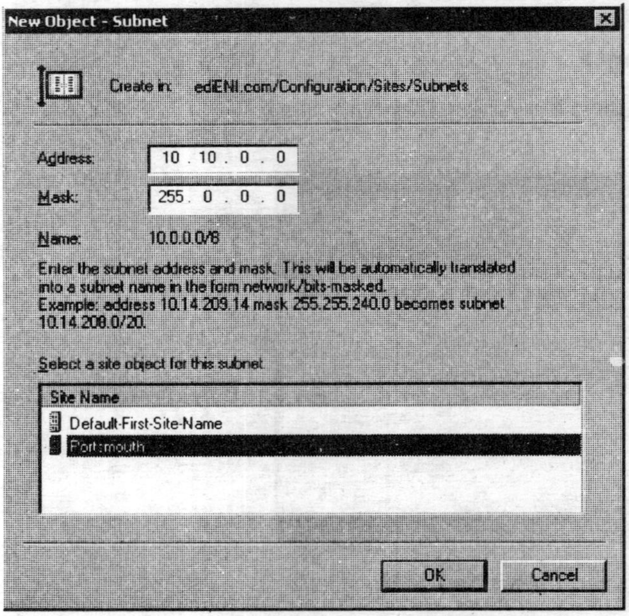

☛ Enter the network address along with that of the mask, and select the site with which the subnet must be associated.

Once you have associated the subnet with the site, when you install a domain controller with an address that corresponds to that of the subnet, then the new domain controller will be added automatically to the site concerned, and not to the **Default-First-Site-Name** site.

On the other hand, if you create sites and subnets after you have installed all the domain controllers, then you must move them into the sites to which they belong. You can carry out this operation as follows:

☛ Open the **Active Directory Sites and Services** console.

☛ Expand the **Sites** folder, followed by the **Default - First - Site - Name** folder.

- Then, expand the **Servers** folder and right-click the server that you wish to move.
- Select **Move.**

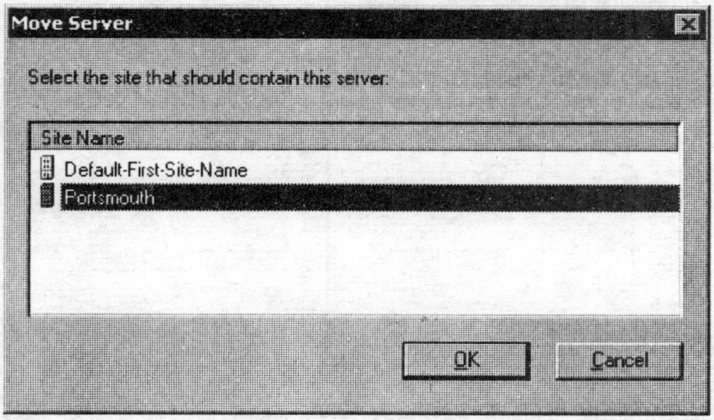

- Select the site to which you want to move the server, and then click the **OK** button.

Repeat this process for all the servers that you want to move.

3. Intra-site and inter-site transport

Intra-site replication

Replication within a site is carried out using RPC (*Remote Procedures Call*), which runs on IP. It provides a relatively quick information transaction and is therefore suitable for intra-site replication. When you modify Active Directory on a domain controller, the domain controller will wait five minutes before sending a notification message to the other domain controllers on the same site. Of course, the domain controller is able to record further modifications during this time. When the domain controllers find out about the notification, they copy the modifications from the domain controller that sent them the message. If no notification is received for six hours, then the domain controllers start the replication process with their partners so as to ensure that no information has been forgotten. However, certain important information is replicated automatically without waiting five minutes. This information includes the modification of such items as the LSA, an account policy, and a user password policy.

With an intra-site replication, replication traffic is not compressed, so as to reduce the workload on the domain controllers.

The KCC organizes the replication amongst all the domain controllers on your site.

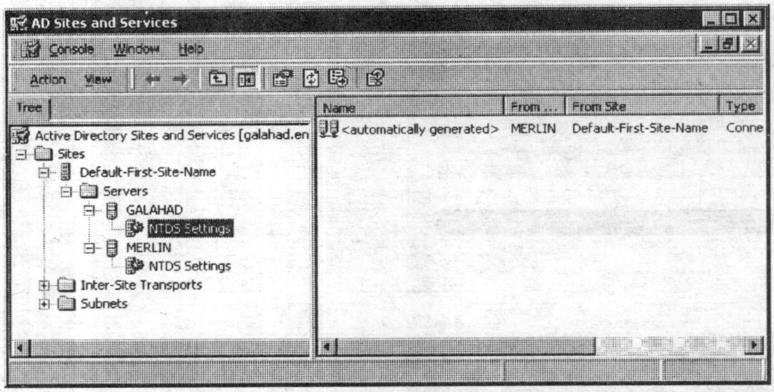

If a domain controller breaks down, then the KCC creates a new replication loop so as to implement a complete replication on the site. Three objects are required in order to make up this loop:

– **Server** object GALAHAD
  Each domain controller has a server object that is independent of the computer account that is created in Active Directory. This object is used to generate the replication.

– **NTDS** Settings object NTDS Settings
  This object contains all the connections that are generated either by the KCC, or by you, for Active Directory replication.

– **Connection** object GALAHAD

This is the direction in which the information is replicated. This is a one-way connection.
Even though KCC generates a replication loop automatically, you can add connection objects so that a specific domain controller will replicate directly with another domain controller. In order to do this, go into the **Active Directory Sites and Services** console and expand the tree down to the **NTDS Settings** object that belongs to the domain controller for which you want to add a new connection. Right-click this object and select **New Active Directory Connection**. Select the domain controller and click **OK**. Then, enter a name for the connection object, and click **OK**.

The **Replication Monitor** *(REPLMON) utility from the resource kit allows you to display the topology of the replication using a graphic interface.*

Inter-site replication

With inter-site replication, you can choose between RPC and SMTP (*Simple Mail Transfer Protocol*) protocols. However, you can use SMTP only for inter-site replication between different domain controllers. The traffic that runs over slow links is compressed by 10 to 15% in order to improve the throughput. However, the domain controllers use more CPU time so as to compress and to decompress the data. Unlike intra-site replication, there are no special provisions for the replication of urgent information, such as passwords for example.

When you create a site, you also create a link for the site. By default, a single link is created. This link is called **Defaultipsitelink**. You can create new links in order to link several sites together, if you do not wish to use the **Defaultipsitelink** link for this purpose.

You can create a new link as follows:

- Go into the **Active Directory Sites and Services** console.
- Expand the **Sites** folder, followed by the **Inter-Site Transports** folder. Then, right-click the **IP** folder, if you wish to create a link that uses RPC. Alternatively, right-click the **SMTP** folder, if you wish to create a link that uses SMTP.
- Select **New Site Link**.

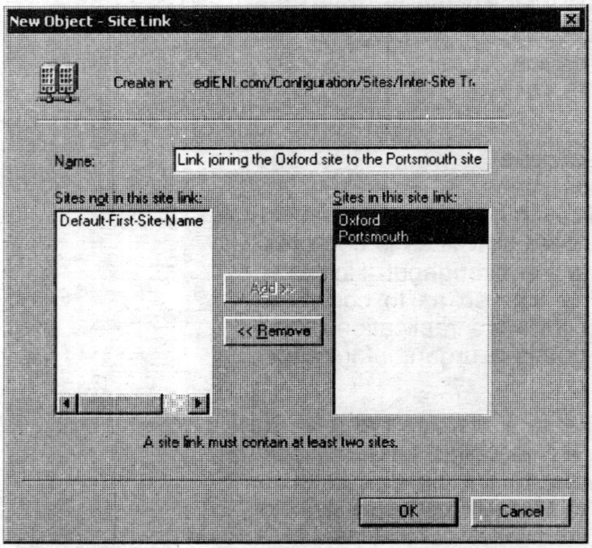

- Enter a name for your link, and then select the sites that you wish to link together. Then, click the **OK** button in order to confirm the operation.
- In order to set up the transit on this link, right-click it and then select **Properties**.

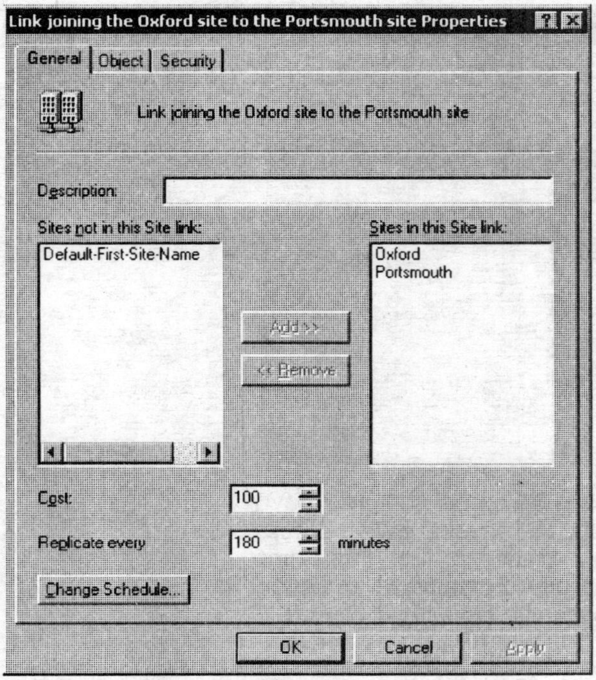

You must define the following items:

– A cost: the smallest cost must be chosen in the case of several links connecting the same sites.
– A replication frequency: If you choose a higher value for this item (in minutes), then the slow link will be used less, but the replication waiting time will be longer.
– A schedule: by clicking the **Change Schedule** button, you can indicate the periods in which the replication can take place on the slow link.

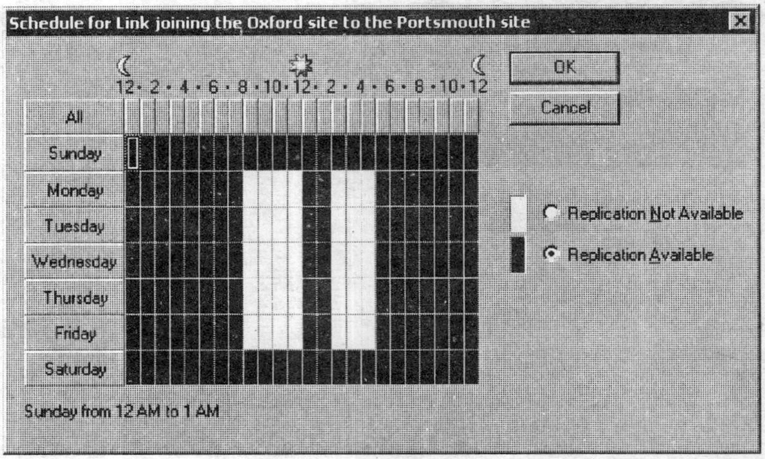

The links between sites are transitive. Suppose that you have three sites, the first called Portsmouth, the second called Oxford and the third called Dover. If you create a link that joins Portsmouth to Oxford, and a link that joins Portsmouth to Dover, then replication will also take place between Dover and Oxford.

Manual replication

You can force replication between domain controllers at any time.

☞ Go into the **Active Directory Sites and Services** console, and expand **Sites**, followed by the site to which you wish to replicate.

☞ Then, expand the server that must replicate the information and click **NTDS Settings**.

☞ Right-click the connection that you wish to use in order to replicate.

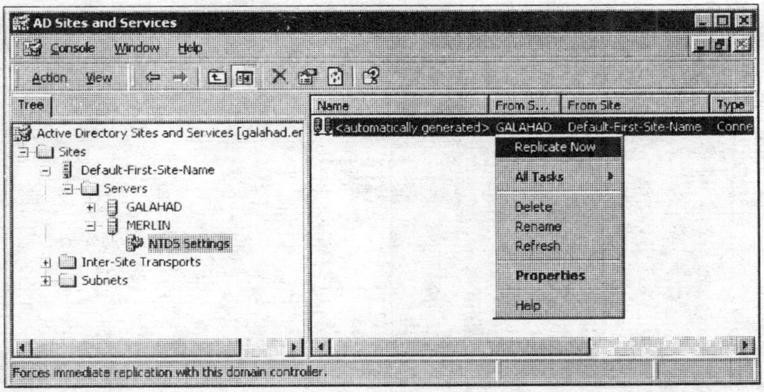

☞ Select **Replicate Now**.

You must remember that the connection objects replicate only one way. If you want to replicate in both directions, then you must carry out the same operation on the other domain controller.

F. Uninstalling

In order to uninstall Active Directory on your server, run the **Dcpromo.exe** command a second time. If you wish to uninstall Active Directory on a domain controller that is acting as global catalog server, make sure that you have another server that is playing this role in the forest, unless you want to delete the domain completely.

☞ Click **OK**.

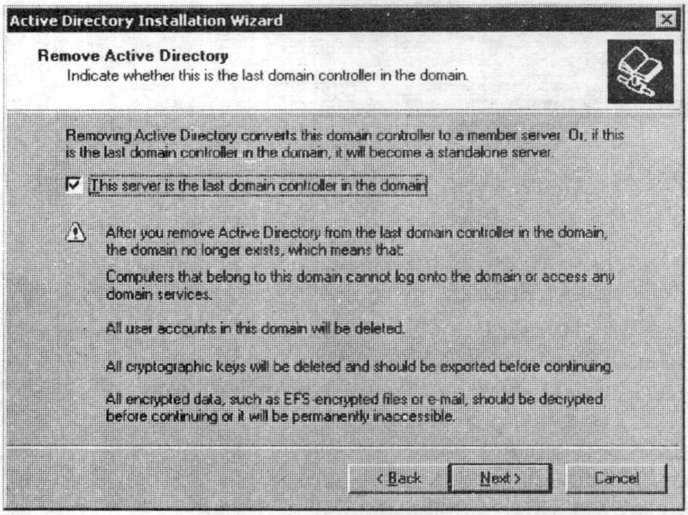

If the server concerned is the last domain controller in the domain, then activate the **This server is the last domain controller in the domain** check box. In this case, all the user accounts and the computer accounts that are in the domain will be deleted, and no one will be able to log on to the domain any more because the domain will no longer exist.

☞ Click the **Next** button.

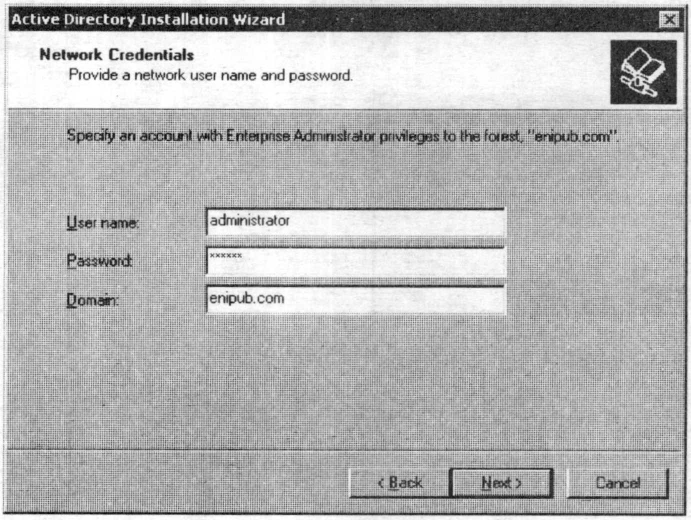

☞ Enter the details of an account that is a member of the company's **Administrators** group, if you must delete the domain.

☞ Click the **Next** button.

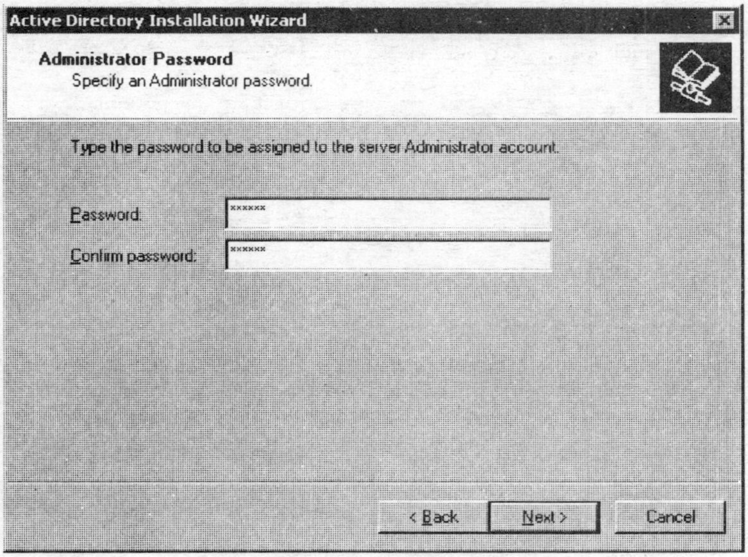

☞ Enter the password for the account of the local machine administrator. Then click the **Next** button.

☞ In the **Summary** dialog box, once again click **Next**.

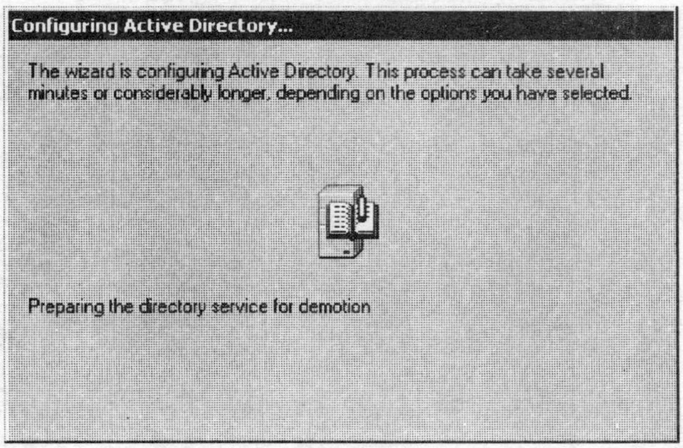

☞ When the uninstall process is completed, restart the server.

Group policies

A. **Overview** 142

B. **Managing GPOs** 142

1. Creating a GPO 143
2. Adding a GPO 144
3. Deleting a GPO 144

C. **Group policy settings** 145

D. **User environment** 147

E. **Applying GPOs** 149

1. Order of application 149
2. Inheriting 150
3. Permissions 152

A. Overview

A group policy is a set of parameters that you can apply to users, to groups of users and to computers. You can define group policies at site level, at domain level or at organizational unit (OU) level. When a group policy applies to such a container, it applies to all the network objects that the container holds.
Group policies allow you, to restrict the capabilities of user's desktops, to apply account and password policies, to deploy applications, to set up security options, to run scripts, to implement audits, and to change user rights.
In summary, group policies provide an administration tool that allows you to reduce the **Total Cost of Ownership** (TCO) by managing the working status of users.
Group policies are implemented in the form of Active Directory objects. These are known as GPOs (*Group Policy Objects*). A GPO is made up of two parts that are stored in different locations:

- GPC (*Group Policy Container*) is an Active Directory object that contains the attributes of the GPO. In order to view the GPC in Active Directory, go into the **Active Directory Users and Computers** console. Then, open the **View** menu and select **Advanced Features** in order to display the **System** folder.
- GPT (*Group Policy Template*) is stored in the **sysvol** directory and contains a template of settings that can be applied to a GPO.

Consequently, when you create a group policy, you will create an Active Directory object that is linked to a container (an OU, a site or a domain). You can link the same GPO to several containers, and you can link several GPOs to the same container.

B. Managing GPOs

As you can apply a group policy to a site, to a domain, or directly to an OU, you must use two different consoles:

- **Active Directory Sites and Services**: in order to apply GPOs at site level.
- **Active Directory Users and Computers**: in order to apply GPOs at domain level, or at OU level.

1. Creating a GPO

You can create a group policy as follows:

- Open, either the **Active Directory Sites and Services** console,

  Active Directory Sites and Services

  or the **Active Directory Users and Computers** console:

  Active Directory Users and Computers

  from the **Administrative Tools** menu.

- Right-click the container to which you want to apply a policy:
  - Either, a domain: enipub.com
  - Or an OU: enipub.com

You can apply GPOs only to organizational units, which are indicated by an icon. You cannot apply GPOs to containers that are indicated by an icon. In fact you can apply group policies to any of the OUs that you create, or to any of the OUs that have already been created, which correspond to the domain controllers.

- Select **Properties** and then select the **Group Policy** tab.

If you carry out such an operation on the domain or on the OU that contains the domain controllers, you must view a default policy in the GPO list.

- In order to create a new policy, click the **New** button.

A new policy appears that has the name **New Group Policy Object**, by default. You can rename this policy in order to call it something that is more meaningful. As you can apply several GPOs to the same container, it is better to give your policy a name that represents the action that is provided by the policy so that you will be able to find it quickly.

2. Adding a GPO

☞ You can link a container to a GPO that already exists, by right-clicking the container, and then selecting **Properties**. Select the **Group Policy** tab, and then click the **Add** button.

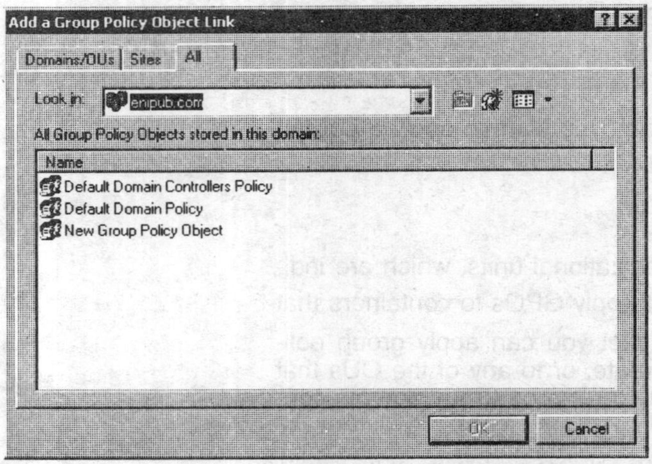

– The **All** tab allows you to view all the GPOs, irrespective of the containers to which the GPOs are linked.
– The **Domains/OUs** tab lists GPOs according to the location to which they are applied.
– The **Sites** tab lists the GPOs that are applied at site level.

☞ Select the policy that you wish to apply to the container and then click the **OK** button.

You may find it useful to create your GPOs in a container that you have designed specially for this purpose, and then deactivate your GPOs for this container. When you have done this you will be able to use the Add button in order to link the policies to the required containers.

3. Deleting a GPO

A policy that is applied to a container is merely a link to the GPC. Consequently, when you delete a policy, you can choose to delete only the link (**Remove the link from the list**), or you can choose to delete the link and the GPO (**Remove the link and delete the Group Policy Object permanently**).

☛ In order to delete a group policy, select it and then click the **Delete** button.

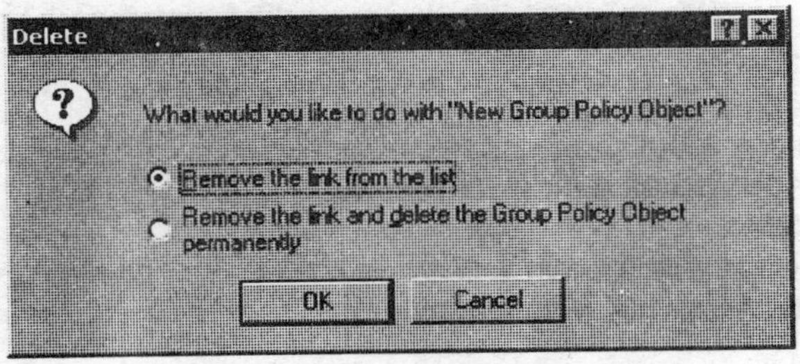

C. Group policy settings

When you have added your GPO, click the **Edit** button. The list of settings that you can modify appears in the **Group Policy** window.

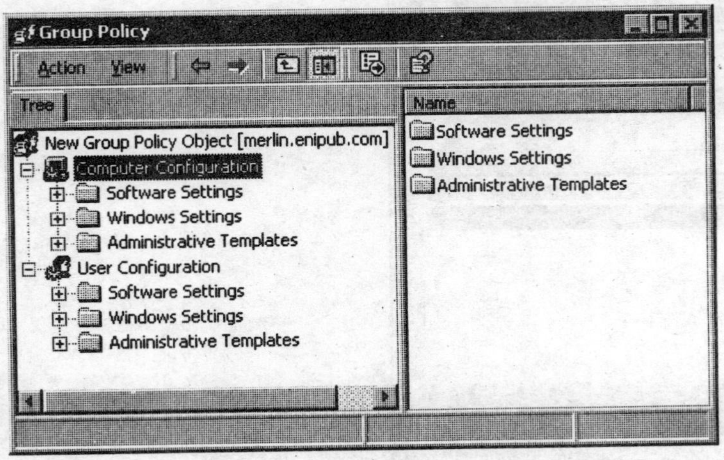

The left-hand pane of this window shows two tree structures: one concerns computer settings, and the other concerns user settings.

Here are the different types of policy that you can implement:

– **Software Settings**: allow you to publish, or to attribute, programs. This type of policy is available in both of the tree structures. This item allows you to deploy programs, either for users or for computers.

- **Administrative Templates**: allow you to set up the user environment (in order to define the level of access to the Control Panel and to the **Start** menu, to enable or disable offline folders, or to define disk quotas).
- **Scripts**: allow you to run scripts, either when users log on or log off (under **Windows Settings** in the User Configuration), or during shutdown or startup of a computer (under **Windows Settings** in the Computer Configuration).
- **Security Settings**: allow you to define the security that you want to apply (including user rights, accounts and passwords policy, and IPSec security).
- **Folder Redirection**: allows you to set up directory redirection.

When a user logs on, the GPOs are consulted so as to find out which settings must be applied, either to the user, or to the computer on which the user is logging on. In order to speed up the logon process, you can deactivate any user or computer settings that are not used.

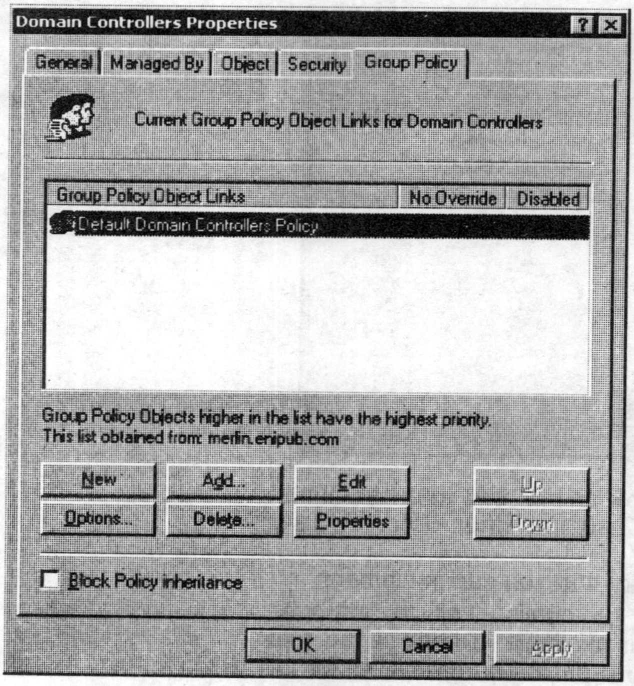

☞ Select the policy concerned and then click the **Properties** button.

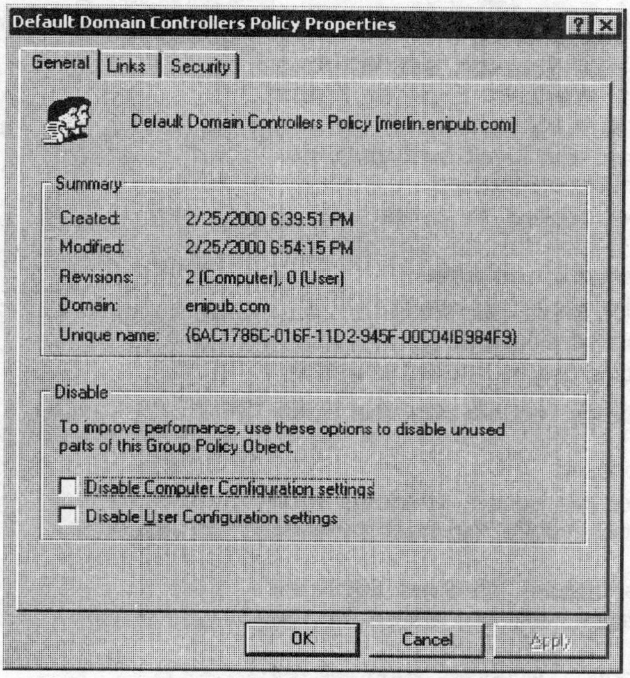

☛ Activate the **Disable Computer Configuration settings** check box, if only the user components are used in the policy. Activate the **Disable User Configuration settings** if only the computer components are used in the policy.

D. User environment

When a user logs on, Windows 2000 consults the **SYSVOL** folder for the domain controller so as to find a policy file that is called **Registry.pol**. Two **registry.pol** files are present in the GPT for each GPO: one of these files contains computer settings, and the other contains user settings.
In order to control user environments, you must use mainly the **Administrative Templates**. These contain registry database values that will be modified locally on the machine on which the user logs on. You can use a graphic interface in order to modify these values. When you apply group policies that concern user settings, you modify **HKEY_ CURRENT_USER** and when you apply computer settings you modify **HKEY_LOCAL_ MACHINE**.

The values that you can set include the following:

- Windows components; for example you can set Windows Installer, Internet Explorer, and Windows Explorer (these values can be applied to users and to computers).
- System; these include disk quotas, and logon settings (these values can be applied to users and to computers).
- Network; (these values can be applied to users and to computers).
- Printers (these values can be applied to computers).
- Control Panel (these values can be applied to users).
- Desktop (these values can be applied to users).
- Start menu & Taskbar (these values can be applied to users).

In order to apply a setting in a policy, double-click the policy concerned.

Then, select one of the following options:

- **Not Configured**: When you select this option, Windows 2000 will ignore this setting and will not modify the corresponding registry database value.
- **Enabled**: When you select this option, Windows 2000 will apply this setting, and the value will be added to the **Registry.pol** file.
- **Disabled**: When you select this option, Windows 2000 will not apply this setting, and the value will be added to the **Registry.pol** file.

In addition to selecting one of these three options, you must add values, for some settings.

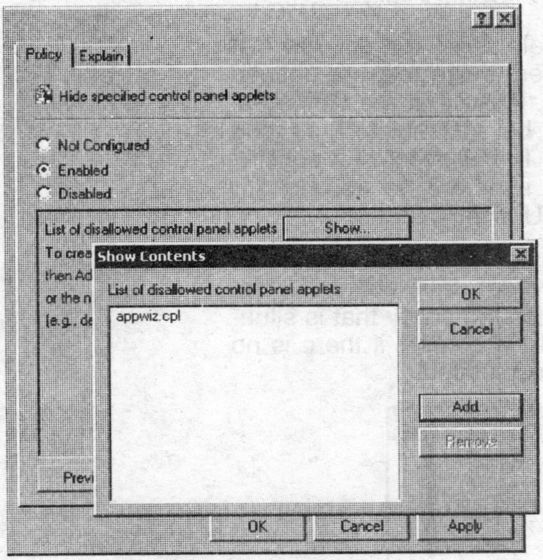

This is the case in the example above. This is the setting that is called **Hide specified control panel applets**. This setting is activated (**Enabled**). By clicking the **Show** button, you can list the applets concerned: **appwiz.cpl** is the **Add/Remove Programs** icon (the **.cpl** filename extension is used for control panel applets). Alternatively, you can enter the name of the icon.

E. Applying GPOs

1. Order of application

When you start up your machine, the settings that have been defined for the computer will be applied, along with the startup scripts. Then, when the user logs on, the user settings are applied, followed by the logon scripts. By default, the logon scripts must finish executing within ten minutes.

Once these policies have been applied, they are refreshed every 90 minutes. By this means, the current policies will always be applied to computers and to users, even if they do not disconnect. On domain controllers and on member servers, these policies are refreshed every 5 minutes.

You can modify these values for the policies in ***Administrative Templates - System - Group Policy.***

Policies can be applied at different levels. First, the policies that are defined at site level are applied, then, those that are defined at domain level are applied, and finally, those that are defined at OU level are applied. The policies will be accumulated, as long as they do not conflict with each other. In the event of a conflict, then the policy that is nearest to the user will be applied (for example, the policy that is defined at OU level).

If several policies have been defined for the same container, then the policies will be read in the list order, from bottom to top. Consequently, in the event of any conflict, the policy that is situated at the top of the list will be applied. Of course, if there is no conflict, then the policy settings will be cumulated.

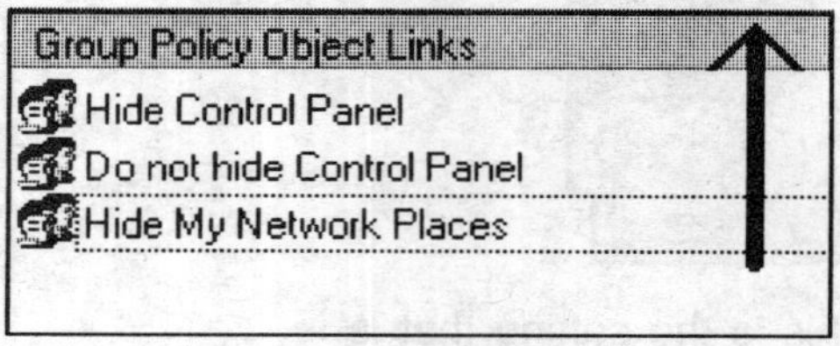

In the example above, if the policy names represent the policy contents, then, for the users of this container, **Control Panel** and **My Network Places** will be hidden. You can change the list position of a policy using the **Up** and **Down** buttons.

2. Inheriting

By default, policies are inherited from parent containers. For example if no policy has been defined for the users of an OU, then settings may be applied that have been defined at site level, at domain level, or even at the level of an OU that is a parent of the container. If you do not want a container to inherit policies that have been defined for containers that are higher in the tree (for parent containers), then you can block the inheritance at the level of the (target) container concerned.

☛ Right-click the container concerned and then select **Properties**. Select the **Group Policy** tab.

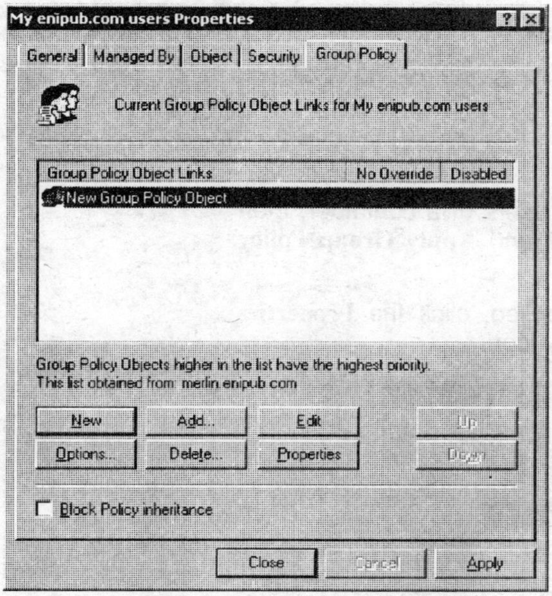

☞ Activate the **Block Policy inheritance** check box.

If you activate this check box, then only the policies that apply to the container will be applied to the objects that are in the container. This rule will apply, except in the case where the **No Override** option has been set for the parent container. This option allows an administrator to force the application of a policy, either in the event of a conflict, or even if the **Block Policy inheritance** option has been set for a child container. In order to set the **No Override** option for a GPO:

☞ Right-click the container, select **Properties** and then select the **Group Policy** tab.

☞ Select the GPO concerned and then click the **Options** button.

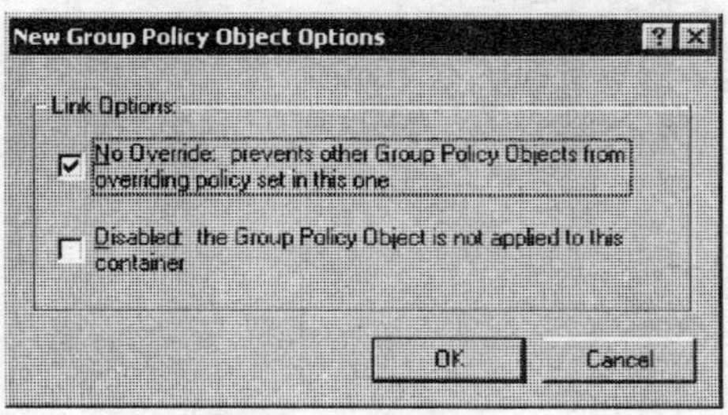

☞ Activate the **No Override...** check box.

It must be noted that this dialog box also allows you to disable a policy for a container.

3. Permissions

So that a policy can be applied to the users of a container, then these users must have at least, **Read** and **Apply Group Policy** permissions.

☞ Select the policy that must be applied, click the **Properties** button, and then select the **Security** icon.

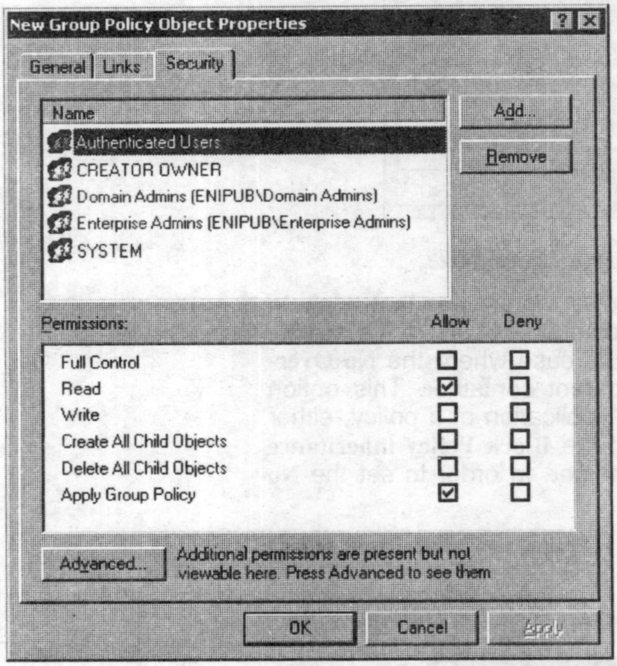

This dialog box allows you to apply policies to a group of users. It also allows you to remove a user from the policy. By default, policies are not applied to administrators.

User and group management

A. Managing a local computer 154

1. Users 154
2. Groups 160

B. Managing a domain 163

1. Managing domain users 163
2. Managing groups 172
3. User profiles 179

You can administer user accounts and groups using two different consoles:

– **Active Directory Users and Computers** in order to manage the domain.
– **Computer Management** in order to manage the accounts and the local groups of a member server, of a stand-alone server or of a Professional workstation.

A. Managing a local computer

1. Users

A local user account is an account that can be used in order to log on locally to a computer. With this type of account, you can access only the local resources of a machine. These accounts are stored in the accounts database of the local computer. This is the SAM database, which is stored under the directory **%systemroot%\system32\config**. These account databases are present only on workstations, and on member and stand-alone servers. On a domain controller, accounts and groups are stored in Active Directory.
If a user who is logged on locally wishes to access resources that are situated on another computer, then the user must have an account on the other machine.

Predefined accounts

When you install Windows 2000, two user accounts are created:

– the Administrator account, and
– the guest account.

Administrator

The administrator has the maximum power on a machine. The administrator manages the system configuration, which includes the following tasks:

– managing security policy,
– managing user accounts and group accounts,
– managing the software configuration of the operating system,
– creating folders and installing files on the hard disks,
– installing and configuring printers,
– administrating the sharing of file and printer ressources,
– logical and physical organisation of data on the disks (including formatting, and partitioning),

– backing up and restoring data.

You cannot delete the **Administrator** account, but you can rename it.

You are recommended to rename the Administrator account because it is more difficult to find the password of an account when you do not know its name.

In addition, it is useful not to display the name of the last user who logged on to a machine. You can do this by adding the value DontDisplayLastUserName: REG_SZ: 1 in the registry location: HKEY_LOCAL_MACHINE\ SOFTWARE\MICROSOFT\Windows NT\current Version \Winlogon\.

Guest

As the name indicates, this account is intended for occasional users, or for inexperienced users. For security reasons, the *Guest* user has a minimum amount of rights on the system.

By default, this account is disabled, and does not have a password. When you enable this account, you introduce a major weak-point into the security system.

Creating a user account

You can create a local user account using the **Local Users and Groups** folder of the **Computer Management** console.

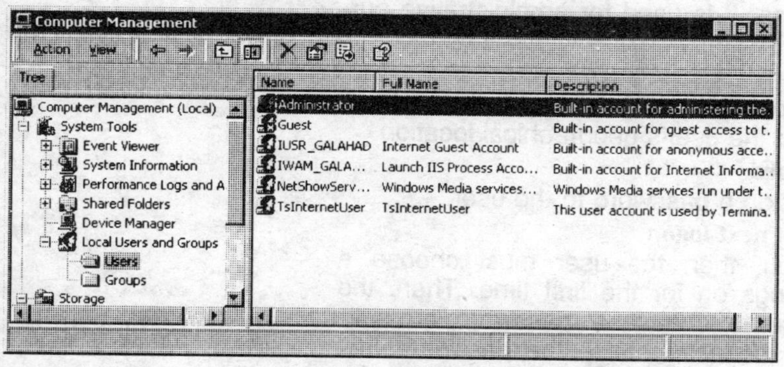

Right-click **Users** and then select **New User**.

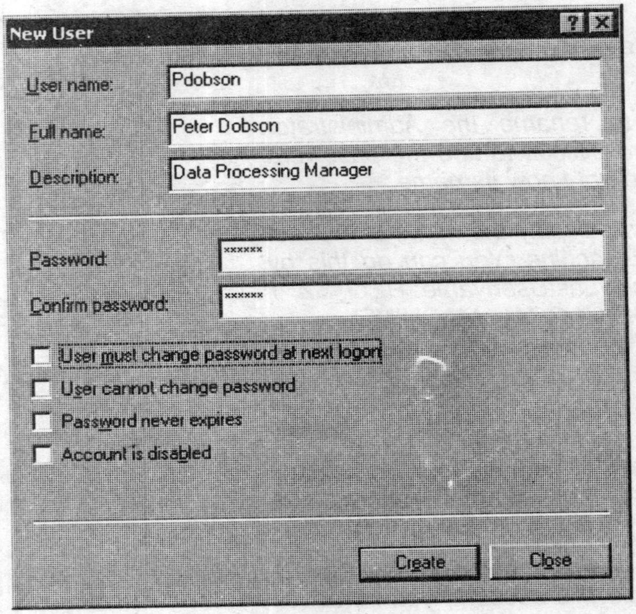

User name

This is the name that the user must enter in order to log on to the machine. This field is obligatory and must not exceed 20 characters.

Full name

This is the user's full name. It is used for administrative purposes.

Description

This field allows you to specify such details as the user's position in the company, and the user's geographical location.

Password and confirm password

The administrator can assign a password to the user.

User must change password at next logon

If you enable this option, then the user must choose a password when he/she logs on for the first time. Then, the user will no longer have to choose a password on subsequent logons, and will be able to use the password that he/she entered upon the first logon. This option allows the administrator to let the user choose his/her own password. However, in this case the administrator will have no unilateral means of finding out a user's password.

User cannot change password

This option is useful so as to fix certain passwords, such as that of the guest user and those of accounts that are user by several people. This option helps the administrator to manage user passwords.

Password never expires

You must use this option if you do not want the password to expire. This option can be useful with an account that is used by an application or by a service.

Account is disabled

You must enable this option if you do not want anyone to use an account (for example, when a user goes on holiday). When you disable an account, a cross appears on the icon ( ).

If you select the ***User must change password at next logon*** *option, then the* ***User cannot change password*** *option, and the* ***Password never expires*** *option, are grayed out.*

Modifying a user account

Once you have created a local account, then it appears in the **Computer Management** console, in the user list under the **users** folder

You can modify the characteristics that you have defined for a user, later. In order to do this, select the user concerned and then press the Enter key. Alternatively, you can open the **action** menu and select **properties.**

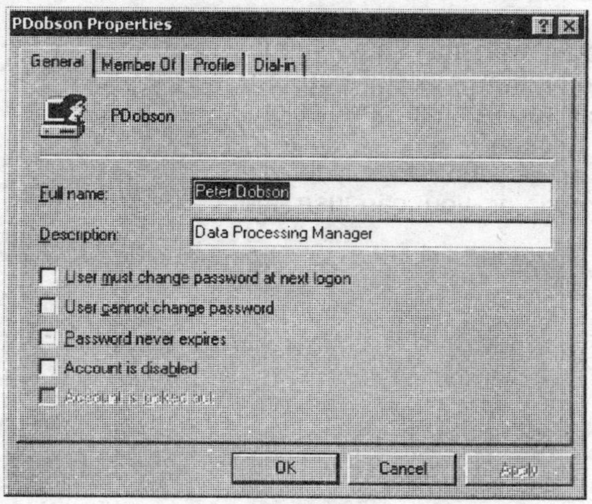

It must be noted that this dialog box contains a new option that is grayed out: **account is disabled**. This option will become available if you define an account policy that indicates that the account must be locked out after a specified number of failed logon attempts.

The User Properties dialog box offers a number of additional tabs:

- The **Member Of** tab indicates the groups of which the user is a member. If you wish to include the user in a new group, then click the **Add** button and select the desired group.
- The **Profile** tab allows you to specify the path of the user's profile. This topic will be covered in greater detail later on in this chapter.
- The **Dial-in** tab allows you to specify how this account must be used via remote network access or via VPN *(Virtual Private Networking)*.

When you rename a user account you do not lose all the information that is associated with the account (such as group memberships and permissions). In fact, when you handle a user account, you use the login name of the user. However, Windows 2000 associates this name with a security identification number (SID). This number is unique, and has the following format:

```
S-1-5-21-527237240-2111687655-1957994488-500
```

When you rename an account you will modify the login name; on the other hand the SID never changes. When you grant permissions to a user account, then these permissions are attributed to the SID that is associated with the account. If you delete an account, and then recreate the account with the same name, then you will have created a new account that is associated to a new SID. Because of this, you will not recover the permissions that had been granted to the previous account.
If you wish to rename, or to delete an account, then you can either right-click the account concerned, or you can use the **Action** menu.

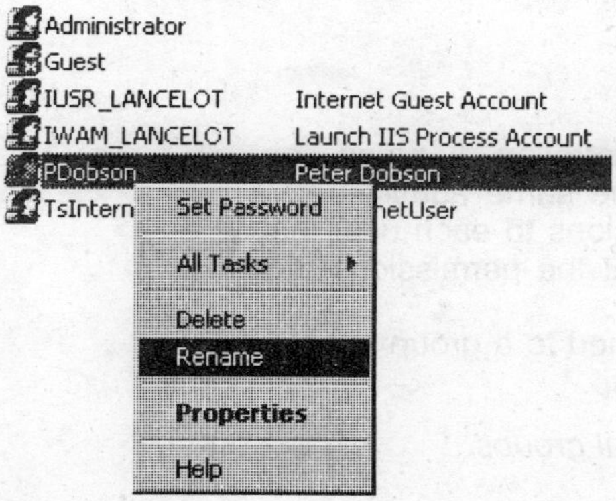

Modifying a password

With Windows NT 4.0, you could change the password that is associated with a user account by modifying the properties of the account. With Windows 2000 however, you must right-click the account concerned and then select the **Set Password** option (alternatively, you can use the **Action** menu).

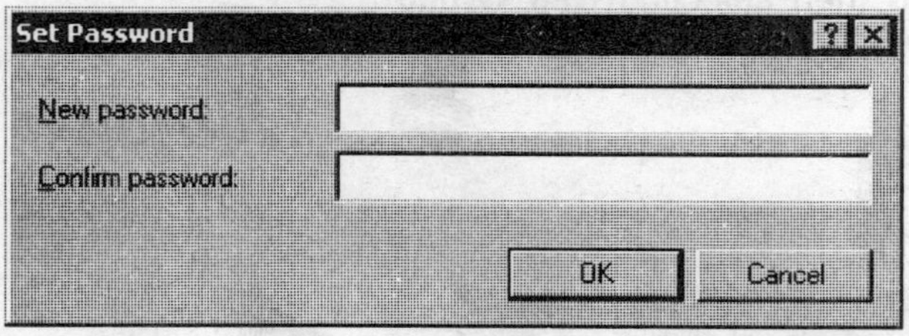

You cannot modify a password via the properties of the account so that the administration of this item can be delegated. With the Windows 2000 approach, you can grant to users, or to groups of users, the sole power of changing their passwords, without allowing them to change any other characteristics of their accounts.

An administrator cannot find out a user's password.

2. Groups

Introduction

Groups allow you to simplify user administration. A group contains a set of user accounts that have the same administrative needs. Thus, rather than granting permissions to each user individually, an administrator can simply grant the permissions to a group.
The permissions and rights that are assigned to a group apply to all the users who are members of the group.

A user can be a member of several groups.

In the local accounts database of a member/stand-alone server, or of a workstation, only one type of group can be created: a local group. Local groups are represented by the icon.

Creating a group

You can create a group by right-clicking the **Groups** folder in the **Computer Management** console, and then selecting **New Group** (alternatively you can select the **Groups** folder and then use the **Action** menu).

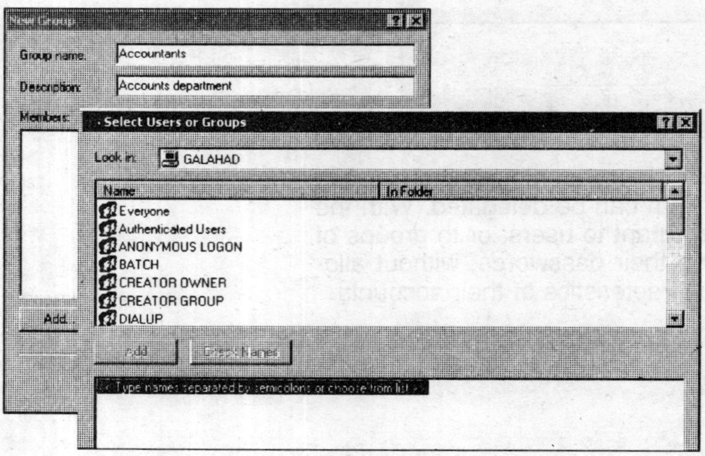

Give the group a meaningful name, and possibly a description, and then click the add button. You can choose, **Add** to include users, either from the local accounts database, or from a domain.

Predefined groups

On member/stand-alone servers, and on Windows 2000 Professional workstations, a number of groups are predefined during the installation of Windows 2000.
These groups have rights that allow them to carry out a certain number of tasks on the local machine, such as making backups, and administering resources.

These predefined groups are as follows:

- **Administrators**: the members of this group can carry out all the computer's administrative tasks. By default, the only member of this group is the administrator account. When you include a workstation, or a stand-alone server, in a domain, then the global administrators group of the domain is included automatically in the local administrators group of your computer. This is done so that the domain administrators can manage all the machines that are in their domain.

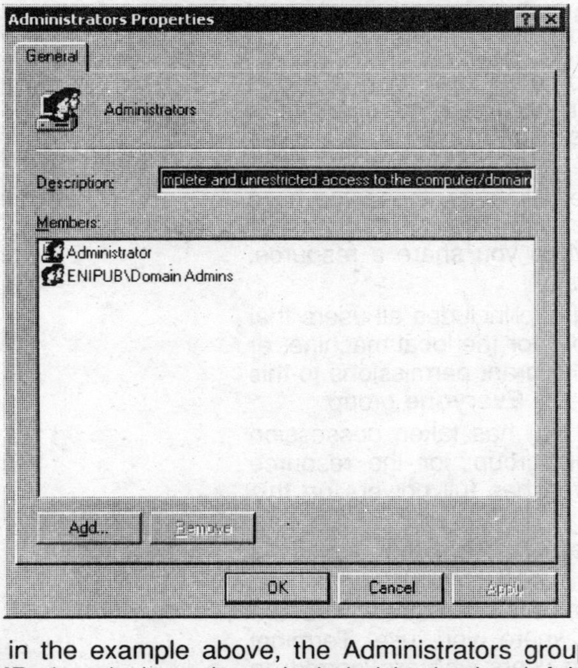

Thus, in the example above, the Administrators group of the **ENIPUB** domain have been included in the local Administrators group of the member server. Thanks to this approach, the domain administrator can administer this computer in the same way as the local machine administrator.

- **Guests**: as the name indicates, this group is used for occasional access. For security reasons, the users of this group are granted only a minimum number of system rights. By default, the **Guest** account is automatically included in this group.
- **Backup Operators**: the members of this group can use the Windows 2000 Backup utility in order to backup and to restore data.
- **Users**: all the user accounts that you create are included in this group. They can carry out only the tasks that you specify and have access only to those resources for which you have granted permissions. When your workstation, or your server joins a domain, the users group of the domain is automatically included in the users group of your machine.
- **Power Users**: the members of this group can share resources, and they can create and modify user accounts from the computer's local accounts database. Thereby, they can carry out certain administrative tasks without being in total control of the machine.

In addition to these groups, every computer that runs Windows 2000 has system groups. You cannot modify the membership of these groups, which reflect the status of your system at a given time.

- **Everyone** group: this group includes all users: those you have created, the guest account, and all the users of the other domains. It must be noted that, when you share a resource, this group has **Full Control** permission.
- **Authenticated Users** group: this group includes all users that have a user account and a password for the local machine, or for Active Directory. It is preferable to grant permissions to this group, rather than granting them to the **Everyone** group.
- **Creator Owner** group: every user that has taken possession of a resource is a member of this group, for the resource concerned. The owner of a resource has full powers on this resource.
- **Network** group: this group includes all users that access a resource via the network.
- **Interactive** group: this group contains all the users who are logged on locally (in the case where you use Terminal Services, this group contains all the users who are logged on to the Terminal Server).

B. Managing a domain

Every person who uses the network must have a user account in order to log on to the domain and thereby have access to the network resources. These user accounts are created in the Windows 2000 directory database.

When a user logs on to the domain, the logon information is sent to the domain controller, which compares it with the information that is contained in the Active Directory database. When the logon has been validated, the user can access all the network resources for which he/she has the permission to access.
When you promote a Windows 2000 server to domain controller (by installing Active Directory), the group and user information that is contained in the SAM database are migrated to the Active Directory database.

1. Managing domain users

Predefined accounts

When you install Windows 2000, two user accounts are created:
– the **Administrator** account, and
– the **guest** account.

Creating a user account

Before you start creating users, you might find it useful to define a naming convention that will allow you to identify each user, and above all, that will allow you to ensure that each logon name is unique in the domain. For example, one possible naming convention could be to use the first letter of the user's first name, followed by the users surname. If this rule leads to a duplication of logon names, one way of solving the problem could be to add the second letter of the first name. For example, suppose you have one user who is called Peter Jenkins and another user who is called Paul Jenkins. Then, you could define their login names as **pejenkins** and **pajenkins**, respectively. In order to create domain user accounts, you must use the Active Directory Users and Computers console. You must create this user object in a container. In order to do this, right-click the organizational unit in which you want to create the account, and then select **New** followed by **User** (alternatively, you can use the **Action** menu).

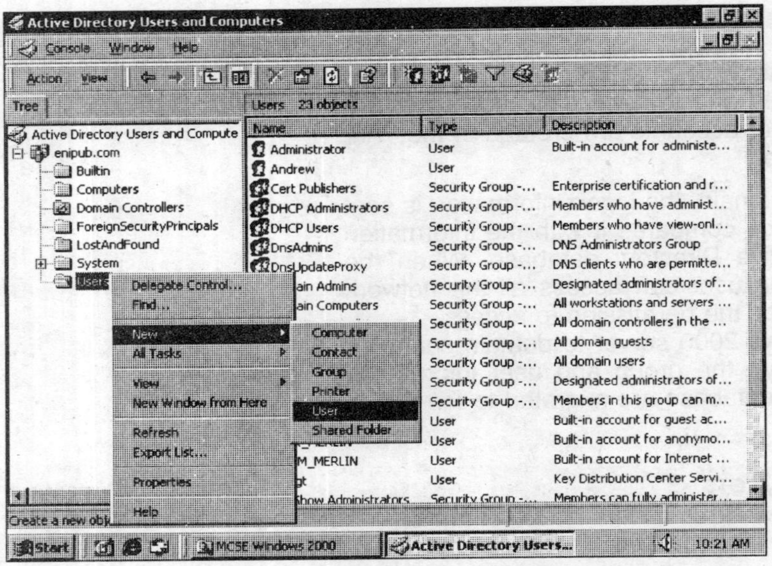

The **New Object - User** dialog box appears:

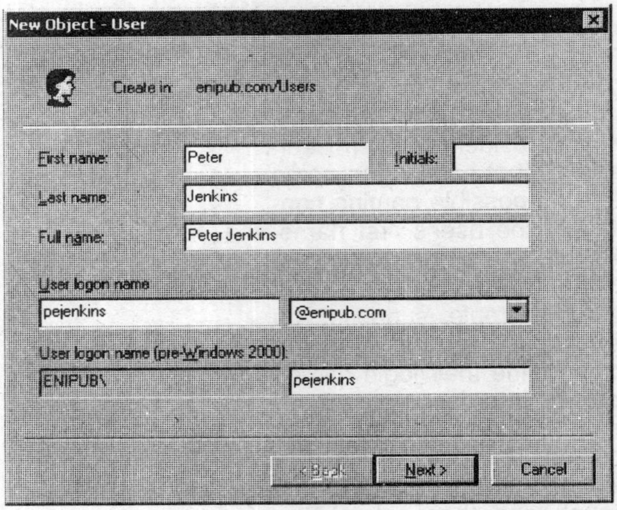

First name

This field is obligatory. It allows you to enter the user's first name.

Last name

The user's surname is also obligatory.

Full name

This name must be unique on the organizational unit in which you are creating the user account.

User logon name

The user will enter this name so that it can be authenticated by the domain controller. This name must be unique in the domain, and must be in conformity with your naming convention. It must be noted that this logon name is followed by the name of the domain in which you are creating the user. In the example above, the user will be able to log on as **pejenkins@enipub.com**.

User logon name (pre-Windows 2000)

Users who work with a pre-Windows 2000 version must log on with this name. This name must not exceed 20 characters.

☛ When you have completed these fields, click **Next**.

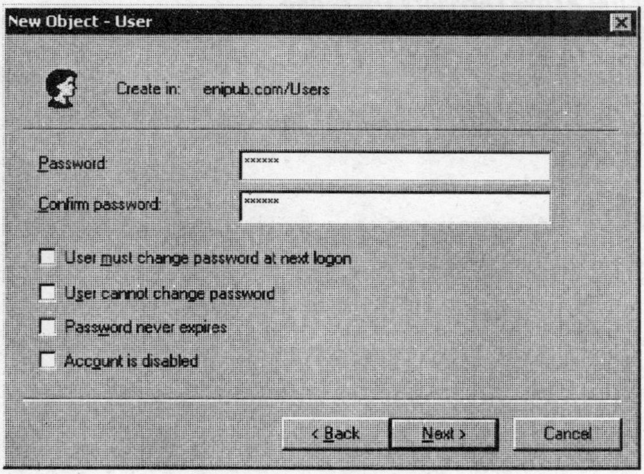

Password and Confirm password

The administrator can provide a password for the user.

User must change password at next logon

If you enable this option, then the user must choose a password when he/she logs on for the first time. Then, the user will no longer have to choose a password on subsequent logons, and will be able to use the password that he/she entered upon the first logon. This option allows the administrator to let the user choose his/her own password. However, in this case the administrator will have no unilateral means of finding out a user's password.

User cannot change password

This option is useful so as to fix certain passwords, such as that of the guest user and those of accounts that are user by several people. This option helps the administrator to manage user passwords.

Password never expires

You must use this option if you do not want the password to expire. This option can be useful with an account that is used by an application or by a service.

Account is disabled

You must enable this option if you do not want anyone to use an account (for example, when a user goes on holiday). When you disable an account a cross appears on its icon.

If the predefined OUs do not suit your needs, then select the name of your domain in the ***Active Directory Users and Computers*** *console, and open the* ***Action*** *menu and select New followed by* ***Organizational Unit****.*

When you create an object it is replicated automatically on all the other domain controllers.

User account properties

Personal properties

Personal properties are the attributes of the user. This information includes such items as the users geographical address, and the user's telephone numbers. This information is stored in the Windows 2000 directory database so that users will be able to find it very easily.

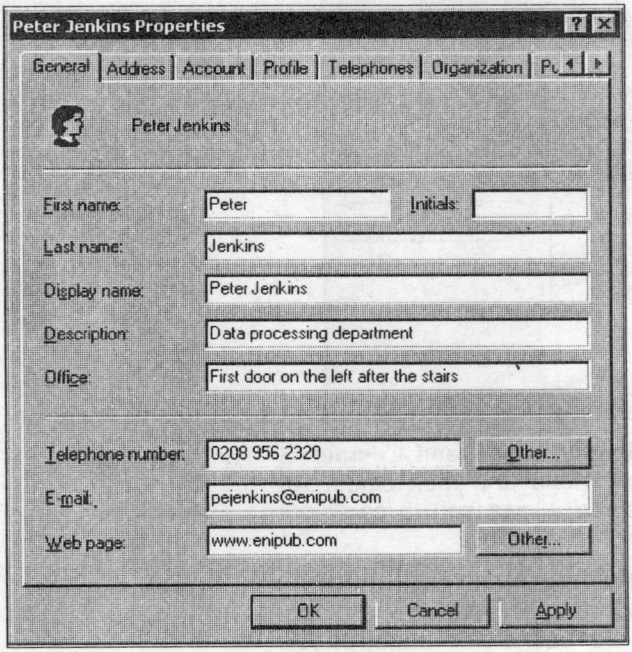

This information allows you to find a user very easily.
You can look for a user in two ways:

- Open the **Start Search For People** menu, and then select **Active Directory** in the **Look in** drop-down list box.

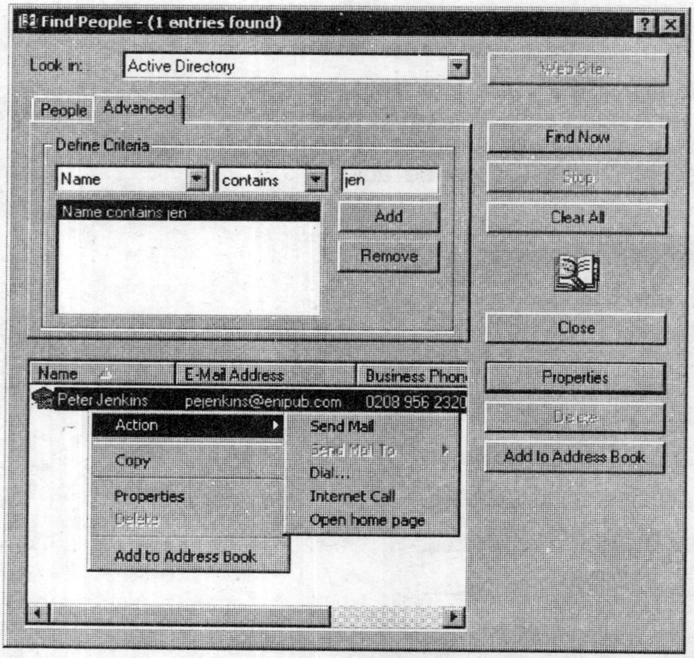

– Alternatively, using the **Active Directory Users and Computers** console you can open the **Action** menu and then select **All Tasks** followed by **Find**. This method allows you to carry out searches according to more advanced criteria.

When you have found your contact, you can carry out a certain number of actions. For example, you can send the user an electronic mail message, you can open the user's web page, or you can view the user's properties in order to find out his/her geographical address.

Account properties

Unlike personal properties, account properties do not supply information on the user. They supply information concerning the running of the account (including items such as time period restrictions, and account expiry).

In order to view or to enter account properties, double-click the user concerned and select the **Account** tab.

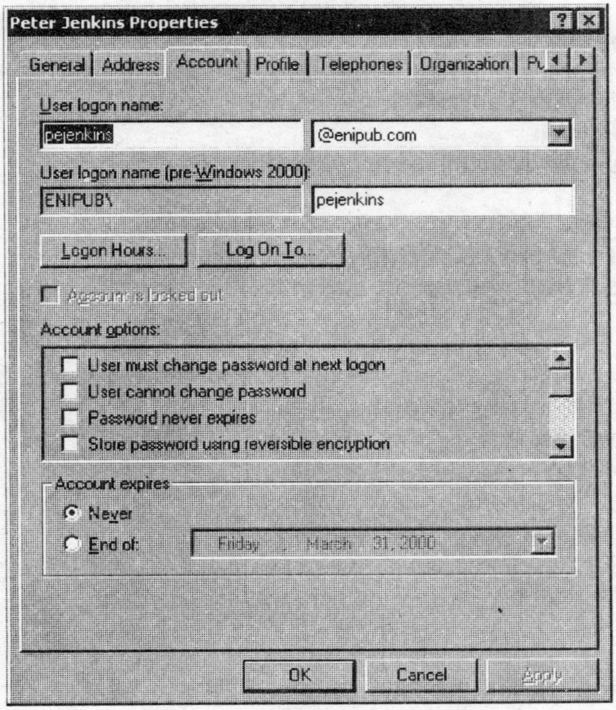

Under **Account options** you can modify the settings that were specified when the account was created. These settings include the following:

- Password never expires,
- User must change password at next logon,
- User cannot change password,
- Account is disabled.

In addition, the following options are also available:

Smart card is required for interactive logon

Windows 2000 allows you to request authentication using a smartcard, provided that your system is equipped with a card reader.

Account is sensitive and cannot be delegated

This option ensures that control of this account will not be delegated.

Account is trusted for delegation

This option allows the user to delegate administrative tasks to other users.

Store password using reversible encryption

You must use this option if there are any users in the Windows 2000 network who work with Apple computers.

Do not require Kerberos preauthentification

You must use this option if the user account uses another version of the Kerberos protocol.

Use DES encryption types for this account

You must enable this check box if you use DES (*Data Encryption Standard*) encryption. DES supports encryption methods such as IPSec, and MPPE.

Account expiry

You can set an account expiry date (this may be useful in the case where you know that a user will leave the company on a fixed date, for example on June 5th, 2000). You can set an expiry date as follows:

☛ Under **Account expires** select the **End of** option, and open the list box so as to display the calendar. Then select the date on which you want the account to expire.

Time period restrictions

For security reasons, you may want to define the time periods during which a user will be allowed to log on. In order to do this, select the **Logon Hours** button.

☛ Select the desired logon hours, and then enable either the **Logon Permitted** or the **Logon Denied** option button according to your requirements.

Access restrictions

You can restrict the access of the user to certain, specified machines. In order to do this, click the **Log On To** button, and then add the names of the computers onto which the user must be allowed to log.

Copying user accounts

If you must create a large number of user accounts with the same characteristics, you may find it quicker to create a template account that includes all the common characteristics, and then to copy it.

When you copy an account, the following settings are maintained:

- Logon Hours.
- The following account options:
  User must change password at next logon,
  User cannot change password,
  Password never expires,
  Account is disabled.
- Access restrictions (Log On To).
- Account expiry date.
- Profile options and the home directory (for these settings you must use the **%username%** variable).
- Group membership.

☞ In order to copy an account, right-click the account concerned, and then select **Copy**.

Modifying an account

Resetting a password

If a user forgets his/her password, then you must reset it (after first verifying the user's identity). You can reset a password by right-clicking the user's account, and then selecting **Reset Password**.

Moving a user object

As the organizational unit tree structure is not fixed, you can move a user account (or any other object) from one OU to another OU. In order to do this, right-click the account that you want to move, and then select **Move**.

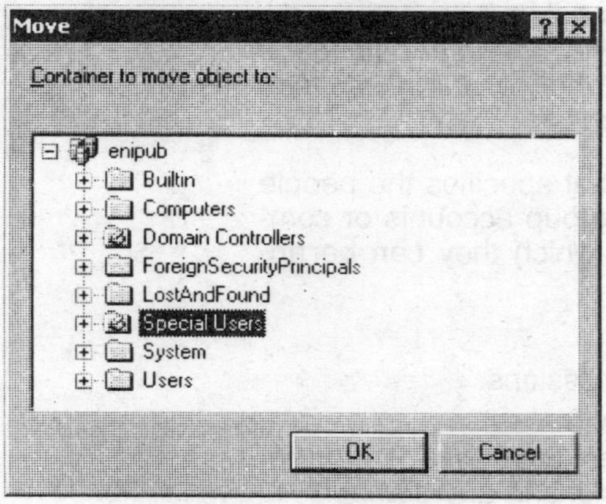

Select the OU to which you want to move the user object, and then click **OK**.
You can move objects from an OU in a domain, to another OU in another domain by using the **MOVETREE** command from the Windows 2000 resource kit.

2. Managing groups

Group Types

As has been discussed earlier on in this chapter, groups help you to manage user accounts so that you can allow them to access resources. Thereby, groups allow you to simplify administrative tasks.
Active Directory has introduced a number of group features that were not avaiable with Windows NT 4.0.

There are two types of group:
- **Security groups**, which are used in order to manage the resources of one or more domains.
- **Distribution groups**, which can be used, for example, to send electronic mail messages to all the users in such groups. These groups cannot be used for security purposes. Applications such as Exchange 2000 work with the Windows 2000 directory database, and can therefore use distribution groups.

Although you can use security groups as you would use distribution groups, you are strongly recommended not to do so, as some applications are able to read only distribution groups. In addition, when a user logs on, Windows 2000 creates an access token that contains the list of all the security groups to which the user belongs. If you use security groups for distribution purposes, then you may slow down the logon process.

Each of these group types has a scope that specifies the people who can belong to them (user accounts, group accounts or computer accounts) along with the extent to which they can be applied.

There are three types of group scope:
- **Domain local**: allows you to apply permissions.
- **Global**: allows you to organize user accounts.
- **Universal**: allows you to group together users that come from any domain, and to grant them permissions in any domain.

The contents of these groups will differ according to whether the domain configuration is in native mode, or in mixed mode.
A mixed mode domain allows Windows NT 4.0 domain controllers to operate in a Windows 2000 domain.

When you have upgraded all pre-Windows 2000 domain controllers, then you can switch to native mode. When you have switched to native mode, you will be able to use universal groups, and you will be able to nest groups inside other groups (for example, a global group can be a member of another global group in native mode).

After you have installed your Windows 2000 domain controllers, your domain will be in mixed mode. Switching to native mode is irreversible. In order to switch to native mode, go into your domain properties in the ***Active Directory Users and Computers*** *console.*

In **mixed** mode:

- A **domain local** group can contain users and global groups that come from any domain.
- A **global** group contains users that come from the same domain as that of the global group.
- **Universal** groups do not exist in mixed mode.

In **native** mode:

- A **domain local** group can contain user accounts, global groups, and universal groups that come from any domain in the forest. It can also contain domain local accounts that come from its own domain.
- A **global group** can contain user accounts and global groups from the same domain.
- A **universal group** can contain user accounts, global groups and universal groups from any domain in the forest.

Domain local groups can obtain permissions on the domain in which it is located.
Global groups and universal groups can obtain permissions on all the domains in the forest.

Creating groups

In order to create these groups, go into the **Active Directory Users and Computers** console.

- Select the OU in which you want to create your group.
- Open the **Action** menu, and select **New** followed by **Group**.

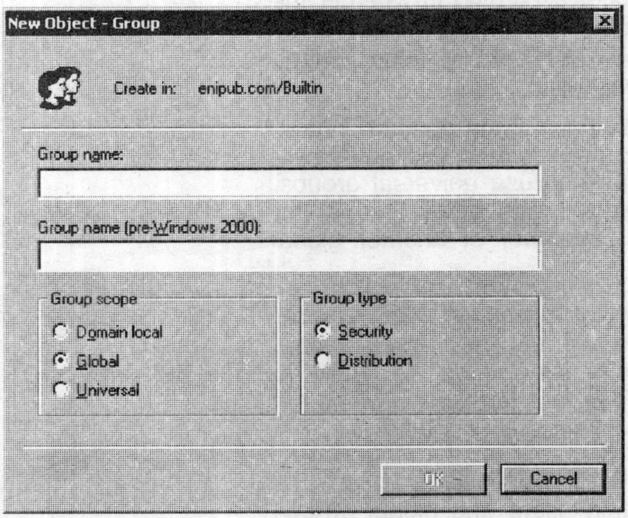

- Select the **Group type** (**Security** or **Distribution**) along with the **Group scope** (**Domain local, Global** or **Universal**).
- Give a meaningful name to the group.

It must be noted that you can specify a different name with which this group may be used on a pre-Windows 2000 machine. When you have created your group, you can double-click it, in order to edit its properties:

If the domain is in native mode, then you will be able to modify the **Group type** at any time. You can also modify the **Group scope**:

- You can change from a global group to a universal group provided that your global group in not a member of another group. This is because, a global group cannot contain a universal group.
- You can change from a domain local group to a universal group provided that your domain local group does not contain any other domain local groups. This is because, a universal group cannot contain a domain local group.

The **Members** tab allows you to view, to add, or to remove, user accounts or computer accounts in this group. An alternative way of adding a user to a group, is to display the properties of the user concerned, and then to use the **Member Of** tab in this dialog box.

The **Member Of** tab allows you to display the list of the groups to which your group belongs. This tab also allows you to insert your group into another group.

The **Managed By** tab allows you to specify the person or the group that must manage your group. For example, a user can view this tab in order to find out the telephone number of the person who is responsible for this group, so as to contact this person if any problem occurs.

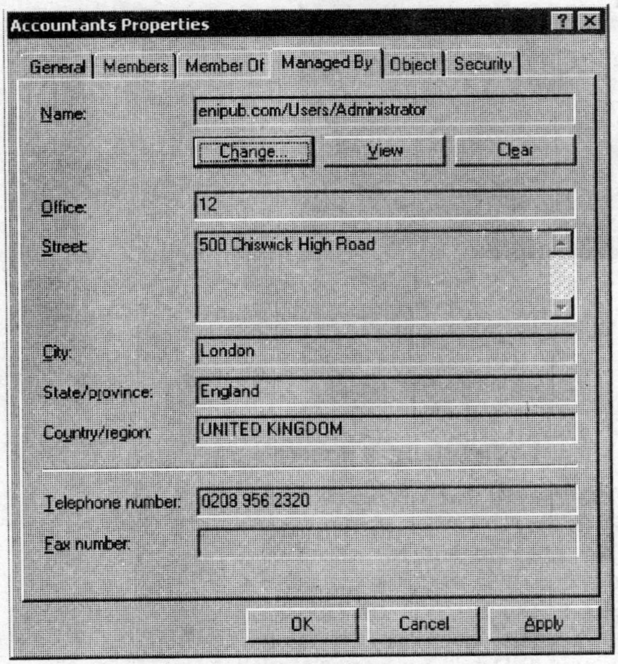

Carrying out actions on a group

Finding a group using Active Directory

If you have many different groups that are in different OUs, then you might find it useful to search for a group using Active Directory so that you can administer the group.

- Open the **Active Directory Users and Computers** console, open the **Action** menu, and select **Find**.
- Enter the name of the group that you seek and then click **Find Now**.

☞ Then, when your group has been found, you can double-click it, or right-click it, in order to administer it.

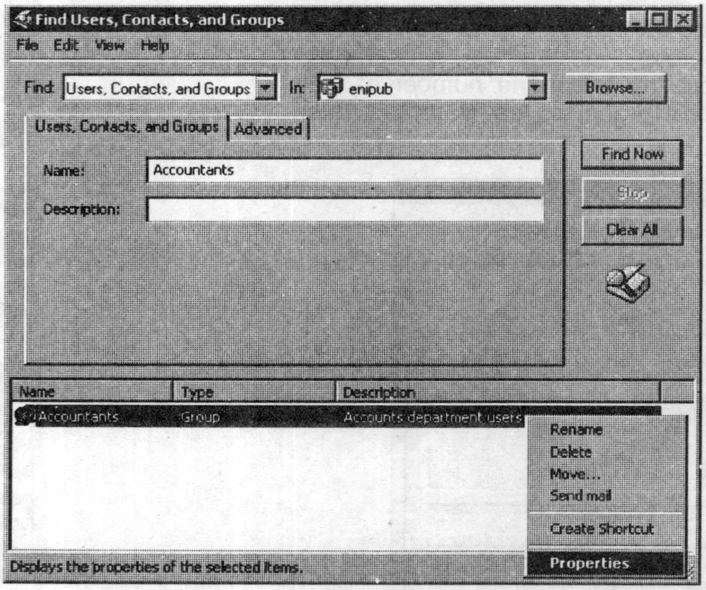

Deleting a group

When you delete a group, you do not delete the accounts that are members of the group.

The rights and the permissions that are associated with this group are deleted. When you create a group, a security identifier (SID) is associated with it. This SID is unique and cannot be re-used. Consequently, if you delete a group, and then create a group with the same name, then a new SID will be associated with this group. The permissions of the former group will not be applied to the new group.

In order to delete a group, right-click it and then select **Delete**. Alternatively, you can use the **Action** menu.

Renaming a group

When you rename a group, you will change the name of the group, but the SID that is associated with the group will stay the same. The members of this group are retained, and they can carry on using the resources for which the group has permissions.

Strategies for using groups

A domain local group can have permissions only on the domain in which it is located. Consequently, whenever possible you must try to organize users into global groups, and then include these global groups (which can come from any domain in the forest) into domain local groups.

Then, you can assign permissions for resources to the domain local groups, and these permissions will automatically apply to the member users of the global groups.

Predefined groups

Remember that all the computers that run Windows 2000 have a certain number of predefined groups, which are created when Windows 2000 is installed.

Predefined global groups

Domain Guests

The **Guest** user account is automatically included in this group. In addition, this global group is itself automatically included in the Guests domain local group.

Domain Users

All the user accounts that you create are included in this group. These accounts can carry out only those tasks that you specify and have access only to those resources for which you grant permissions. These accounts are automatically included in the **Users** domain local group.

Domain Admins

The Administrator account belongs to this group, which itself is included in the Administrators domain local group. In fact, the Administrator user account has no particular rights as a user account. The **Administrator** obtains its rights by being a member of this global group, which itself belongs to the Administrators domain local group.

Enterprise Admins

The members of this group have administrator rights on the whole network (they are not limited to the domain).

Predefined domain local groups

Account Operators

The members of this group can administer user accounts and groups (they can add, remove and modify these items). However, they cannot touch the Administrator account, nor can they touch the accounts of the other members of the **Account Operators** group.

Server Operators

The members of this group can share resources, and they can back up and restore data on the domain controllers.

Print Operators

The members of this group can manage the network printers of the domain controllers.

Administrators

The members of this group can administer the domain controllers, along with any machine that is included in the domain. By default, the **Domain Admins** global group and the Administrator account belong to the Administrators domain local group.

Guests

This group includes the **Domain Guests** global group and the Guest user account. Members of the **Guests** domain local group have few rights.

Backup Operators

The members of this group can backup and restore on all of the domain controllers.

Users

This group includes the **Domain Users** global group. You can use this group in order to apply rights and permissions to everybody that has an account in the domain.

By default, the different operator groups do not have members. You can include user accounts in these groups in order to assign specific rights to your users.

If a user must carry out backup operations, then it is better to include this user in the Backup Operators group, rather than in the Administrators group. In order to control security, it is preferable to limit a user's rights to those functions that the user must carry out.

It must be remembered that, in addition to these groups, every computer that runs Windows 2000 has system groups. You cannot modify the membership of these groups, which reflect the status of your system at a given time.

- **Everyone** group: this group includes all users: those you have created, the guest account, and all the users of the other domains. It must be noted that, when you share a resource, this group has **Full Control** permission.
- **Authenticated Users** group: this group includes all users that have a user account and a password for the local machine, or for Active Directory. It is preferable to grant permissions to this group, rather than granting them to the **Everyone** group.
- **Creator Owner** group: every user that has taken possession of a resource is a member of this group, for the resource concerned. The owner of a resource has full powers on this resource.
- **Network** group: this group includes all users that access a resource via the network.
- **Interactive** group: this group contains all the users who are logged on locally (in the case where you use Terminal Services, this group contains all the users who are logged on to the Terminal Server).

3. User profiles

User profiles

Local user profiles

A local user profile is a file that is stored locally in a folder that bears the user's logon name. This folder is stored in the **Documents and Settings** directory. When no roaming profile exists for a user on a server, a new folder is created locally with the name of the user, and with the contents of the **Default user** profile. The user environment is then built up by adding the information that is contained in the **All Users** folder. All modifications that are made by the user are saved in the new user profile. The initial **Default user** profile is unchanged. If the user has the same account name in order to log on locally and to log on to the domain, then two separate folders are created. Notably, this is the case for the administrator:

The user's environment is contained in each of these folders. The profile file is called **ntuser.dat**.

The profile provides the user's environment (including such items as screen background colours, and customized **Start** menu) each time that the user logs on.

Roaming user profiles

With local profiles, the user will go into his/her environment only if the user logs on to the machine on which his/her environment has been configured.

In many networks, users move from machine to machine. It is useful then, for the user to be able to go into his/her environment on whatever machine to which the user logs on. This can be achieved by configuring roaming profiles.
When a user logs on, Windows 2000 automatically downloads the user's profile. However, before it does this, Windows 2000 compares the user's profile with that which is on the machine on to which the user is logging. This approach allows Windows 2000 to download only the differences between the two profiles, so as to speed up the logon process.

Roaming personal profiles

Here are the steps that you must follow in order to create a roaming profile:

- Open the **Active Directory Users and Computers** console, and double-click the user for whom you wish to create a roaming profile.
- In the user's **Properties** dialog box, select the **Profile** tab and input the path that leads to the user profile (before doing this you must have created a shared directory on the server concerned, in which the profiles can be placed).

The path that leads to a profile must have a UNC name (**server name\share**\).
If you use the **%username%** variable, then a directory will automatically be created with the name of the logon account. This approach is especially useful if you have to create a large number of user accounts. In this case, you could create a template account, in which you use this variable so as to specify the path that leads to each user. Windows 2000 will replace this variable with the logon name of the user.

Every user who logs on has a listed profile, as in the example below:

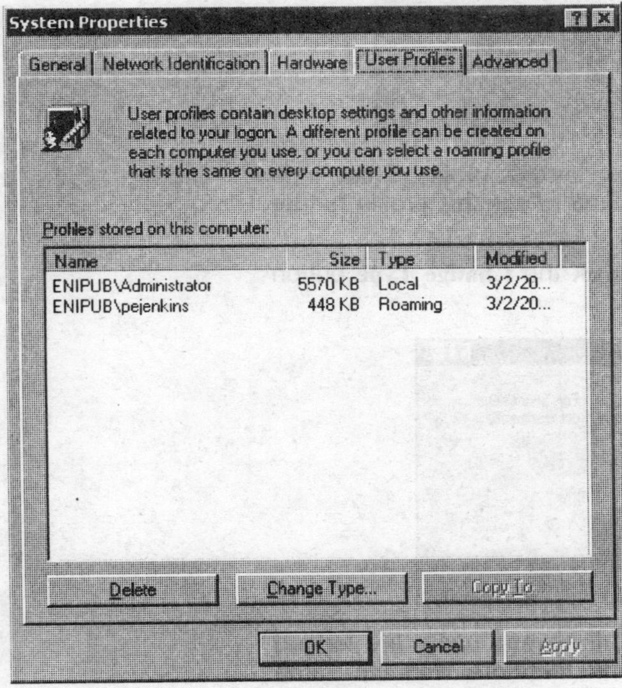

In order to access this dialog box, go into **Control Panel** and open the **System** icon. Then, select the **User Profiles** tab.

This dialog box allows you to copy a user profile to another user profile, replacing the contents of the latter. In order to do this, click the **Copy To** button, so as to display the following dialog box:

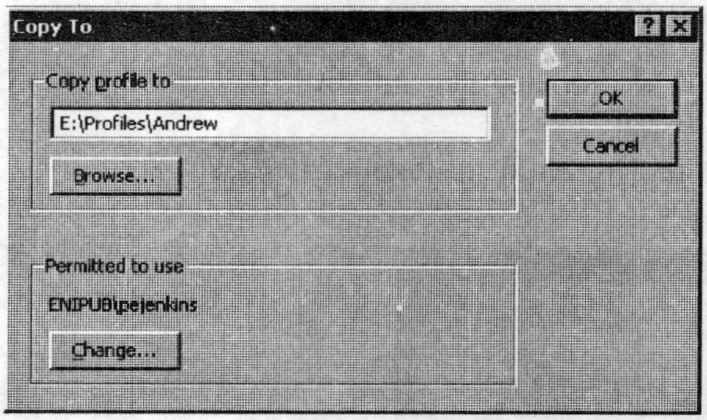

Input the path to which you want to copy this profile. Then, indicate as necessary who must be allowed to use this profile (under **Permitted to use**).

In order to define the profile type, click the **Change Type** button under the **User Profiles** tab.

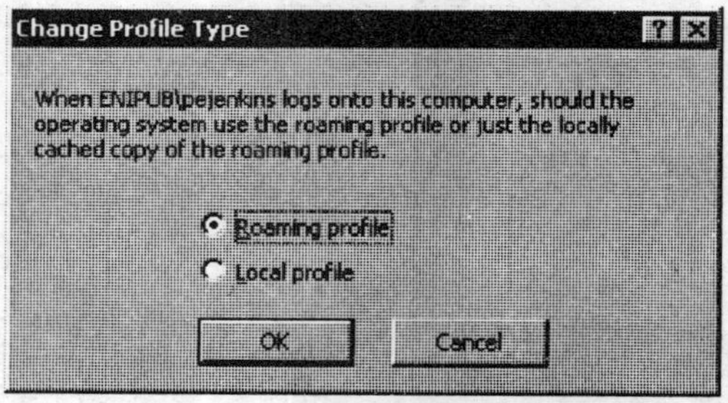

The profiles are saved upon log-off. If several users are logged on with the same user account, and therefore with the same profile, then the profile that will be saved is that of the last user to log-off.

Mandatory roaming profiles

If you use the same profile for all your users, then you must create a mandatory roaming profile. This type of profile is compulsory for the user, and is in read-only mode. In fact, if a user modifies his/her profile, then this profile will not be saved upon log-off.

This approach is very useful when there are several users who must have a common desktop (for example, with the same shortcuts that lead to the same applications, and the same reference letters so as to connect to network devices).
In order to transform a roaming profile into a mandatory roaming profile, rename the **ntuser.dat** file as **ntuser.man** (with 'man' as in mandatory).

The following example creates a mandatory roaming profile that is stored on a server called **Galahad**.

- Log on with the account that must be used as a template.
- Organize the user environment so that it will be suitable for the users concerned. For example, you may wish to add network connections, or to modify the **Start** menu by adding shortcuts onto the desktop.
- When you have finished configuring the desktop, log off so as to save the profile.
- Then, log on as the administrator, and create the shared directory in which you will save the profile. For example, create a **profiles** directory, and then share it, using the same name as the share name. Then, create another directory, and save the common profile. You could call the directory "common", for example
- Go into the **Control Panel**, open the **System** icon, and select the **User Profiles** tab.
- Select your template profile, and then click **Copy To**, so as to save it in the "common" directory.
- In order to do this, input the path that leads to the shared directory, and then authorize the **Everyone** group to use this profile.
- In order to make the profile mandatory, rename the **ntuser.dat** file as **ntuser.man**, in the directory into which you have just copied the profile (using Windows Explorer, display the file name extensions so that you will not confuse the two ntuser files!).
- Open the **Active Directory Users and Computers** console and specify the path that leads to the profile for the users concerned.

- In the properties dialog boxes for the users that must use this profile, select the **Profile** tab, and enter the path that leads to the profile: **\\galahad\profiles\common**.
- Finally, log on with the account of the user to whom you have applied the profile, in order to verify that the operation was carried out successfully.

You are strongly recomended to place roaming profiles on a computer that does not act as a domain controller. This approach will speed up logons, as it will allow the resources of the domain controller to be used solely for the logon process.

Home directory

The home directory of a user, is the user's reception folder. It can be either a local path, or a network path. If you use a network path for this purpose, then you can save your data in your home directory, irrespective of the machine on to which you are logged. In addition, this technique eases backup operations.

If you use an NTFS partition in order to accomodate the home directories, then you can use the **%username%** variable so as to create a user's home directory automatically, according to the user's logon name. In addition, the user will have access to his/her home directory. The NTFS Full Control permissions will be assigned automatically to the user, and to the administrator.

Under the **Profile** tab of the user properties:

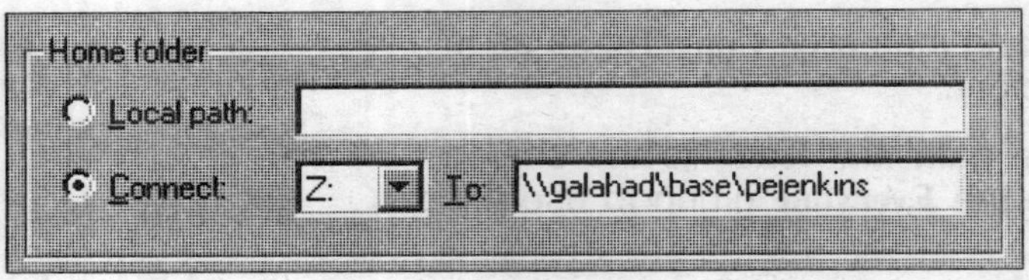

This example creates on the **Galahad** server, a directory called "base" that is shared with **Full Control** permissions for the **Everyone** group. The **%username%** variable ensures that the user's home directory will be created automatically in the "base" directory. Thereby, if the "base" directory was created on an NTFS partition, then, apart from the administrator, only the user will have access to his/her own home directory.

The home directories on Windows 2000 have improved with respect to those on Windows NT 4.0. With Windows NT, when you explore the disk that is associated with your home directory, you view the list of all the home directories of all the users, even though you do not have the permissions to access them. This approach is inconvenient when there are a lot of users. With Windows 2000, the drive letter that is associated with the home directory, directly references the home directory.

Managing disk resources

A. **File systems** 188

1. FAT16 188
2. FAT32 188
3. NTFS 5.0 188
4. Choosing the most suitable file system (FAT or NTFS) 189

B. **Sharing folders** 190

1. Sharing a folder 191
2. Ceasing to share a folder 196
3. Connecting to a shared resource 198
4. Checking shares 200
5. Advice for sharing folders 202

C. **Access security** 202

1. NTFS Permissions 203
2. Taking ownership of files and folders 210
3. Copying and moving files and folders 212

D. **DFS** 212

E. **Managing disk quotas** 219

A. File systems

1. FAT16

This file system is present on a large number of operating systems:
- OS /2
- MS-DOS
- Windows 3.x
- Windows 95/98
- Windows NT
- Windows 2000

The FAT system was designed for low-volume partitions (nowadays, for partitions of up to 500 MB). For partitions of this size, FAT uses only a very small amount of disk space for its internal management.

The FAT structure is very simple. One reason for this simplicity is that the FAT does not manage an Access Control List (ACL) for each file and folder.

2. FAT32

FAT32 is a development of FAT16 file systems. Whereas FAT16 does not support partitions of over 2 GB, FAT32 allows you to go beyond this limit. This file system is used with OSR2 versions of Windows 95, and also with the Windows 98 operating system. Windows NT 4.0 does not recognize FAT32. However, Windows 2000 does support this file system.

3. NTFS 5.0

NTFS *(NT File System)* allows you to manage security locally using ACLs. NTFS also supports, individual compression, disk quota management, and file encryption by public key/private key.

NTFS offers a transactional mode at file system level. This mode allows NTFS to ensure that the internal structures will be coherent, in most cases. This is possible because all actions that are carried out on the file system are logged. In addition, NTFS supports 64-bit addressing. This feature allows NTFS to divide its partitions into elementary allocation units, which are known as clusters. Not only does this technique allow NTFS to manage larger partitions, but it also allows this file system to waste less disk space when it manages small files.

With NTFS, search operations are much quicker thanks to the use of a B-tree structure. This structure, which is complicated to set up, allows you to write algorithms that have Log N complexity, whereas classical algorithms offer a complexity that is a function of N/2.

In other words, if you want to look for an item amongst N items (for example, N=100), then with classical algorithms you will need to search for a length of time that is proportional to N/2 (for example 100/2 = 50). On the other hand, with B-tree structures you will need to search for a length of time that is proportional to Log N (for example Log 100, which equals 2). Suppose that your reference time is one second. Then, with classical N/2 algorithms your search will take 50 seconds, whereas with B-trees your search will take only 2 seconds.

The higher the value of N, the greater this difference will be.

When a file is fragmented, then fewer disk accesses that will be necessary in order to re-assemble it with NTFS, than would be necessary with FAT.

NTFS uses a particular table called the *Master File Table*. This table allows you to accommodate small files, and to access them very quickly.

You can extend an NTFS volume, or an NTFS disk stripe. This technique allows you to increase the size of a data volume, without losing information.

Finally, with NTFS, there is no specific limitation on the number of directories that you can create.

4. Choosing the most suitable file system (FAT or NTFS)

For partitions that are smaller than 500 MB, the FAT file system is the most suitable.

NTFS is particularly suitable for high-volume disks. You must use NTFS when you want to:
– implement data security (for files or for folders),
– compress individual items,
– have a stable file system,
– manage data encryption,
– apply disk quotas,

– make your server a domain controller (in order to store Active Directory).

B. Sharing folders

The main purpose of a network is to allow you to access files that are situated on another computer, a workstation or a server. By default, operating systems such as Windows for Workgroups, and the different versions of Windows 95, do not share directories (folders) or files that are on the hard disk, for security reasons. The administrator must set up the sharing of the resource in order to allow users to access it via the network. According to the users who must access it, this resource is shared with different rights (for example, write, read, or delete).

Resource level security

On Windows for Workgroups operating systems, access security is ensured by a password. A password is allocated per resource and per type of access, independently of the users. For example, no password is necessary for read-only access, whereas a password is necessary in order to allow full access (read and write).

User level security

With Windows 98, you can operate with user level security, or with resource level security.
With Windows NT and Windows 2000, only user level security can be used. In this mode, initial authentication is compulsory. Thereby, a user is designated as being authorized to access a resource, according to a particular type of access. For any given resource, you can designate several users, and/or groups of users, and you can define a specific type of access for each of them.

It must be noted that, with Windows for Workgroups and Windows 98, you can share resources only if you have explicitly enabled this feature by activating the options **I want to be able to give others access to my files** and **I want to be able to allow others to print to my printers.**

When you have activated these options, and after you have restarted your machine, the server service that allows you to share these resources is loaded into memory.

With FAT, sharing folders is the only means of ensuring the security of network access to resources.

1. Sharing a folder

On Windows 2000, the files are not shared. Only the folder that contains the files can be shared.
By default, certain resources are shared on Windows 2000. These are administrative shares that are reserved for the configuration management of remote workstations. These files are hidden, and only the administrator can access them.

Shared Folder	Shared Path	Type
ADMIN$	E:\WINNT	Windows
C$	C:\	Windows
D$	D:\	Windows
E$	E:\	Windows
IPC$		Windows
print$	E:\WINNT\System32\spool\drivers	Windows

C$, D$, E$, device_letter$	This share provides the administrator with full access to drives. The administrator can connect to a remote machine by entering **\\computer_name\c$**.
Admin$	This share is used in order to manage a workstation via the network. This refers to the **%systemroot%** directory.
IPC$	This share allows processes to communicate with each other. It is used in order to administer a workstation remo- tely, or in order to consult a shared directory.
Print$	This share is used in order to administer printers remotely.

It must be noted that the names of administrative shares finish with a **$** sign, which causes them to be hidden. You can add this symbol at the end of a share name so as to hide the share concerned.

In order to share a folder, right-click the folder that you want to share, and then select the **Sharing** option.

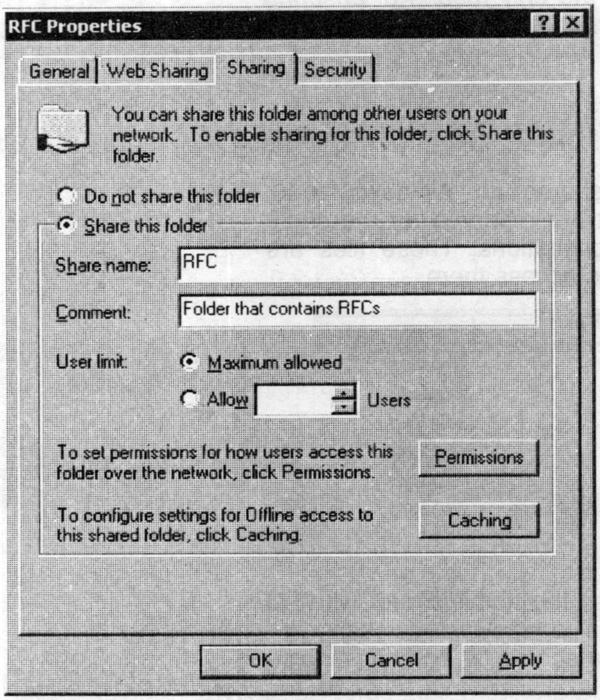

Enable the **Share this folder** option. You can then change the name of your share, if you wish. This is the name that will be seen via the network. By default, the share name is the same as that of the folder, but this is not obligatory. You can also add a comment that is useful in order to describe the folder's contents.

On Windows 2000, a shared folder is reserved for certain users. In order to access a shared folder on a domain controller, you must be a member, either of the administrators group, or a member of the server operators group. On a Windows 2000 member server, or an a Windows 2000 Professional workstation, you must be either a member of the administrators group, or of the power users group.

You can choose to restrict the number of simultaneous connections on this share.

If you have MS-DOS or Windows for Workgroups clients, then you must use short names (in the 8.3 character format).

In order to modify network access permissions, click the **Permissions** button.

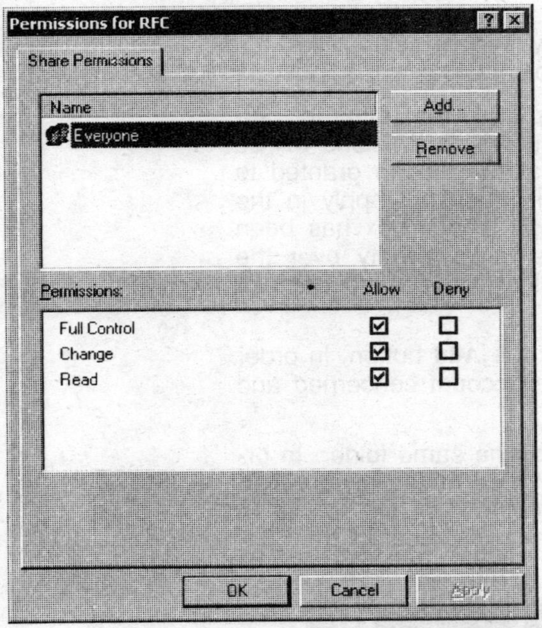

This dialog box displays the share permissions that are currently applied to the folder. Note that the system grants **Full Control** permission to the **Everyone** group, by default.

Under **Permissions**, the list of permissions that apply to the shared folder is displayed. These permissions are as follows:

- **Read**: The user that has this permission is allowed to read the files, to run the programs, and to browse the subfolders.
- **Change**: The user that has this permission, has the **Read** permission, plus the right to modify, and to delete, folder and files.
- **Full Control**: The user that has this permission, has the **Change** permission, plus the right to change share permissions.

In order to apply these permissions to the users, you can use two columns of check boxes:

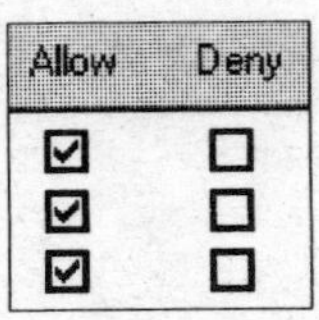

In order to grant a permission, click the corresponding check box in the **Allow** column. In order to deny a permission, click the corresponding check box in the **Deny** column.

If a user is a member of several groups to which different permissions have been granted, then the users permissions will be the combination of the permissions that have been granted to the different groups. However, this rule does not apply in the case of a permission for which the **Deny** check box has been enabled. The **Deny** check box always takes priority over the **Allow** check box (you must be careful of this consequence of using the **Deny** check box).

In order to add a group or a user, click the **Add** button. In order to delete a user or a group, select the account concerned and then click the **Remove** button.

You can create several share names for the same folder. In order to do this, you can click the **New Share** button (in order to make this button appear, you may need to click **OK** so as to close this dialog box, and then re-open it and reselect the **Sharing** tab).

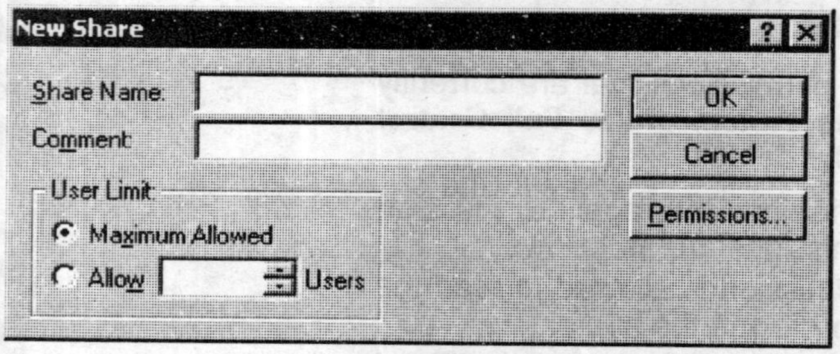

Alternatively, you can use the **Computer Management** console in order to share a folder.

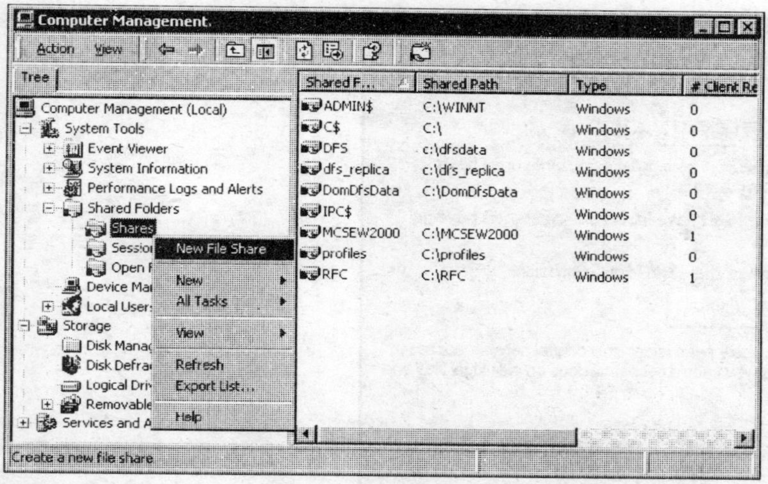

Right-click the **Shares** folder and then select **New File Share**.

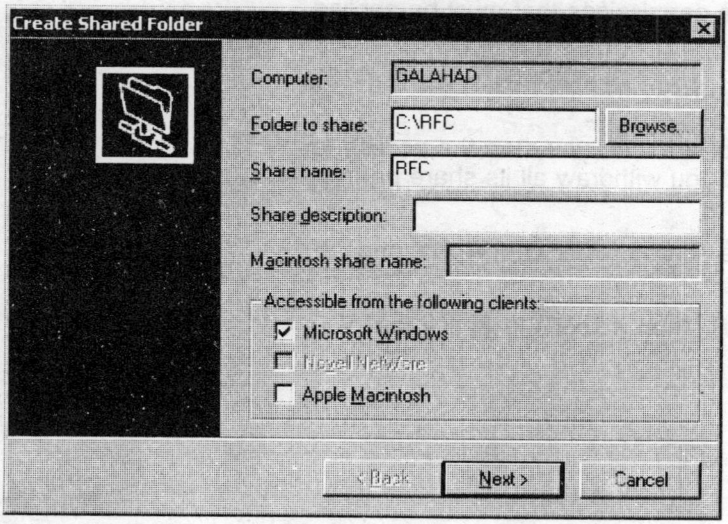

Fill in the different fields and then click **Next**.

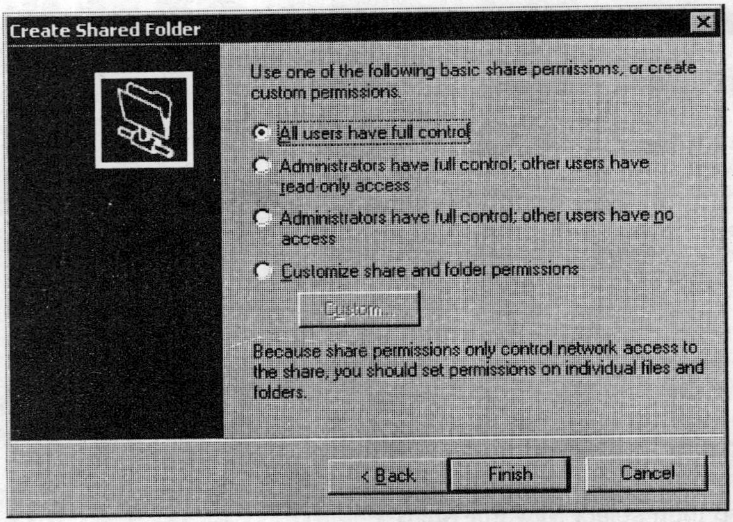

You can then specify the share permissions that must be applied to this folder.

2. Ceasing to share a folder

When you cease the sharing of a folder, you stop the access to this folder via the network, and you withdraw all its share permissions.

- ☞ Right-click the name of the shared folder concerned, and select the **Sharing** option.
- ☞ If there are several shares, then select the share that you wish to remove.

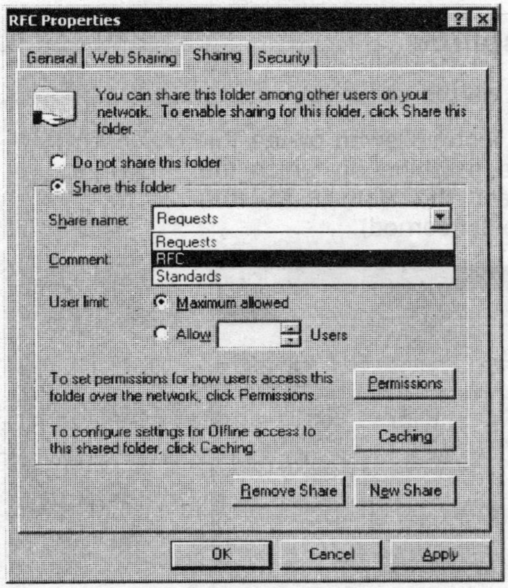

☞ Click the **Remove Share** button, then click **OK**.

☞ If you have only one share name for the folder, or if you want to stop sharing the folder, whatever the share name, then click the **Do not share this folder** option.

Alternatively, you can cease a share using the **Computer Management** console:

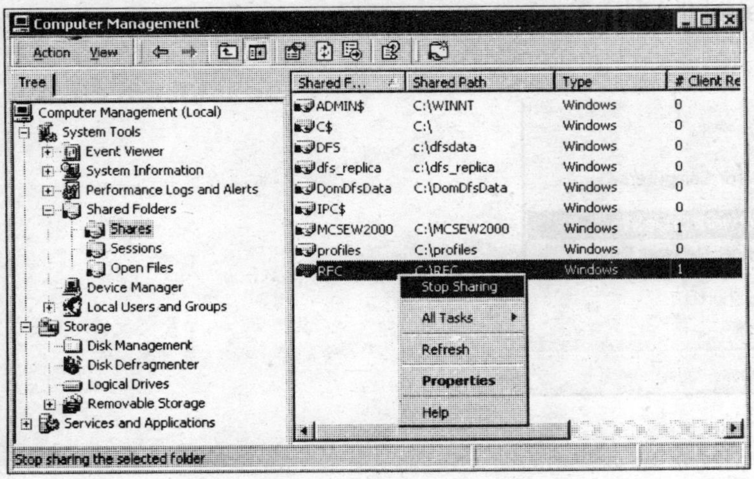

Managing disk resources

3. Connecting to a shared resource

Once a folder is shared, it is accessible via the network.

☞ Double-click the **My Network Places** icon, followed by the **Entire Network** icon. Then select the machine on which the shared resource is located (select the domain or the workgroup, followed by the machine concerned).

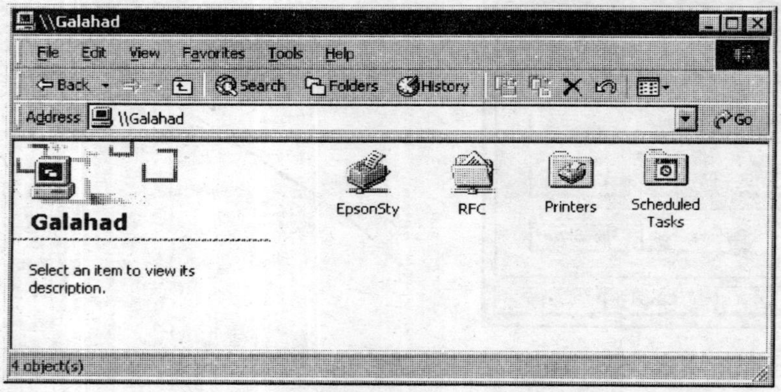

☞ Double-click the icon that represents the computer concerned. You will be able to access a shared resource if you have the necessary permissions.

In order to connect a drive letter to a shared resource, right-click the **My Network Places** icon, or, go into **Windows Explorer** and open the **Tools** menu, then select the **Map Network Drive** option.

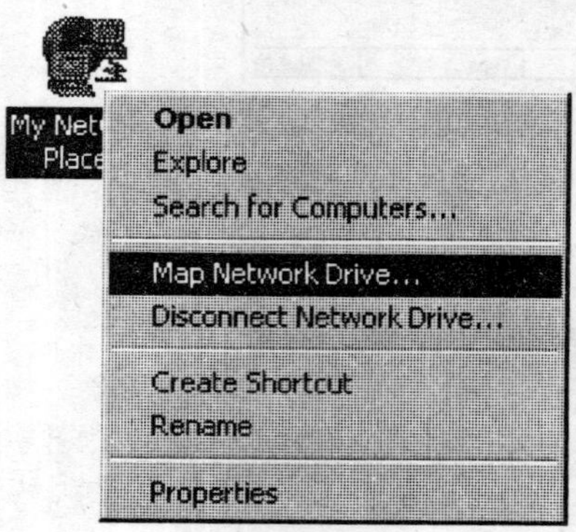

The following dialog box appears:

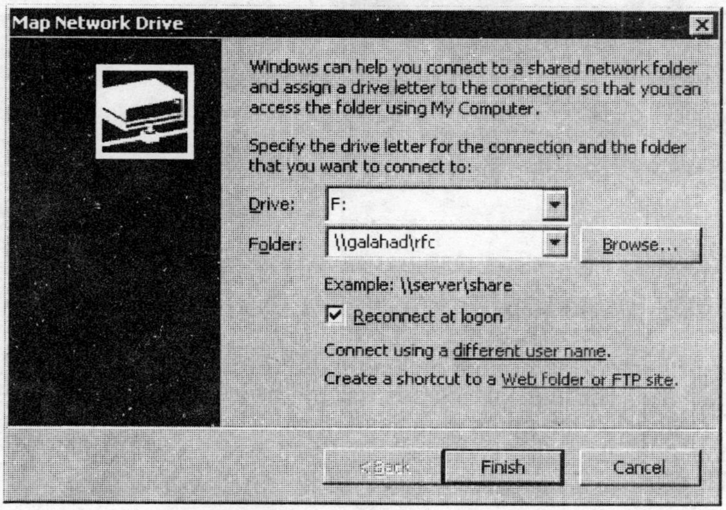

- Choose the drive letter that you want to use as a reference to the shared resource on the target computer.
- Enter the path that leads to the resource concerned. This must be a UNC path (**\\server\share**).
- Enable the **Reconnect at logon** check box if you want to continue using this drive letter the next time that you log on.
- You can connect to the resource using the permissions of another user account. In order to do this, click **different user name**, and then, in the dialog box that appears, enter the user name and the password for the account that you want to use for this connection.
- The **Web folder or FTP site** option allows you to add the connection to this shared folder, into **My Network Places**.

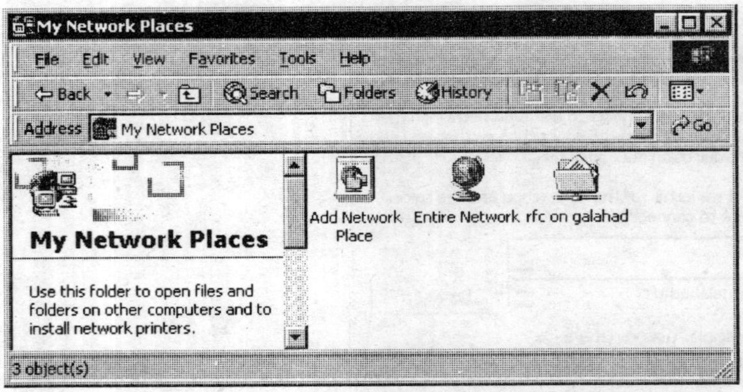

You can now access the shared directory by double-clicking the **My Network Places** icon. You can also add network places using the **Add Network Place** icon. In addition to paths that lead to shared directories, you can also add as network places, URLs that point to Web sites or to FTP sites.

4. Checking shares

Checking shares allows a user or the administrator to display the list of network users who are accessing the shared resources, and to control the access to these resources.

☞ Open the **Computer Management** console.

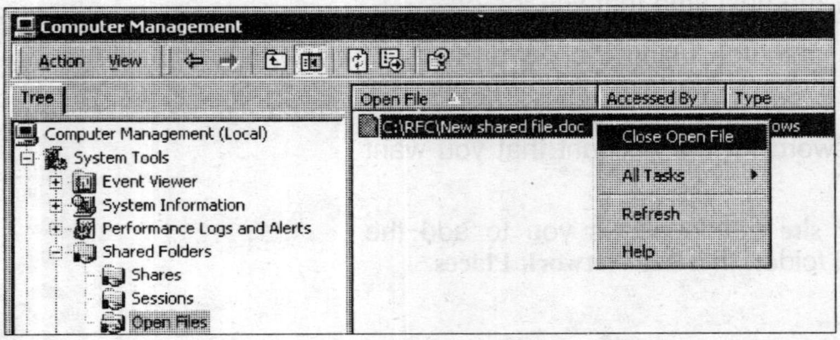

– The **Open Files** folder allows you to view the list of all the files from shared folders that are open on the server. It also allows you to close these shared resources. If you close a file that was open in read/write mode, then any modifications that had been made will be lost. The user still has the right to access the resource. The disconnection is temporary however, as the user can re-access the resource immediately.

This passive disconnection technique allows the system to ensure fault tolerance even when the network temporarily fails.

- The **Sessions** folder allows you to view all the sessions that are open on the computer. This folder then, lists all the people who have logged on to the computer via the network. All the connections that a user has made are represented by a single session, no matter how many times the user has logged on to the machine. This feature is particularly useful when you want to shutdown a computer, as it allows you to warn all the users who are currently logged on to it.
- The **Shares** folder allows you to share, or to cease sharing a resource (as discussed earlier in this chapter).

This console allows you to connect to remote computers in order to administer them. For example, you can create new shares remotely, or cease sharing remote resources.

Sending administrative messages

If you want to stop a service in order to carry out maintenance work, then you must warn the users who are connected so that they will be able to save their data.
You can send a message to all the users who are connected to your server.

- Open the **Computer Management** console, and right-click **Shared Folders**.
- Select **All Tasks**, followed by **Send Console Message**.

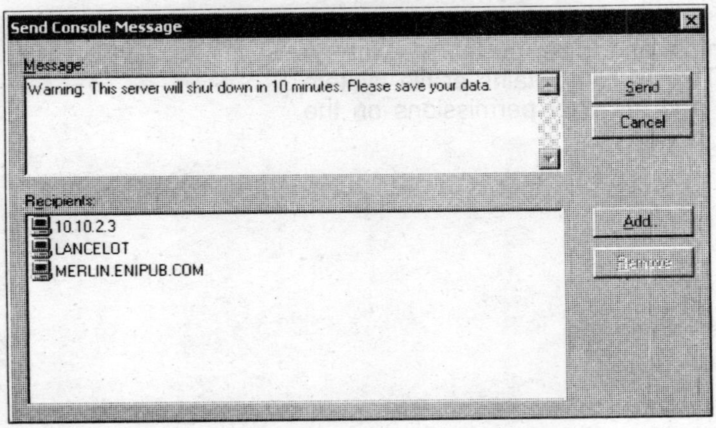

Your message will be sent to all the machines that are listed under **Recipients**.

5. Advice for sharing folders

In order to ease the access to resources via the network, you must take into account the following points:

- Choose share names carefully and provide comments on the shares.
- Remember that if the share name exceeds 8.3 characters, then the users of machines that run MS-DOS, Windows 3.x or Windows for Workgroups will not see the shares and will not be able to access them.

C. Access security

The permissions that have been described so far in this chapter are applied to enable users to access resources via the computing network. They do not provide protection when users access a computer locally.
This chapter will now cover the security features that allow users to protect their own data from unauthorized access, both locally and via the network. These security features also allow you to protect the operating system from accidental deletion by uninformed users, or by users who are insensitive to system warnings when the system is about to delete files. In order to use these Windows 2000 features, you must be using the NTFS file system. Only NTFS allows you to implement security and to audit attributes on folders and files.

NTFS allows you to keep each file and folder up to date with an Access Control List, or ACL. This ACL maintains at file system level, the user numbers (SID) and the user permissions on the resource.

1. NTFS Permissions

NTFS distinguishes between folder permissions and file permissions.

Conditions for attributing NTFS permissions

In order to apply NTFS permissions for a file or for a folder, you must either be the owner of the item concerned, or you must be the administrator, or you must have the necessary permissions. The permissions that are required are **Full Control**, **Change Permissions** or **Take Ownership** (which allows you to become the owner of the object).

Permissions for a folder

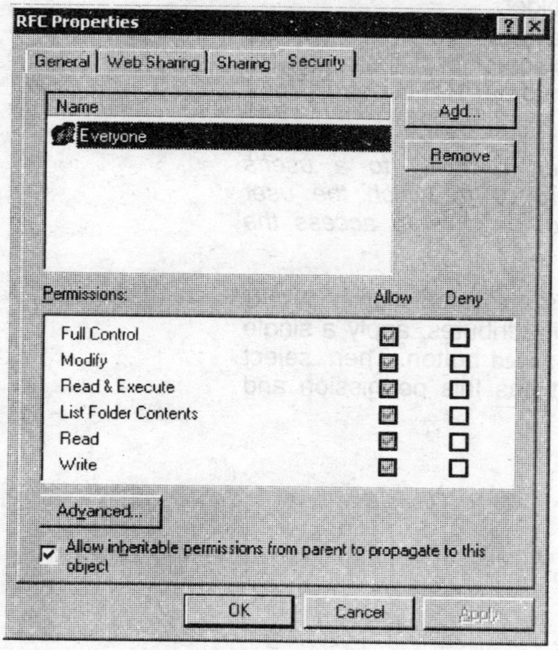

In order to apply NTFS permissions for a folder, right-click the folder concerned, select **Properties**, and then select the **Security** tab.

The following permissions appear:

– **Write**: users who have this permission can create files and folders, and they can also modify the attributes of these items (for example: **Read-only**, and **Hidden**).

A user who has this permission must also have read permission so as to be able to access the folder.

- **Read**: users who have this permission can read the contents of the folder and also the contents of the files that are in the folder. This permission also allows users to read the attributes.
- **List Folder Contents**: this permission covers **Read** permission, plus the right to browse the folder's contents
- **Read & Execute**: this permission covers **Read** permission, plus **List Folder Contents** permission, plus the right to navigate across folders so as to reach other folders and files.
- **Modify**: this permission covers **Read & Execute** permission, and it also allows you to delete the folder.
- **Full Control**: this permission allows you to change permissions for the folder, to take ownership of the folder, to delete the folder, and it covers all the other NTFS permissions as well.

If permissions are not applied explicitly to a user's account, or to one of the groups to which the user belongs, then the user will not be able to access the resource.

In reality, each of these permissions is an association of NTFS attributes. In order to find out the list of attributes, apply a single permission to a user and click the **Advanced** button. Then, select the **Permission Entry** for the user that has this permission and click the **View/Edit** button.

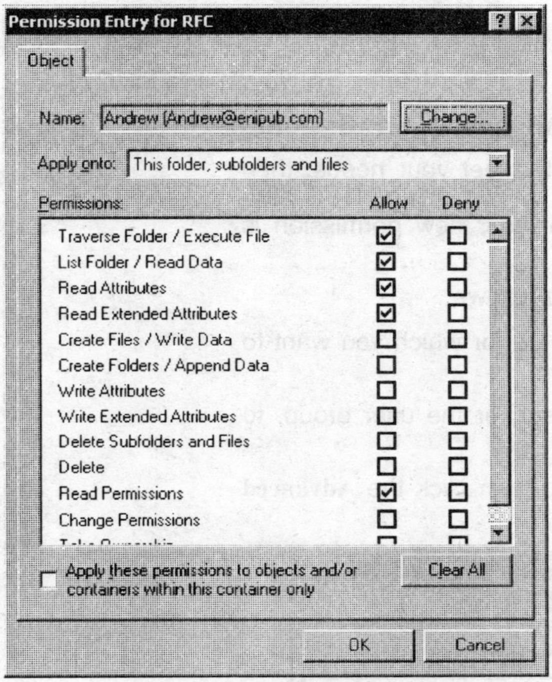

Permissions for a file

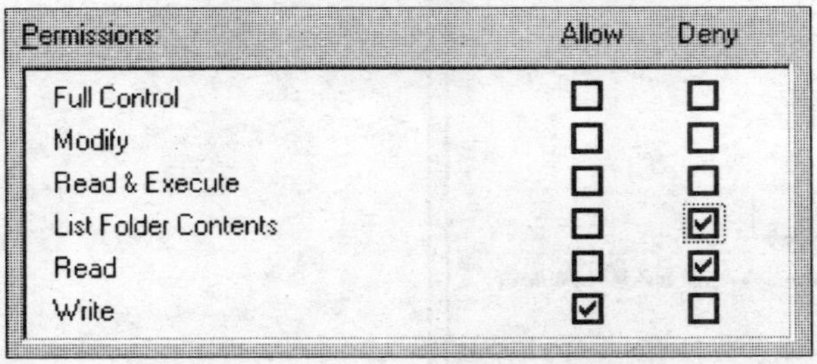

- **Write**: allows you to write in the file, to change its attributes, and to display the permissions and the owner of the file.
- **Read**: allows you to read the file contents, its attributes, the permissions that are associated with the file, and the name of its owner.
- **Read & Execute**: This permission provides **Read** permission, and it also allows you to run programs.
- **Modify**: This permission provides **Read & Execute** permission, and it also allows you to delete the files.

– **Full Control**: This permission covers **Modify** permission, and it also allows you to take ownership of the file and to change its permissions.

Advanced permissions

If the standard permissions do not fully meet your needs, then you can create your own permissions by combining NTFS attributes. However, you must ensure that your new permission is coherent.

You can customize your permissions as follows:

☞ Display the properties of the resource for which you want to apply NTFS permissions.

☞ Under the **Security** tab, add the user, or the user group, to which the permission must apply.

☞ Select this user, or this group, and then click the **Advanced** button.

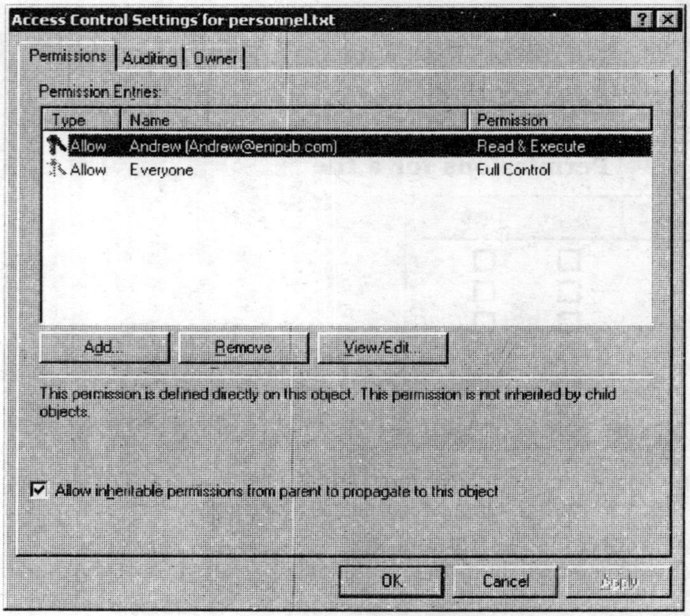

☞ This dialog box shows the list of all the NTFS attributes that have been granted to each user.

☞ Click the **View/Edit** button.

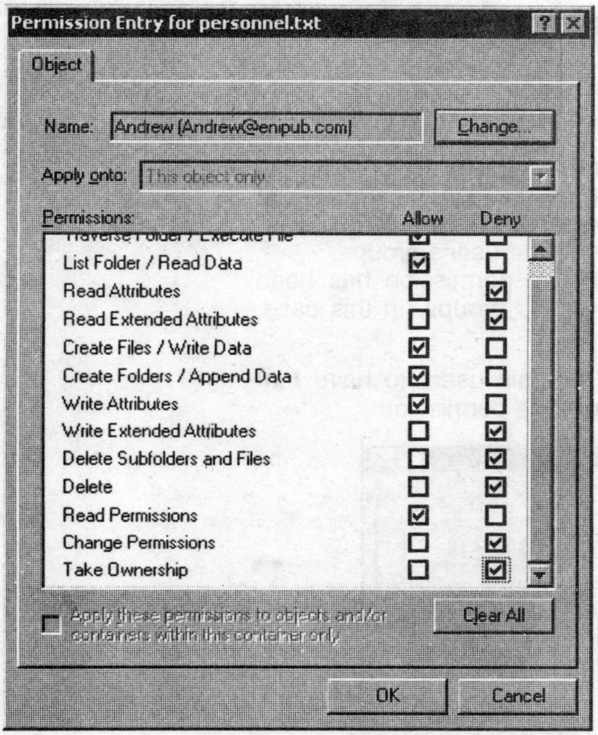

- Choose the NTFS attributes that you require.
- You can also specify the scope of your permissions.

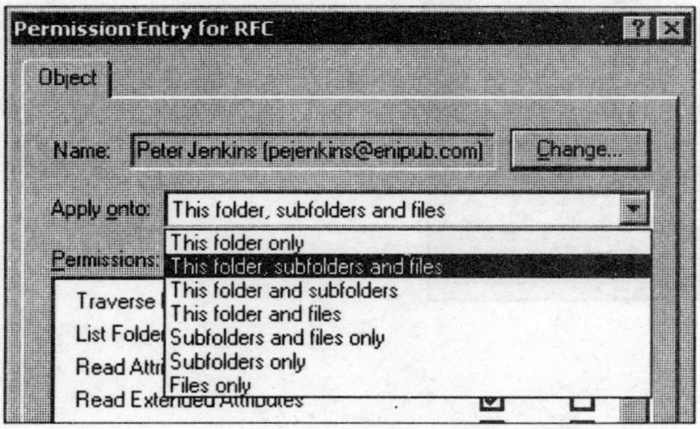

Multiple application

You can apply NTFS permissions for a file or for a folder, to users or to groups of users.
When a user is a member of several groups to which different permissions have been attributed, then the user's permissions that will be effectively applied to the user will be the combination of all the permissions that are applied to the user's groups.
An exception to this rule occurs when a permission has been denied to the user or to one of the user's groups. In this case, the deny always takes priority.

For example: suppose you want all domain users to have **Full Control** permission for a file. You apply this permission:

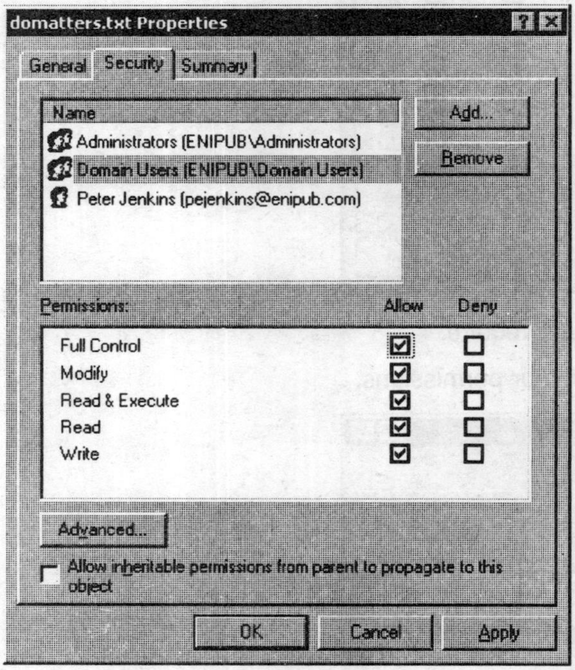

However, you do not want the user **Peter Jenkins** to be able to access this file. You deny **Full Control** permission for this user:

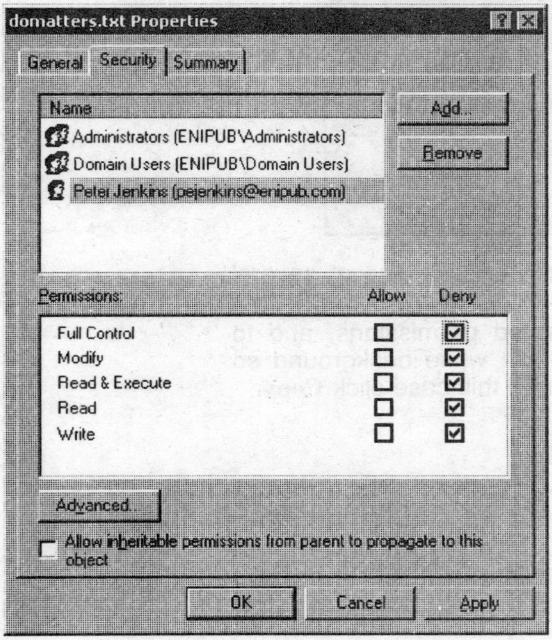

Inheriting permissions

When you create a file or a folder, then the file or the folder inherits the permissions of the parent container. This inheritance is represented by a series of check boxes that are grayed-out.

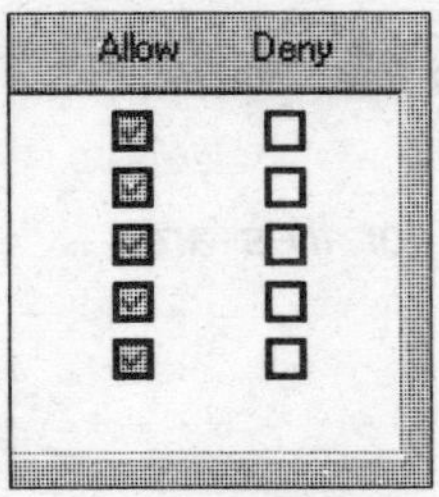

In order to cancel this inheritance, disable the following check box:

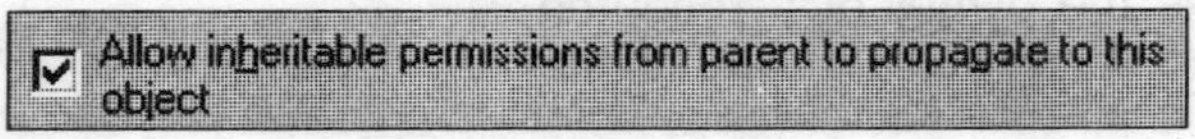

The following message then appears:

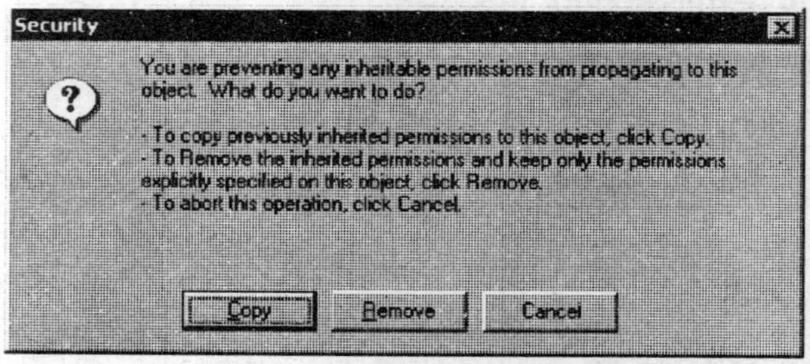

In response to this dialog box, you can choose one of several options:

– You can choose to keep the inherited permissions, and to make their check boxes appear with a white background so that you will be able to change them. In this case click **Copy**.

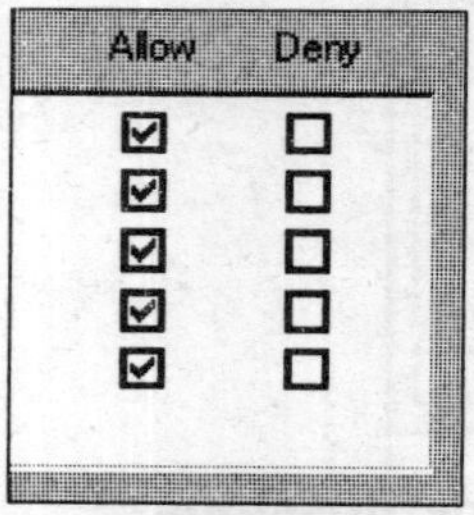

– Alternatively, you can choose to remove the inheritance, and to keep only those permissions that you have attributed for the file or the folder. In this case click **Remove**.

If you remove an inheritance, you can recover it again by re-enabling the Allow inheritable permissions from parent to propagate to this object check box.

By default, the permissions for folders and for files are inherited from the parent container.

2. Taking ownership of files and folders

Each file or folder that is located on an NTFS volume has an owner. By default, the owner of a resource is the user that created the resource, who is automatically a member of the **CREATOR OWNER** group. When a user is the owner of a resource, he/she can always modify the permissions, such as those that allow users to read or to write.

A user cannot become the owner of a resource, unless he/she has the special **Take Ownership** permission. Although a user that has this permission can become the owner of a resource, he/she cannot make another user the owner of the resource.

Here are the steps that you must follow in order to take ownership of a resource:

- Right-click the name of the file, or of the folder, of which you want to take ownership, and select the **Properties** option.
- Select the **Security** tab and then click the **Advanced** button.
- Select the **Owner** tab.

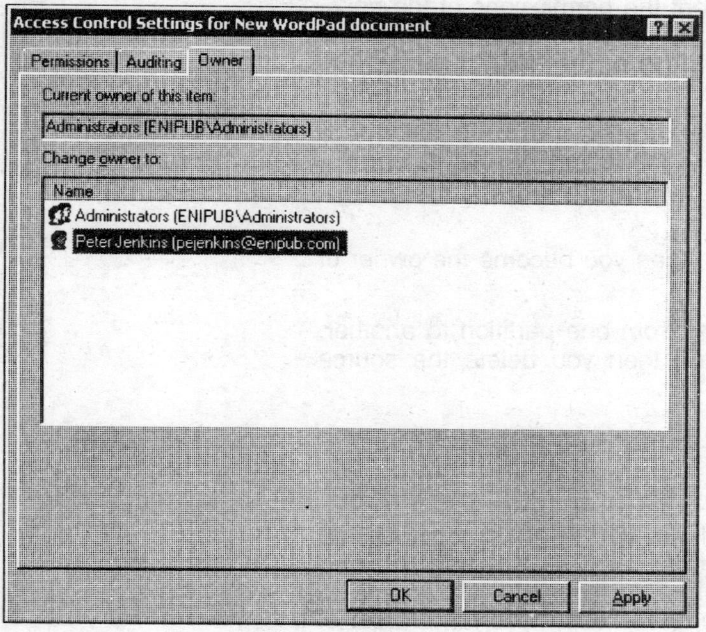

If the user has **Take Ownership** permission, then the user's account will appear in the list under **Change owner to**. The user must select his/her account and then click the **Apply** button.
Unlike Windows NT 4.0, with Windows 2000 when a user who belongs to the administrators group takes ownership of a resource, then it is the user's account that becomes the owner.

3. Copying and moving files and folders

In order to copy or move an item to an NTFS partition, a user must have the necessary permissions.

For example, a user can move a file between NTFS partitions only if the user has **Write** permission for the destination folder, and **Modify** permission for the source folder.

If you copy a file or a folder to a different NTFS partition, or to the same NTFS partition, then the file or the folder will inherit the permissions of the destination container folder.

If you move a file or a folder to a different NTFS partition, then the file or the folder will also inherit the permissions of the destination container folder. However, if you move a file or a folder to the same NTFS partition, then the file or the folder will keep the same permissions.

If you copy or move files or folders from an NTFS partition to a non-NTFS partition, then the file or the folder will lose its permissions, as these permissions are supported only on NTFS partitions.

When you copy a file or a folder, then you become the owner of the copy that you have made.

When you move a file or a folder from one partition to another, then you copy the item first, and then you delete the source item.

D. DFS

DFS (*Distributed File System*) allows you to group together into one tree structure, several directories that are physically situated at different places in the network. This technique allows you to group together into one structure all the information that a set of users require, without the users having to worry about where their data is physically located.

You can configure two types of DFS systems:

– **Stand-alone DFS**, with which the DFS topology resides on a single server.
– **Fault-tolerant DFS** (or domain DFS), with which the DFS topology is recorded in the Active Directory database.

Terminology

A DFS topology comprises at least two items:
– A root node, which provides the entry point.
– Child nodes that point to different shared folders.

When you create a DFS topology, the first thing that you must do is to create a root node under which all the child nodes will be created. You can create a DFS topology an NTFS file system, or on a FAT file system. However, you must remember that if you use an NTFS system, then you will enhance the security of your data.

Stand-alone DFS

You can create a stand-alone DFS structure as follows:

- Open the **Distributed File System (DFS)** console, open the **Action** menu, and select **New Dfs Root**.
- Select **Create a standalone Dfs root**, and click **Next**.
- Then enter the name of the server that must accommodate the DFS topology.

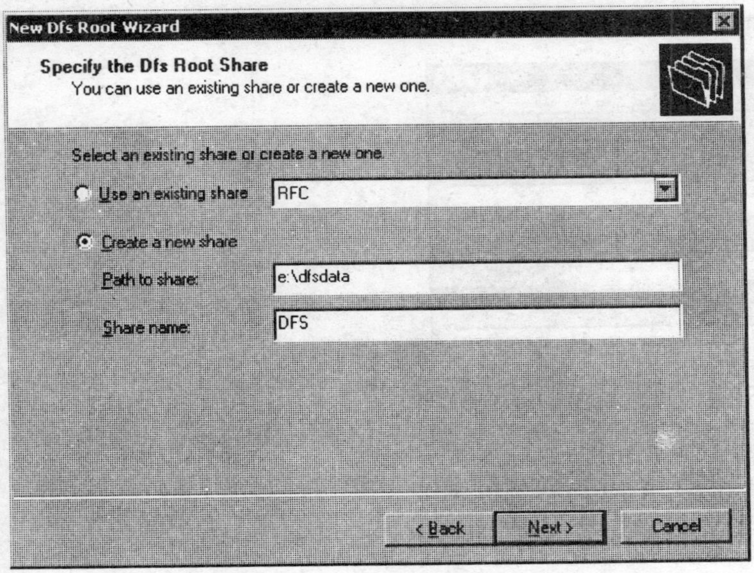

- In order to specify your DFS root share, you can either select an existing share, or you can choose to create a new share.

When the operation is finished your root will be created. All that you need do now is to create the child nodes.

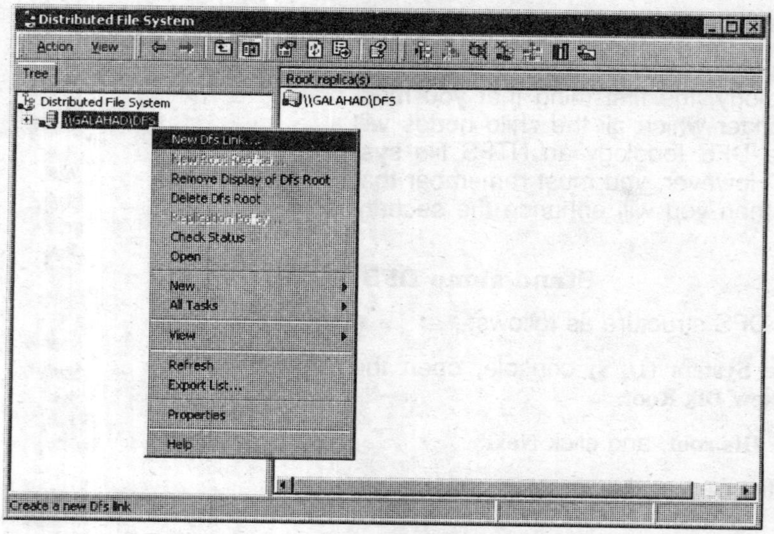

☞ Right-click the DFS root and then select **New Dfs Link.**

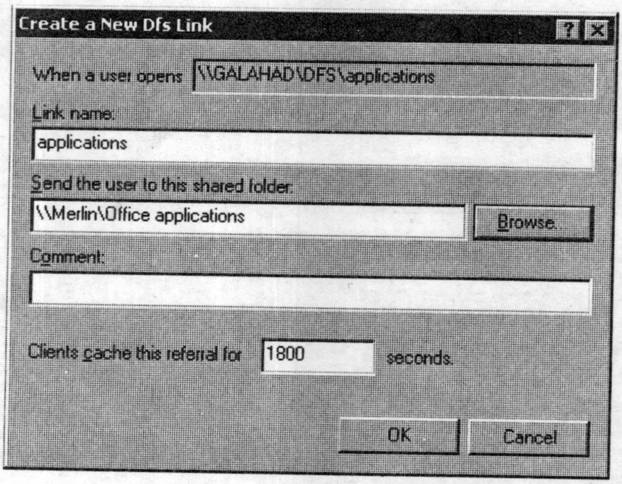

- Give a name to the child node. This name will be that which the users will view when they browse the DFS topology. Then, indicate a UNC path for the shared folder to which you want to point. You can add a comment, and you can change the length of time that the child node reference will be kept in the cache of the client computers.
- Use the same procedure in order to add your other child nodes.

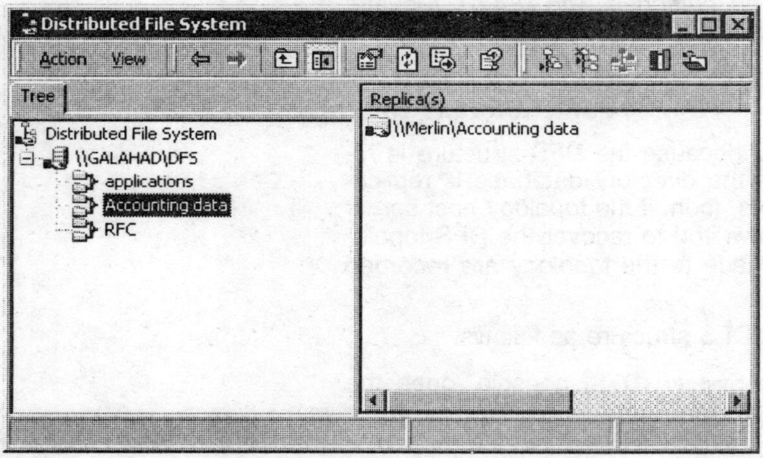

When users access the share that is called DFS on the **Galahad** server, via the network, they will see the following window:

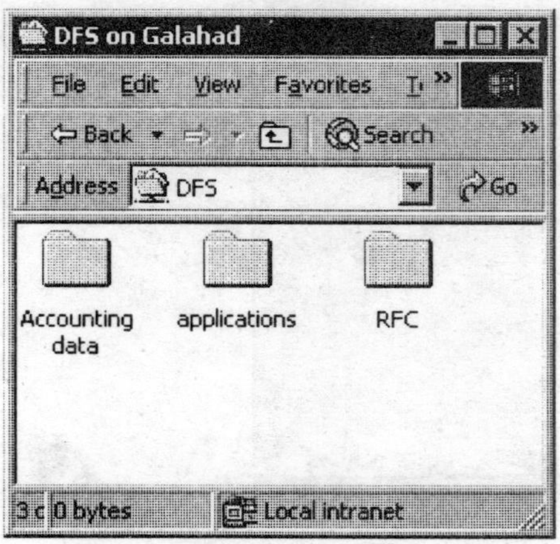

Clients that run Windows NT 4.0, Windows 98 and Windows 2000 can access DFS topologies. Clients that run Windows 95 must install the DFS client software. In order to do this you must install the Active Directory client for Windows 95 that is located on the Windows 2000 Advanced Server CD-ROM Windows. This client allows you to use DFS, and it also allows you to carry out searches in Active Directory. However, the Windows 95 workstation must be equipped with IE4.01 (or later version) and the Active desktop snap-in must be enabled.

Fault-tolerant DFS

The fault tolerance is obtained because the DFS structure is recorded in Active Directory. As the directory database is replicated on all the domain controllers, then, if the topology host server fails, then Active Directory allows you to recover the DFS topology. All the changes that are made to the topology are recorded in the directory database.

You can create a fault-tolerant DFS structure as follows:

- Open the **Distributed File System (DFS)** console, open the **Action** menu, and select **New Dfs Root.**
- Select **Create a domain Dfs root.**

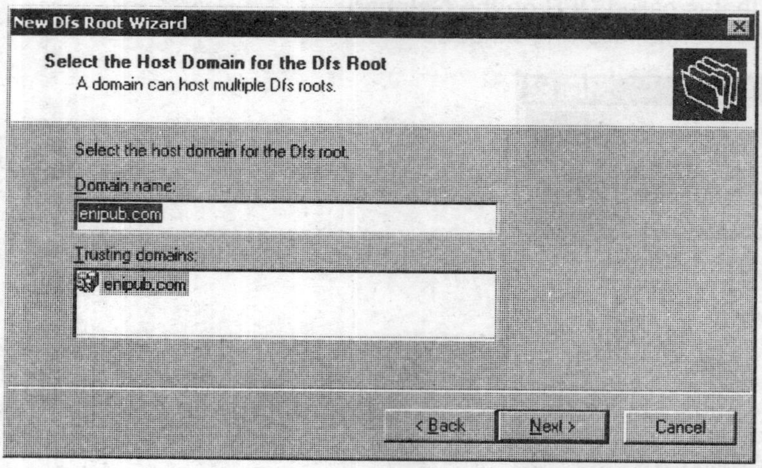

- Select the domain that must accommodate the DFS topology.

- Then, indicate the domain server that must accommodate your DFS topology.
- As with the creation of a stand-alone DFS structure, you must now specify the path of the DFS root share, along with its share name.
- Then, create the child nodes in the same way as you created them for the stand-alone DFS topology.

After you have installed a DFS topology, you can create replicas of your root. The purpose of a replica is to provide fault tolerance in the case where a client is unable to connect to a DFS root. When this happens, the system will automatically connect the user to the DFS root replica.

In order to create a replica you must carry out the following steps:

- Right-click the fault-tolerant DFS structure.
- Select **New Root Replica**.
- Enter the name of the host server for the replica.
- Finally, you must indicate the shared folder on the server that you indicated above that must host the DFS root replica.

When you configure Active Directory, you define the sites that group together the computers in your network that communicate over fast links. The purpose of these sites is to regulate the traffic that runs over slow links. As the DFS system recognizes these sites, then it will always try first to connect the user to a replica that is located on the user's site.

This section has just described how you can introduce fault tolerance using a DFS root. If a user connection to a DFS root fails, then the connection will be set up with a replica of this root. However, what will happen if a user is able to connect to a DFS root, only to find that the servers that host the child nodes are unavailable? In this case, the user will be unable to access the required resources. In order to safeguard against this situation, you must create replicas of the child nodes. This technique will then provide you with fault tolerance that is reasonably complete.

You can create a replica of a child node as follows:

- Right-click the child node for which you want to create a replica, and select **New Replica**.

↓ personal notes ↓

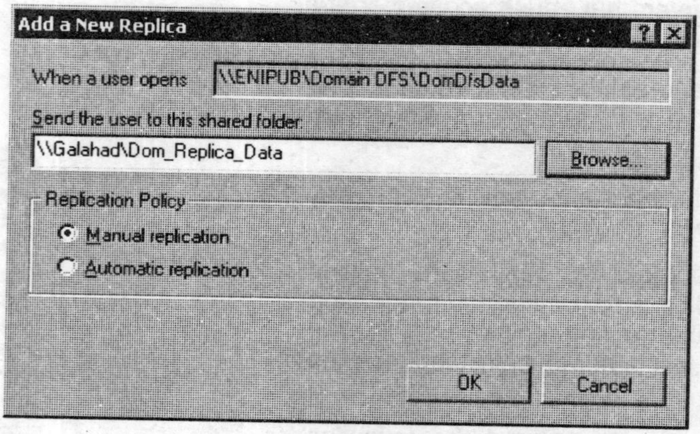

- Enter the path for the folder to which the users must be redirected, when necessary.
- When you have finished configuring your replicas, all that you need do is to replicate the contents of the child nodes to all the replicas (you can do this either manually, or automatically).

In order to ensure that you have identical data in each replica, you must configure the replication. To do this, right-click the child node, and select **Replication Policy**. Then, select the share that must be the master replica, and click the **Set Master** button. When you have done this, select the other replicas that must participate in the replication and click the **Enable** button. If you do not want to replicate with one of the replica members, then select it and click the **Disable** button. You can replicate only with members that are situated on NTFS partitions, and on machines that run the replication service.

In addition to providing fault tolerance, creating replicas of child nodes allows you to spread the workload. This is because the DFS topology server will forward the client queries to all the servers that act as child node replicas.

Each child node can have up to 32 replicas.

E. Managing disk quotas

With a network environment in which the users save their data on the servers, it is useful to be able to control the amount of disk space that is used by each user. Thanks to its NTFS file system, Windows 2000 allows you to manage disk quotas on each partition. Not only can you limit the amount of data that the users can store, but you can also set alerts, and monitor for each user, the amount of disk space that has been used, and the amount of disk space that remains available. Windows 2000 uses file and folder ownership in order to calculate its quotas. Thereby, when a user takes ownership of a file or a folder, then the space that is required by the file or the folder is added to the amount of space that is already occupied by this user. In its quota calculations, Windows 2000 does not take into account any compression that you may have carried out. Also, although you can apply disk quotas to compressed partitions, the space that is calculated by Windows 2000 will not take account of this compression.

Enabling disk quotas

Disk quotas are not enabled by default. In order to enable them, you must carry out the following steps:

☞ Right-click the drive letter that corresponds to the partition to which you want to apply the disk quotas. Select **Properties** and then select the **Quota** tab.

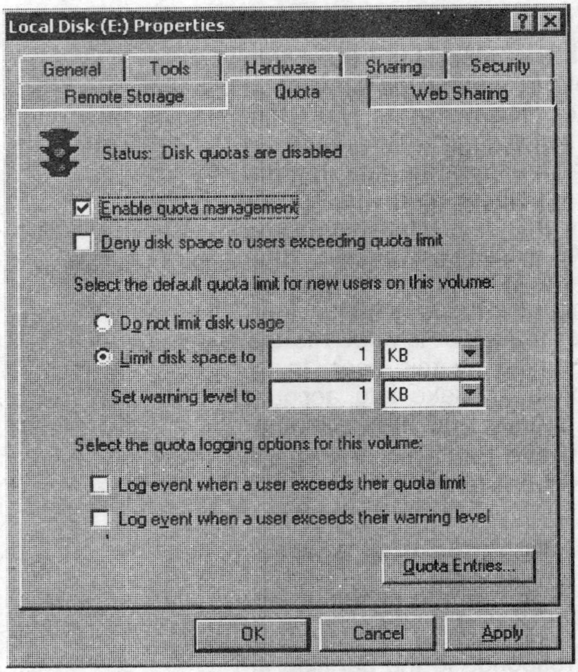

☞ As the quotas are not enabled by default, activate the **Enable quota management** check box.

The  icon is at red whilst the quotas have not been enabled. When you have activated the **Enable quota management**. Enable quota management check box, click **Apply** and watch what happens to this icon. It shows amber to indicate the initialization of the quotas, and finally it turns to, and stays on, green when the quotas are enabled.

Activate the **Deny disk space to users exceeding quota limit** check box in order to to implement this option.

When the disk quota system is active, you can define the amount of disk space that must be allocated to each user. For any users that have no quota entries, you can choose not to limit the amount of disk space that they use. Alternatively, you can set a limit that must be applied to all of these users.

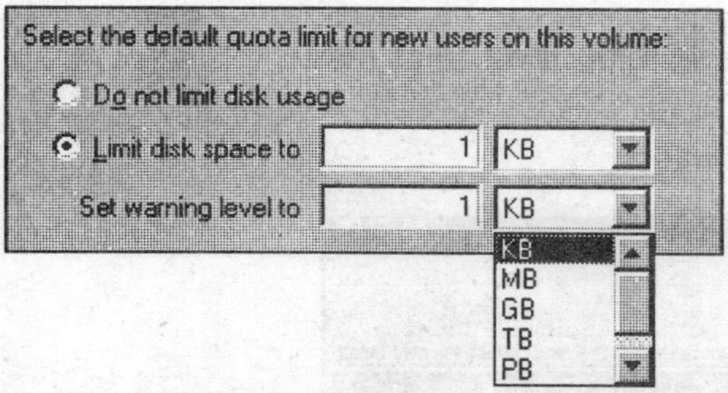

The warning level defines the amount of information that can be stored before Windows 2000 writes an error message in the quota entries.

If you wish to log any occurrences either of users who exceed their quota limits, or of users who exceed their warning levels, then activate the corresponding check boxes:

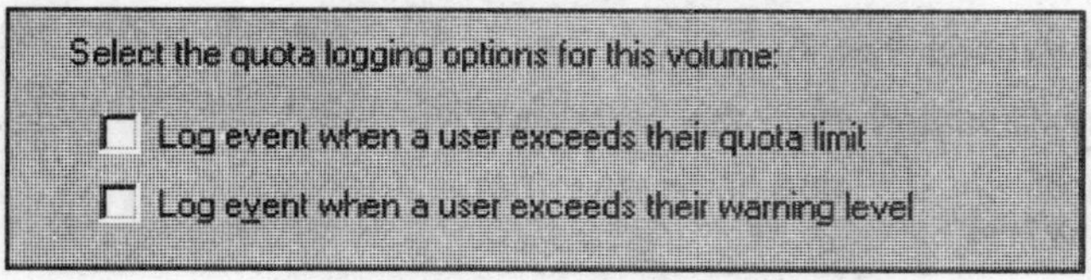

Creating a new entry

Creating an entry allows the administrator to define the amount of disk space that a user is allowed to occupy on a partition.

- In order to create a new entry, click the **Quota Entries** button.
- Open the **Quota** menu, and select **New Quota Entry**. Then select the user(s) to whom you wish to apply the entry.

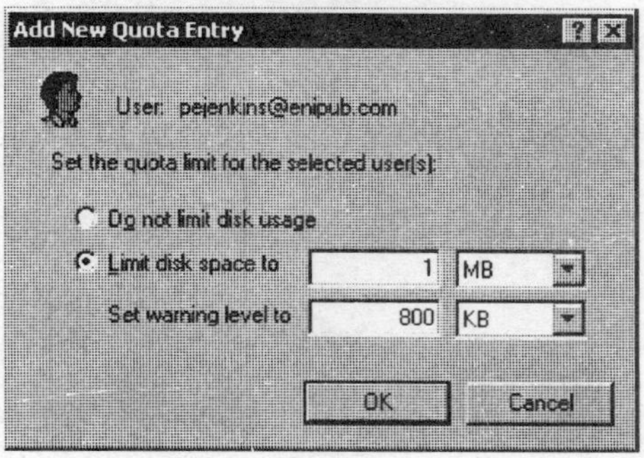

☞ Select the disk space limit, and the warning level, and then click **OK**.

The user then appears in the quota entries list.

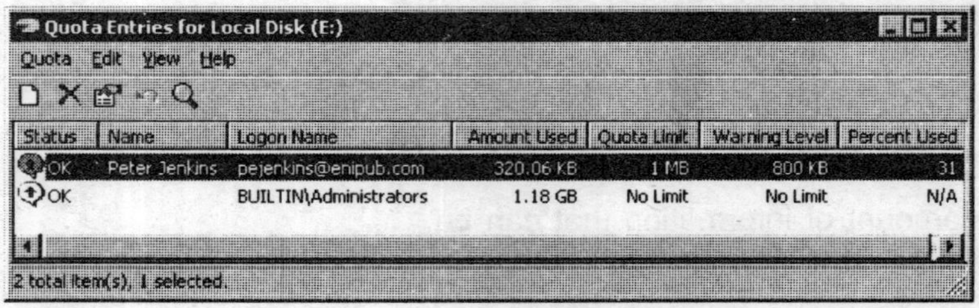

This list tells you for each user, how much disk space is currently occupied, the limit that is set by the quota, the warning level, and the percentage used.

In the **Status** column, an icon indicates that the user is under his/her warning level, an icon indicates that the user has exceeded his/her warning level, and an icon indicates that the user has exceeded his/her quota limit.

The **Quota Entries** window allows you to delete documents so as to free up disk space.

In order to do this, right-click the user for whom you wish to free the disk space, and click **Delete**.

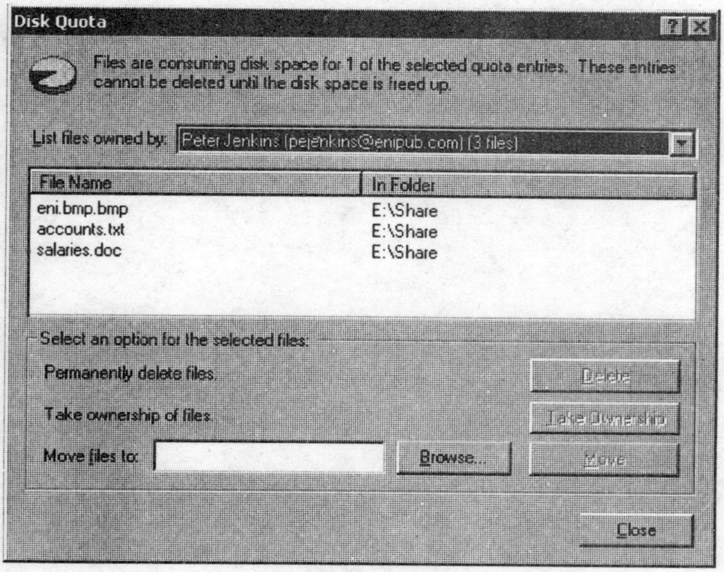

Select the files, either that you want to delete, or for which you want to take ownership, or that you want to move.

You cannot delete the administrator's documents in this way.

Configuring disks, partitions and volumes

A. **Basic disks** 226
1. Creating a primary partition 227
2. Creating an extended partition 229
3. Creating logical drives 229

B. **Dynamic disks** 231
1. Upgrading to a dynamic disk 231
2. Simple volume 233
3. Extending a simple volume 235
4. Spanned volume 236
5. Striped volumes 237

C. **Fault tolerance** 239
1. Overview of RAID technology 239
2. RAID 1: disk mirroring 239
3. Implementing mirrors 240
4. Booting on a secondary mirror disk 243
5. Repairing an original system disk 243
6. Mirroring a basic disk 245
7. RAID 5: stripe set with parity 245
8. Choosing the best fault tolerance solution 248

The disk management of Windows 2000 has evolved with respect to earlier Windows versions. Although there is nothing new about the contents of primary partitions, extended partitions and other logical drives, you can now optimize your disks by creating volumes.

A. Basic disks

With Windows 2000, a basic disk is a disk structure on which you can create primary partitions and extended partitions.
There is a limit to the number of partitions that a basic disk can support. On a basic disk, you cannot have more than:
- 4 primary partitions,
- or, 3 primary partitions and 1 extended partition. In this extended partition you can create one or more logical drives.

On Windows 2000, you can manage your disks using the **Disk Management** snap-in that is situated under the **Storage** node of the **Computer Management** console tree.
Alternatively, you can create your own console and add the **Disk Management** snap-in into it.

Enter the name of the computer for which you want to manage the disks, and then repeat the operation for any other machines for which you want to manage the disks.

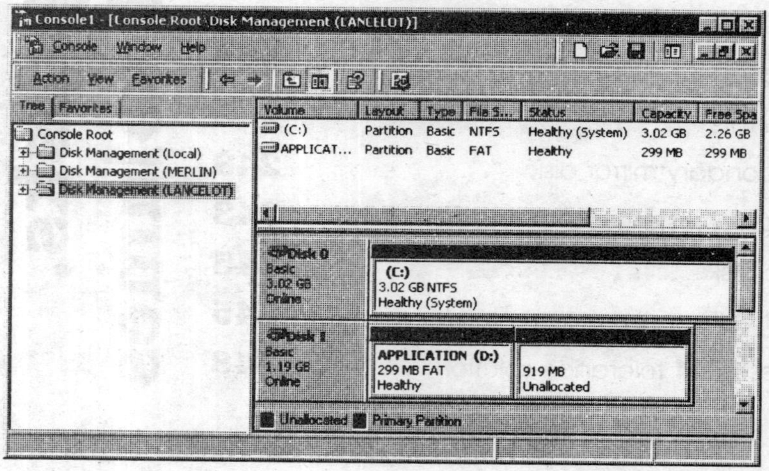

You can now use this console in order to carry out operations on your physical disks such as creating and deleting partitions.

1. Creating a primary partition

In order to create a primary partition, right-click an unallocated disk space:

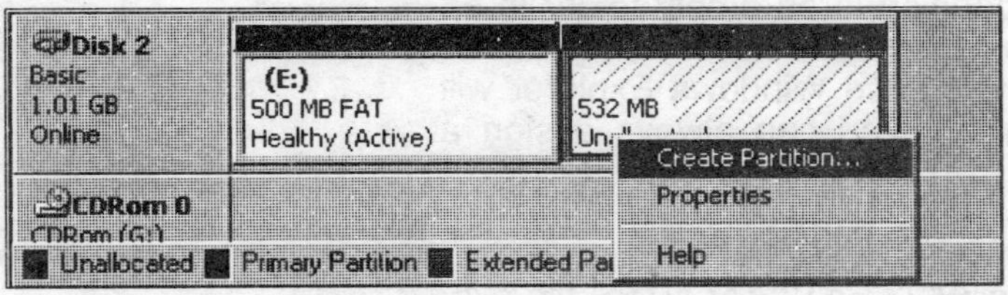

Then, select **Create Partition** so as to start up the **Create Partition Wizard.**

Select **Primary partition**. Note that the **Logical drive** option is grayed out. This is because you can create a logical drive only within an extended partition.

Click the **Next** button.

Enter the size that you want for the principal partition. If you decide to create a partition that will occupy all the available disk space, then you should leave at least 1 MB of free space, as you will need this should you want to convert your basic disk into a dynamic disk. This is because the conversion processes will need this space in order to store their working information.

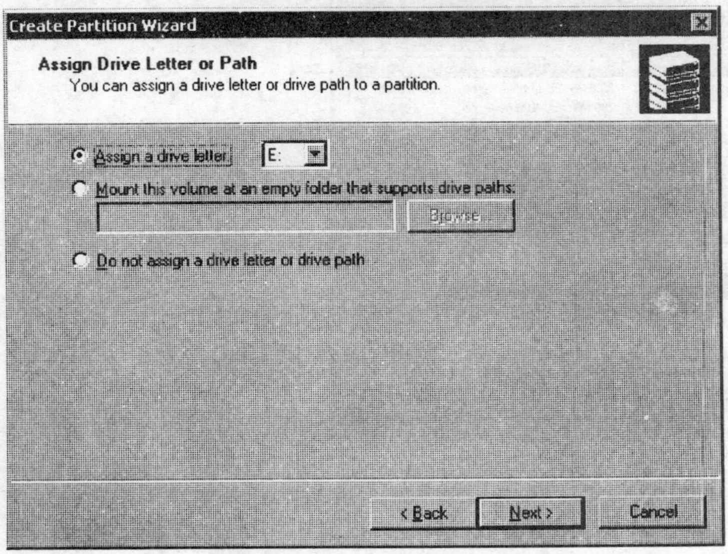

Windows 2000 suggests a drive letter for this partition, by default. If you wish, you can choose another letter that is not being used by the other drives. You can change this drive letter after the partition has been created.
You can choose to mount your partition in an empty folder in an NTFS partition. Alternatively, you can choose not to assign either a drive letter or a drive path. In this case Windows Explorer will not be able to access this partition (you can always assign a drive letter later).

The next step consists of formatting the partition.

You can choose to use either the FAT, FAT32 or NTFS file systems. In addition, you can customize the size of the allocation unit. If you choose to format your partition in FAT with a cluster size of over 32 KB, then your partition will not be compatible with previous operating system versions. Be careful of this point then, if you have a multiple boot facility. However, pre-Windows 2000 operating systems would still be able to access the resources that are located on this partition via a network share.
Note that you can choose to enable file and folder compression if you format your partition in NTFS.
When you have finished indicating your settings, the system will format your partition. When your partition is ready to be used it will be marked as being **Healthy**.

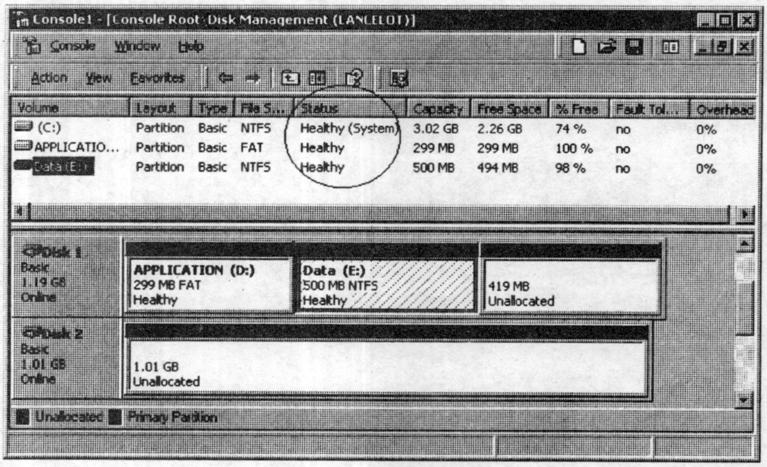

In addition to allowing you to carry out such operations as creating and deleting partitions, this **Disk Management** program provides information concerning disk type (basic or dynamic), file systems, capacities, free space, percentage of free space, and whether or not your partitions belong to a fault-tolerant set.

2. Creating an extended partition

If you have already three primary partitions on your disk, then your extended partition must occupy the rest of the available space (leaving 1 or 2 MB in order to allow for possible conversion to a dynamic disk). Otherwise, you will lose any remaining space because you cannot create more than four partitions on your disk.
In order to create an extended partition you must carry out the following steps:

- Right-click an unallocated space and then select **Create Partition**.
- Select **Extended partition** and then click **Next**.
- Enter the size that you require for your extended partition and click **Next**.

The extended partition is then created and appears in the Disk Management console in green (when standard colors are used). This extended partition is no longer considered as being **Unallocated**, but it is considered as **Free Space** (free for the creation of a logical drive).

3. Creating logical drives

After you have created an extended partition, you must create one or more logical drives. You can create as many logical drives as you have drive letters that are available.
In order to create a logical drive, right-click the extended partition and then select **Create Logical Drive** so as to start the **Create Partition Wizard**.

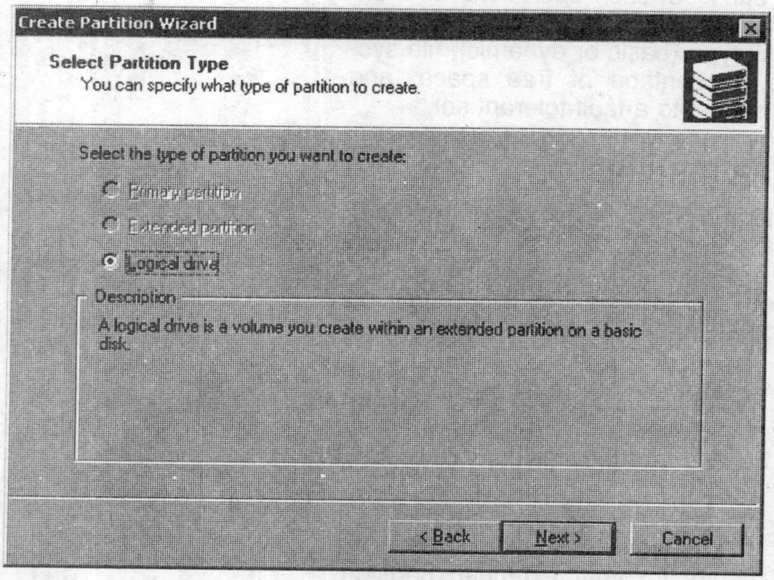

The **Logical drive** option is then selected automatically.

- Choose the size that must be allocated to this logical drive. If you wish to create several logical drives within this extended partition, then do not take up all the available space in order to create the first one!
- The following step involves, either choosing the letter that you want to assign to this drive, or deciding not to assign a letter, or mounting the drive at an empty folder in an NTFS partition.
- Then, define the type of formatting (FAT.i.FAT;, FAT32, NTFS, and the cluster size) and click **Finish**

The system then formats the logical drive. If you have not used all the free space for the creation of this logical drive, then you can use the rest of the free space in order to create other logical drives. Once the drive has been formatted it is marked as **Healthy**.

You can change the letters that are attributed to your partitions or to your logical drives at any time. In order to do this, right-click the partition or the drive for which you want to change the drive letter and select ***Change Drive Letter and Path****.*

Removable storage devices contain only primary partitions. You can create neither extended partitions nor volumes on this type of storage device. In addition, you cannot mark as active, a partition that is on a removable storage device.
You can alter the colors and the schemes that are used to represent the different partitions using the **View - Settings** menu option.

B. Dynamic disks

A dynamic disk does not have partitions, it has volumes. A volume is a part of a disk that runs like a separate physical disk. The information concerning the disk is not written in the registry, but on the disk itself.
Here are the advantages of dynamic disks:

- You can use fault tolerance (without having to restart the computer),
- You can create as many volumes as you like,
- You can extend NTFS volumes.

You can still use the partitions on basic disks, which ensures compatibility with existing configurations. However, volumes cannot be read by pre-Windows 2000 systems.

1. Upgrading to a dynamic disk

You can upgrade from a basic disk to a dynamic disk without losing data. However, once you have upgraded to dynamic disks, if you wish to return to basic disks, then you will have to delete all the disk volumes (therefore, you must remember to back up your data first).
On a dynamic disk, you can have the following volume types:

- Simple volumes
- Striped volumes
- Spanned volumes
- Mirrored volumes
- RAID 5 volumes

If there are partitions on your basic disks when you upgrade them to dynamic disks, then they will become volumes as follows:

- A primary partition will become a simple volume.
- Each logical drive of an extended partition will become a simple volume.
- The free space of an extended partition will become unallocated space (you can then create volumes using this space).
- A partition mirror will become a mirrored volume.
- Stripe sets with parity will become RAID 5 volumes.
- Stripe sets will become striped volumes.
- Partition stripes will become spanned volumes.

In order to upgrade from a basic disk to a dynamic disk, go into the **Disk Management** program and right-click the disk that you want to upgrade:

☞ Then, select **Upgrade to Dynamic Disk**.

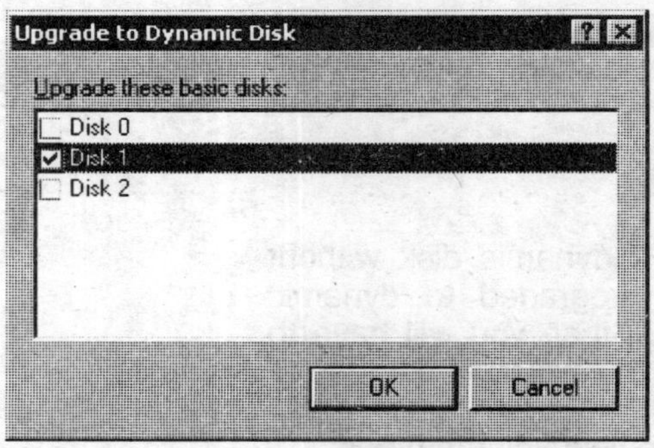

☞ Select the disk(s) that you wish to upgrade, and then click **OK**.

☞ In the dialog box that appears, If you click the **Details** button, a further dialog box appears that indicates all the partitions of the disk that must be upgraded.

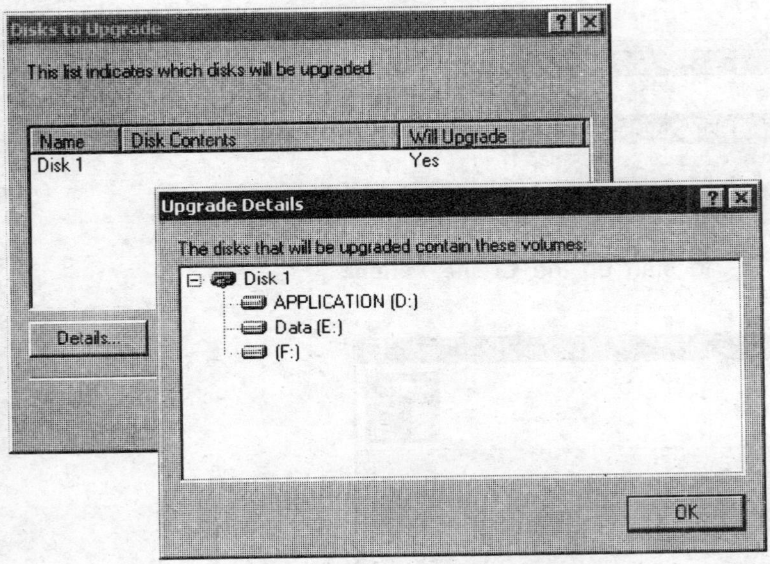

☞ Click **OK** so as to return to the previous dialog box, and then click the **Upgrade** button in order to start the upgrade process.

When the upgrade operation has finished, the modifications are updated in the **Disk Management** console.

2. Simple volume

A simple volume corresponds to the space of a single disk. Unlike partitions, volumes are limited neither to a maximum size nor to a maximum number.
On a dynamic disk, simple volumes can be formatted in NTFS, FAT 16 or FAT 32.
A simple volume that is formatted in NTFS can be extended in order to create a volume that will cover the initial space of the volume, plus one or more unallocated disk spaces that can either be contiguous or not.
In order to create a simple volume, right-click part of a dynamic disk that is not allocated.

↓ personal notes ↓

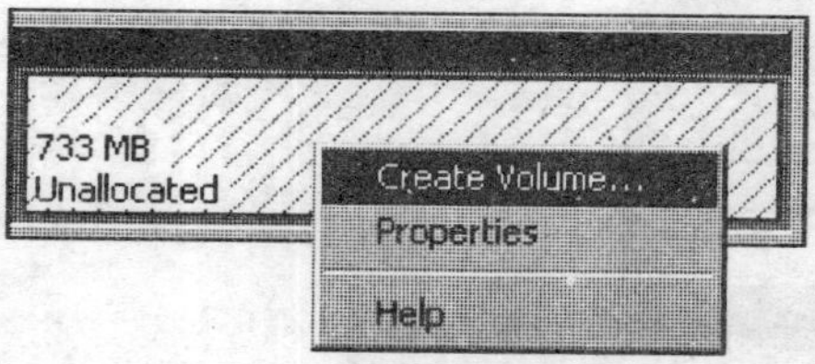

☞ Select **Create Volume** so as to start up the **Create Volume Wizard.**

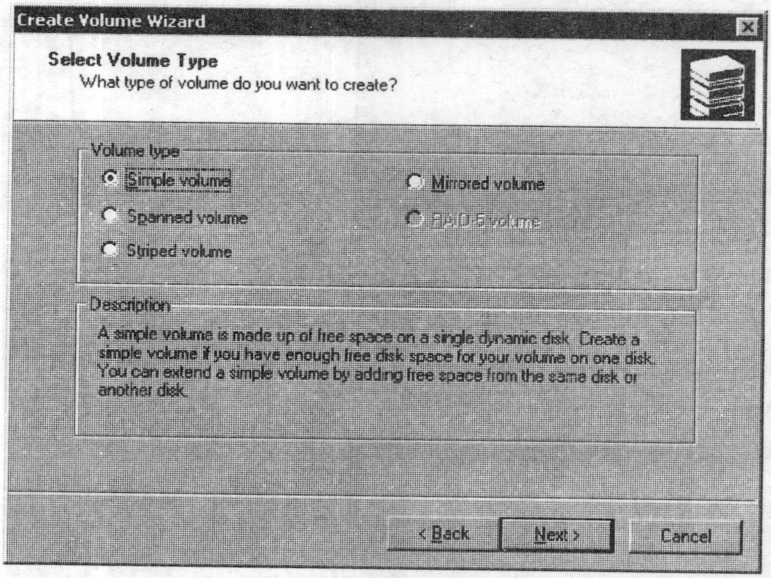

☞ Select **Simple volume** then click **Next.**

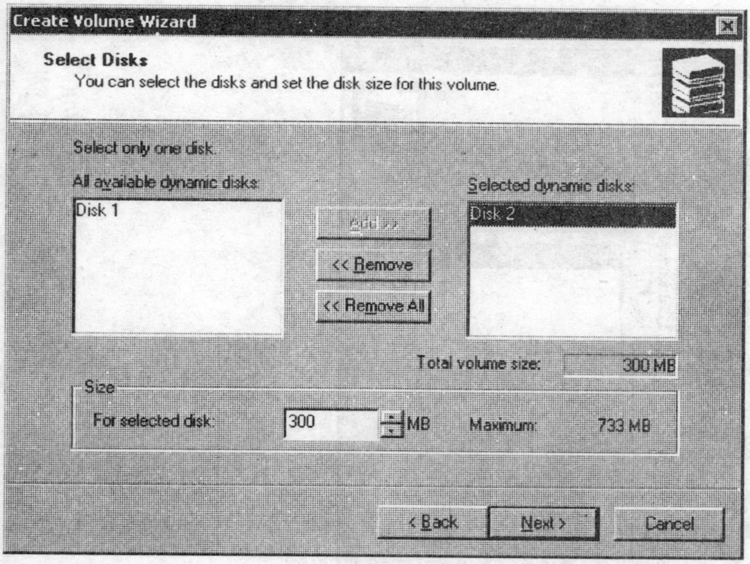

In order to create a simple volume, you must select only one disk and set the size for this volume.

- The next step consists of assigning a drive letter (or not assigning a drive letter), or mounting the volume at a folder.
- Then, select the file system that must be used for this volume.

3. Extending a simple volume

If your volume is formatted in NTFS, then you can extend it by combining the disk space that is occupied by the volume with one or more unallocated spaces.
The new size of the volume will then be the initial size of the volume, plus the sum of all the spaces that have been added.

In order to extend your volume, right-click it and then select **Extend Volume**.

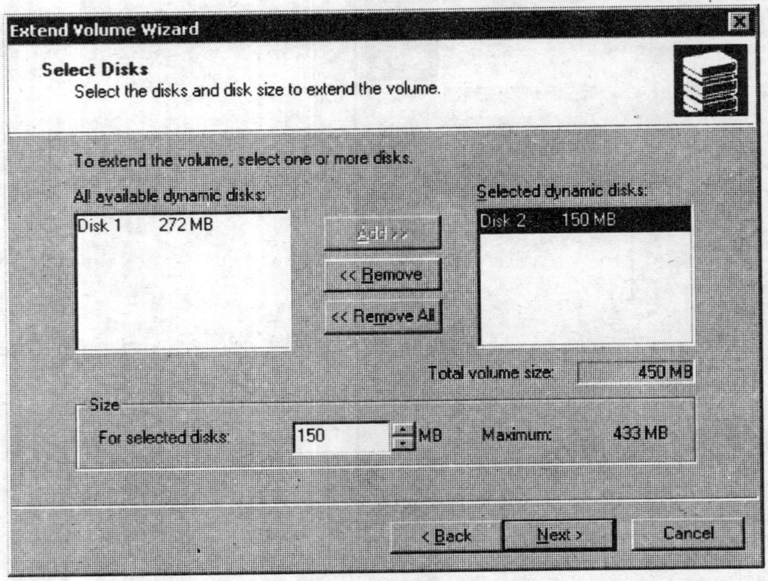

As you can extend your volume over unallocated portions of dynamic disks, you must select the disk(s) on which you want to extend your volume. When you have selected a disk, click the **Add** button so as to add the disk concerned under **Selected dynamic disks**. Then, set the extra size that you want to add to your initial volume. If you are extending your volume using unallocated spaces from several disks, then you can define a different size that must be added from each space.

If you extend your volume over unallocated spaces on another disk, then your volume will become a spanned volume.

You cannot extend a volume that is the result of an upgrade from a partition. The volume must have been created on a dynamic disk. This means that you cannot extend system volumes or boot volumes.

4. Spanned volume

A spanned volume is a composed of unallocated spaces that have been grouped together from a minimum of 2 disks, and a maximum of 32 disks. Data is written first to free space on one disk and, when this disk is full, data is written to free space on the next disk.

In order to create a spanned volume, right-click an unallocated space and then select **Create Volume**.

☛ Select **Spanned volume** and then click **Next**.

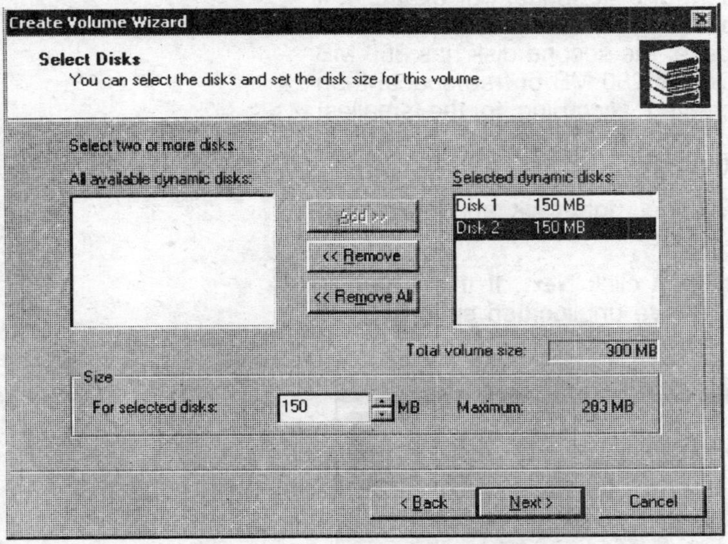

You must select at least two dynamic disks so as to create a spanned volume. Indicate the size that you want to use for each disk, and then click **Next**.

Assign a drive letter or a mount point. Finally, you must specify the file system that must be used for this spanned volume so as to finish the operation.

As with simple volumes, you can extend a spanned volume.

You cannot re-use a space that is situated on a disk that is included in a spanned volume, without deleting all the volume. Before you carry out this operation then, you must back up the volume, as all the data will be lost.

5. Striped volumes

A striped volume groups together into one logical volume, unallocated space from at least 2 disks and at most 32 disks. The data is written to stripes of 64 KB. This means that 64 KB will be written to the first disk, the next 64 KB will be written to the second disk, and so forth. This type of volume optimizes read and write access.

However, it must be noted that this type of volume does not provide fault tolerance. If a disk fails, then all the data that is written to all the member disks of the striped volume will be lost.

As all the data is written in striped sets, each of the stripe members must have the same amount of disk space. For example, if you want to create a striped volume on three disks, for which the first disk has 300 MB of free space, the second disk has 350 MB of free space, and the third disk has 280 MB of free space, then your striped volume will be created according to the smallest amount of disk space. In this example, the size of the striped volume will be 840 MB (3 x 280 MB).

In order to create a striped volume, right-click an unallocated space and then select **Create Volume**:

☞ Select **Striped volume**, and then click **Next**. If this option is grayed out, then you do not have unallocated spaces on at least two different dynamic disks.

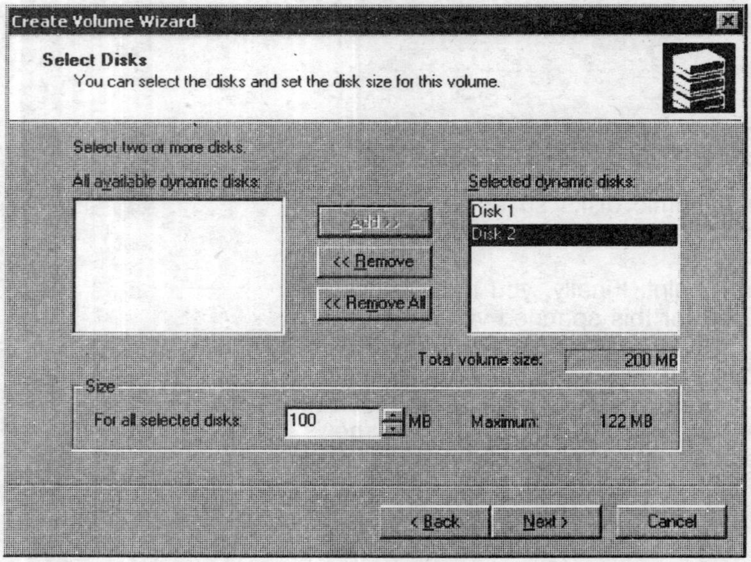

Add the disks on which you want to create the striped volume.
Then select either a drive letter for your striped volume, or a mount point.
Finally, choose the format for your volume (FAT16, FAT32 or NTFS).

You can neither extend nor mirror a striped volume.

C. Fault tolerance

With Windows 2000, fault tolerance can be implemented only on dynamic disks. Windows 2000 supports software fault tolerance.

1. Overview of RAID technology

RAID (*Redundant Array of Inexpensive Disks*) was devised when people realized that it is less costly to have several disks that are reasonably priced and that contribute to system security, than it is to use a single disk that is built to a high specification.

There are six RAID levels that vary according to the management method that is used. Some of these levels are variations, or intermediate phases, of the primary levels. Amongst the RAID levels 0 to 5, the two levels that are used most are RAID 1 and RAID 5.

It must be noted that RAID 0 corresponds to the implementation of a striped volume and it does not implement fault tolerance!

2. RAID 1: disk mirroring

This solution is expensive in terms of storage space with respect to cost. On the other hand, it is easy to implement and to manage.
The data is written identically to two disks, in a way that is transparent to the user.
If an incident occurs, then the mirror is broken, the defective disk is replaced, and the mirror is re-implemented. Consequently, no information is lost.

Two mirroring strategies can be used:

Mirroring

This solution involves one disk controller and two disks. Consequently, it has a vulnerable link!

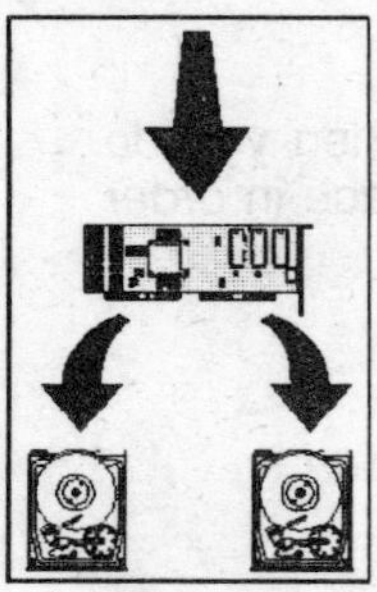

Duplexing

This solution involves two disk controllers and two disks. As a separate controller handles each disk, this method offers improved reliability and performance. This strategy is used with SCSI controllers.

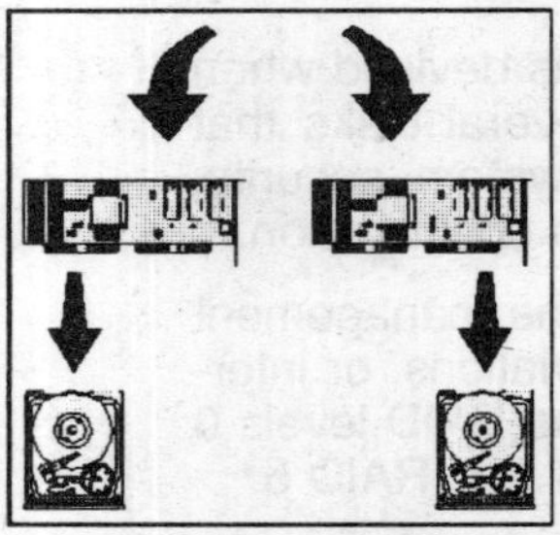

Windows 2000 manages both of these methods in such a way that their operation is transparent to the user.

A further advantage of RAID 1 is that it can cover the system partition.

3. Implementing mirrors

- Right-click the volume that you want to mirror.

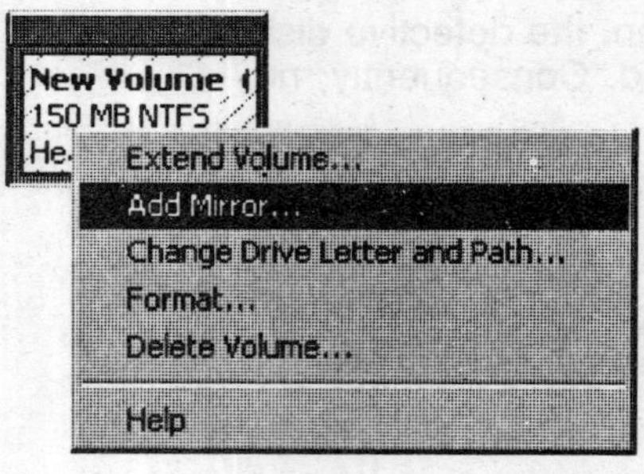

- Select **Add Mirror**. If this option is unavailable then you do not have a dynamic disk that has enough free space in order to create a mirror.

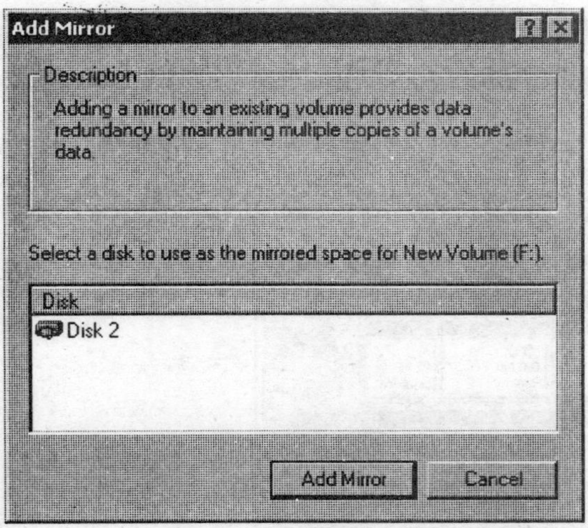

☞ Select the disk on which you want to set up your mirror, and then click the **Add Mirror** button.

The system then regenerates the data that is situated on the initial disk, onto the mirror disk.

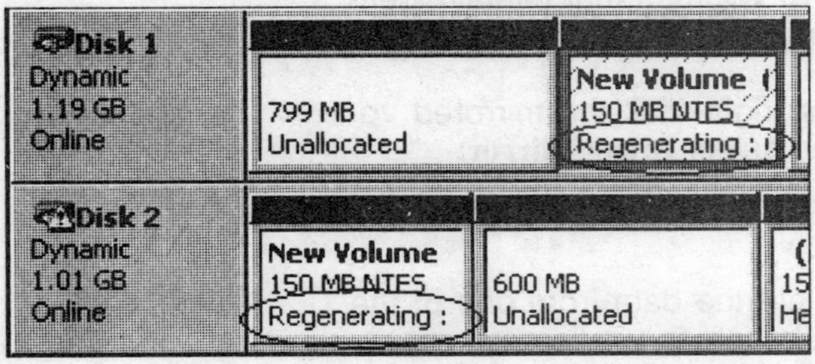

Unlike Windows NT4.0, Windows 2000 does not require you to restart your computer after you have created a mirror.

You can check that the mirroring was implemented:

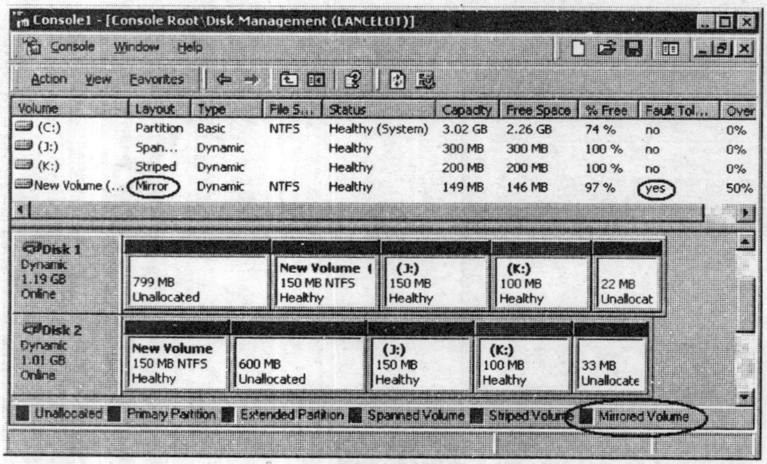

Breaking and removing a mirror

You can break or remove a mirror at any time. When you break a mirror, you keep the data intact on both members of the mirror. The mirror then, is separated into two volumes that contain identical information. However, this configuration no longer provides fault tolerance.

In order to break a mirror, you must right-click the mirrored volume that you wish to break and then select **Break Mirror**.

A new drive letter is then assigned to the volume on which you carried out this operation.

When you remove a mirror, you delete the data from one of the mirrored volumes. This volume then becomes unallocated space. In order to remove a mirror, right-click the mirrored volume that you wish to remove, and then click **Remove Mirror**.

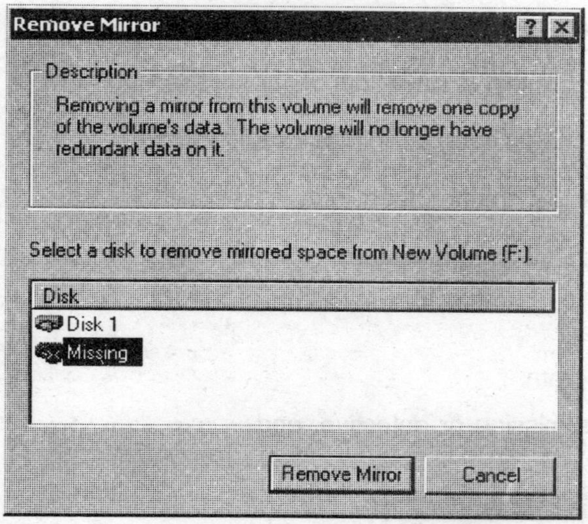

Select the mirror volume that you want to remove, and then click the **Remove Mirror** button.

4. Booting on a secondary mirror disk

As you can mirror the system partition, you must be able to boot on the secondary mirror disk if the primary mirror disk fails.
In order to do this you must create a bootable diskette. This diskette must be formatted using a Windows 2000 or a Windows NT 4.0 operating system. For an INTEL type machine, this diskette must contain the following files:

- NTLDR
- NTDETECT.COM
- NTBOOTDD.SYS (in the case where the BIOS of the SCSI controller is disabled)
- BOOT.INI (the chapter: ,"Backing-up, restoring and troubleshooting" describes the contents of the BOOT.INI file)

5. Repairing an original system disk

When a mirrored volume fails, the other mirrored volume will continue to run, but it will no longer provide fault tolerance. Consequently, you must repair the mirror. When a disk fails, it is marked in the **Disk Management** console as **Missing, Offline**, or **Online (Errors)**.

If an error occurs on one of the mirrored volumes, then right-click the volume concerned, and select the **Reactivate Volume** option.
If this technique is ineffective, then you must remove the mirror and then re-create it.
This is a delicate operation. It is described here for information purposes only, and if you decide to carry it out, then you must do so at your own risk! You must use this solution then, only as a last resort when all else fails, and you must try it out first on a test machine before you use it on an operational machine.

- Boot the machine using a bootable diskette, and select the partition on the disk that is still intact.
- Start up the **Disk Management** program.
- Select the mirrored volume that is missing or defective, and then select **Remove Mirror.**

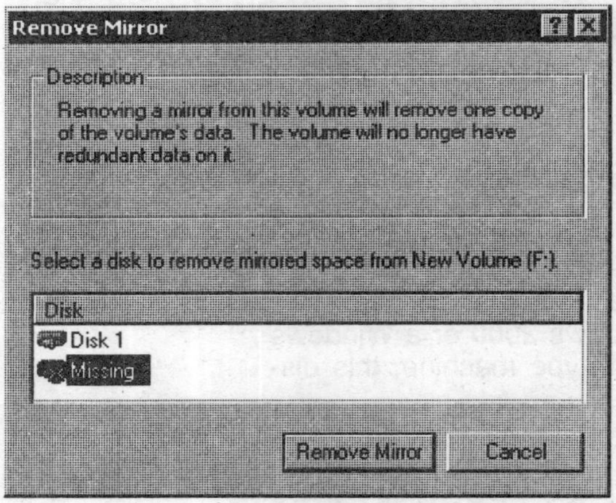

- Check that you have selected the disk that has the problem, and then click the **Remove Mirror** button.

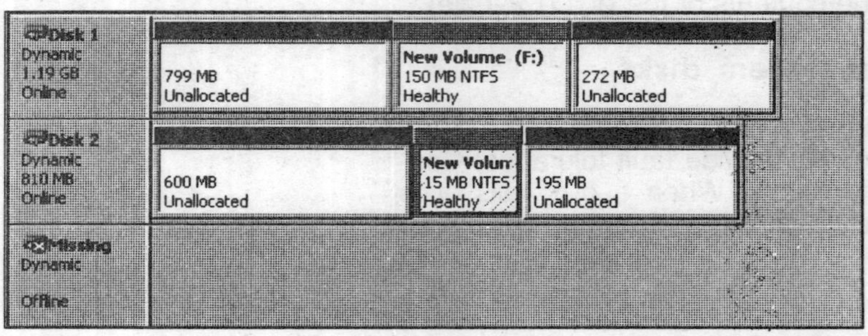

The mirror is then removed.

☛ Modify the **boot.ini** file as necessary, then replace the defective disk so that you can recreate the mirror.

6. Mirroring a basic disk

When you upgrade from Windows NT 4.0 to Windows 2000 then any disk mirroring that was implemented on the machine will be conserved. This is the only case in which you can have RAID 1 fault tolerance on basic disks with Windows 2000. Your mirror will continue to operate as it did before you upgraded your system.

You can carry out the following actions on a basic disk:

- Repairing: if you wish to repair your mirror, then you will need another basic disk for your new mirrored-member. You cannot use a dynamic disk in order to repair a mirror that is situated on a basic disk.
- Resynchronizing a mirror: When you have repaired a mirrored disk, if the disk does not return to **Healthy** status, then you must resynchronize the mirror in order to update the information on the mirrored members.
- Breaking a mirror: If you no longer want to implement fault tolerance for the information that is concerned on your disks, then you can break your mirror at any time. In order to do this, right-click the mirror and then select **Break Mirror**. The two halves of the mirror then become two independent partitions that contain the same data.
- Removing a mirror: in order to be able to re-use both partitions independently of each other, right-click the mirror and then select **Remove Mirror**. The mirrored information is then deleted.

7. RAID 5: stripe set with parity

This solution is less expensive than mirroring, in terms of the disk space that is occupied by the security information. However, it requires at least three disks, as the parity information must be stored for each stripe. This solution allows you to record extra parity information that is calculated using saved data. This technique enhances read/write performance.

The disadvantage of a software solution such as that offered by Windows 2000, is that it is unable to cover the system partition. However, a number of vendors do offer hardware solutions that cover the system partition, and that cover it in a fully transparent manner.

Nevertheless, the software solution is much less expensive in money terms.

Creating stripe sets with parity

Right-click an unallocated space, and select **Create Volume.**

Then, select **RAID-5 volume**, and click **Next.**

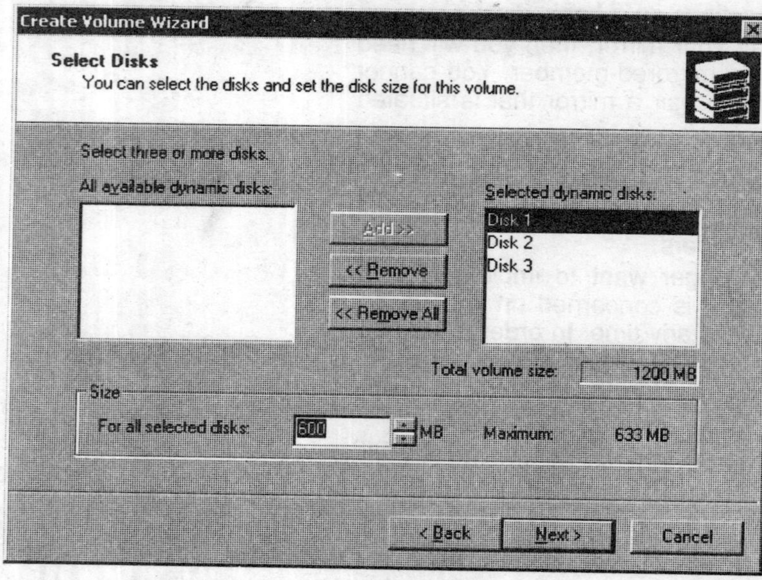

In order to create a RAID 5 volume you must, have at least three disks. As with stripe sets, the volumes that must be used for RAID 5 must all be of the same size. If you have unallocated spaces of 800 MB on the first disk, 750 MB on the second disk and 600 MB on the third disk, then the stripe set with parity will have a size of 3 x 600 which equals 1800 MB (this calculation is based on the smallest space that is available on any of the disks that will be used for RAID 5).

As with the creation of other types of volume, you must then choose a drive letter and a file system format.

Repairing a defective RAID 5 volume

If you have a problem with one of the stripe set members, then you will still be able to access the data. However, the fault tolerance driver, **ftdisk.sys**, must regenerate the missing parts (using the parity information), which will result in a slight deterioration in system performance.

In order to solve the problem, you must repair the defective stripe set member. If the volume concerned has either an **Offline** or a **Missing** status, then right-click it and select the **Reactivate Volume** option.
If the volume status is **Online (Errors)**, then try following the same procedure as for the other defective statuses. However, if the operation is ineffective, then you must replace the defective disk. In order to do this, right-click the RAID 5 volume that is on the faulty disk, then select **Repair RAID-5 volume**. A dialog box then asks you to select the disk that must replace the defective disk.

RAID 5 on basic disks

As with RAID 1, you will conserve your stripe sets with parity when you upgrade from Windows NT 4 to Windows 2000. Your stripe sets with parity will be implemented on basic disks, and this is the only way in which you can obtain RAID 5 level fault tolerance with this type of disk on Windows 2000.

You can carry out the following actions:

- Removing: when you remove a stripe set with parity on a basic disk then the data is deleted along with the partitions that make up the stripe set with parity.
- Repairing: in the case of **Failed Redundancy**, you must repair the stripe set with parity. In order to do this you must have another basic disk. You cannot use a dynamic disk in order to repair a stripe set with parity that is implemented on basic disks. In order to repair your stripe set with parity, right-click it and then select **Repair Volume**. If the status of the stripe set with parity does not return to **Healthy** when this regeneration is finished, then right-click the stripe set with parity and select **Regenerate Parity**.

8. Choosing the best fault tolerance solution

RAID 1 versus RAID 5

Both of these solutions support FAT and NTFS.

Mirroring :
- can be used with system volumes and boot volumes,
- requires two hard disks,
- offers good read/write performance.

Stripe set with parity :
- can be used only with data volumes,
- requires at least 3 hard disks and at most 32 hard disks,
- offers excellent read performance.

Data backup strategies

Data must still be backed up with either of these fault tolerance solutions.
With either of these solutions, and notably with a RAID 5 solution, if more than one of the disks fails then you can repair the problem only by restoring the data, which you must have backed-up previously.

Cost of RAID 1 and RAID 5 solutions

For both of these solutions, it is useful to measure the cost in terms of the percentage of the disk that is used. For the mirror solution, disk consumption is important, as the data is written twice, which means that only 50% of the available space is *useful* disk space
With a RAID 5 solution, the more disks that you have, the more the cost decreases. If you have n disks, then this 'useful' disk space ratio is *(n-1)/n*.

For example, with a RAID 5 solution that uses 5 disks each of which has a size of 1 GB, then the disk space that is effectively available is 4 GB (the 'cost' ratio is 4/5).

Choosing the best fault tolerance method

You can implement both RAID 1 and RAID 5 solutions on the same server.
It is common practice to use a mirror solution for the boot volume (the volume that contains the system files), and to use a stripe set with parity solution in order to protect the data volumes.

Security

A. **Encrypting documents** 250
1. Introduction 250
2. Implementation 251

B. **Security of IP network traffic** 255

C. **Accounts and password security** 257
1. Account lockout policy 259
2. Password policy 261

D. **Audit** 263

E. **User rights** 269

F. **Security options** 270

A. Encrypting documents

1. Introduction

In order to enhance resource security, Windows 2000 allows you to encrypt your data in the context of NTFS file systems. This technique ensures that the contents of your documents will be accessible only by users who have the key that allows them to decrypt them.

Once you have encrypted a document, users who are authorized to decrypt it will have transparent access to it. Although this encryption is applied according to NTFS permissions, it is independent of the NTFS permissions that are applied to the same document.

The encryption that is used on Windows 2000 is called EFS (*Encrypting File System*). In response to an increasing need for security, EFS allows you better to protect sensitive data. Even though it is difficult to by-pass NTFS permissions, an element of risk is always involved. For example, on the Internet you can obtain utilities that allow you to access NTFS partitions by booting your computer on a simple MSDOS diskette. In this case, NTFS permissions no longer apply.

EFS uses symmetric encryption (this means that the same keys are used for encryption and for decryption). The list of these keys itself is encrypted with a public key from the user's X.509 v3 certificate. This list is integrated into the document. In order to decrypt the document, you must use the user's private key that was used to encrypt the document so that you can extract the list of keys that are used. Only the user knows this private key. This technique is known as asymmetric encryption (the public key that is used in order to encrypt the document is different from the private key that is used in order to decrypt the document).

Files are encrypted block by block, and each block is encrypted using a different encryption key.

EFS allows you to encrypt files or folders that are on a computer. It does not allow you to encrypt data that is transferred on the network. For this purpose, Windows 2000 offers solutions such as IPSec and SSL (Secure Sockets Layer). IPSec will be covered later on in this chapter.

2. Implementation

Encrypting

- Open Windows Explorer and then right-click the file or the folder that you want to encrypt on an NTFS partition or volume. Then select **Properties**.
- Click the **Advanced** button.

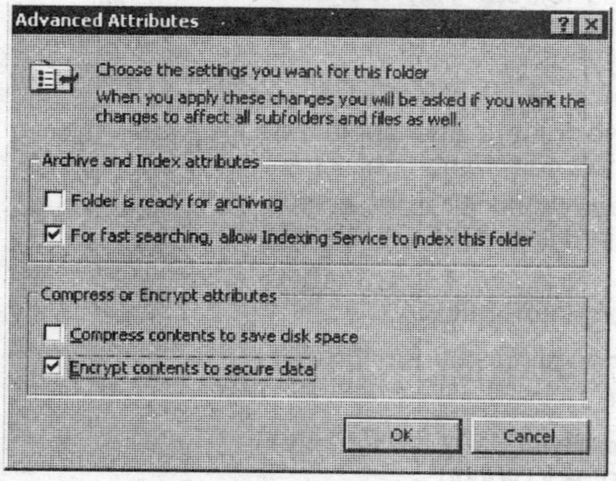

- Activate the **Encrypt contents to secure data** option, and then click **OK**.

If you encrypt a folder that contains files or subfolders, then you must choose whether you want to encrypt only the folder, or whether you want to encrypt the folder and its contents.

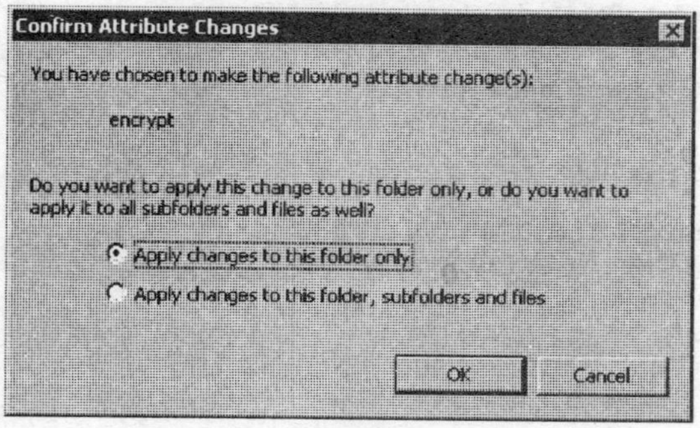

You cannot encrypt a file or a folder, and compress it. If you encrypt a file that is compressed, then the file will lose its compression attribute.

You can also use a command prompt utility in order to encrypt or to decrypt files or folders. This utility is called **cipher.exe**.

Using cipher.exe

- `/e` Encrypts the folders that are specified, and encrypts also any files or folders that will be added later to the specified folders.
- `/d` Decrypts the specified folders. Any folders or files that are added later to the specified folders will not be encrypted.
- `/s:dir` When combined with **/e** or **/d**, this switch encrypts or decrypts the folders and subfolders that are specified in the command line.
- `/i` By default cipher stops when an error occurs. This switch forces cipher to continue its operations.
- `/q` Reports only important information.
- `/k` Generates a new encryption key for the user that is running cipher.

If you run the cipher utility without specifying any switch, then cipher will return the status of the current encryption.

```
E:\>cipher /e /s:data1

 Setting the directory data1 to encrypt new files [OK]

 Encrypting directories in E:\data1\

data2                  [OK]

 Encrypting directories in E:\data1\data2\

2 directorie(s) within 3 directorie(s) were encrypted.

E:\>
```

If you decide to encrypt a file that is located in a directory that is not encrypted, then you can choose either to encrypt only the file, or to encrypt the file and its parent folder.

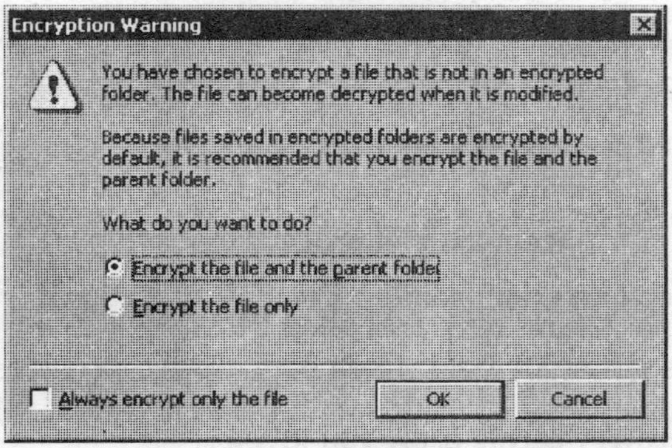

Stop encrypting

If you want to stop encrypting (decrypt) a file or a folder, go into Windows Explorer, right-click the folder or the file that you want to decrypt, select **Properties** then click the **Advanced** button. Then, deactivate the **Encrypt contents to secure data** option.

If you decrypt a folder that contains files or subfolders, then you must choose whether or not you want to decrypt the contents of the folder.
You can also use the cipher.exe utility for this purpose, specifying the switch /**d**.

Copying and moving

When you copy or move an encrypted document, then the document will stay encrypted, whether the destination folder is encrypted or not.
Similarly, if you backed up encrypted documents using the Windows 2000 backup utility, then these documents will remain encrypted after you have restored them.
If you copy, or move, an unencrypted file to a folder that is encrypted, then the file will also be encrypted. You can apply a policy that will prevent the encryption of files that are moved to an encrypted folder that is situated on the same volume.

In order to do this, you must use the policy that is situated in the **Group Policy** snap-in, in the folder **Computer Configuration - Administrative Templates - System.**

It must be noted that if you copy or move an encrypted file to a file system other than NTFS, then the file will not be encrypted at the destination. You may find this technique useful so as to issue a document that you have encrypted.

When a document has been encrypted by another user, you can copy or move it only to an NTFS file system.

A user who has the right to delete a file will be able to delete an encrypted file.

Recovery agents

Only the user who has encrypted a document can read it. But, what happens if the user account of the person who encrypted the document is deleted? It would appear that the data would be permanently lost!

In order to deal with such situations, **recovery agents** allow you to decrypt documents. Each encrypted document contains the list of the keys that were used in order to encrypt the document. This list is itself encrypted with the user's public key, and normally, it can be decrypted only with the private key of the user who encrypted the document. However, this list is also encrypted with the recovery agent's public key. Consequently, it can be decrypted by the recovery agent's private key. Thereby, when a user's private key fails, you can use the recovery agent in order to recover the documents concerned.

Who are they?

The first administrator who logs on to a domain after the domain has been created becomes the recovery agent for that domain. The first administrator that logs on to a workstation, or to a stand-alone server, becomes the recovery agent for the workstation or the server.

Recovering a document

A recovery agent decrypts a document using his/her private key:

- Either, you must copy the recovery agent's private key onto the computer on which you want to recover the encrypted document (you are strongly advised not to use this method for security reasons),
- Or, you must send the document that must be decrypted to the recovery agent, so that the recovery agent can use his/her private key that is located on his/her own machine.

If you decide to send the document to the recovery agent, then back up the document using the Windows 2000 backup utility, and send the backup to the recovery agent, who can restore it on his/her own machine. Then, the recovery agent will be able to open the document transparently.

B. Security of IP network traffic

With Windows 2000, Microsoft allows you to encrypt the IP traffic that circulates on your LAN, or even across extended networks. The main objective of this feature is to provide security for data that circulates on a network that is not itself secure, like Internet for example.
Windows 2000 uses **IPSec** (*IP Security*) for this purpose. This is an open standard, and not a proprietary invention. Because of this, a Windows 2000 machine is able securely to communicate with any type of computer (client, server, or router) that runs IPSec.

IPSec is described in RFC 1825.

It is very simple to implement IPSec. You can implement IPSec, either machine-by-machine, or using group policies.

- Right-click **My Network Places** and then select **Properties.**
- Right-click the **Local Area Connection** for the network interface card on which you want to enable IP security.
- Select **Properties**, then select **Internet Protocol (TCP/IP)**, and click the **Properties** button.
- Then, click the **Advanced** button.

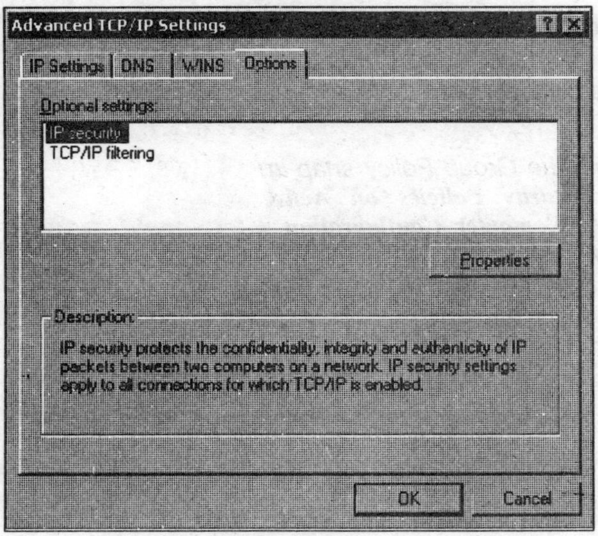

☞ Click the **Options** tab, then select **IP security** and click **Properties.**

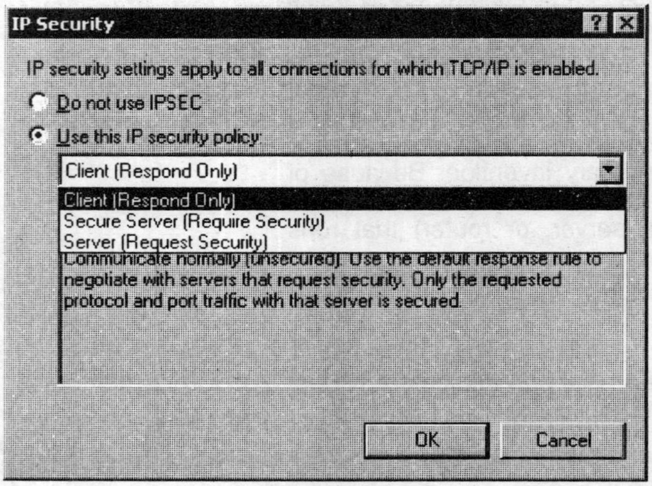

By default, IP security is not enabled. You can choose from three security levels:

Client (Respond Only)

This option allows IP traffic to circulate normally. Encrypted response is provided to clients that request it.

Secure Server (Require Security)

This option does not allow unsecured communication.

Server (Request Security)

This option implements encrypted messages, but accepts unencrypted client requests.

*You can implement IPSec with the Group Policy snap-in. For this purpose use **IP Security Policies on Active Directory** that is located in **Computer Configuration - Windows Settings - Security Settings**.*

C. Accounts and password security

You can define accounts and password security using group policies. Several templates are provided that offer different levels of security. You can modify existing templates, or you can create new ones, in order to meet your own specific security needs.
Once you have configured a template it is imported into the group policy so that it can be applied to users or to computers.
You can access security templates by creating an MMC and adding into it, the **Security Templates** snap-in.

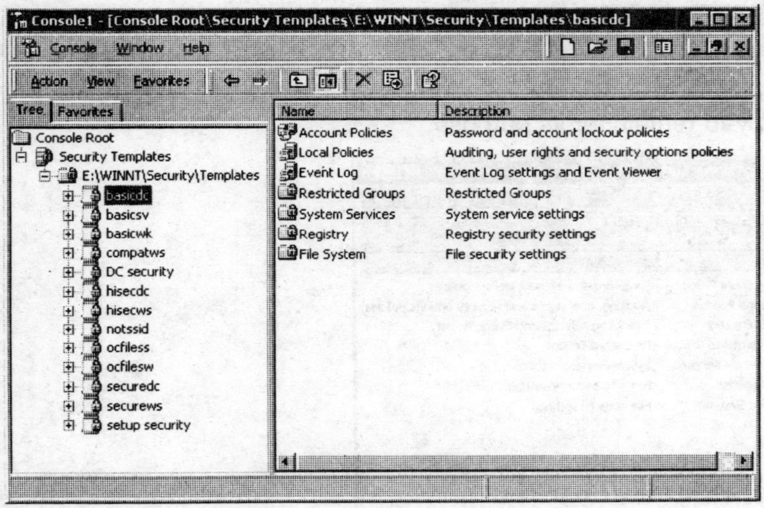

The security templates are text files that have .inf name extensions. They are located in the directory **%systemroot%\security\templates**.

You can display a description of the contents of a template by right-clicking the template concerned and selecting the ***Set Description*** *option.*

In order to create a new template, right-click **%systemroot%/security/template**, and then select **New Template**.

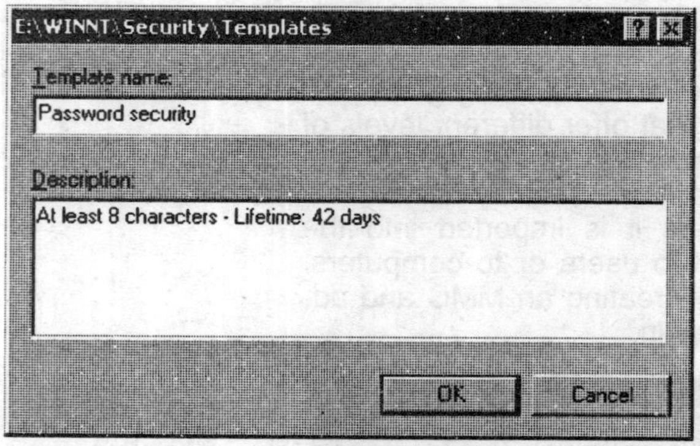

Give a significant name to your new template, along with a description that will help you quickly to remember its purpose.

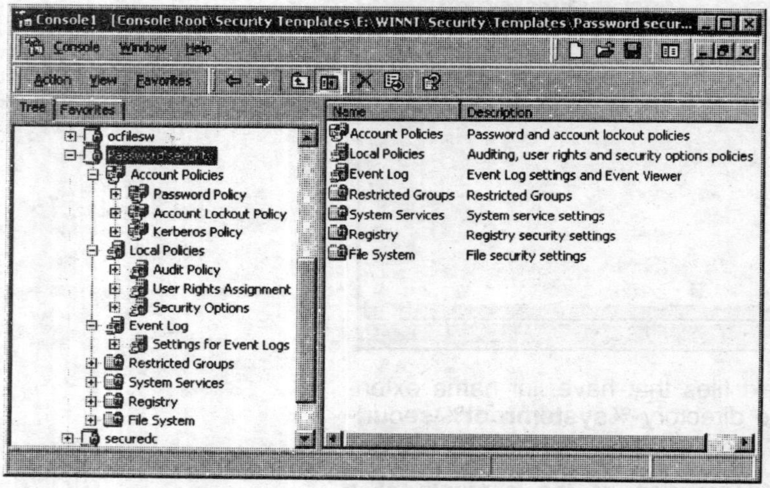

Finally, you must set up the security actions that your template must implement.

In order to apply a security model to a group policy, you must use either the **Active Directory Sites and Services** console, or the **Active Directory Users and Computers** console.

- Right-click the container for which you want to apply the policy.
- Select **Properties** then select the **Group Policy** tab.
- Select, or create a policy, then click the **Edit** button.

☞ Right-click **Security Settings** (under **Computer Configuration - Windows Settings**), then select **Import Policy**.

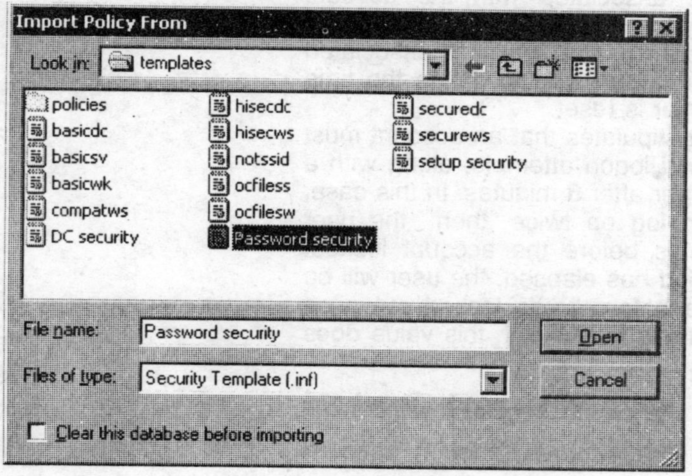

☞ Select the security template that you wish to import and then click the **Open** button.

1. Account lockout policy

Now that this chapter has described how to apply a security template to a group strategy, it will cover more closely the settings that must be applied to an account policy.

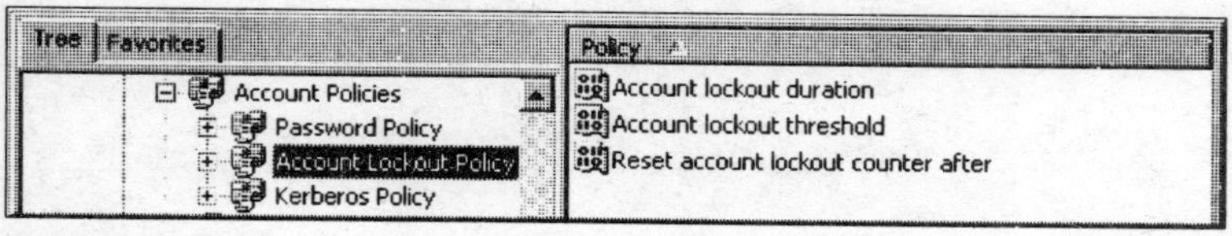

Account policies allows you to define the conditions in which user accounts will be locked out. When an account has been locked, no one can use it until it has been unlocked.

Account lockout duration

Activate the **Define this policy setting in the template** check box so that you will be able to define the length of time for which the account will be locked out.
If you want to retain full control over account lockouts, then do not activate this check box.

Reset account lockout counter after

A counter and a duration are associated with the account lockout. The counter allows you to count the number of unsuccessful logon attempts. The duration, which is associated with the account lockout counter, allows you to define the time that must elapse before this counter is reset.
Suppose you define a policy that stipulates that an account must be locked out after 3 unsuccessful logon attempts, along with a reset of the account lockout counter after 5 minutes. In this case, if a user unsuccessfully tried to log on twice, then the user would have to wait for 5 minutes before the account lockout counter was reset. After this period has elapsed, the user will be able to try to logon again twice before being locked out once more. However, when the account is locked out, this value does not apply.

Account lockout threshold

You must indicate the number of unsuccessful logon attempts before the account is locked out.
If a user reaches this number of consecutive unsuccessful logon attempts, then the user will receive a message saying that the user's account has been disabled and that the user must contact the administrator. In the properties of this account, the **Account is locked out** check box will no longer be grayed out, and will be activated.

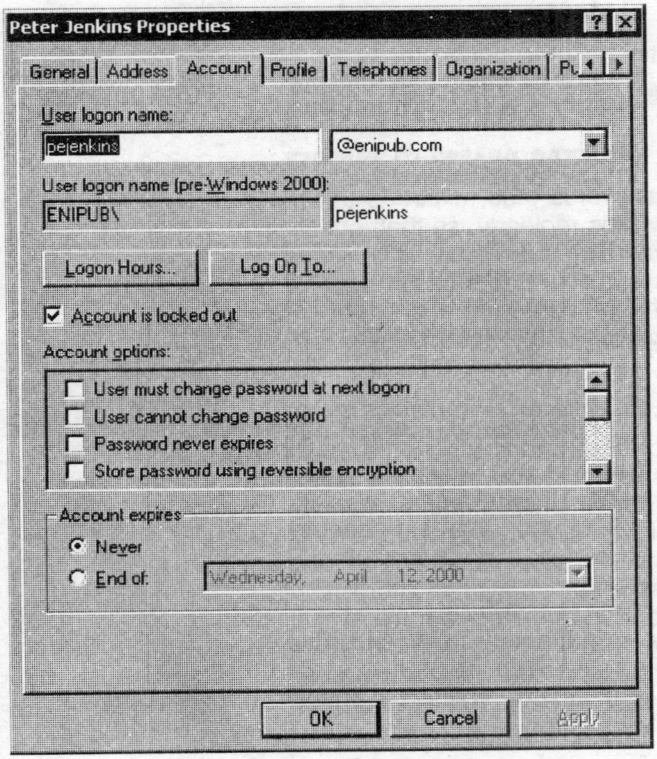

Before you unlock the account, check the user's identity along with the reasons for which the account was locked out. In order to unlock the account, deactivate the **Account is locked out** check box.

2. Password policy

- Enforce password history
- Maximum password age
- Minimum password age
- Minimum password length
- Passwords must meet complexity requirements
- Store password using reversible encryption for all users in the domain

Maximum password age

This setting allows you to indicate the time period for which a user's password will remain valid. When this period has elapsed, the user must change password.

Enforce password history

The purpose of stipulating that passwords must expire is to ensure that users change their passwords regularly, so that, should a pirate discover a password, he/she will be unable to continue infiltrating the network with this user account. It is useful then, to ensure that when a user has to change password, the user cannot choose the same password again. For this purpose, you can keep a password history.

Minimum password age

This setting indicates the period of time during which the users do not have to change their passwords. If you defined a policy that remembers former passwords, then, when the user changes password, he/she will not be able to use a password that is stored in the password history. However, there is nothing to stop the user from changing his/her password immediately afterwards, and in this case, there is nothing to stop the user from re-using a former password. In order to prevent this, you can forbid users from modifying their passwords for x days. The value of x should be as close as possible to the number of days that must elapse before the password expires.

Minimum password length

Longer passwords are more difficult to guess. Remember that passwords are case sensitive.

Passwords must meet complexity requirements

If you enable this setting, then passwords must contain lower case and upper case characters, along with numbers or punctuation marks. A password cannot be the user's account name nor can it be the user's full name.

Store passwords using reversible encryption for all users in the domain

You must use this parameter if you have Macintosh clients who do not use the Microsoft client software. Macintosh clients cannot encrypt passwords by using the same method as that used by Windows 2000. Consequently, the password is stored in Active Directory, and the server can decrypt it so that it can compare it with the password that the client sends.

D. Audit

The audit is a system tool that allows you to log the events and the activities that are carried out either by the system or by the users that you want to monitor. Events can be audited when they are successful, and/or when they are unsuccessful.
The results of these audits are stored in the **Security** log of the **Event Viewer**. They provide information on the action that was carried out, they tell you by whom it was carried out, and they tell you whether the action was successful, or whether it was unsuccessful.
You can define an audit policy by defining a security template and then importing it into a group policy. Alternatively, you can define your audit policy directly in the group policy, using the **Active Directory Users and Computers** console. As audit policies must be applied computer by computer, then it is better to define a group policy for an organizational unit that contains the computers that must be audited (these are generally the servers).

- Open the **Active Directory Users and Computers** console, and right-click the container to which you want to apply the audit policy.
- Select **Properties** and activate the **Group Policy** tab.
- Create a new policy, or select an existing one and then click the **Edit** button.
- Expand **Computer Configuration, Windows Settings, Security Settings, Local Policies,** and **Audit Policy**.

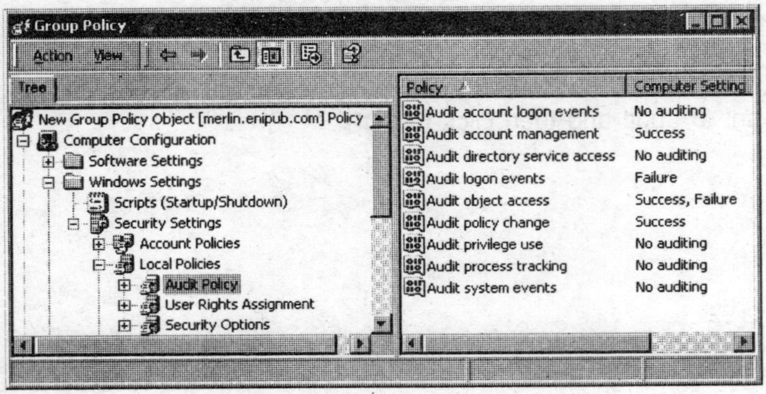

- Double-click the event that you want to audit.

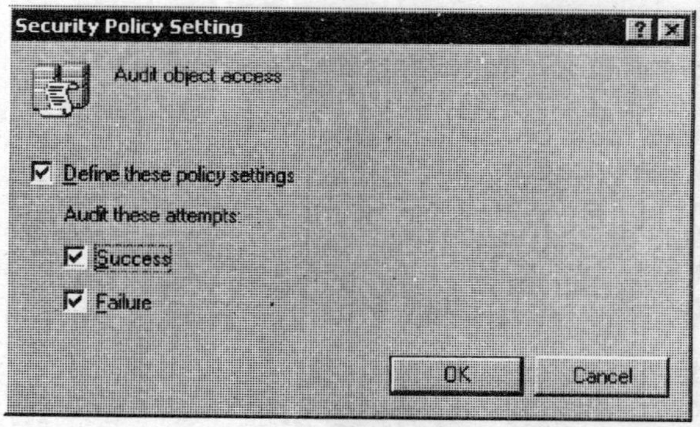

- Activate the **Success** check box, and/or the **Failure** check box.

Do not choose to audit all the types of event on success and on failure, as this will make it more difficult to extract relevant information from the Event Viewer.

If you want to audit the actions that are carried out on your resources (such as files, folders, printers and drives), then you must activate the **Audit object access** policy, and set up the audit on the resource concerned. You can do this as follows:

- Edit the properties of the resource.

You can audit only files and folders that are located on NTFS partitions or volumes.

- Select the **Security** tab, and click the **Advanced** button.
- select the **Auditing** tab, and click the **Add** button.
- Add the users that you want to audit and then click the **OK** button.

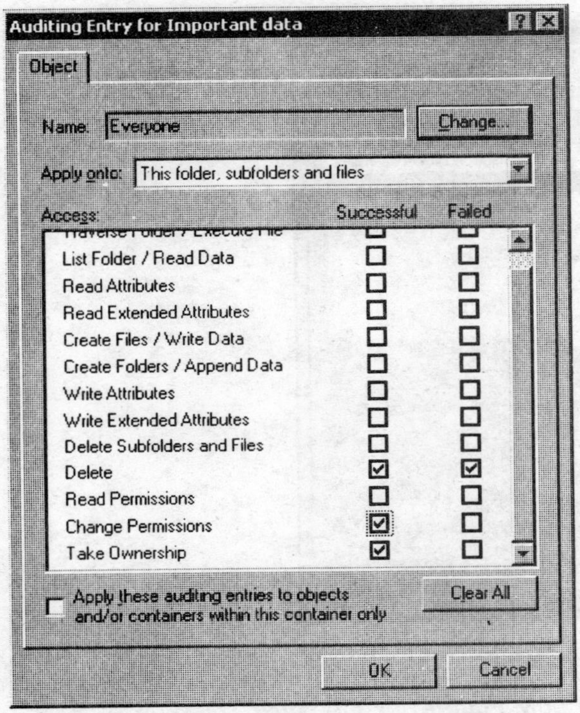

- Enable the actions that must be audited when they are successful, and/or when they fail, and then click **OK**.

Security

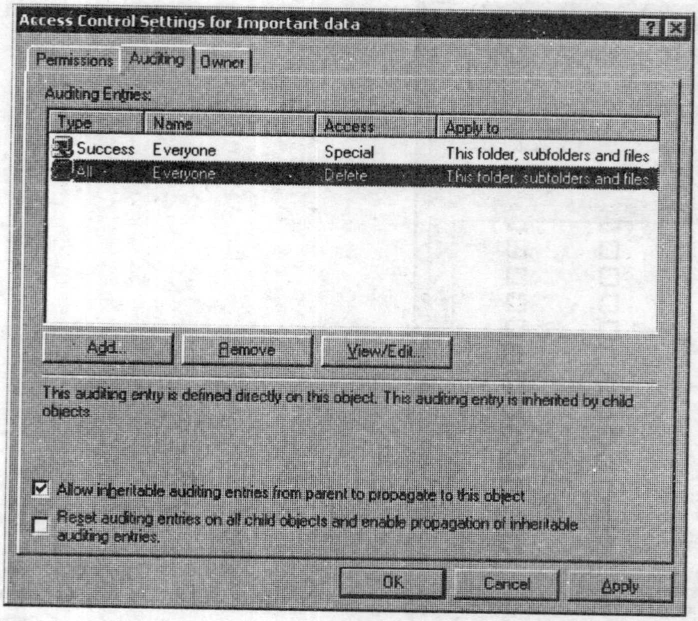

☛ Click **OK** in order to finish the operation.

Important note: If you select only ***Failure*** *for the* ***Audit object access*** *policy, then you will not be able to audit the events that are successful, even if you define them as such at resource level.*

You can audit a printer for invoicing purposes, for example. You can audit the following actions for a printer: Print, Manage Printers, Manage Documents, Read Permissions, Change Permissions and Take Ownership.

Auditing Active Directory

Audit policies allow you to audit actions that are carried out on the Active Directory database. In order to do this, set up the **Audit directory service access** event in the Audit Policy. Similarly to Audit object access, you must go into the directory database in order to specify the items that you want to audit.

☛ Open the **Active Directory Users and Computers** console.

☛ Right-click the object that you want to audit, and select **Properties.**

- Select the **Security** tab, and click the **Advanced** button.
- Select the **Auditing** tab, and click the **Add** button.
- Add the users that you want to audit (you are advised to add the **Everyone** group), and then click the **OK** button.

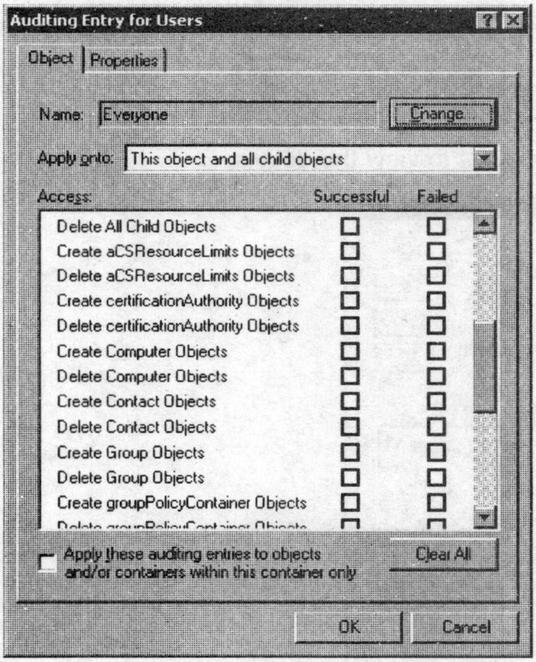

- Enable the check boxes that correspond to the events that you want to audit, and the click **OK** twice so as to confirm you choice.

Viewing the audited events

You can consult the audited events using the **Security** log of the **Event Viewer**.

The  icon represents failure, and the  icon represents success.

- Open the **Event Viewer** console that is situated in the **Administrative Tools** menu.
- Click the **Security Log**. The list appears of all the actions that have been audited.

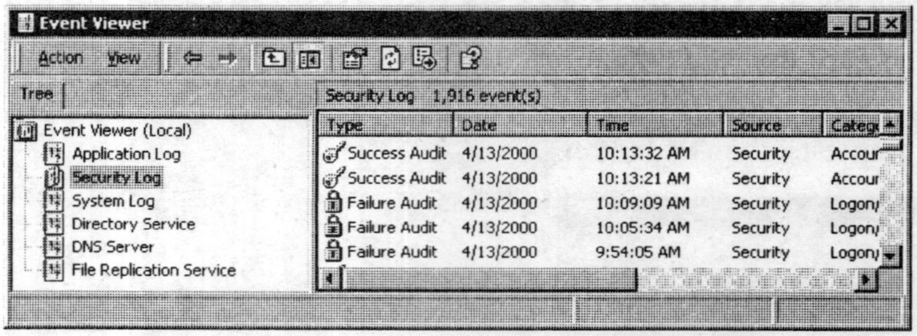

☞ Double-click the event for which you want to view the details.

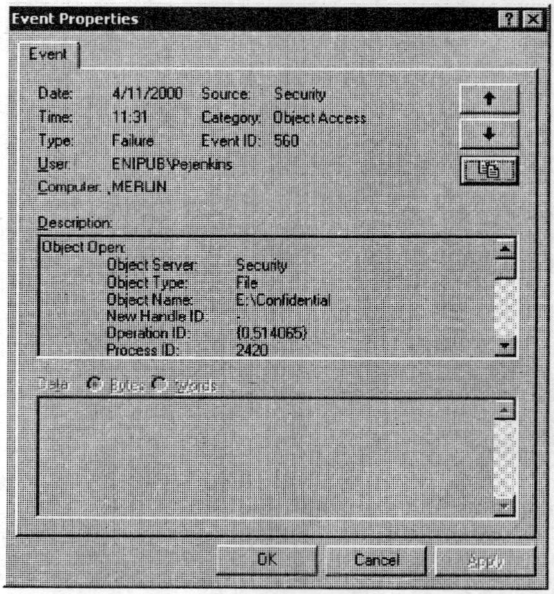

This dialog box shows information on the action concerned, and provides the name of the user that carried it out. If you click the  button, then you will take a copy of the description that you can then insert into a text file.

You define audit policies in order to monitor your network so as to counter any intrusions or incorrect usage. Consequently, it is important that you cover all the relevant events. Group policies allow you to set up the Event Viewer in order to:

– Stop the computer when the security log is full. This technique allows you to ensure that you will not miss any event audit.

- Set a maximum size for the security log, the system log and the application log.
- Set a time period, during which log data will be stored in the different logs.
- Define how you want to store the different logs (by overwriting events that are older than a certain number of days, by overwriting events when necessary, or by not overwriting events at all).

You can define these settings in the **Event Log** of the group policies, under **Security Settings**.

E. User rights

You can use group policies, in order to modify certain rights on the operating system. These user rights include the rights to log on locally, to change the system time, to shut down the system, to add workstations to domain and to manage auditing and security log.
In order to modify these rights, select the container concerned and then go into the group policies.

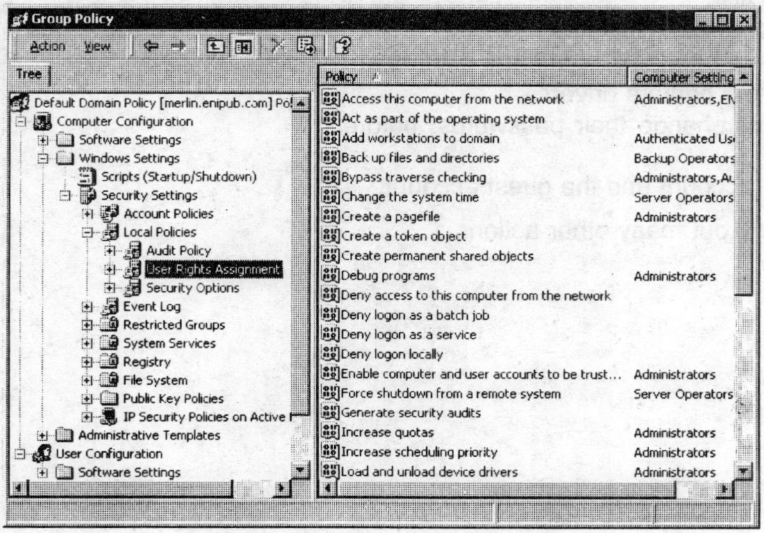

For example, suppose that you want to grant the right to log on locally onto a domain controller to a specific user (by default, only the administrators and the operators have this right on domain controllers). In order to do this, select the organizational unit that represents the domain controllers, then modify this group policy so as to add the user concerned for the **Log on locally** right, in the **User Rights Assignment** that is situated under **Local Policies.**

F. Security options

In addition to account, password and auditing options, group policies allow you to add an extra security level using the **Security Options**, which are situated under the **Local Policies.**

These security options allow you:

- not to display the logon name of the user who last logged on (this policy allows you to prevent users from guessing the name of the administrator, in the case where you renamed this account),
- to display a logon message title,
- not to allow unsigned drivers to be installed,
- automatically to log off users when their logon time expires,
- to prevent users from installing printers drivers,
- to warn users that they must change their passwords, before their passwords expire,
- to rename the administrator account and the guest account,

And they also allow you to carry out many other actions.

A. Dynamic Host Configuration Protocol 272

1. Installing DHCP server 273
2. Authorizing a DHCP server 274
3. Creating address scopes 275
4. Configuring a client machine to use DHCP . . . 280
5. Processing DHCP queries 280
6. New features offered by the Windows 2000 DHCP service 284
7. DHCP relay agent 288

B. Windows Internet Name Service 289

1. Installing the WINS service 290
2. Static configuration of WINS clients 291
3. Dynamic configuration of WINS clients 292
4. Configuring static entries 293
5. Displaying the WINS Server database 294
6. Using a WINS proxy agent 296
7. Replication partners 296
8. Setting up the WINS server 298

C. Remote access 299

1. Transport methods 299
2. Configuring a remote access server 301
3. Authentication 311
4. Remote access policy 313

Network services

A. Dynamic Host Configuration Protocol

In the preceding chapters, you will have noticed the main difficulty that you meet when you implement TCP/IP on a network of any reasonable size. Each machine must be perfectly configured, and the risk of conflicting addresses will always be present. Another point that is even more important is that you must change the addresses of portable machines each time that you move them to another network.

The DHCP protocol, which is defined in the RFC 1533, 1533, 1534, 1541 and 1542, allows you centrally to configure the machines in a network. It does this by providing the local network with a server that is able to supply the client machines with their TCP/IP settings. These settings include:

- IP address,
- Subnet mask,
- Default gateway,
- Addresses of name servers (NetBIOS/WINS or Internet/DNS),
- NetBIOS node type (the way in which a network interface card resolves a NetBIOS name into an IP address),
- Internet domain name.

This technique reduces the risk of conflicting addresses. In addition, when you use DHCP you no longer have to reconfigure your portable computers each time they are used in another network.
In addition, when you configure an IP workstation you need activate only one check box, as the server provides all the IP settings.
The administrator can easily find out the addresses that have been allocated to DHCP clients. The addresses are allocated according to a **lease** that can run either for a limited time period, or for an unlimited time period. Each machine keeps the same address until the end of the lease, and will renew the lease with the same address if this address is available.

The following machines can be DHCP clients:

- Windows 2000 Professional, and Server versions,
- Windows NT, Server and Workstation,
- Windows 95,
- MS-DOS 3.0 Client,
- Windows for Workgroups 3.11.

plementation issues

You can search for a DHCP server using a broadcast. You must have one DHCP server per segment, unless you use a DHCP relay agent. It is advisable that you have two DHCP servers available, for fault tolerance reasons.

Some routers can let through DHCP broadcasts that are based on BOOTP (RFC n1542). In this case, a DHCP server can provide addresses to machines throughout the whole network.

1. Installing DHCP server

- On the Windows 2000 server, go into the Control Panel and double-click the **Add/Remove Programs** icon.
- Click the **Add/Remove Windows Components** icon, click the **Components** button, select **Networking Services**, and then click the **Details** button.

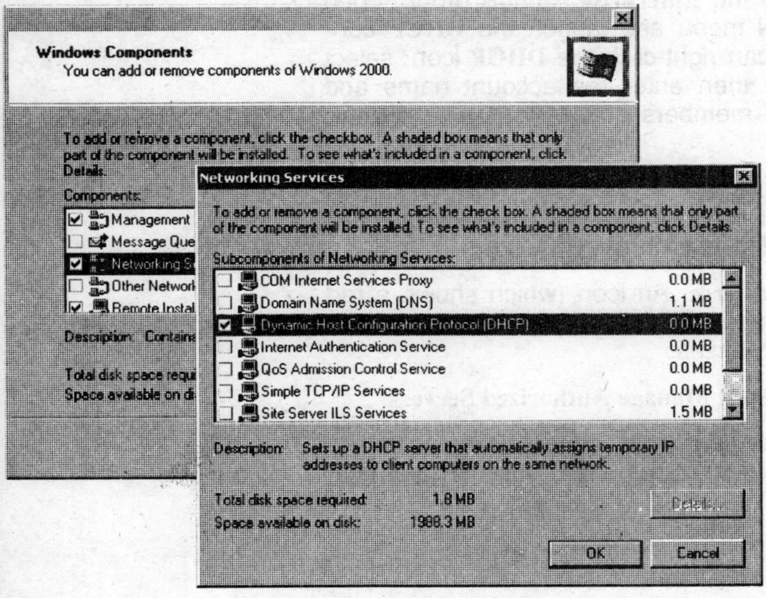

- Enable the **Dynamic Host Configuration Protocol (DHCP)** check box, and click the **OK** button.
- Click the **Next** button in order to launch the installation.

When you have installed the DHCP server service, you can start creating address scopes that will be attributed to clients who ask for them. However, before clients will be able to obtain IP configurations from a DHCP server, the DHCP server must first be authorized in the Active Directory to attribute IP leases.

2. Authorizing a DHCP server

It is important to control the machines that are able to act as DHCP servers, and consequently to control the machines that are able to attribute IP leases that could conflict with the IP addresses of the other DHCP servers. For this purpose, a member of the **Enterprise Admins** group (in the root domain of the forest) must authorize DHCP servers to attribute IP configuration to clients. In addition, this approach allows the administrator to control the IP addresses that will be distributed to clients.
The following steps allow you to authorize a DHCP server in Active Directory:

- Log on as a member of the **Enterprise Admins** group, open the **Administrative Tools** menu and launch the **DHCP** console. Alternatively, you can right-click the **DHCP** icon, select the **Run as** option, and then enter the account name and password of one of the members of the **Enterprise Admins** group.
- If your server does not appear in the **Tree** pane, right-click **DHCP**, and then select the **Add Server** option. Enter the name of your server and then click the **OK** button.
- Select your server under **Tree**. An icon (which shows a red arrow pointing downwards) indicates that your server is not authorized to attribute IP leases.
- Right-click **DHCP** and select **Manage Authorized Servers**.
- Click the **Authorize** button and enter either the name of the DHCP server that you want to authorize, or its IP address. Then click the **OK** button.

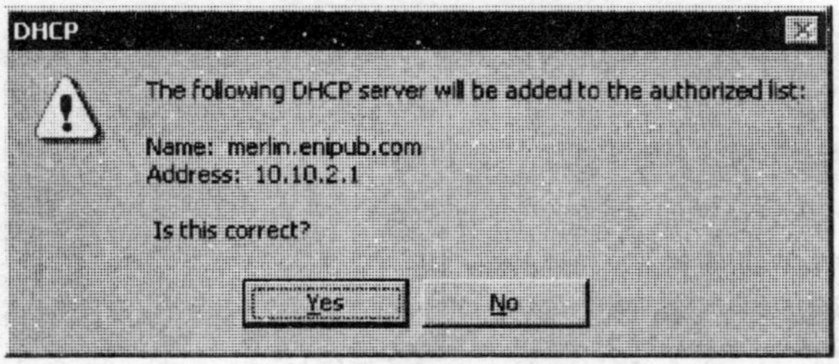

- If the information is correct, then click the **Yes** button.
- The icon that appears before the name of the DHCP server then appears as follows (a green arrow pointing upwards).

A DHCP server sends broadcasts regularly so as to check that the authorization status has not changed

Creating address scopes

n address scope contains the IP addresses that must be allo-ated to the client, the subnet mask, the lease period of this ;ope, along with any addresses that must be excluded, if any achines already use addresses that are contained in this ;ope.

there are several DHCP servers in the network, then they must ot have scopes that overlap each other or else the dynamic ddress allocation could offer conflicting addresses.

ou can create an address scope as follows:

- Go into the **DHCP** console, right-click the name of the DHCP server, and select **New Scope**.
- Click the **Next** button, and give a name and a description that corresponds to your scope.
- Enter the start address and the end address of your scope. By default, a mask is assigned that corresponds to the class of your addresses. However, you can change this mask so that you will be able to create subnets. In this case, indicate the number of bits that you want to use for your mask. Alternatively, you can enter the value of the mask directly in decimal.
- Click the **Next** button.

- Enter any addresses or address ranges that you want to exclude from your scope, and then click the **Next** button.
- Indicate the duration of your scope, and then click the **Next** button.

Remember that a DHCP client will try to renew its IP lease half way through its lease period, and again when 87,5% of the lease period has elapsed, if it was unable to renew its lease half way through the lease period. Consequently, the longer the lease, the less traffic that will be generated by these lease renewal queries. On the other hand, you must be careful not to set the lease period too long if you have a lot of mobile clients. In any case, lease renewal queries do not generate a very high volume of network traffic!

The next screen asks you whether you want to continue your configuration by specifying further scope options now, or whether you prefer to configure these options later.

- Enable **No, I will configure these options later**, and then click the **Next** button, followed by the **Finish** button.

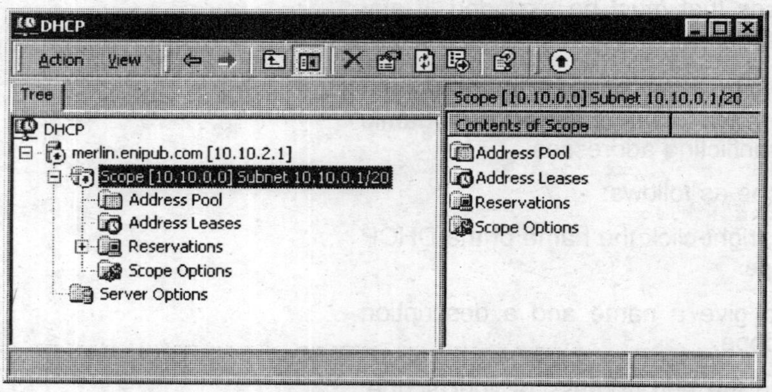

By default, when you create a scope, your scope is not activated. In order to make your scope operational, you must activate it by right-clicking it and then selecting **Activate**. Until you carry out this operation, the DHCP clients will not be able to obtain an IP lease.

When you install the DHCP service, two new groups are created. The ***DHCP Users*** *group allows its members to access the information in the DHCP console in read-only mode. The* ***DHCP Administrators*** *group allows its members to administer the DHCP server.*

Adding options to a scope

This chapter has described how you can attribute a standard IP configuration to DHCP clients. However, it is also useful to provide DHCP clients with other settings, such as their default gateway address, and the addresses of their DNS and WINS servers.

You can do this in two ways:
– either, you can configure identical settings for all the scopes.
– or, you can configure different settings for each scope.

Creating specific options for each scope

One of the scope options is the IP address of the gateway.

☞ Right-click the **Scope Options** folder that is situated under the scope folder concerned, and select **Configure Options**.

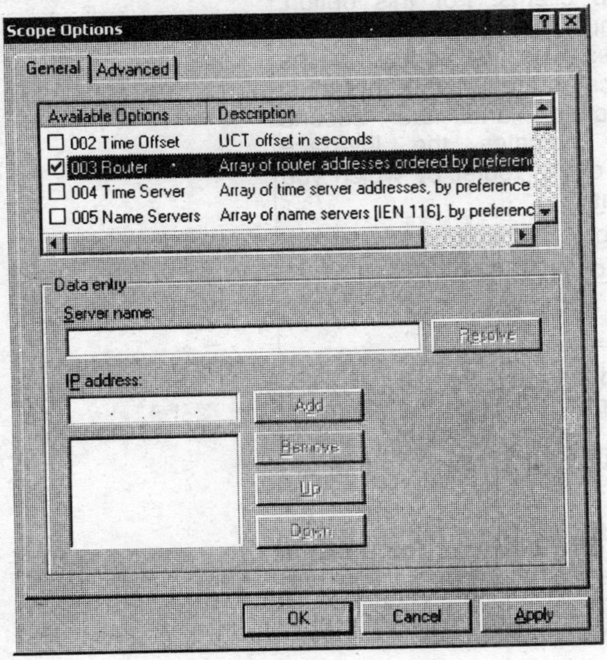

- Enable the check box of each of the options that you wish to add, and then indicate its value.

Creating global options for all the scopes

Unlike the scope options, the global options, or **Server Options** apply to all the scopes that are created on the server.

- Right-click the **Server Options** folder and select **Configure Options.**
- Enable the check box of each of the options that you wish to add, and then indicate its value.

Principal DHCP options

Option	Role
003 Router	Default gateway address.
006 DNS Servers	Addresses of name servers.
015 DNS Domain Name	Name of Internet domain.
028 Broadcast Address	Allows you to specify a broadcast address.
033 Static Route Option	Allows you to distribute static routes to clients. For this option, you must specify pairs of addresses. The first address of the pair indicates the network that must be reached, and the second address indicates the interface address of the router by which you must pass.
035 ARP Cache Timeout	Lifetime of ARP mappings.
044 WINS/NBNS Servers	Address of WINS server(s).
046 WINS/NBT Node Type	NetBIOS node type.

Some of these options were introduced by the DHCP RFC n°2132 implementation. These new options include the means of indicating one or more default Web servers to clients, and of listing the addresses of SMTP, POP3, or NNTP servers that are available for DHCP clients.

Reserving a specific address for a client

If you want a client to obtain a specific IP address, you can reserve an address for the client using the client's MAC (physical) address. You can do this as follows:

- Right-click the **Reservations** folder that is situated under the scope from which you want to reserve an address, and then select **New Reservation**.

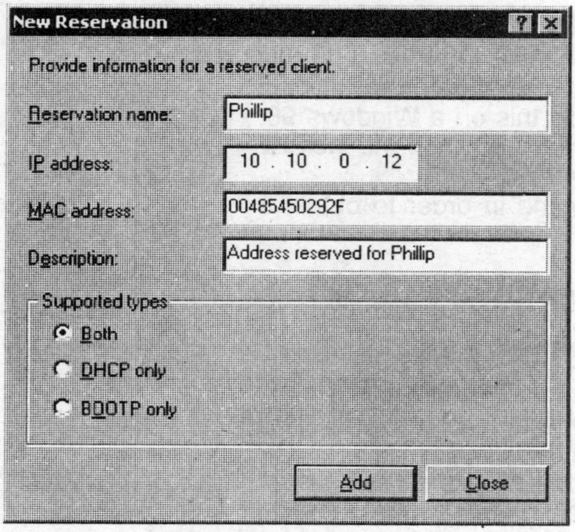

- You must enter the following items: the IP address that you want to reserve, the MAC address that is defined on 48 bits with Ethernet, a reservation name and a description. Note that you can specify whether this reservation will be used for a DHCP and/or for a BOOTP client.

- By right-clicking this reservation, you can configure options that are specific to this address.

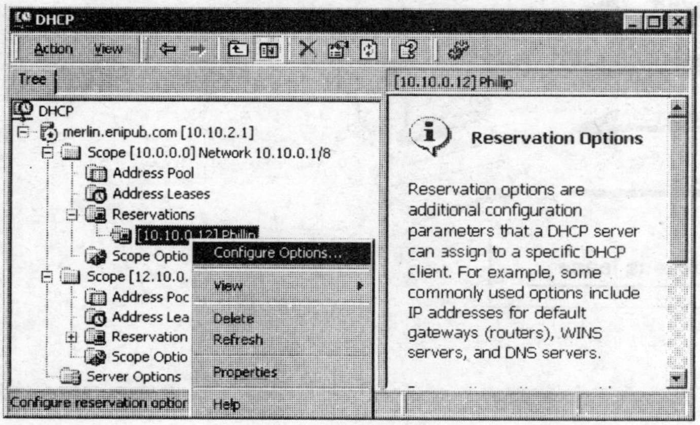

You can find out the MAC address of a machine by entering ipconfig /all in the command prompt.

Lease renewal or freeing by the user

You can force your computer to free its lease. In order to do this on a Windows 2000 or Windows NT machine, you can use the **Ipconfig/Release** command. In order to do this on a Windows 98, you can run the **WINIPCFG.EXE** program and click the **Release All** button, which is provided for this purpose.
You can use the Ipconfig/Renew command in order to obtain a new IP lease.

4. Configuring a client machine to use DHCP

- Edit the TCP/IP properties of the machine.
- Enable the **Obtain an IP address automatically** option. Note also that you can manually enter the IP address of a DNS server, even if you obtain your IP configuration via a DHCP server. In order to obtain the IP address of the DNS server using the scope options of the DHCP server, select **Obtain DNS server address automatically**.

The TCP/IP properties that are manually defined on the client machines take priority over the DHCP options.

5. Processing DHCP queries

Queries

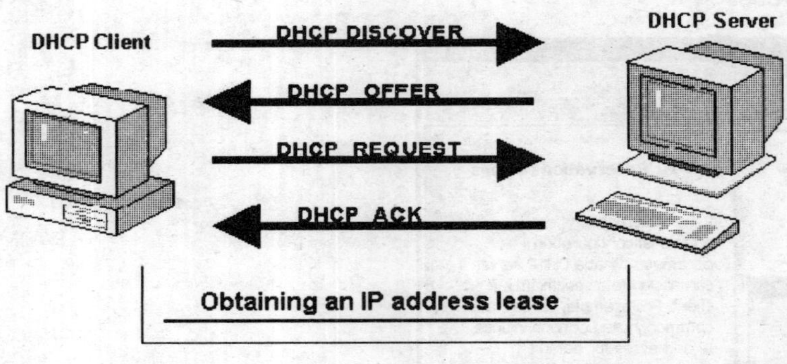

DHCP Discover

Strange as it may seem, even when a client has no TCP/IP settings, it will still execute a limited version of these protocols in order to obtain these configuration setting.
The DHCP client broadcasts a first frame so as to look for the DHCP server. This frame is called **DHCP DISCOVER**.
The client sends a broadcast to look for the DHCP Server because it does not know which machine it is: physically, this broadcast frame is sent to the MAC address FF.FF.FF.FF.FF.FF, and logically it is sent to the address 255.255.255.255.
As a sender, the client identifies itself with its own physical MAC address, and with a logical IP address of 0.0.0.0, whilst the client does not have its IP address.

The client uses the UDP protocol in order to send the broadcast. This protocol allows you to connect to UDP port 67 (BOOTP server), as a BOOTP client (UDP port 68).

This process is carried out each time that it is needed. Notably, it is used in the following circumstances:
– When TCP/IP is initialized for the first time on a DHCP client,
– When the DHCP client requests a specific IP address, and this address is refused. In this case the DHCP client must send a new **Discover** in order to find another server,
– When the client's lease expires and the client must request a new one.

DHCP Offer

All the DHCP servers in the network must make an offer to the client, provided that they have IP addresses that are available for the IP network number that is requested.

The scope is chosen according to the origin of the IP packet. For example, for a server that has several IP addresses, then the scope is chosen according to the IP network number that is associated with the network interface card that received the broadcast. In the case of a DHCP Relay Agent$IDHCP Relay Agent, the scope will be chosen according to the agent's IP address.

This is the **DHCP OFFER** step. In principle, the client can choose to take up the offer of any of the servers. However, in practice, the client will proceed with the first offer that it receives.

The DHCP servers transmit the following information in this frame:

- The client's MAC address,
- The IP address that is offered,
- The associated mask,
- A lease duration,
- The DHCP Server's own IP address.

It must be noted that this frame is also broadcast on the network and that the client's MAC address is not used directly.

If none of these attempts are successful, then it tries again every 5 minutes.

DHCP Request

The client responds to one of the offers from one of the servers. It does this by sending a broadcast in which it indicates that it accepts the offer. This is called a **DHCP REQUEST**. The client sends this broadcast so as to inform all the DHCP servers of the choice that it has made. In fact, the client chooses the first offer that it receives.
Following this broadcast, each of the DHCP servers whose offer has not been chosen by the client withdraws its offer.

DHCP Acknowledgement

Finally, when the DHCP Server receives the DHCP request from the client accepting the offer that was made by the Server, it confirms the lease by sending a DHCP ACK (or **DHCP Acknowledgement**). The DHCP Acknowledgement stipulates the lease duration, and it includes the DHCP options if these are necessary.

***DHCP ACK** must not be confused with DHCP NACK. A **DHCP NACK** is sent by a DHCP Server in order to withdraw TCP/IP settings that have been leased. For example, the DHCP Server will do this when the lease expires, or if the client has moved to a different physical network. Thereby, the server no longer acknowledges the lease that it allocated previously. Then, the client must restart the lease query process, as the client no longer has an IP address.*

The client can now set up its TCP/IP using all the information that it has received.

This information is stored in HKEY_LOCAL_MACHINE\ System\CurrentControlSet\Services*Network_Interface_card_name*\ Parameters\Tcpip.

On Windows NT, you can view these settings using the ipconfig /all command.

Renewing a lease

Upon machine start-up

When a machine that is configured as a DHCP client starts-up, it will try to renew its lease with the same server, using the same settings that it obtained previously, by making a **DHCP REQUEST**.
If the request is unsuccessful, then the client will continue to use these settings until the lease expires.

Half way through the duration

When half of the lease duration has elapsed, the DHCP client will try to renew its lease, before it is no longer able to use its IP settings. In this way, the client can exchange frames directly, without having to make costly broadcasts on the network.
This approach greatly simplifies the DHCP query procedure, as the client can make its renewal query by sending a **DHCP REQUEST** directly to the server with which it set up its current lease.
If the server is available, then it responds by returning a **DHCP ACK** acknowledgement, along with any settings that may have changed.
If the server is not available, then the client will not be able to renew its lease. However, the client will be able to continue to work with its IP settings until its lease expires.

7/8ths of the way through the duration

If the client was unable to renew its lease half way through its duration, then it will make a final attempt to renew its lease when 87.5% of the duration has elapsed. In this case, the client will send its DHCP query to all the DHCP servers. The client no longer sends its request specifically to its previous DHCP server, as this server did not renew its lease upon the previous request.

Thus, a **DHCP REQUEST** message is broadcast in order to contact any server that is available.
If the DHCP lease is not renewed before the end of the lease, then the client will lose its IP settings and it will no longer be able to use IP communication.

You can monitor the IP leasing mechanism by running the **Network Monitor** so as to capture the frames that are exchanged between the DHCP client and the DHCP server.

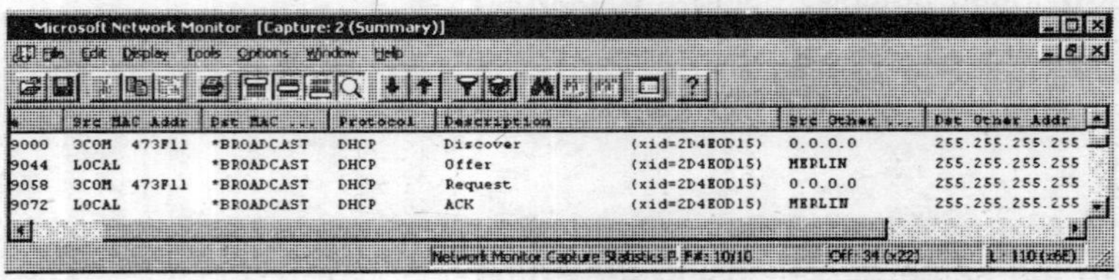

6. New features offered by the Windows 2000 DHCP service

Dynamic update of DNS servers

When a DHCP server allocates an IP address to a machine, then, provided that the DNS server supports the dynamic update protocol, it will inform the DNS server so that this server can update the DNS Server database.
By default, the client updates the host name "A" resource record, and the DHCP server updates the "PTR" resource record.
When the lease expires, the DHCP server deletes both of these records in the DNS database.

☛ Go into the **DHCP** console, right-click the DHCP server name and select **Properties**. Then activate the **DNS** tab.

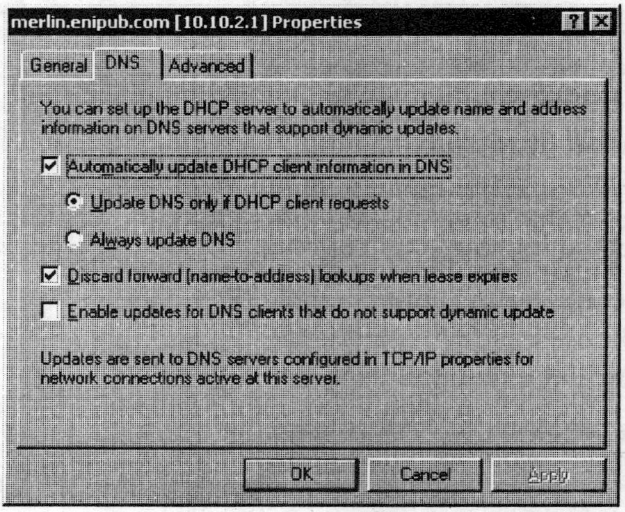

- Enable the **Automatically update DHCP client information in DNS** check box (this check box is enabled by default).
  - The **Update DNS only if DHCP client requests** option means that the DHCP server will update the PTR record, and the DHCP client will update the A record.
  - The **Always update DNS** option indicates that the DHCP server will update both records (A and PTR).

If you disable this dynamic update feature, then the DHCP clients will try to update both A and PTR records. However, if the DHCP client computer updates the PTR record, then the DHCP server will not be able to delete it. This can result in a build-up of old, out-of-date records in the DNS database.

The clients that are allowed to update their DNS records are those for which the extension 81 appears in the DHCP query frame. Windows 2000 DHCP clients have frames with this extension.

Superscopes

Superscopes, or global scopes, allow you to attribute IP addresses from several logical subnets, to DHCP clients that are situated on the same physical segment. Thereby, you can administer all the scopes that belong to the global scope, in the same way as you would administer a single scope. Superscopes are useful when you do not have enough addresses for a subnet.

You can configure a superscope as follows:

- In the **DHCP** console, right-click the server name, and select **New Superscope**.
- Enter a name for your superscope, and then click the **Next** button.

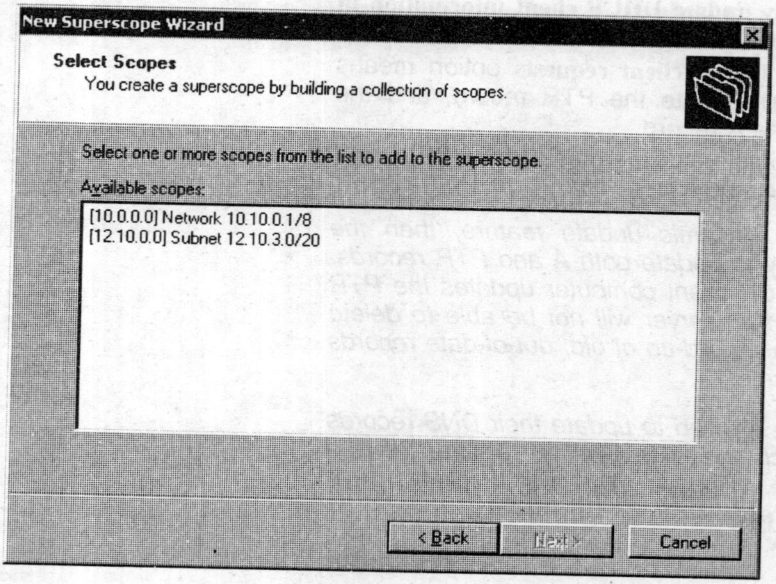

- Select the scopes that must be included in the superscope. You can use the Ctrl key in order to help you to select several scopes.
- Click the **Next** button followed by **Finish**.

Once your superscope has been created, you can add new scopes to it at any time by simply right-clicking it and selecting **New Scope**.
When you delete a superscope you do not delete the scopes that it contains.

Multicast scopes

The Windows 2000 DHCP service allows you to use class D multicast addresses (from 224.0.0.0 to 239.255.255.255). This type of address is used by videoconference type applications. The objective is to broadcast information to different clients by sending a single message. This approach also allows you to avoid using broadcasts that needlessly use the resources of all the machines.

You can create a multicast scope as follows:

- Go into the **DHCP** console, and right-click the DHCP server name.
- Select **New Multicast Scope**.

- Click the **Next** button and enter a name and a description for your multicast scope. Then click the **Next** button.
- Enter the start IP address and the end IP address, and then click the **Next** button.
- Indicate any addresses that you wish to exclude from this scope, and then click the **Next** button.
- Specify the duration of your multicast scope lease, and click **Next**. Then select the **Yes** option in order to activate your multicast scope.
- Click the **Next** button, followed by the **Finish** button.

In its properties, you can indicate a time-to-live for your multicast scope.

Multicast runs on IGMP (Internet Group Management Protocol) protocol.

Automatic private IP addressing

As with Windows 98, Windows 2000 allows you to allocate an IP address to a workstation without having to configure the workstation manually, and without even having a DHCP server. In order to do this, you must configure the client as a DHCP client in the TCP/IP properties. If no DHCP server responds then Windows 2000 will automatically apply an IP address from the range 169.254.0.1 169.254.255.254. With such an address, a machine can communicate with all the other machines to which IP addresses have been allocated using the same method. In order to prevent the same address being allocated to several machines, when a machine generates an address in this way it broadcasts it. Then, if no computer responds then the machine will apply the address. The DHCP client will continue to use this address for as long as it does not detect a DHCP server on the network.

Automatic private addressing provides only an IP address and its mask. It does not provide any other information. Because of this, clients that have obtained such an address are able to communicate only with machines that have received an address by the same mechanism, and that are located on the same network segment.

*You can use the registry in order to deactivate the allocation of an automatic private address. In order to do this you must reset the **IPAutoconfigurationEnable** value of the **REG_DWORD** type, to zero. This value is located under **KKLM\SYSTEM\CurrentControlSet\Services\Tcpip\Parameters\Interfaces\Network_Inter-face_Card_GUID**.*

7. DHCP relay agent

DHCP clients obtain a lease by broadcasting for a DHCP server. If you have several network segments that are separated by routers, then you must normally have one DHCP server per segment. However, you can overcome this constraint by having a server that acts as a DHCP relay agent.

A DHCP relay agent must be configured with a static IP address, and it must know the IP address of the DHCP server. It interprets the DHCP broadcasts that are sent by the clients, in order to route then to the DHCP server. The DHCP server knows from which scope it must select an address to be returned to the DHCP relay agent, as the server knows the agent's IP address. When the DHCP relay agent receives this address, it broadcasts it on its segment. In this way, the DHCP relay agent is able to attribute an IP address that corresponds to its own IP address scope.

You can implement a DHCP relay agent as follows:

- Open the **Routing and Remote Access** console.
- If the routing is not active on your server, then right-click the name of your server and select **Configure and Enable Routing and Remote Access.**
- Select **Manually configured server** and then click the **Next** button.
- Click the **Finish** button in order to start the service.
- Expand the icon that represents your server, followed by the **IP Routing** folder.
- Right-click **DHCP Relay Agent,** and select **New Interface.**
- Enable the **Relay DHCP packets** check box.

*If the **DHCP Relay Agent** does not appear under **IP Routing**, then right-click the General folder and select **New Routing Protocol**. Select **DHCP Relay Agent** and click the **OK** button.*

Now, you must indicate the DHCP server to which the agent must relay the packets.

- Right-click the **DHCP Relay Agent** icon, and then select **Properties.**
- Enter the address of the DHCP Server(s).

B. Windows Internet Name Service

The WINS service (NetBIOS name server, or NBNS), resolves NetBIOS names into IP addresses. This service is an Internet standard, and it has been part of the Microsoft implementation of TCP/IP for a long time. Each Windows machine has a NetBIOS name and a host name. Therefore, you must not confuse the WINS service with the DNS service. By default, the host names correspond to the NetBIOS names of the machines. However, this is not compulsory, and these two services are complementary.

When a Windows machine starts up, it registers its name with its WINS server. Then, each WINS client can call the server so as to resolve a NetBIOS name into an IP address. For example, this happens when you start **Network Neighborhood** on Windows NT, or **My Network Places** on Windows 2000. The WINS service allows you to install DNS very easily. If DNS is unable to resolve a name, it queries the WINS server so as to resolve it. As all clients automatically register with WINS, then DNS is able to resolve all names, and you do not need manually to provide this information to the DNS server. However, it must be noted that this feature is valid only in an environment in which the machines run with NetBIOS (these are essentially Microsoft machines, and Unix machines that use SAMBA).

When a machine registers its name with its WINS server, then the WINS server consults its database so as to check that another machine has not already registered with this name. The WINS server returns to the client, a message confirming the registration. This confirmation message contains a value called TTL (*Time-To-Live*) that indicates for how long the registration will be valid. If the client does not renew its registration before the TTL elapses, then it will be deleted from the WINS server database. Similarly, when a WINS client shuts down, it informs the WINS server so that the WINS server can delete the registration.

By default, the client renews its name when half of the TTL has elapsed. Also by default, the TTL is set at six days, and the client renews its name after three days. When the client renews its name, it receives from the server a new confirmation message with a TTL of six days.

When a client needs to resolve a NetBIOS name into an IP address (after the user enters a **net view**, or a **net use** command) it must first consult its local NetBIOS cache. If the name does not appear in its cache (because the name has not previously been resolved), then it must interrogate its WINS server. If the WINS server cannot answer the query, then the client will send a broadcast so as to resolve the name.

Although the Windows 2000 WINS service is an improved version, it is compatible with pre-Windows 2000 versions. In fact, in an environment that is entirely composed of Windows 2000 components, the main name resolution method is DNS, which runs dynamically. In addition, as this book indicated at the beginning, with Windows 2000 NetBIOS is no longer compulsory, and it is quite possible to deactivate it.

1. Installing the WINS service

Before you install the WINS service, check that the WINS server has a static IP configuration.

☞ Go into the control panel, and double-click the **Add/Remove Programs** icon.

☞ Click the **Add/Remove Windows Components** icon, and then click the **Components** button.

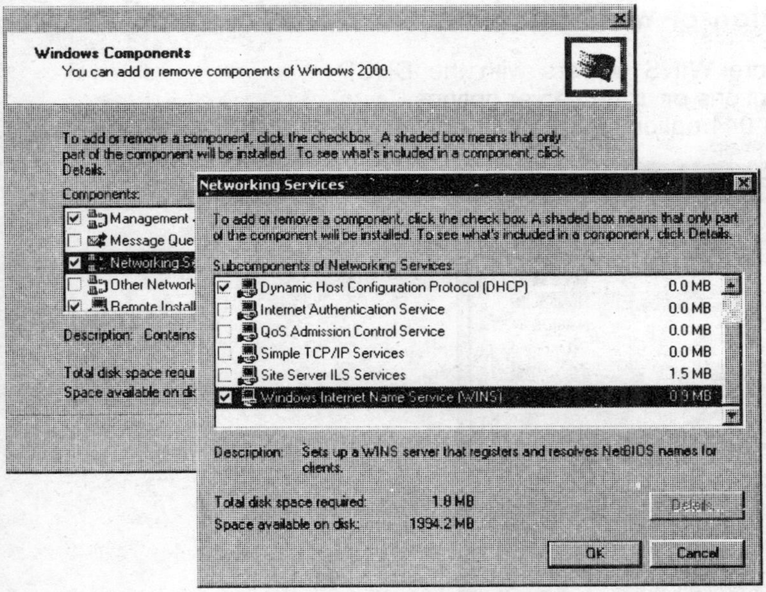

- Select **Networking Services** and then click the **Details** button.
- Enable the **Windows Internet Name Service (WINS)** check box, and then click the **OK** button, followed by the **Next** button.

2. Static configuration of WINS clients

When a machine does not use DHCP in order to obtain its IP configuration, you must manually configure the address of its WINS server(s).

- Display the TCP/IP **Properties**.
- Click the **Advanced** button.
- Click the **WINS** tab, and then click the **Add** button.
- Enter the address of the primary WINS server, and repeat the operation if you want to add other WINS servers (for fault tolerance reasons). You can add up to 12 WINS servers.

Unlike Windows NT, on Windows 2000 you do not need to restart your machine after you have configured your WINS.

3. Dynamic configuration of WINS clients

You can attribute one or more WINS servers with the DHCP console, either using scope options or using server options.
In this case you must add the 044 option and the 046 option:

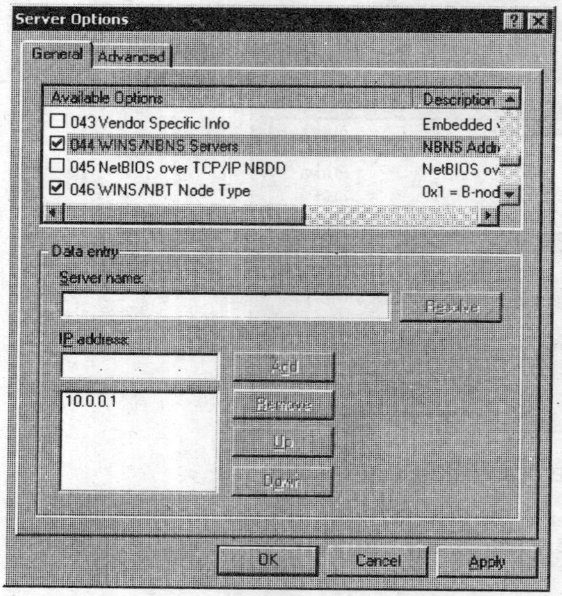

☞ Enable the **044 WINS/NBNS Servers** check box, and indicate the IP address(es) of the WINS server(s).

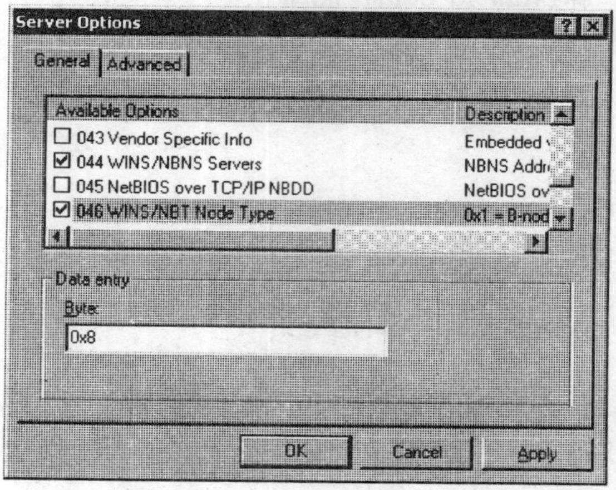

- Enable the **046 WINS/NBT Node Type** check box and indicate the value that corresponds to the node type that you want to assign to the client for name resolution:
  - **0x1: B-node**. Clients will use broadcasts in order to resolve NetBIOS names into IP addresses.
  - **0x2: P-node**. Clients will use a name server so as to register, and so as to resolve NetBIOS names into IP addresses.
  - **0x4: M-node**. With mixed mode, clients will first try broadcasting. Then, if this is not enough, they will use a name server.
  - **0x8: H-node**. With hybrid mode, clients will use a name server, followed by a broadcast, if necessary.

*The node type corresponds to an entry in the registry database in **HKLM\System\CurrentControlSet\Services \Netbt\ Parameters**. This is the NodeType value, which has a **REG_DWORD** type.*

4. Configuring static entries

If you have any non-WINS clients in your network, then you can register them manually in the WINS database so that their names can be resolved.

- Open the **Administrative Tools** menu and then activate the **WINS** console.

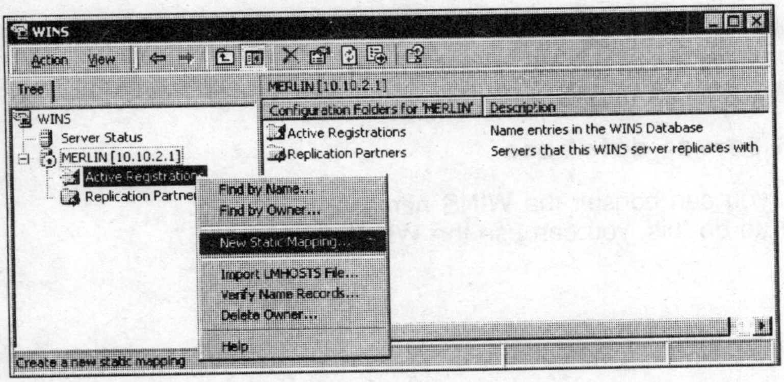

- Right-click the **Active Registrations** folder and select **New Static Mapping**.

Network services

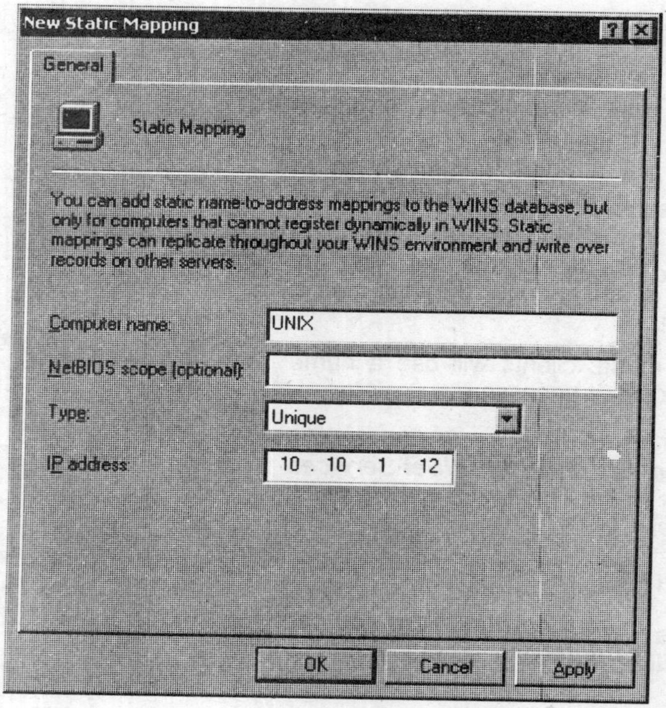

☞ Enter the name of the machine along with its IP address, and then click the **OK** button.

As the name implies, it must be noted that static mappings are not dynamic! Consequently, they must be updated as soon as any change occurs.

5. Displaying the WINS Server database

As the network administrator, you can consult the WINS names database at any time. In order to do this, you can use the **WINS** console.

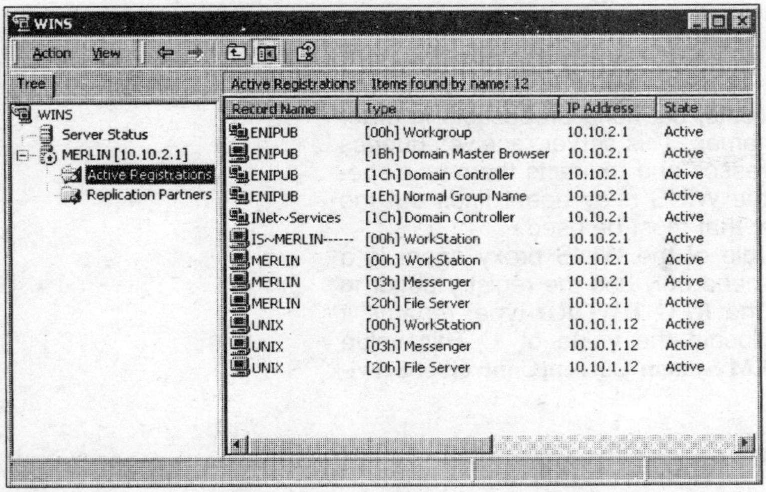

You can make searches by right-clicking the **Active Registrations** folder.

This console allows you to find out which network resources the machines are using. For example, when a workstation registers with its WINS server, in addition to its NetBIOS name and its IP address, it registers a NetBIOS name that corresponds to the server service and to the workstation service of the machine. This service is identified by the 16th byte of the NetBIOS name. Here is the list of the main NetBIOS names:

- computer_name [00h]: the name that is registered for the workstation service of the WINS client.
- computer_name [03h]: the name that is registered for the Messenger Service on the WINS client.
- computer_name [20h]: the name that is registered for the Server Service on the WINS client.
- user_name [03h]: the name of the user who logged on to the computer. The 16th byte of this record has the value of 03h. The net send command uses this record in order to send a message to a user.
- domain_name [1Bh]: the name of the domain that is registered by the domain controller that is acting as Domain Master Browser.

6. Using a WINS proxy agent

The WINS relay agent, or WINS proxy agent, is used when NetBIOS clients are not WINS clients, but send broadcasts in order to resolve IP addresses into names. This server receives queries to resolve names into IP addresses and redirects them to a specific WINS server. Thereby, the WINS relay agent finds out the IP address of the WINS server that must be used.

The machine that plays the role of the WINS proxy agent is a client of a WINS server. You need only use the registry editor in order to create a value with the **REG_DWORD** type, rename it as **EnableProxy**, and then allocate the value of **1**. This value must be situated in **HKLM\System\CurrentControlSet\Services\NetBT\ Parameters.**

7. Replication partners

You can add a replication as follows:

- Open the **WINS** console. Right-click **Replication Partners** and then select **New Replication Partner**.

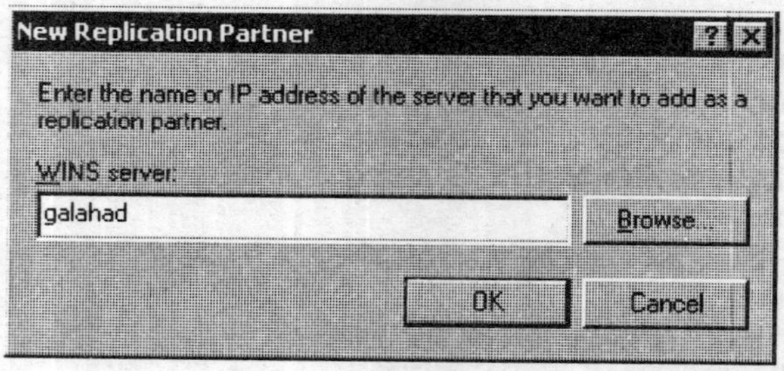

- Enter the name or the IP address of the server that you wish to add as a replication partner (a name can be used only if the LMHOSTS file contains the necessary information, or if the WINS server is in the same network).
- When you click **OK**, the replication partner server appears in the list in the right-hand pane of the **WINS** console.

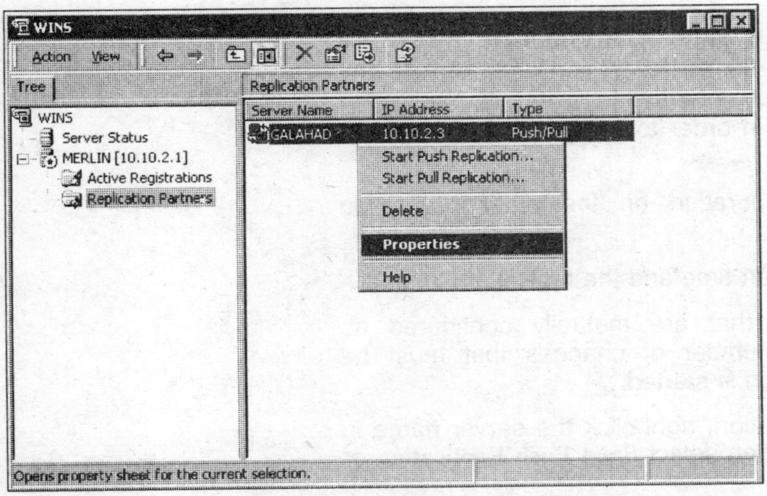

☛ Right-click this list entry, and select **Properties** so as to set up the role that the server must play in the replication (by default it is a **Push/Pull** server).

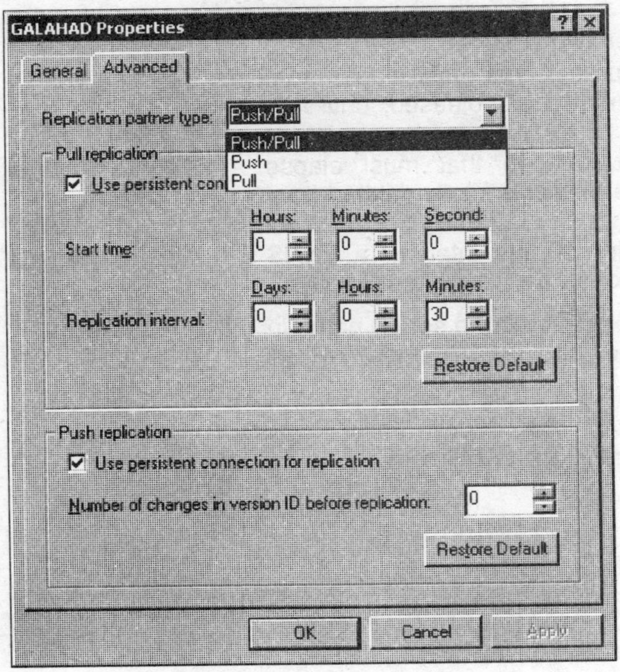

- Activate the **Advanced** tab, and select **Push/Pull** so that this server will send notifications to the other WINS server, and so that it will also obtain information when its replication partner sends it a query in order to notify it that a modification has been made.
- Carry out the same operation on the other replication partner.
- Indicate the replication start time and the replication interval.
- For replication partners that are mutually configured as **Push/Pull**, indicate the number of changes that must be made before the replication is started.
- In order to force a replication, right-click the server name in the **WINS** console, and then select **Start Push Replication** or **Start Pull Replication.**

8. Setting up the WINS server

You can configure a set of intervals for a WINS server:

- **Renew interval**: This is the **Time-To-Live** value (the frequency with which a WINS client must renew its name).
- **Extinction interval**: This is the duration that must elapse from the moment when an entry is marked as released, until it is marked as extinct.
- **Extinction timeout**: This is the duration that must elapse before an entry that is marked as extinct is finally deleted from the database.
- **Verification interval**: Upon expiry of this interval, a WINS server will check that the names of its partners are still active.

In order to configure these settings, right-click the server name in the **WINS** console, select **Properties** and activate the **Intervals** tab.

*You can stop and restart the WINS service by right-clicking the server name in the **WINS** console.*

C. Remote access

Windows 2000 allows users to access a company's network remotely (from a hotel, or from home, for example). You can configure a Windows 2000 server so that it will act as a remote access server and a VPN server. On the client side, the user will connect to the server using the remote access client. The two sides must be linked using a communications medium that is suitable for remote communication. Therefore, a WAN link must be used. This can be a Switched Telephone Network (STN), an Integrated Services Digital Network (ISDN), an X25 medium (packet switching), a frame relay (frame switching) or an Asynchronous Transfer Mode (ATM) connection. You can even use a serial cable in order to link together the two computers. A WAN link communication protocol must be used on this physical medium. With Windows 2000, you can use PPP, Microsoft RAS, ARAP and SLIP protocols.

1. Transport methods

In order to send data between the remote client and the server, you must encapsulate it in a suitable protocol.

WAN link protocol

You need a specific protocol in order to transmit information across remote links. Microsoft allows you to use several protocols:

- **SLIP** (*Serial Line Internet Protocol*): You must use this protocol in order to connect to a SLIP server via a modem. This is an old communication standard that is used in UNIX environments. It was originally written in order to support low throughput networks. It does not support automatic negotiation of the network configuration and can encapsulate only the IP. It does not support encrypted authentication either.

Windows 2000 includes a SLIP client but it does not support the role of SLIP server as this lacks the security and the efficiency of PPP.

- **PPP** (*Point to Point Protocol*): This is an improvement on SLIP. Unlike SLIP, which supports only IP, PPP allows you to encapsulate other protocols such as IPX/SPX, and NetBEUI, in addition to TCP/IP. The great advantage of PPP is that it is not a proprietary protocol. Because of this, any client that supports PPP can connect to a Windows 2000 remote access server.

Network Services

– **Microsoft RAS**: This proprietary protocol allows Windows for Workgroups clients, Windows NT 3.1 clients, MS-DOS clients and Lan Manager clients that use NetBEUI protocol to access a Windows 2000 remote access server. The Windows 2000 remote access server acts as a gateway for these clients in order to allow them to access the server, even if the server uses another protocol.
– **ARAP**: Windows 2000 can act as a remote access server for Macintosh clients. Macintosh clients use the ARAP protocol to connect to Windows 2000 servers.

Windows 2000 clients cannot connect to an ARAP remote access server.

LAN protocol

The section above describes the different protocols that allow you to set up a connection with the remote access server. Once the connection has been set up, the client uses resources as if they are located on the local network. In order to allow this, the data is encapsulated in a local network protocol. Windows 2000 allows you to use TCP/IP, Nwlink IPX/SPX, NetBEUI and Apple-Talk protocols. In turn, these LAN protocols are encapsulated into a WAN link protocol such as PPP so that they can be transmitted on the remote links.
Thereby, you can use Windows 2000 remote network access services in order to allow a client that runs the NetBEUI protocol for example, to communicate with a UNIX server that is located on the company's local network. In this way, the remote access server acts as a NetBEUI/TCP-IP gateway. However, both of these protocols must be installed on the remote access server.

Virtual Private Networks (VPN)

The main advantage of virtual private networks is that you can use them in order to connect together two computers irrespective of the physical level (LAN or WAN connection). Thereby, you can create a VPN between two machines using either the Internet, or simply the local network as the communication medium. VPNs use tunneling protocols. Windows 2000 allows you to use VPNs with PPTP or with L2TP. The purpose of these two protocols is to provide encrypted tunnels in an insecure network (such as the Internet).
– **PPTP** (*Point to Point Tunneling Protocol*): This protocol allows you to interconnect networks using an IP network.

– **L2TP** (*Layer Two Tunneling Protocol*): This protocol allows PPTP to interconnect networks when the tunnel offers a packet oriented point-to-point connection. They allow you to operate on an IP network using Frame Relay, X25, ATM, and IP Permanent Virtual Circuits (PVC).

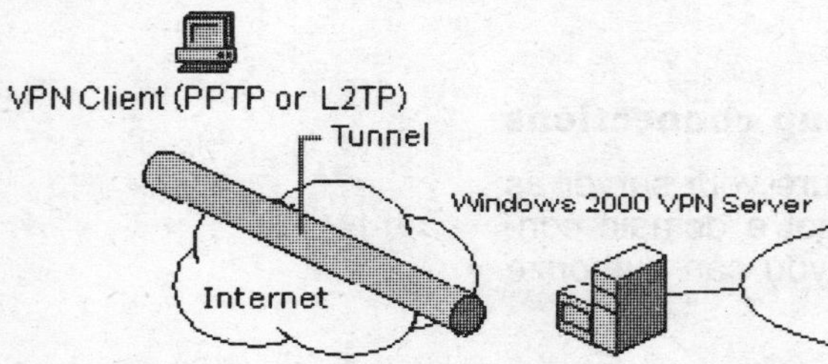

Both PPTP and L2TP use PPP protocol in order to transfer data (IP, IPX/SPX...). They provide an extra envelope for data transport via VPNs. This envelope adds headings that allow you to transport the information.
L2TP offers the following advantages:

– It allows you to compress headers (4 bytes, instead of 6 bytes with PPTP)
– It allows authentication to take place in the tunnel.

These two protocols offer different levels of security. PPTP uses the encryption that is offered by PPP. L2TP uses IPSec in order to encrypt data. However, IPSec and L2TP are totally independent from each other. You can use L2TP without IPSec.
If you use IPSec in a PPTP tunnel then the PPTP will provide authentication in the tunnel, in the same way as L2TP does.

2. Configuring a remote access server

Windows 2000 provides two utilities that allow you to configure remote network access:

– **Network and Dial-up Connections**
– and the **Routing and Remote Access** console.

You can use this console in order to configure incoming connections when your server is either a domain controller or a domain member.

If this is not the case, then you can configure both incoming and outgoing connections using the **Network Connection Wizard**. You can access the **Network Connection Wizard** by opening the **Start - Settings** menu and then selecting **Network and Dial-up Connections.**

Incoming connections

Network and dial-up connections

When you authorize incoming calls, you configure your server as a remote access server. On a server that is not a domain controller and that does not belong to a domain, you can authorize incoming calls as follows:

- Open the **Start - Settings** menu and then select **Network and Dial-up Connections.**
- Double-click the **Make New Connection** icon.
- The welcome screen of the **Network Connection Wizard** appears. Click the **Next** button.
- Select **Accept incoming connection**, and then click the **Next** button.

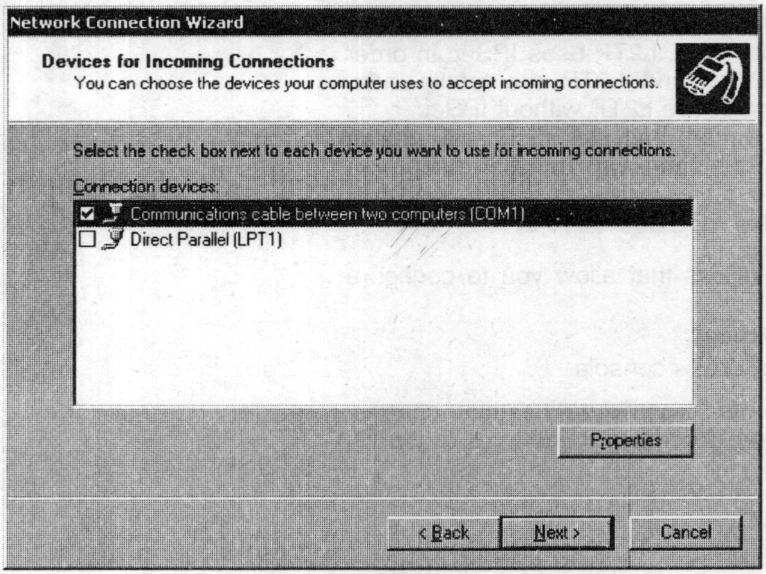

☞ Select from the list, the devices that you want to use for your incoming connections. If your modem does not appear in the list, then you can install it using the **Phone and Modem Options** program that is located in the **Control Panel**. Click **Next**.

☞ Indicate whether or not you want to allow VPN connections, and then click the **Next** button.

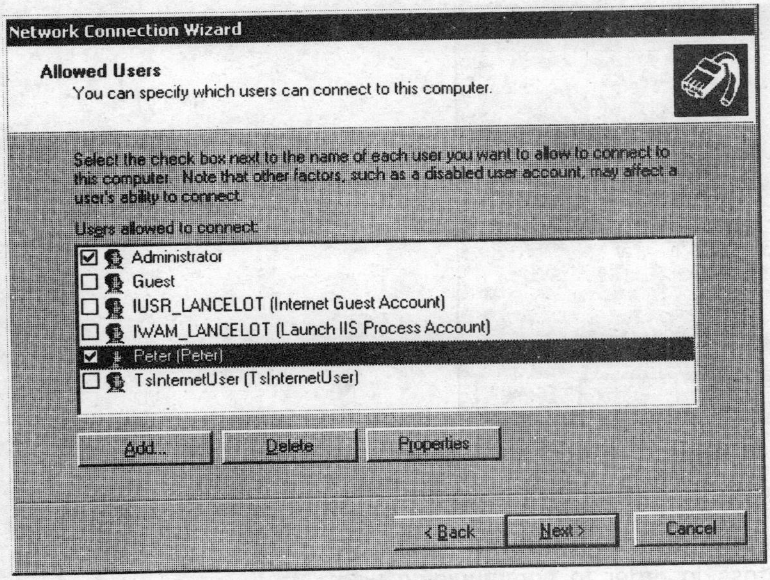

☞ Select the users that will be allowed to use the remote access. You can grant permission to other users at any time by displaying the properties of the accounts concerned, and selecting the **Dial-in** tab.

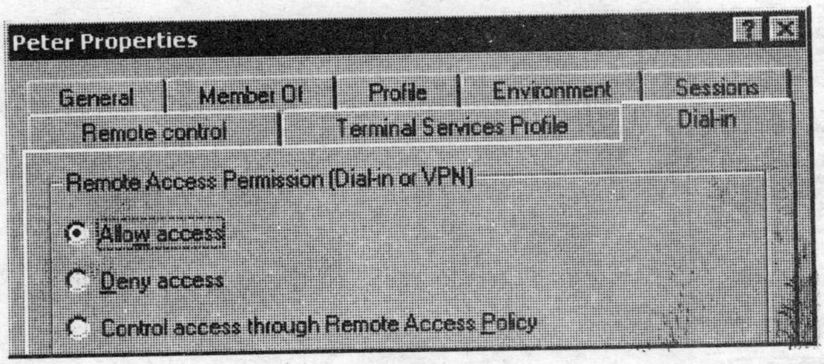

Users who dial in to a server that is not a domain controller must have an account in the SAM database of this server.

☞ The next step allows you to modify the dial-in properties, such as the LAN protocol that must be used.

Thus, you can add a new protocol, or set up the addresses that must be used by remote access clients. In order to do this, select the **TCP/IP** protocol and then click the **Properties** button.

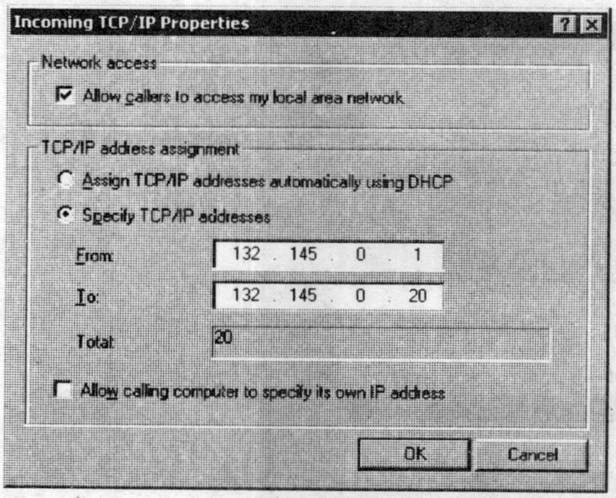

You can use DHCP in order to attribute IP addresses to remote clients automatically or to specify a range of addresses for these clients. In this case, the first address in the range will be assigned to the remote access server. This technique allows you to use a different network address in order to communicate with remote clients.

```
D:\>ipconfig /all

Windows 2000 IP Configuration

        Host Name . . . . . . . . . . . . : merlin
        Primary DNS Suffix  . . . . . . . :
        Node Type . . . . . . . . . . . . : Broadcast
        IP Routing Enabled. . . . . . . . : Yes
        WINS Proxy Enabled. . . . . . . . : No

Ethernet adapter Local Area Connection:

        Connection-specific DNS Suffix  . :
        Description . . . . . . . . . . . : Addtron AEF-380TXD PCI Fast Ethernet
 Adapter
        Physical Address. . . . . . . . . : 00-40-33-AA-02-85
        DHCP Enabled. . . . . . . . . . . : No
        IP Address. . . . . . . . . . . . : 10.0.1.30
        Subnet Mask . . . . . . . . . . . : 255.0.0.0
        Default Gateway . . . . . . . . . :
        DNS Servers . . . . . . . . . . . :

PPP adapter RAS Server (Dial In) Interface:

        Connection-specific DNS Suffix  . :
        Description . . . . . . . . . . . : WAN (PPP/SLIP) Interface
        Physical Address. . . . . . . . . : 00-53-45-00-00-00
        DHCP Enabled. . . . . . . . . . . : No
        IP Address. . . . . . . . . . . . : 132.145.0.1
        Subnet Mask . . . . . . . . . . . : 255.255.255.255
        Default Gateway . . . . . . . . . :
        DNS Servers . . . . . . . . . . . :

D:\>
```

- Click the **Next** button, and then click the **Finish** button so as to complete the operation.

Routing and Remote Access

In order to accept incoming connections on a domain controller or on a member server, you must use the **Routing and Remote Access** console.
When you use this console for the first time, you must enable the Routing and Remote Access service.

- Right-click the name of your server, and select **Configure and Enable Routing and Remote Access.**
- Click the **Next** button in the welcome window that appears.
- Select **Remote access server**, and click the **Next** button.
- Then, check the list that appears in order to make sure that it contains all the protocols that you require, and click the **Next** button.
- Indicate whether you use a DHCP server so as to assign IP addresses to your remote clients, or whether you prefer to specify a range of addresses. If you prefer the latter option, then enable **From a specified range of addresses**, and click the **Next** button.
- Click the **New** button, and then enter a start address and end address for your address range.

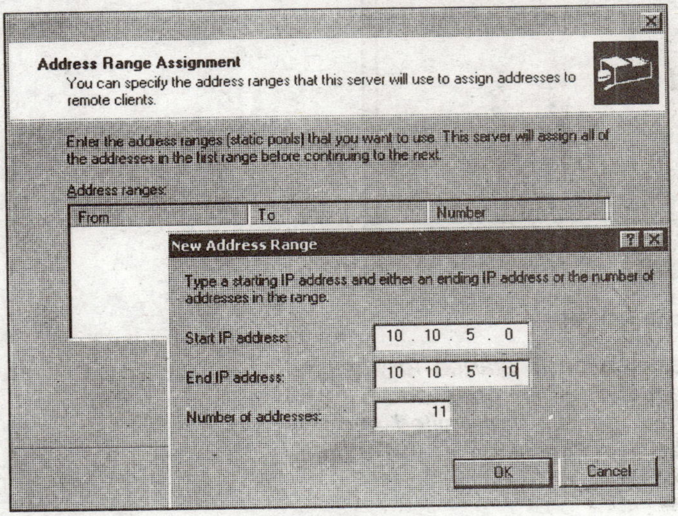

- Click the **OK** button, followed by the **Next** button.
- For the last step, you are asked if you want to install the RADIUS server. Select **No, I don't want to set up this server to use RADIUS now**, and click the **Next** button followed by the **Finish** button.

If you have used this console already for a reason other than for the remote access service (for example in order to configure a DHCP relay agent, or to configure a router), then you can configure your remote access server by right-clicking it's icon in this console and selecting ***Properties****.*

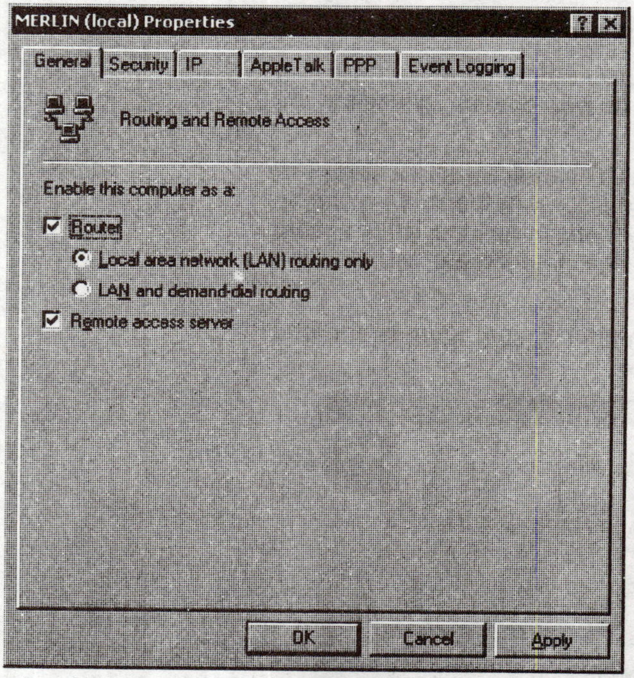

Activate the **Remote access server** check box.

When the remote access service is started for the first time, it automatically creates 5 PPTP ports and 5 L2TP ports. The number of these ports is not limited and you can configure them using the Ports icon in the ***Routing and Remote Access*** *console.*

Outgoing connections

In order to access a remote access server, you must configure an outgoing connection. You must use the **Network Connection Wizard** for this purpose. In order to access this wizard, you must open the **Start - Settings** menu, select **Network and Dial-up Connections** and double-click the **Make New Connection** icon.

You can configure three types of outgoing connections:

- Remote access connection (which covers the options, **Dial-up to private network** and **Dial-up to the Internet**).
- Connection to a virtual private network.
- Direct connection using a cable.

Remote access connection

The **Dial-up to private network** option allows remote clients to connect directly to the remote access server using a modem.
In this case you must know the telephone number of the server to which you want to connect.

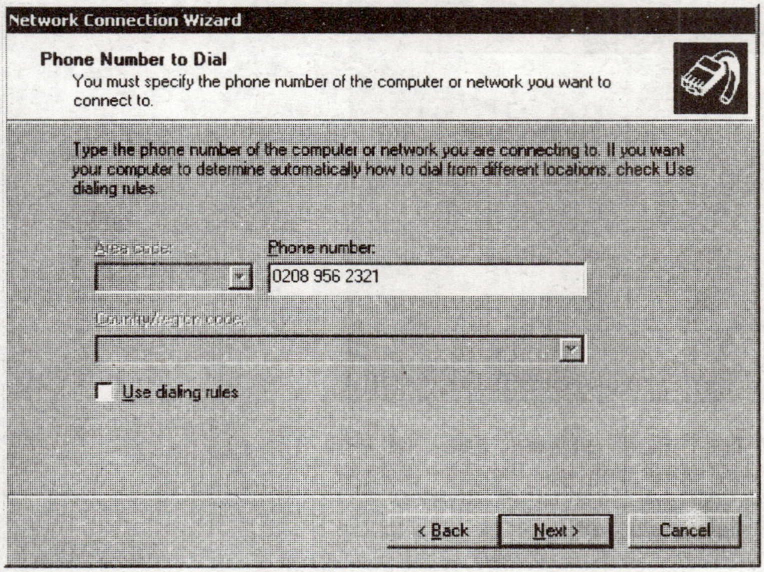

The **Dial-up to the Internet** option allows you to connect to an Internet Service Provider (ISP). The **Internet Connection Wizard** will help you to set up this connection. You can connect via your LAN, in which case you must indicate the address of your proxy server. Alternatively, you can use your modem in order to connect to your ISP.

Connecting to a Virtual Private Network (VPN)

In order to create a virtual private network you need to know only the IP address of the destination machine. Select the **Connect to a private network through the Internet** option, and then click **Next**.

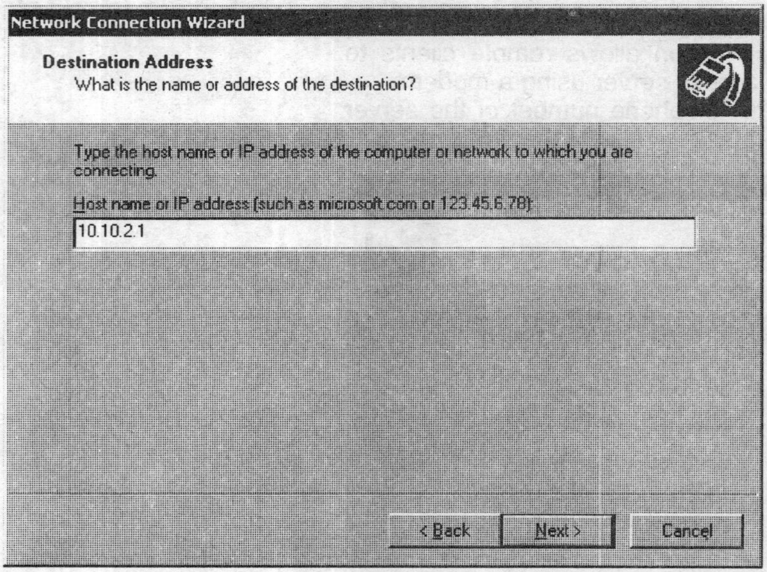

☞ Indicate the host name or the host IP address, and click the **Next** button. Then, indicate whether only you must be able to access the connection that you are creating, or whether you want to share it with other users, who will then be able to log on to your machine.

☞ The next step allows you to share this connection with other users of your LAN. Click **Next**, enter a name for this connection, and then click the **Finish** button.

The wizard creates a new icon in the **Start** menu:

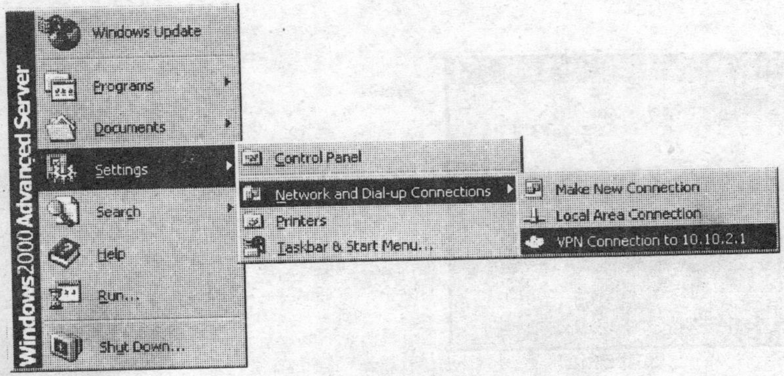

In order to connect, click the icon that represents the connection.

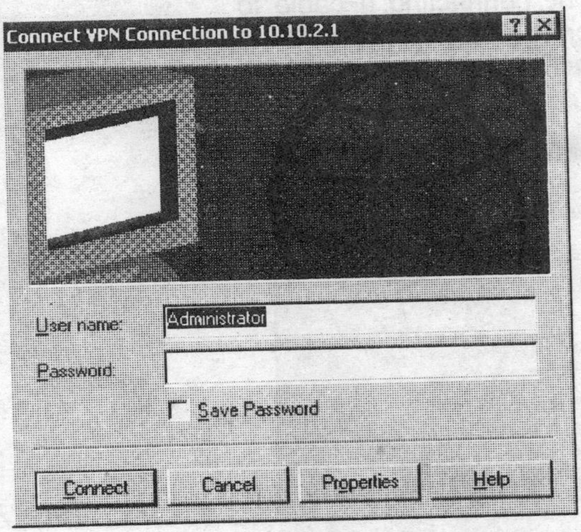

Enter a user name and a password for an account that has dial-in permission, and then click the **Connect** button.

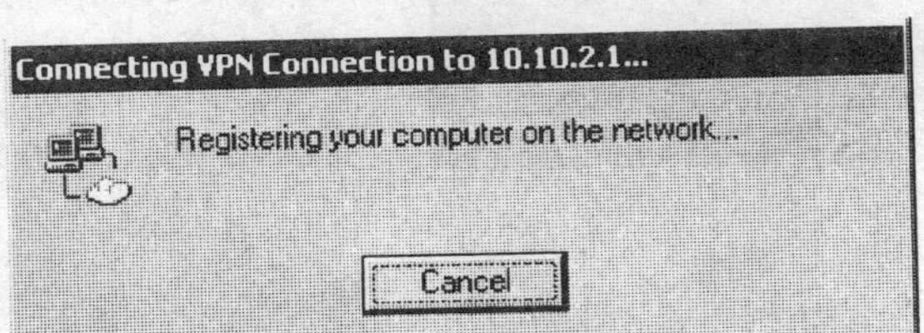

When the connection has been set up you will receive the following message:

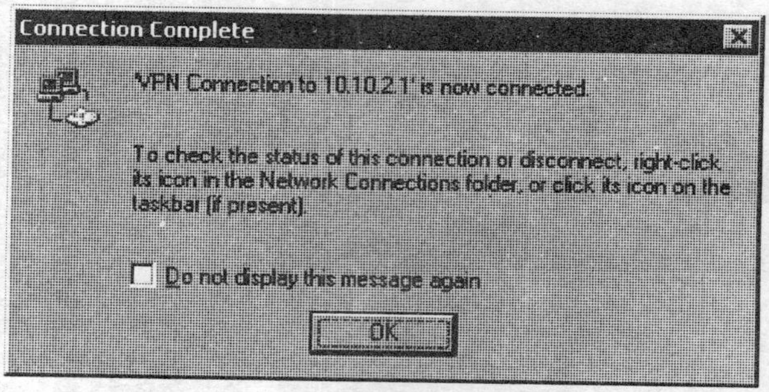

Connecting directly using a cable

You can link two computers together by connecting a cable to the serial ports, to the parallel ports or to the infrared ports. In this case, select **Connect directly to another computer**, and then click the **Next** button.

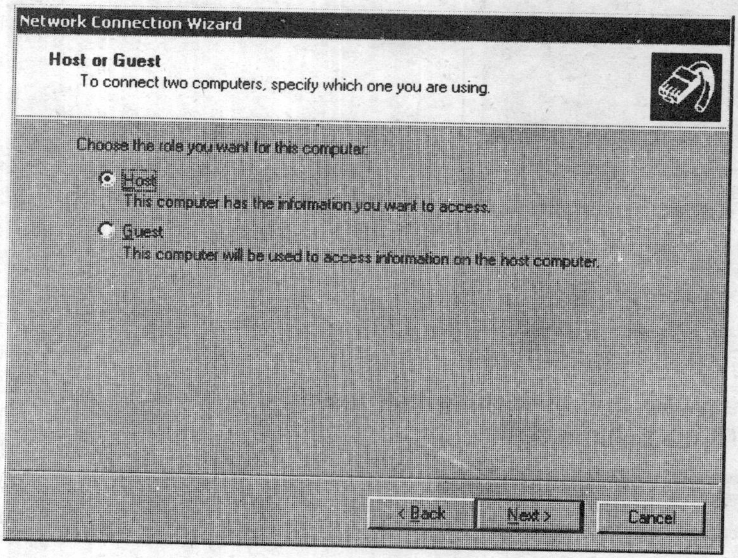

In order to make this type of connection work, then one of the computers must be configured as a **Host**, and the other computer must be configured as a **Guest**. The host computer will act as a sort of access server, and the guest computer will act as the client. With both of these configurations, you must specify the device that will be used for the connection (and also the port that will be used for the connection). In addition, for the host you must indicate the users that will be allowed to connect.

3. Authentication

When you allow remote network access connections, you must implement an authentication mechanism that will run during the logon process, so as to prevent any unauthorized people from getting into your company's network.
Logging on via a WAN takes place in three phases:

- Setting up a physical link. This first phase allows the two parties to negotiate the connection by sending LCP (*Link Control Protocol*) packets. These packets contain the connection's negotiation settings on the physical level, such as the compression, the type of authentication that is used, and whether links are shared or not.
- The second phase covers the authentication. It runs after the line has been set up, and before the network level is set up.
- When the authentication has been completed, then the network level-3 protocol that must be used (IP for example) is negotiated. NCP (*Network Control Protocol*) packets are sent for this purpose.

Here are the layers of the PPP architecture:

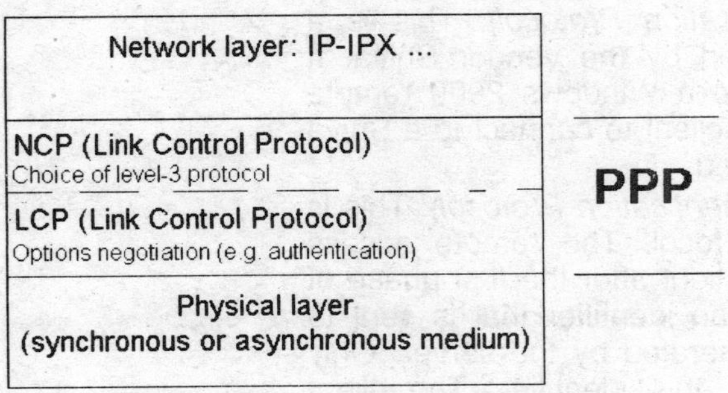

Windows 2000 supports several authentication methods that offer differing security levels. You can configure these authentication methods using the **Routing and Remote Access** console.

- Right-click the name of your remote access server and then select **Properties**.
- Select the **Security** button and then click the **Authentication Methods** button.

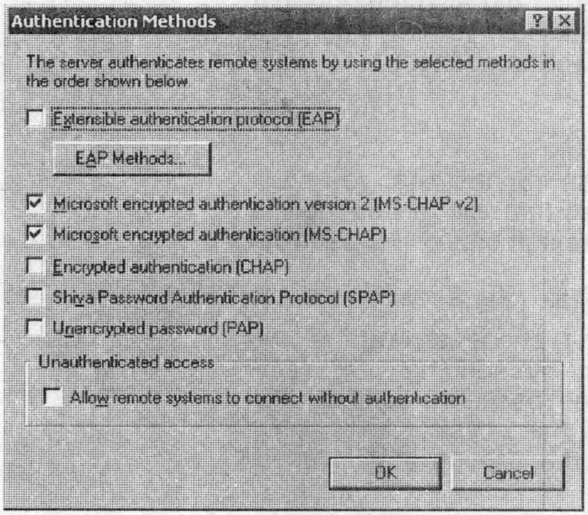

Several authentication protocols are provided:

- **PAP** (*Password Authentication Protocol*): This method is relatively simple, and not very secure. The remote client sends the password as clear text. The client sends the user name and password to the remote access server. The remote access server then checks this information against its own information.
- **SPAP** (*Shiva Password Authentication Protocol*): This is a proprietary protocol that is supplied by the vendor Shiva. It allows a Shiva client to connect to a Windows 2000 remote access server, or a Windows 2000 client to connect to a Shiva server. The passwords are encrypted.
- **CHAP** (*Challenge Handshake Authentication Protocol*): This is a sophisticated authentication protocol. The remote access server sends a "challenge" to the client after the first phase of the logon has completed. This is an identifier that is sent to the client after being randomly generated by the server. Only the remote access server knows this identifier. The client sends its password in a hashed format, together with the "challenge" that was sent by the server. This method is called hashing (it is used by MD5: *Message Digest*). The server

restores the message and checks that the password corresponds to the user name.

– **MS-CHAP** (*Microsoft Challenge Handshake Authentication Protocol*): This protocol uses the same principle as CHAP. In addition, MS-CHAP allows you to use MPPE (*Microsoft Point-to-point Protocol*) encrypting in order to secure data on PPP or PPTP links.
– **MS-CHAP version 2**: This is a development of MS-CHAP. It is more secure than MS-CHAP v1. It is the most secure authentication protocol that Windows 2000 offers. You can use this protocol only if you have Windows 2000, Windows NT 4.0 or Windows 95/98 clients.
– **EAP** (*Extensible Authentication Protocol*): This is not a single protocol. It is a set of protocols that provide other methods in order to authenticate PPP protocol. Notably, EAP is used for smart-card authentication by TLS (*Transport Layer Security*) protocol, by MD5-CHAP protocol, and by other authentication methods that have not yet been developed such as biometric recognition.

As with the MS-CHAP protocol, you can use MPPE encryption with the TLS protocol.

4. Remote access policy

The remote access server and the IAS sever use remote access policies in order to control how users log on. Unlike group policies, remote access policies are not stored in Active Directory. This means that you can apply different remote access policies on different remote access servers.
These policies are combinations of **conditions**, of **authorizations** and of a **profile**.

Conditions

The conditions of a policy are a set of attributes that allow you to decide whether or not the connection must be accepted.
You can set up conditions as follows:

☞ Open the **Routing and Remote Access** console. Right-click **Remote Access Policies**, and then select **New Remote Access Policy**.

☞ Enter a name that represents your policy, and then click the **Next** button.

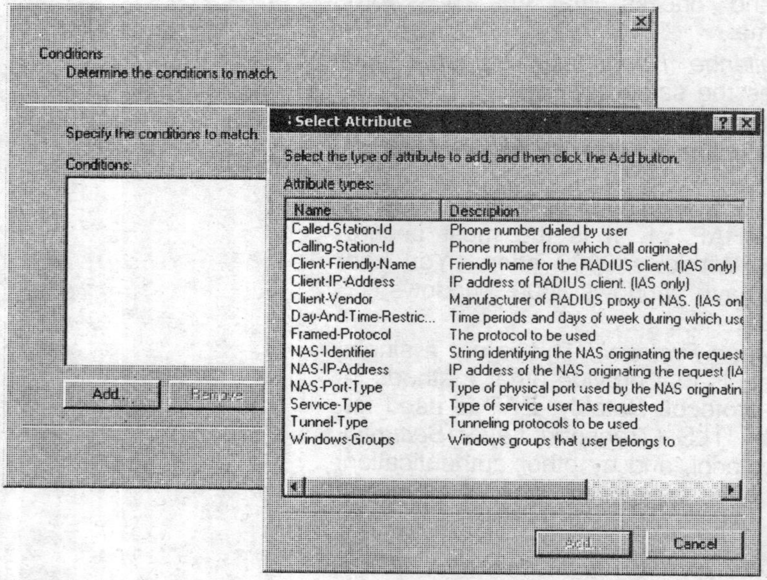

☞ Click the **Add** button, then add the attributes that you want to include in your policy. For example, you can specify the type of the connection. In order to do this select **Tunnel - Type** and then click the **Add** button.

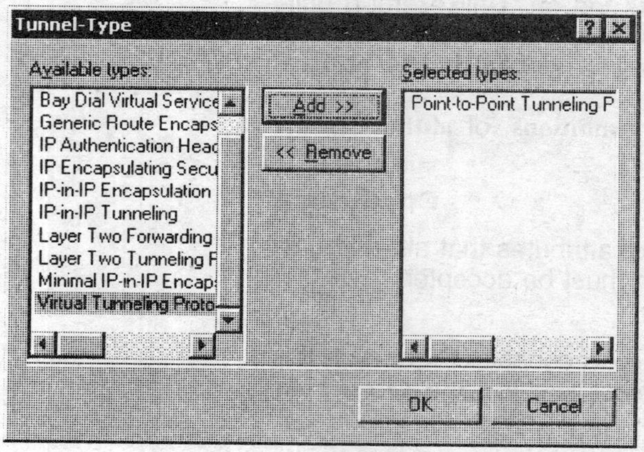

☞ Select the protocol(s) that will be used as conditions from the list in the left-hand pane, then click the **Add** button.

- Repeat the operation with all the conditions that you want to add to your policy. All the conditions that you specify will appear in the following window:

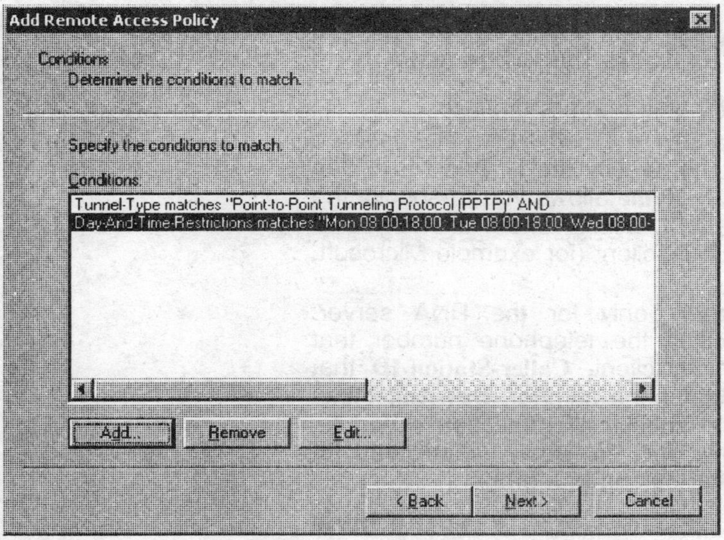

- Click the **Next** button.

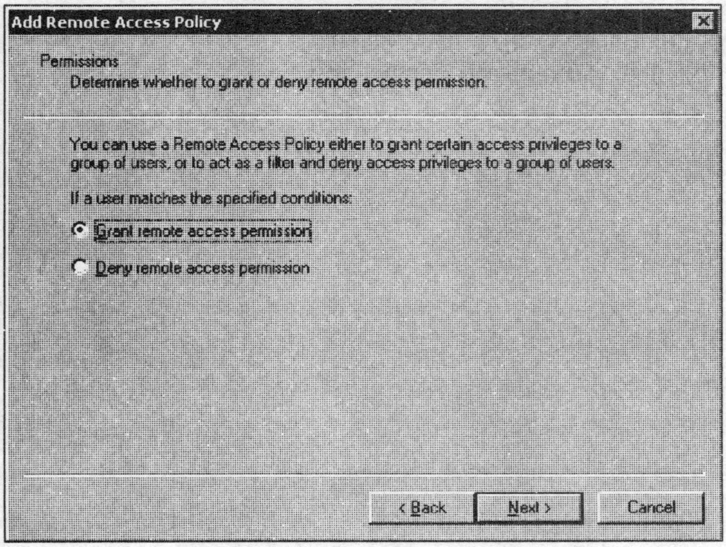

☞ Indicate whether you want to grant, or to deny, the connections that correspond to your conditions, and then click the **Next** button.

☞ Then, you can choose to edit your profile, or to click the **Finish** button. You can always modify your profile later.

Here is a list of some of the attributes that are offered:

- Attributes that you can apply only for the IAS server: **Client-IP-Address** allows you to specify the IP address of the RADIUS client, **Client-Friendly-Name** allows you to specify the name of the RADIUS client, and. Client-Vendor allows you to specify the make of the RADIUS client (for example Microsoft, Cisco, or 3COM).
- Attributes that you can apply only for the RNA server: **Calling-Station-ID** that specifies the telephone number that must be dialed by the remote client, **Caller-Station-ID** that corresponds to the caller's telephone number, **Day-And-Time-Restrictions** that allow you to specify a connection schedule, **Windows groups** that allow you to apply restrictions or authorizations to the users that belong to a group.

Authorizing

On Windows 2000 you can define remote access permissions in the properties of user accounts, and you can also define them in remote access policies.

In order to change the connection permissions for a user, display the **Properties** dialog box for the user account and select the **Dial-in** tab.

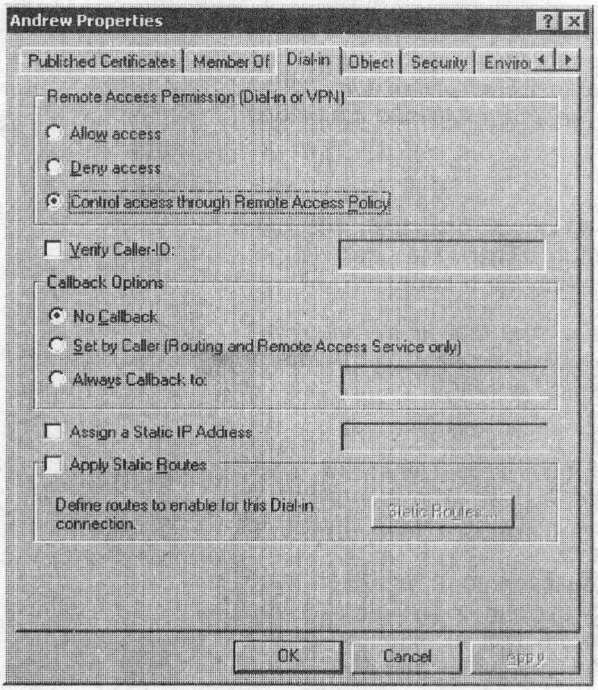

Remote Access Permission (Dial-in or VPN)

You can allow, or deny, access to a user explicitly. However, as user access permissions are defined both in the user account properties and in the remote access policies, if you explicitly allow access to a user, then the user may still not be able to connect, as this will also depend on the conditions, and on the profile of the policy. Notably, this approach allows you to grant access to a group of users, but to deny access to one specific user who is a member of this group. In order to do this, you must specify the **Windows Groups** attribute as a condition of the remote access policy, and then explicitly **Deny access** to the user in the properties dialog box for the user account concerned. For the other members in the group, you can explicitly **Allow access** in their user account properties, or you can simply allow them access using the remote access policy.

The **Control access through Remote Access Policy** is available only for user accounts in a domain that is in **native mode**. It allows you to grant or to deny access according to the permissions that are defined in the remote access policy.

The permissions that are defined at remote access policy level correspond to the **Grant remote access permission** *option or to the* **Deny remote access permission** *option according to whether or not the users fulfill the conditions of the policy.*

Verifying Caller-ID

If you activate the **Verify Caller-ID** check box, then you can specify the caller's telephone number. Then, the user will not be able to connect from another telephone number.

Use this option only if you are sure that all the elements of your connection will accept the caller ID. If this is not the case then the connection will fail.

Callback Options

Callback options allow you to call back a user when the user tries to connect. This option allows a user, who is working at home, to connect to the company network without having to meet the communication expenses.

In addition, you can force the callback to a predetermined number. This provides an additional level of security, as you will be sure that user who is connecting is situated on the specified number. If this is not the case, then the connection will fail.

IP routing

You can assign an IP address to a user that connects to the remote access server by activating the **Assign a Static IP Address** check box. For example, if you apply the following settings for a user:

Then, when the user connects, his/her IP settings will be as follows:

```
Microsoft Windows 2000 [Version 5.00.2195]
(C) Copyright 1985-1999 Microsoft Corp.

D:\>ipconfig

Windows 2000 IP Configuration

        Connection-specific DNS Suffix  . :
        IP Address. . . . . . . . . . . . : 10.0.1.38
        Subnet Mask . . . . . . . . . . . : 255.0.0.0
        Default Gateway . . . . . . . . . :

PPP adapter Virtual Private Connection:

        Connection-specific DNS Suffix  . :
        IP Address. . . . . . . . . . . . : 192.145.0.15
        Subnet Mask . . . . . . . . . . . : 255.255.255.255
        Default Gateway . . . . . . . . . : 192.145.0.15

D:\>
```

You can also update the routing table of the remote client by adding static routes that the client may need. In order to do this, you must activate the **Apply Static Routes** check box.

When you are in mixed mode you cannot check the caller's ID, as the options that allow you to assign IP addresses and static routes are not available. Neither can you control access via the remote access policy.

Profile

You can set up profiles using the **Routing and Remote Access** console. A profile allows you to specify the connection settings that must be applied to the client, once the conditions have been validated.

- Go into the **Routing and Remote Access** console and select **Remote Access Policies**.
- In the right-hand pane, right-click the policy for which you want to modify the profile.
- Select **Properties** and then click the **Edit Profile** button.

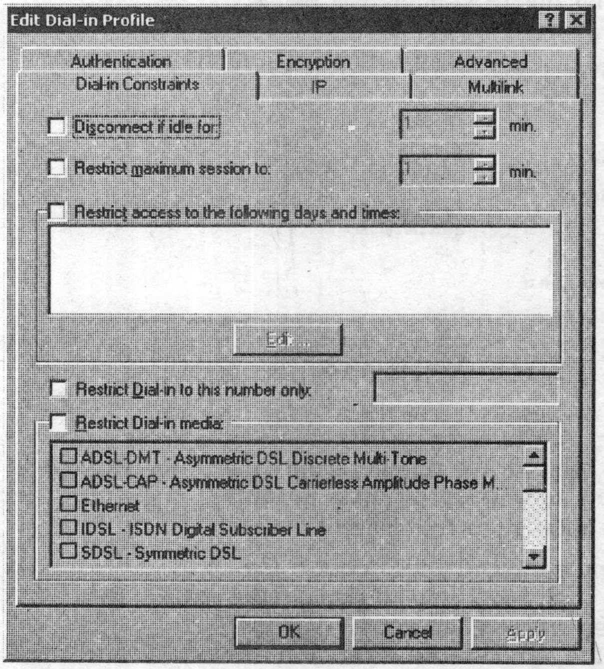

Dial-in Constraints

Using this tab you can specify how long users can stay connected, and you can indicate the idle time that must elapse before a session is disconnected. You can also restrict access during certain time periods, to a certain telephone number, and to a certain types of media (such as X25, Ethernet, VPN, or ISDN).

IP (Filtering IP traffic)

Using the **IP** tab, you can filter packets that come from clients, or that go to clients. You can apply these filters according to the type of protocol (for example, ICMP, UDP, or TCP). You can apply these filters either according to the port number of the source, or according to the port number of the destination. This tab also allows you to configure the way in which IP addresses must be assigned to clients.

Authentication

You can use the **Authentication** tab in order to specify the protocol that must be used for connections that use this policy. The protocol that you select must be configured in the properties of the server.

Encryption

The **Encryption** tab allows you to specify the type of encryption that must be used for connections that use this policy. You can apply two different types of encryption:

- MPPE (*Microsoft Point-to-Point Encryption*), which is used by PPP and PPTP connections.
- IPSec (*IP Security*), which is used by VPN L2TP connections.

Enable the **Basic** check box in order to activate 56-bit DES encryption for IPSec and 40-bit encryption for MPPE.

Enable the **Strong** check box in order to activate 56-bit DES encryption for IPSec and 56-bit encryption for MPPE.

Multilink

Windows 2000 allows you to use several physical links in order to create a single logical link, so that you can increase the bandwidth. You can use this feature only if PPP Multilink Protocol has been installed on both the server, and on the clients. In order to allow multilinks, go into the **Routing and Remote Access** console, display the **Properties** of the server, activate the **PPP** tab, and enable the **Multilink connections** check box. Windows 2000 has improved the basic principles of multilinks by adding the BAP (*Bandwidth Allocation Protocol*). This protocol allows you to allocate bandwidth dynamically according to needs. This protocol then, allocates bandwidth on demand. BAP runs in combination with PPP.

Consequently, the **Multilink** tab allows you to set up the BAP protocol.

Application order of conditions, permissions and profile

When you try to connect, the system consults policy conditions first, followed by the permissions, and finishes with the profile. The following diagram illustrates the different phases of setting up a connection.

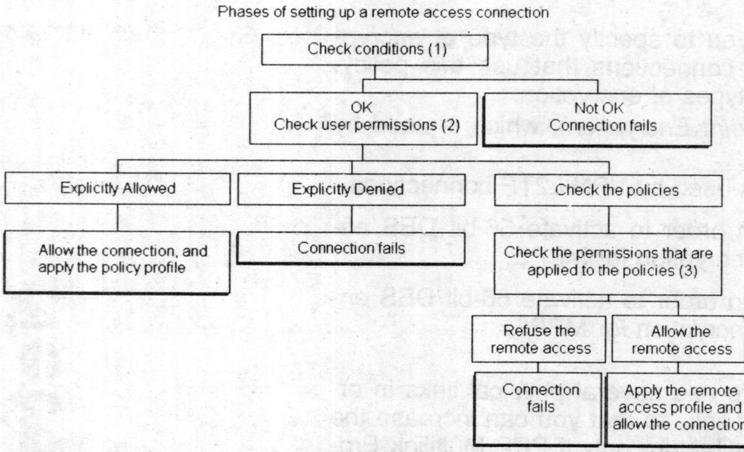
Phases of setting up a remote access connection
Check conditions (1)
OK
Check user permissions (2)
Not OK
Connection fails
Explicitly Allowed
Explicitly Denied
Check the policies
Allow the connection, and apply the policy profile
Connection fails
Check the permissions that are applied to the policies (3)
Refuse the remote access
Allow the remote access
Connection fails
Apply the remote access profile and allow the connection

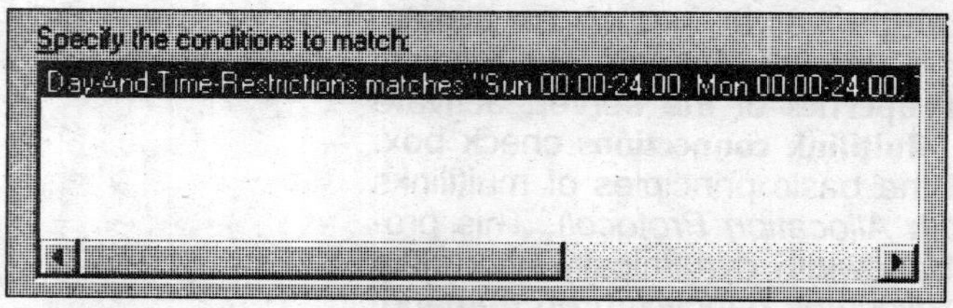
Specify the conditions to match:
Day-And-Time-Restrictions matches "Sun 00:00-24:00; Mon 00:00-24:00;

(1)

Remote Access Permission (Dial-in or VPN)
Allow access
Deny access
Control access through Remote Access Policy

(2)

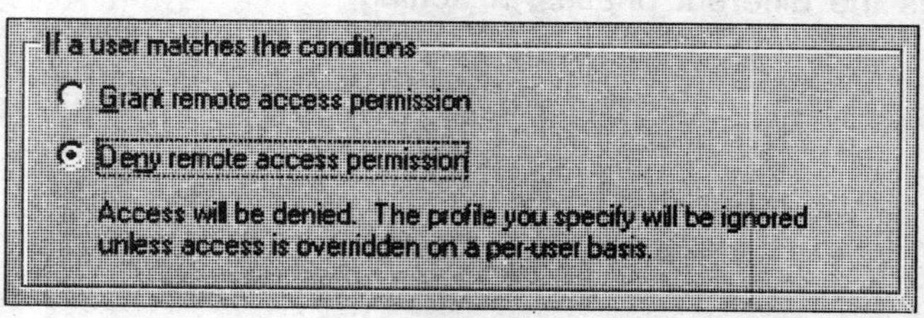
If a user matches the conditions
Grant remote access permission
Deny remote access permission
Access will be denied. The profile you specify will be ignored unless access is overridden on a per-user basis.

(3)

When you install the **Routing and Remote Access** service, then you create a policy by default. This policy refuses access for all uses that have **Control access through Remote Access Policy** Control access through Remote Access Policy permission. In fact, the default policy stipulates that connections will be refused 24 hours a day. Consequently, in order to allow users to connect, either you must grant explicit permission in the **Dial-in** tab of their account **Properties** dialog box, or you must change the policy. This rule applies only if your domain is in native mode. It does not apply in mixed mode because users cannot have **Control access through Remote Access Policy** permission in mixed mode. However, remote access policies will still be applied in a mixed mode domain, as even if you explicitly allow users to connect, then they will still have to fulfill the policy conditions in order to be able to connect.

*When you change from mixed mode to native mode, then the explicit **Deny access** permissions become **Control access** through Remote Access Policy permissions, and the explicit Allow access permissions stay the same.*

You can create several remote access policies. However, if you do this you must ensure that all the users who must have remote access are in accordance with at least one of the policies.

Backing up, restoring and troubleshooting

A. **Backing up** **326**

1. Backing up data **326**
2. Backing up the system state **330**
3. Scheduling **330**

B. **Restoring** **331**

1. Restoring data **331**
2. Restoring the system state **333**

C. **Troubleshooting** **335**

1. Startup steps **335**
2. Contents of the BOOT.INI. sections **337**
3. Last known good configuration **338**
4. Starting from a floppy disk **338**
5. Using an emergency repair disk **339**
6. Other startup options **339**
7. Recovery console **340**

↓ personal notes ↓

A. Backing up

Windows 2000 provides a tool that allows you to backup and to restore system data (such as the Active Directory, and the registry). This utility is called **Backup** and is located in the **Start - Programs - Accessories - System Tools** menu. The Backup utility is very easy to use and provides a graphic interface that is very user friendly and intuitive. Not only does it allow you to backup and to restore, but also it allows you to schedule these activities. This tool has been greatly improved since the Ntbackup tool of Windows NT 4.0.
You can backup to tape devices, to logical drives, to removable disks or to CD-ROM writer drives. You can backup from volumes that are formatted either in FAT.i.FAT; or in NTFS.
You can backup and restore manually. Alternatively, you can use a wizard that will guide you step by step through the procedure of creating the necessary jobs. This wizard also allows you to create an emergency repair disk.
It is, of course, extremely important that you back up regularly, system data, and other essential information. In addition, it is just as important that you test your backups. You must regularly carry out restore tests, so as to be sure that your storage devices will operate correctly on the day when you need to restore.

1. Backing up data

Every file and every folder has an archive attribute. When this attribute is set, it indicates that the file or the folder has not been modified since the last backup. When you modify a file, the system sets this attribute, and will backup this file when it runs the next backup procedure.
You can access this attribute by opening the properties of the file, or of the folder, and then clicking the **Advanced** button.

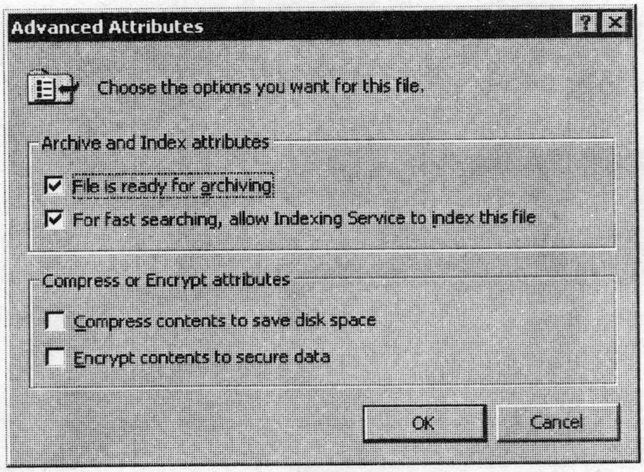

If the **File is ready for archiving** check box is enabled, then the archive attribute is set. If this attribute is disabled for a file or a folder then the system will automatically enable it when you modifiy the file or the folder.

You can make five types of backup:

Normal
: Backs up all the files that you have selected and sets their archive attribute.

Copy
: Backs up all the files that you have selected and does not set their archive attribute.

Incremental
: Backs up all the files that you have selected that have been modified since the last backup. This type of backup sets the archive attribute.

Differential
: Backs up all the files that you have selected that have been modified since the last backup. This type of backup does not set the archive attribute.

Daily
: Backs up all the files that have been modified during the day that the backup is made. This type of backup does not set the archive attribute.

A differential backup takes longer than an incremental backup. However, a differential backup takes less time to restore than an incremental backup.

In order to back up data you must carry out the following steps:

- Go into the **Start - Programs - Accessories - System Tools** menu, and then select **Backup**.

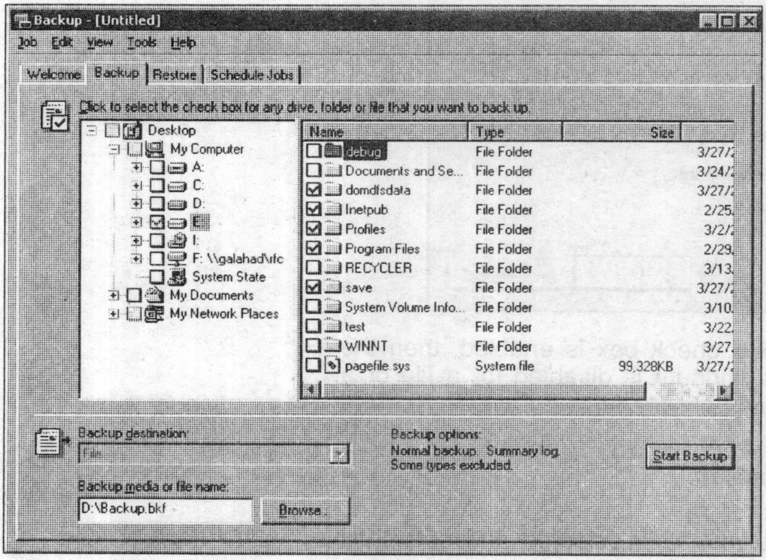

- Activate the **Backup** tab, and then select the folders and the files that you want to back up.
- Open the **Tools** menu and select **Options**.
- Activate the **Backup Type** tab and select the backup type that you want to implement.
- The **Backup Log** tab allows you to specify the level of detail that you want to log during the backup process.
- Click the **OK** button.
- Enter the name of the backup file, along with the identification of the drive onto which you want to back up.

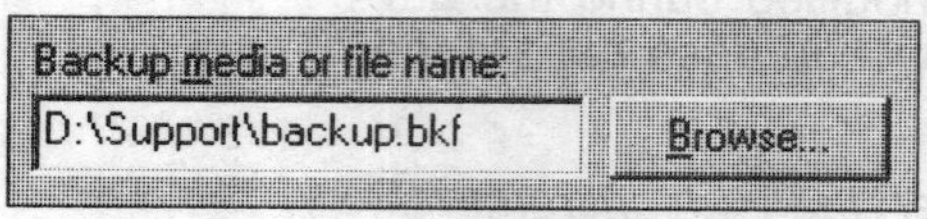

- Click the **Start** button in order to start the backup.

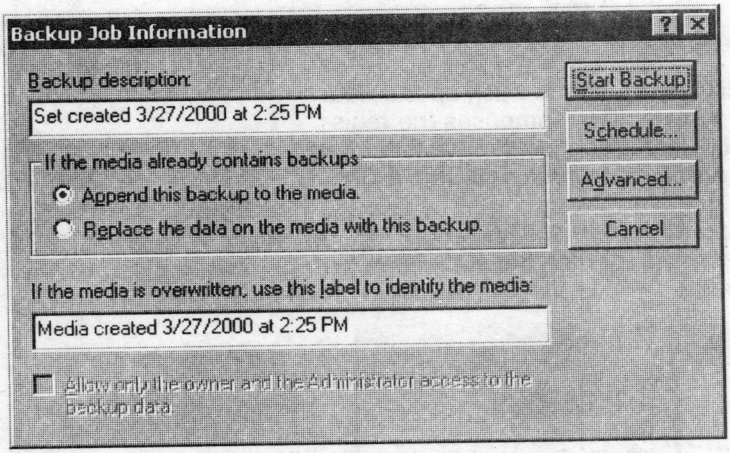

- Enter a description for your backup (the description by default includes the creation date and time). The **Advanced** button allows you to select the backup type. This button is useful if you have not already selected the backup type using the **Tools** menu.
- Click the **Start Backup** button. When your backup has finished it is represented by an icon.

If you back up NTFS files, the NTFS permissions that are associated with the files and the folders will be maintained when these files and folders are restored onto an NTFS partition. Similarly, files that have been encrypted will remain encrypted after you have restored them.

Before you carry out your backup, make sure that nobody is using the files that you have selected. The backup process will ignore any files that are being used. These files will be indicated in the backup log. Nevertheless, Windows 2000 can backup files that are being used by the system when it backs up the System State.

2. Backing up the system state

The Windows 2000 Backup utility allows you to back up the data that concerns the state of your system. This comprises the registry database, the system startup files, the Active Directory, the sysvol files, the certificates service database and the COM+ Class Registration database.
You cannot back up these components individually.
In order to back up these components, go into the **Backup** utility, and activate the **System State** check box.

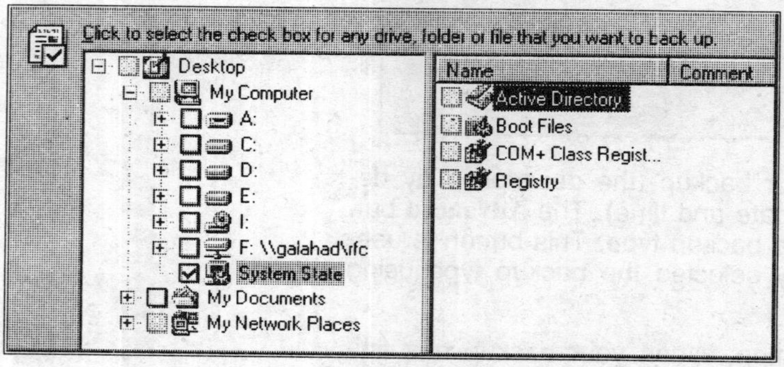

3. Scheduling

One of the improvements that the Windows 2000 Backup utility offers, with respect to the Windows NT version, is that Windows 2000 Backup allows you to schedule your backup jobs, using a graphic interface.

- Click **Schedule Jobs**, in the **Backup** utility.
- Click the **Add Job** button in order to start the Backup Wizard.
- Follow the steps of the Backup Wizard.

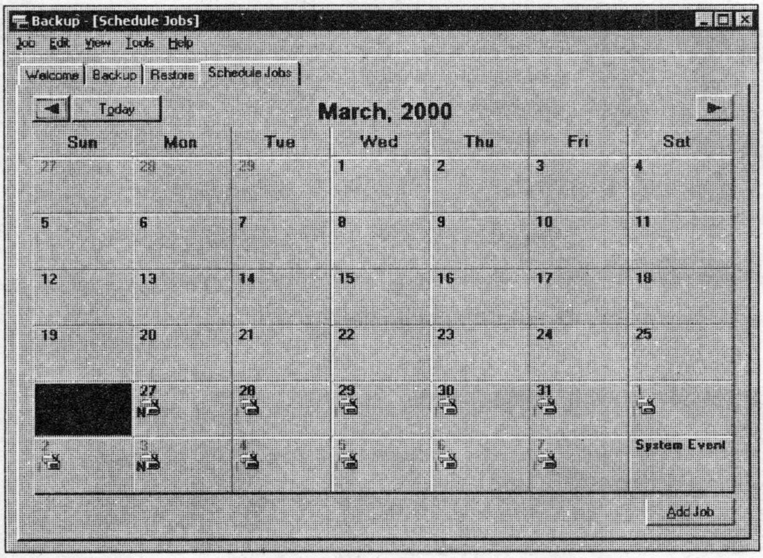

In this schedule, the system will carry out a normal backup every Monday, and an incremental backup every other day of the week.

B. Restoring

1. Restoring data

In order to restore data, you can use the Restore Wizard, or you can restore manually. For this purpose, activate the **Restore** tab in the **Backup** utility. Then, select the backup that you want to restore. If no backup media appear in the list, then this is probably because you have deleted the catalog that corresponds to the media catalog by selecting **Delete Catalog** from the **Tools - MediaTools** menu. In this case you must import the catalog that corresponds to the backup. You can do this by opening the **Tools** menu and then selecting **Catalog a backup file**.

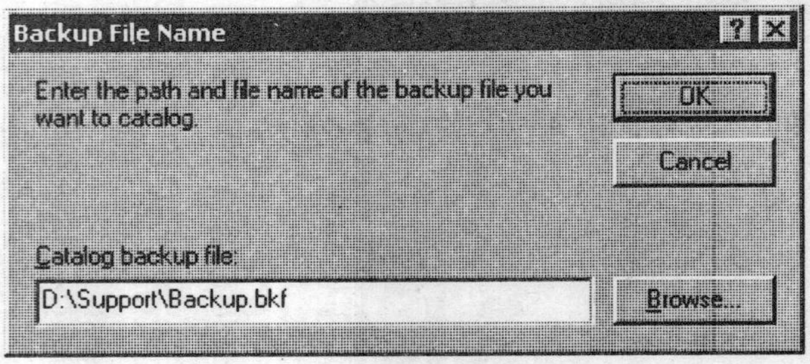

☞ Enter the name of the path that leads to your backup files and then click **OK**.

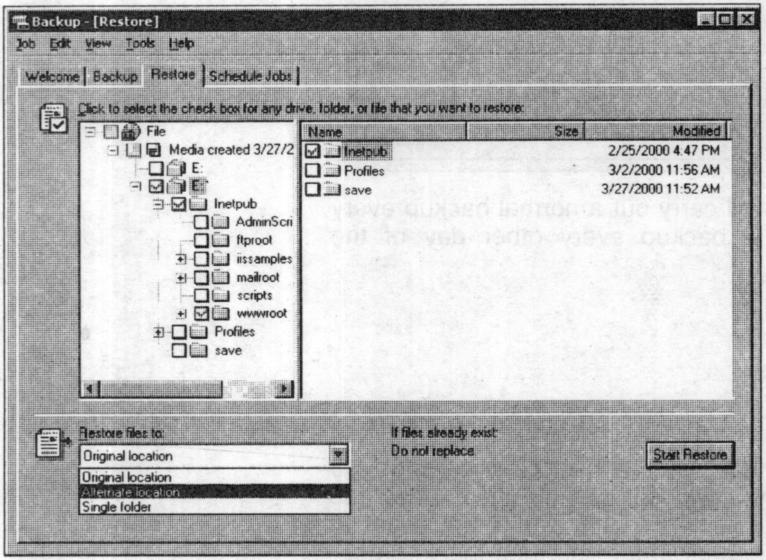

☞ Open the media and select the files that you want to restore from the backup set. Then, indicate whether you want to restore your backup to the original location, or whether you want to restore your backup to an alternate location.

☞ Click the **Start** button.

☞ Click the **Advanced** button if you want to specify advanced settings, and click **OK** in order to start restoring.

2. Restoring the system state

When you restore the system state, Windows 2000 deletes the current system state and replaces it with the system state from the backup. Consequently, you must backup the system state regularly in order to avoid losing data.
So as to restore the state of your system on a domain controller, you must restart your server in **Directory Services Restore** mode. In order to do this you must press the 8 key when the system prompts you to do so and then select the **Directory Services Restore Mode (Windows 2000 domain controllers only)** menu. Log on using the local administrator account that you created when you installed Active Directory. This startup mode allows you to start Windows 2000 without loading Active Directory. In fact, if you want to restore the system state, then the Active Directory database must not be loaded. Then, you can use the **Backup** utility so as to restore Active Directory (System State). Restart the server so that Windows 2000 will re-index and update the Active Directory database.

Restoring Active Directory objects

If you want to restore Active Directory objects that you have inadvertently deleted, then you must follow a different procedure. Windows 2000 marks all deleted objects and stores them in the directory database for 60 days. Each object has a serial number that is called the USN (*Update Sequence Number*). This USN is used for replication. If you restore an object in Active Directory, then you will restore it with a USN that is smaller than that of the object that you deleted. Therefore, during the replication process, the object will be marked as deleted.
The mechanism that allows you to restore objects into Active Directory is called **forced restore**. When you force a restore, you restore the objects that have the largest USN numbers. This allows you to restore them and to replicate them without any problems.

In order to restore individual objects, you must carry out the following steps:

- Restart your domain controller in **Directory Services Restore Mode (Windows 2000 domain controllers only)**.
- Restore the latest backup that concerns the system state using the **Backup** utility.
- When the restore has finished, close the **Backup** utility, and open a command prompt.

- Then, enter **ntdsutil**.
- Then, enter **authoritative restore**.
- Then type:
restore subtree *full_object_name*.

```
Microsoft Windows 2000 [Version 5.00.2195]
(C) Copyright 1985-1999 Microsoft Corp.

E:\>ntdsutil
ntdsutil: authoritative restore
authoritative restore: restore subtree OU=newusers,DC=ENIPUB,DC=COM

Opening DIT database... Done.

The current time is 04-13-00 19:17.37.
Most recent database update occured at 04-13-00 18:13.50.
Increasing attribute version numbers by 100000.

Counting records that need updating...
Records found: 0000000002
Done.

Found 2 records to update.

Updating records...
Records remaining: 0000000000
Done.

Successfully updated 2 records.

Authoritative Restore completed successfully.

authoritative restore: _
```

The example above illustrates the restore of the **GROUPS** organizational unit, in the **enipub.com** domain.

- Quit the **ntdsutil** program by entering the Quit command twice, and then restart the server.

Restoring the system on a new server

If your server breaks down completely, and you must re-install it, then you can restore the system state of the old server, onto the new server so that it will have exactly the same characteristics (for example, it will have the same name, the same registry database and the same directory database).
In order to do this, re-install the Windows 2000 system. You must accept the default install options, as you will set up your system again later. Make your server a stand-alone server and re-install all the applications that were present on the server previously. Then, go into the **Backup** utility and restore the system state from the latest backup.

C. Troubleshooting

1. Startup steps

After your computer has tested its hardware components (using the POST.i.POST (Power On Self Test);, or Power On Self Test, sequence on Intel platforms), the first action that it will carry out is to read the MBR: Master Boot Record.i.MBR (Master Boot Record);. Then, this MBR will examine the partitions table in order to find the active partition in this table that contains four entries. The boot sector in the active partition is run: this is the operating system preloader. The preloader then loads the operating system loader, which will then load the operating system.
Here are the steps of a Windows 2000 boot:

- **Step 1**
  Reading NTLDR (for MS-DOS, IO.SYS is the first file that is read). **Ntldr** switches the processor from real mode to 32-bit linear memory mode. Then it starts up the FAT and NTFS system drivers, which allow it to access the file systems in order fully to start up Windows 2000. **Ntldr** then reads **BOOT.INI** so as to build the boot loader menu.
- **Step 2**
  BOOT.INI: This is a text file that allows Windows 2000 to boot, or to start up on another operating system.

Here is an example of the **boot.ini** file. You can use this file in order to boot Windows 2000:

```
[boot loader]
timeout=30
default=multi(0)disk(0)rdisk(0)partition(1)\WINNT
[operating systems]
multi(0)disk(0)rdisk(0)partition(1)\WINNT="Microsoft Windows 2000
Advanced Server" /fastdetect
```

ARC Names

ARC names have the following structure:

SCSI(x)disk(y)rdisk(0)partition(n)

or

MULTI(x)disk(0)rdisk(z)partition(n)

SCSI(x) or MULTI(x)

The value x denotes the SCSI hardware controller number in their initialization order. It must be noted that some SCSI discs appear with the name MULTI (those for which the SCSI controller BIOS has not been disabled), according to the BIOS management mode.

`DISK(y)`	For Multibus SCSI adapters, this corresponds to the bus number. It is always equal to zero for MULTI controllers.
`RDISK(z)`	For MULTI components, z indicates the disk number on the adapter. For SCSI disks it is always equal to zero.
`PARTITION(n)`	n indicates the partition number on the disk, from 1 to n.

Thereby, on a disk that is handled by an IDE controller, or by a SCSI (BIOS activated) controller, the second partition that is on the second physical disk of the first controller will be referenced by: multi (0) disk (0) rdisk (1) partition (2). In this case disk (0) is a constant.

Important note: an incorrect ARC name will generate the following message,
"Windows 2000 could not start because the following file is missing or corrupt:
%Systemroot%\System32\ntoskrnl.exe
Please re-install a copy of the above file"
*In most cases, you can solve this problem simply by editing the **boot.ini** file.*
An incorrect ARC name can occur after you have created a new main partition, when the Windows 2000 boot partition is in a logical drive of an extended partition.

– **Step 3**
NTDETECT.COM: hardware detection program.

***NTDETECT.COM** allows you to generate the HARDWARE volatile key.*

*If you select an operating system other than Windows 2000, then the **BOOTSECT.DOS** file allows you to run the preloader of this other system (**BOOTSECT.DOS** is a copy of the former boot sector before Windows NT was installed).*

– **Step 4**
The **Hardware Profile/Configuration Recovery** startup menu, followed by loading of the Windows 2000 system.

2. Contents of the BOOT.INI. sections

This file is hidden, and is in read-only mode (S, H, R attributes). With Intel platforms, it is created automatically on the system partition when Windows 2000 is installed.

[boot loader] Section

`timeout` Defines the number of seconds that must elapse before Windows 2000 loads the default operating system.
A value of 0 causes the system to start immediately.

*You can modify **boot.ini** directly, and set a value of 1. In this case the system will wait indefinitely for you to select an option.*

*In most cases, you should use the **Control Panel System** icon, activate the Advanced tab, and then click the **Startup** and **Recovery** button, in order to modify this value.*

If you want to modify this file after you have started MS-DOS, then you must simultaneously disable the three attributes S,H, and R. Before you modify the file, you must reset theses attributes using the following command:
attrib -S -H -R BOOT.INI
After you have modified the file, you must reset these attributes using the following command:
attrib +S +H +R BOOT.INI

`default` This parameter corresponds to the path of the default operating system. This path must be present in the [operating systems] section.

[operating systems] section

This section allows you to define the paths to the boot sectors of the different operating systems that are available, such as: Windows 2000, Windows NT, Windows 95/98, MS-DOS and OS/2.

3. Last known good configuration

Internally, Windows 2000 manages several sets of system configurations (it manages three in general).
In most cases, Windows 2000 starts up with the default configuration, or **CurrentControlSet** (see HKEY_LOCAL_MACHINE\System).

*In fact, Windows 2000 records a configuration as the **last known good configuration** as soon as a user is able to log on with it (even if it generates many errors!).*

When a problem occurs following a new installation, then the message **At least one driver or service failed during system startup** will warn you of the problem, before you log on. In this case, you must stop and restart the machine, without logging on, so as to restart using the **Last known good configuration** option.

You can access this option as follows:

– When you start up Windows 2000, press the F8 key when you are prompted to do so. Then, use the arrow keys in order to select the **Last known good configuration** option.

When you apply the last known good configuration, you lose all the configurations from the previous session.

4. Starting from a floppy disk

You can start up Windows 2000 using a FAT diskette, whether Windows 2000 uses FAT or whether it uses NTFS!

For this purpose, you must use a diskette that you have formatted on a Windows NT 4.00 system, or on a Windows 2000 system (this is necessary so that the NT preloader will be installed on the diskette, and ready to load **NTLDR**). You must then copy the files **NTLDR**, **BOOT.INI**, **NTBOOTDD. SYS** (if the BIOS of the SCSI controller is deactivated) and **NTDETECT.COM**, which are situated in the root of the Windows 2000 system partition. Startup steps 1 to 3 are carried out on the diskette instead of the hard disk.

5. Using an emergency repair disk

As the administrator, you can repair the system by starting up on the Windows 2000 installation startup diskettes. You can create these 4 diskettes by selecting the bootdisk directory on the Windows 2000 CD-ROM, and entering the command **makeboot a** in a command prompt:

After you have inserted the fourth diskette, you can carry out an emergency repair by pressing the **R** key. However, in order to do this you need previously to have created an emergency repair diskette on the system that you want to repair. You can create this diskette using the **Welcome** tab of the **Backup** utility. You can also repair the installation using the recovery console (by pressing the **C** key).

After you have pressed the **R** key, you can repair manually, so that you can choose the options that you want to use. Alternatively, you can choose to carry out a fast repair. In this case the following options will be chosen for you:

Inspect startup environment

This option checks the presence of the files that are needed in order to start up Windows 2000 (such as **boot.ini**, and **ntldr**).

Verify Windows 2000 system files

This option is needed if any Windows 2000 files have been deleted, or if the disk has been altered. The **SETUP.LOG** file that is contained on the emergency repair disk allows the program to copy the files from the CD-ROM onto the hard disk.

Inspect boot sector

This option recreates the boot sector (so that it will point to the first **ntldr** file).

You can also run an emergency repair by booting on the Windows 2000 CD-ROM, without using the startup diskettes.

6. Other startup options

Windows 2000 can run in different modes. This feature allows you to troubleshoot any operational problems that the system may have. You can access the menu that allows you to choose these modes by pressing the F8 key when you are prompted to do so during the startup process of your system.

Safe Mode

This option allows you to start up your system by loading the essential drivers that you need for this purpose. A file called Ntbtlog.txt is created in the **%systemroot%** directory. This file allows the system to detect the drivers that have been loaded, and the drivers that have not been loaded.

Safe Mode with Networking

This is the same as **Safe Mode**, except that the drivers that the system needs for networking are loaded as well.

Safe Mode with Command Prompt

When you choose this option, Windows 2000 runs in **Safe Mode** without loading the graphic interface.

Enable VGA Mode

With this option, Windows 2000 runs with the standard VGA graphic drivers. You must choose this option when you have a problem with you graphic card driver.

Enable Boot Logging

When you choose this option Windows 2000 starts up normally, and produces a report on all drivers and services that have been loaded during the start up. This report is written to the **Ntbtlog.txt** file, which is located in the **%systemroot%** directory.

Directory Services Restore Mode (Windows 2000 domain controllers only)

As we saw previously, this mode allows you to start up Windows 2000 without loading Active Directory, so that you will be able to restore it.

Debugging Mode

When you choose this option, the system sends debugging information to another computer via a serial cable.

7. Recovery console

The recovery console is a text mode interface that allows you to repair your system when you can no longer boot Windows 2000. You can use this console, so as to stop or to start services that could prevent the system from starting up, so as to format hard disks and so as to read data that is situated on FAT or NTFS disks. In order to go into this console, you must indicate the installation that you wish to repair, along with the password of the local administrator of the server (if your machine is a domain controller, this is the local administrator that you indicated when you installed Active Directory).

You can run the recovery console in two ways:

– You can start up the system, either using the 4 startup diskettes, or using the Windows 2000 CD-ROM. Then, when you are prompted to do so, you must press the C key so as to start up the recovery console.
– Alternatively, you can access the recovery console using the Windows 2000 startup menu. However, before you can do this, you must first install this console.

Installing the recovery console

☞ Start up a command prompt.

☞ Access the **I386** directory of the Windows 2000 CD-ROM.

☞ Input the command **winnt32 /cmdcons**.

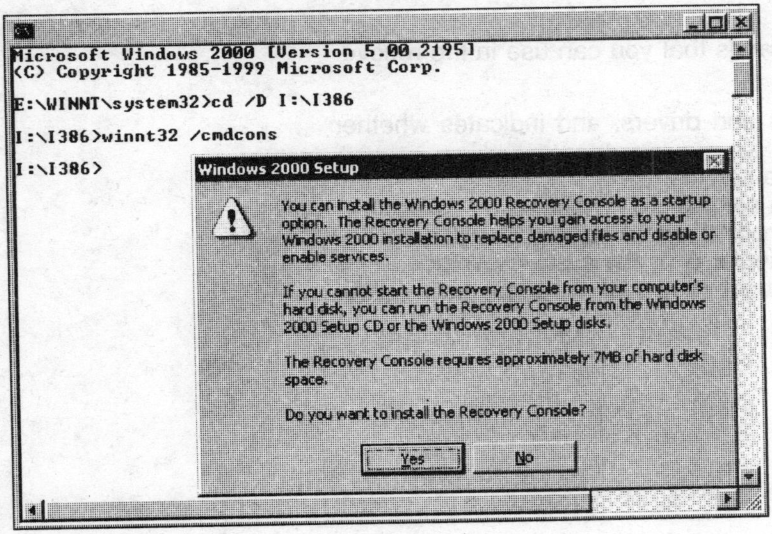

☞ Click the **Yes** button.

☞ Restart your computer. You will notice that the **Microsoft Windows 2000 Recovery Console** option now appears in the startup menu along with other options (such as **Microsoft Windows 2000 Advanced Server**, for example).

*The **boot.ini** file has been modified and will now look like the following example:*

```
[boot loader]
timeout=30
default=multi(0)disk(0)rdisk(1)partition(1)\WINNT
[operating systems]
multi(0)disk(0)rdisk(1)partition(1)\WINNT="Microsoft Windows 2000 Advanced
Server" /fastdetect
multi(0)disk(0)rdisk(0)partition(2)\WINNT="Microsoft Windows 2000 Advanced
Server" /fastdetect
multi(0)disk(0)rdisk(0)partition(1)\WINNT="Windows NT Server Version 4.00"
multi(0)disk(0)rdisk(0)partition(1)\WINNT="Windows NT Server Version 4.00
[VGA mode]" /basevideo /sos
C:\="Microsoft Windows"
C:\CMDCONS\BOOTSECT.DAT="Microsoft Windows 2000 Recovery Console" /cmdcons
```

When you have entered the recovery console, enter the Help command in order to display the list of available commands.

Here are some of the commands that you can use in the recovery console:

listsvc: lists all the services and drivers, and indicates whether they are started or not.
Disable: allows you to stop a service.
Enable: allows you to start a service
Systemroot: sets **%systemroot%** as the current directory.
Fixboot: writes a new boot sector onto the system partition.
Fixmbr: repairs the master boot record of the main boot sector of the partition.

Index by subject

!

32-bit Microsoft operating system, 29
32bit applications, 17

A

Account expiry, 170
Account lockout policy, 259, 260
Accounts and passwords
- resetting a password, 171
- security, 257

ACL (Access Control List), 188, 202
Active Directory, 14, 15, 88, 108, 163
- adding a child domain, 119
- adding a domain controller to an existing domain, 119
- adding a tree into an existing forest, 120
- auditing, 266
- choosing a domain mode, 121
- client, 12
- creating a new, or root, domain, 116
- installing, 113
- Objects, 111
- replication, 128
- uninstalling, 137

Active Directory Domains and Trusts Console, 124
Active Directory Schema console, 111, 125
Active Directory Schema console, 111
Active Directory Sites and Services console, 127, 130, 132, 133, 136, 143, 258
Active Directory Users and Computers console, 142, 143, 173, 175, 180, 183, 258, 263
Add/Remove Hardware, 49
Add/Remove Programs, 48
Address scopes
- creating, 275

Administrative Tools, 16, 59
Adminpack.msi, 126
AppleTalk, 66, 300
Application Log, 269
Application mode, 10
ARAP protocols, 299, 300

ARC name, 336
Architecture (kernel mode, user mode), 10
ARPA, 87
ARPANET, 79
ASMP, 9
ATM (Asynchronous Transfer Mode), 299
Audit, 263
 auditing Active Directory, 266
 viewing the audited events, 267
Authenticated Users, 162
Automatic configuration, 70

B

B-tree structure, 189
Backing up, 326, 327, 330
 scheduling, 330
 strategies, 248
 system state, 330
 troubleshooting, 335
 types of backup, 13, 16, 327
Backup domain controllers, 15
Backup Operators, 162
BIOS management mode, 336
BOOT.INI, 243, 335, 337
BOOTP, 279, 281
BOOTSECT.DOS, 336
BSD, 79

C

Certificate service, 16
CHAP (Challenge Handshake Authentication dProtocol), 312
Cipher.exe, 252
Class, 16, 111
Client for Microsoft networks, 28
Client/server systems, 10
Cluster
 configuration, 18
 mode, 11
 service, 27
Common Name, 112
Computer Management, 59, 155, 160, 200, 226

Configuring devices, 48
Connecting directly using a cable, 310
Copying and moving, 253
Creator Owner group, 162, 210

D

DARPA, 79
Data encryption, 22
Database servers, 10
Dcpromo.exe, 113, 137
Decision aids, 18
Default gateway, 69
Default-First-Site-Name, 130
DES (Data Encryption Standard), 170
Desktop, 17
Device Manager, 54
DFS (Distributed File System), 12
    child nodes, 217
    console, 213
    fault tolerance, 216
    root replica, 217
    stand-alone, 212, 213, 217
DHCP (Dynamic Host Configuration Protocol), 28, 82, 108, 272, 304
    acknowledgement, 282
    address scopes, 275
    Automatic private IP addressing, 287
    client, 277, 279, 287
    configuring a client machine, 280
    console, 275, 292
    discover, 281
    dynamic update, 284
    installing, 273
    lease, 272
    multicast, 286
    new features, 284
    offer, 281
    processing DHCP queries, 280
    relay Agent, 288
    request, 282
    reservation, 278
    RFC, 272

Index by subject

superscopes, 285
DHCP (Dynamic Host Configuration Protocol
client, 16
DHCP ACK, 283
DHCP Administrators group, 277
DHCP NACK, 282
DHCP REQUEST, 283
DHCP server, 277, 287
authorizing, 274
installing, 273
DHCP Users group, 277
Directory database, 12, 117
Directory Services Restore, 333
Disk
basic disks, 226
cleaning up, 13
creating a partition, 226, 229
creating logical drives, 229
defragmenter, 13
dynamic, 231
mirrored volumes, 231
RAID 5, 231, 247
repairing a defective RAID-5 volume, 247
simple, spanned and striped volumes, 231
Disk duplication tool, 13
Disk Management, 20, 229, 232, 243
Disk Management snap-in, 226
Disk mirroring
booting an a secondary, 243
breaking and removing, 242
implementing, 240
mirroring a basic disk, 245
Raid 1, 239
see also mirroring, 245
Disk quota management, 13
creating a new entry, 221
enabling, 219
managing, 219
Disk stripe, 189
Distinguished Name, 112
Distributed link tracking, 13
DLC (Data Link Control), 65

DNS (Domain Name System), 15, 81, 16, 108, 16, 73
creating records manually, 99
creating subdomains, 100
dynamic updating, 95
implementing, 88
server, 289
zone, 92
DoD (Department of Defense), 78
Domain, 24
managing, 163
planning, 24
Domain Component, 112
Domain controllers, 14, 15
roles, 123
Domain local group, 173
Domain Name System, 86
Domains, 109
Dotted decimal notation, 68
Duplexing, 240
Dynamic disk
upgrading to, 231

E

EAP (Extensible Authentication Protocol), 313
EDU, 87
EFS (Encrypting File System), 250
EMA (Enterprise Memory Architecture), 10, 18
Emergency repair disk, 339
Encrypting
cipher.exe, 251
recovery, 254
stop, 253
Encryption types, 250
Energy options, 12
Enhancing network services, 16
Enterprise Admins group, 274
Environment variables, 57
Ethernet, 320
Event Log, 269
Event Viewer, 23, 263, 267, 268
Everyone group, 162, 183

Execute mode, 10
External hard disks, 13

F

FAT see File Systems
FAT16 see File Systems
FAT32 see File Systems
Fault tolerance, 16, 18
  choosing, 248
  duplexing, 240
  mirroring, 239
  overview, 239
  RAID 5, 245
File encryption
  private key, 14
  public key, 14
File Systems, 188
  FAT/FAT32, 22, 116, 228, 248, 335, 340
  FAT16, 13, 188
  FAT32, 13, 22, 188, 228, 230
  NTFS, 13, 22
Files and folder
  ceasing to share, 196
  copying, 212
  moving, 212
  permission, 203, 205
  sharing, 202
  taking ownership, 210
Files and folders
  properties, 326
Forests, 109
FQDN (Fully Qualified Domain Name), 86, 88
Frame Relay (frame switching), 299, 301
Ftdisk.sys, 247
FTP (File Transfer Protocol), 80

G

Global catalog, 126
Global group, 173
GOV, 87
GPOs, 149
GPOs (Group Policy Objects), 142, 143

adding, 144
creating, 142
deleting, 144
managing, 142
GPT (Group Policy Template), 142
Group
creating, 160, 173
deleting, 176
distribution, 172
finding, 175
predefined domain local, 178
predefined groups, 160, 177
renaming, 176
scope, 172
security, 172
strategies for using, 177
types, 172
Group policies
order of application, 149
Administrative Templates, 147
applying, 149
inheriting, 150
permissions, 152
registry.pol, 148
settings, 145
user environment, 147
Group Policy snap-in, 253
Guest, 162

H

HAL (Hardware Abstraction Layer), 34
Hardware Configuration, 53
HARDWARE volatile key, 336
Hardware Wizard, 51
Hashing, 312
HCL (Hardware Compatibility List), 14, 17, 20, 26
Hives, 44
Home directories, 184
HOSTS, 85
HPOV, 82

I

I386 directory, 341
ICMP, 320
IDE controller, 336
IETF (Internet Engineering Task Force), 14
IGMP (Internet Group Management Protocol), 287
IIS (Internet Information Services, 10, 27
Index service, 16
Installation
    answer files, 31
    disk duplication, 36
    switches, 29
    WINNT.EXE, 29
    Winnt32.exe, 29
INT, 87
Intel, 18
Inter-site replication, 133
Interactive group, 162
Internet, 12, 79
Internet Activity Board, 79
IP (Internet Protocol), 78, 81, 301
    Address, 69
    Configuration, 69
    routing, 69
IP addressing
    automatic private, 287
IP network traffic
    security, 255
Ipconfig, 280, 283
IPP (Internet Printing Protocol), 12, 16
IPSec (IP Security), 14, 170, 250
    EPS, 255
ISDN (Integrated Services Digital Network), 299, 320

J

Jet Blue aka ESE database, 113

Index by subject

K

KCC, 132
Kerberos authentication method, 14
Kerberos authentification method, 108, 170
Kernel mode, 10

L

L2TP, 300
LAN, 14, 69
LAN protocol, 300
Last known good configuration, 338
LCP (Link Control Protocol), 311
LDAP, 108
    protocol, 15
    server, 89
LDIF, 108
Lease, 272
    renewing, 283
Licensing mode, 20
    everyone group, 23
    per seat, 23
    per server, 23
Link, 133
LMHOSTS, 84
LMHOSTS.SAM, 84
Load sharing, 16
Local Area Connection, 64
Local loopback address, 68
Logical disks, 13
LSA, 131

M

MAC address, 280
Makeboot.exe, 25, 339
Managing a local computer, 154
Managing disk resources
    choosing the most suitable file system, 189
Manual configuration, 71
Manual replication, 136
Master File Table, 189
MD5":" Message Digest, 312

Member server, 25, 39
Metric, 73
MIB (Management Information Base), 82
Micro-kernel, 10
Microsoft RAS, 299, 300
Microsoft Windows 2000 Recovery Console, 341
MIL, 87
Minimal hardware requirements, 20
Mirroring, 231, 239, 248
Mixed mode, 121
MMC (Microsoft Management Console), 16, 257
MPPE (Microsoft Point-to-point Protocol), 170, 313
MS-CHAP (Microsoft Challenge Handshake Authentication Protocol), 313
MSDOS, 22, 26, 192, 202
Multicast extensions, 16
Multiprocessing
 asymmetric, 9
 symmetric, 9
Multitasking
 co-operative, 8
 pre-emptive, 8
Multithreading, 9
My Computer, 37

N

Native mode, 121, 317
NBNS (Net BIOS name server), 289
NCP (Network Control Protocol), 311
NDIS 5.0, 65
NET, 87
Net use command, 290
Net view command, 290
NetBEUI (NetBIOS Extended User Interface), 65, 300
NetBIOS, 23, 73
Network and dial-up connections, 302
Network Connection Wizard, 307
Network group, 162
Network interface cards, 62, 69
Network monitor, 17, 284
Networking Connection Wizard, 12
NFS (Network File System), 81

NIC (Network Information Center), 68
NNTP servers, 278
NTBOOTDD.SYS, 243
Ntdetect.com, 45, 243, 336
NTDS.DIT, 113
Ntdsutil, 334
NTFS, 21, 26, 116, 184, 188, 203, 228, 230, 248, 326, 335, 340
NTFS file systems, 22
NTLDR, 21, 243, 335
NTLM protocol, 14
NTP, 108
Ntuser.dat, 179, 183
Ntuser.man, 183
Nwlink IPX/SPX/Netbios, 65, 300

O

OnNow/ACPI technology, 11
Open View, 82
Operations masters, 123
Optimizing bindings, 73
ORG, 87
OS/2, 65
OSI model, 79, 82
OU (Organizational Unit), 110, 142, 143, 171
Outgoing connections, 307

P

Paging file, 55
PAP (Password Authentication Protocol), 312
Partition
    boot, 21
    extended, 227, 229
    primary, 227
    system, 21
Password policy
    enforce password history, 262
    password age, 262
Peer-to-peer network, 24
Permission
    advanced, 206
    file, 205

Index by subject

folder, 203
inheriting, 209
modify, 212
NTFS, 208
write, 212
PING, 86
Plug-and-Play, 11, 12
POP3 servers, 278
Power Users, 162
PPP (Point to Point Protocol), 299
PPTP (Point to Point Tunneling Protocol), 300
Predefined accounts, 163
Primary domain controller, 15
Primary WINS Server, 291
Print services for Macintosh and Unix, 27
Processor quotas, 10
PROFILE
Local and home directories, 179
PVC (Permanent Virtual Circuits), 301

R

RADIUS authentication server, 306
RAID (Redundant Array of Inexpensive Disks), 239
RAID 1, RAID 5, 231, 248
cost of, 248
on basic disk, 247
repairing a defective RAID-5 volume, 247
Real mode, 335
Recordable CDROMs, 13
Recovering a document, 254
Recovery agents, 254
Recovery console, 340
Registry
regedit.exe, 46, 48
REGEDT32.EXE, 42
Registry.pol, 147
Relative Distinguished Name, 111
Remote access
application order of conditions, permissions and profile, 321
authentication, 311
authorizing, 316

conditions, 313
configuring, 301
connection, 307
policy, 299
profile, 319
Remote Installation Service, 27
Remote network access, 16
Remote Storage, 27
Remote storage service, 16
Replication
inter-sites, 128
intra-sites, 128
KKC, 128
sites, 128
Required Configuration, 20
Restoring
active Directory and objects, 333
authoritative restore, 334
data, 331
system on a new server, 334
system state, 333
troubleshooting, 335
Reverse Lookup Zone, 92
Reversible encryption, 170
RFC (Requests For Comment), 14, 95, 272
RIP (Routing Internet Protocol, 80
RIS (Remote Installation Service), 13, 16, 32
Routing, 17
Routing and Remote Access console, 288, 301, 305, 311, 319, 321
RPC (Remote Procedures Call), 131, 133

S

SAM (Security Account Manager, 15, 45,
database, 303
Samba, 289
Scandisk, 13
Schema, 111
Scope
adding options to, 277
creating global options for, 278
creating specific options for, 277

Index by subject

multicast scopes, 286
principal DHCP options, 278
reserving a specific address for a client, 278
superscopes, 285
Script Debugger, 27
SCSI (Small Computer System Interface), 26
SCSI controller, 336
Security, 250
encrypting, 251
access, 202
account lockout policy, 259
accounts and passwords, 257
password policy , 261
resource level, 190
template, 257
user level, 190
User rights, 269
Security Log, 263, 267, 269
Server
member, 25
stand-alone, 25
Services, 18
dependencies, 59
Setup Manager, 31
Setup.exe, 25, 26
SETUP.LOG, 339
setupcl.exe, 38
Shared resource
connecting, 198
Shared System Volume, 116
SID (Security IDentifier), 176
Signature, 52
Simple volume, 231, 233
extending, 235
SLIP (Serial Line Internet Protocol), 299
Smartdrv, 29
SMB (Server Message Block), 23
SMP, 9, 18
SMTP (Simple Mail Transfer Protocol, 81
SMTP (Simple Mail Transfer Protocol), 133
SMTP servers, 278
SNMP (Simple Network Management Protocol, 82

SOA (Start of Authority), 96
Spanned volume, 231, 236
SPAP (Shiva Password Authentication Protocol), 312
SRV, 89
SSL (Secure Sockets Layer), 250
Stand-alone server, 25, 39
Starting from a floppy disk, 338
Startup options (modes), 339, 340
STN (Switched Telephone Network), 299
Stripe set with parity, 248
Striped volume, 231, 237
Subdomain
    delegation, 101
    forwarders, 102
Subnets, 69, 130
Subtrees, 43
SUN, 81
Super-extensions, 16
Sysprep.exe, 13, 36, 38
Sysprep.inf, 38
System Log, 269
System properties, 50
Sysvol, 147

T

Task Manager, 9
TCO (Total Cost of Ownership), 15, 142
TCP (Transfer Control Protocol), 78, 320
TCP/IP (Transmission Control Protocol/Internet Protocol), 65, 78, 108, 300, 304
    UDP see UDP
Telnet, 80, 86
Terminal Services, 10, 17, 27
TFTP (Trivial File Transfer Protocol), 80
Threads, 9
TLS (Transport Layer Security), 313
Transport
    inter-site, 131
    intra-site, 131
Transport methods, 299
Trees, 43, 109

Trust relationships, 14
TTL (Time To Live), 289
Types of backup, 13, 16
Types of trust relationship, 110

U

UDP (User Datagram Protocol), 78, 81, 281, 320
Unattend.udf, 36
UNC (Universal Naming Convention)
  path, 215
Universal groups, 173
Unix servers, 289, 300
User account
  access restrictions, 170
  account properties, 168
  copying, 170
  creating, 155, 163
  expiry, 170
  modifying, 157, 159, 171
  moving a user object, 171
  personal properties, 167
  time period restrictions , 170
User mode, 10, 11
User Principal Name, 112
User profiles
  local user, 179
  mandatory roaming, 182
  roaming personal, 180
  roaming user, 180
User rights, 269

V

VPN (Virtual Private Network), 12, 14, 300, 320
  connecting to, 308
  L2TP, 300
  PPTP, 300

FIREWALL MEDIA

(An imprint of Laxmi Publications Pvt. Ltd.)

Computer Books *for School, BCA, MCA, IGNOU, DOEACC and Engineering Students and Professionals*

ISBN	TITLE	AUTHOR	PRICE	PAGES
	.NET			
8170087155	**Building Business Intelligence Applications with .Net**	Robert Ericsson	Rs. 295.00	404
8170083567	**Learning VB.Net Through Applications**	Clayton Crooks	Rs. 295.00	450
8131800865	**Magic of C# with .Net Frame Work**	Shibi Panikkar, Kumar Sanjeev	Rs. 495.00	950
8170082471	**Magic of ASP.Net with C#**	Shibi Panikkar, Kumar Sanjeev	Rs. 395.00	828
8170089662	**ASP.Net Interview Questions and Answers**	J. Rajaram	Rs. 95.00	175
	A TO Z SERIES			
8170083214	**Access 2002 from A to Z**	Julia Kelly, Stephen L. Nelson	Rs. 75.00	185
8170083222	**Excel 2002 from A to Z**	Stephen L. Nelson	Rs. 75.00	193
8170083230	**Front Page 2002 from A to Z**	Heather Williamson	Rs. 85.00	219
8170083249	**Outlook 2002 from A to Z**	Stephen L. Nelson	Rs. 75.00	202
8170083257	**Page Maker 7 from A to Z**	Marc Campbell	Rs. 75.00	202
8170083265	**PowerPoint 2002 from A to Z**	Stephen L. Nelson	Rs. 75.00	202
8170083273	**Windows XP from A to Z**	Pat Coleman	Rs. 95.00	249
8170083281	**Word 2002 from A to Z**	Stephen L. Nelson	Rs. 75.00	199
817008329X	**XML from A to Z**	Heather Williamson	Rs. 75.00	200
8170083303	**Dreamweaver 4 from A to Z**	Heather Williamson	Rs. 85.00	215
	BEGINNERS & GENERAL INTEREST			
817008248X	**Shortcuts to Success in Computing**	Dheeraj Mehrotra	Rs. 55.00	110
8170083311	**Pictorial Computer Dictionary**	Dheeraj Mehrotra	Rs. 45.00	156
8170083486	**Pocket Net Browser**	Dheeraj Mehrotra	Rs. 95.00	302
8170084261	**1000 IT Quizzes**	Dheeraj Mehrotra	Rs. 75.00	120
8131800679	**Information Technology Bible**	Remesh Bangia	Rs. 295.00	567

Please write for a free color Firewall Media Catalog for details on the above books.

ISBN	TITLE	AUTHOR	PRICE	PAGES
8131800377	**Fundamentals of Information Technology Including MS Office**	Dinesh Maidasani, Jai Narayan Yadav	Rs. 175.00	356
813180089X	**Fundamentals of Information Technology Including MS Office (Hindi Medium)**	Dinesh Maidasani, Jai Narayan Yadav	Rs. 175.00	425
8170089719	**Foundations of Computer Science**	Ashok Arora	Rs. 250.00	386

CALL CENTERS

ISBN	TITLE	AUTHOR	PRICE	PAGES
8170082196	**Call Centers Made Easy**	Stephen Medcroft	Rs. 195.00	310

CISCO

ISBN	TITLE	AUTHOR	PRICE	PAGES
8170087481	**Enabling IP Routing with Cisco Routers**	R. Das, K. Chakrabarty	Rs. 295.00	486
817008749X	**Designing Networks with Cisco**	H. Pasricha, D. Jagu	Rs. 195.00	316
8170087503	**Cisco IP Routing Protocols: Troubleshooting Techniques**	V. Anand, K. Chakrabarty	Rs. 295.00	409

DATABASES

ISBN	TITLE	AUTHOR	PRICE	PAGES
8170089530	**DBMS—Complete Practical Approach**	Sharad Maheshwari, Ruchin Jain	Rs. 350.00	656
8170082404	**Learn to Program Visual Basic-Examples**	John Smiley	Rs. 295.00	482
8170082412	**Learn to Program Visual Basic-Databases**	John Smiley	Rs. 325.00	653
8170082420	**Learn to Program Visual Basic-Objects**	John Smiley	Rs. 325.00	670
817008475X	**IT Resources-Access 2002 VBA Programming Access**	Michele Amelot	Rs. 195.00	424
8170084512	**The Power of Oracle 9i**	Rajiv Parida, Vinod Sharma	Rs. 475.00	1035
8170088518	**Principles and Implementation of Data Warehousing**	Rajiv A. Parida	Rs. 295.00	487
817008864X	**DBA Study Guide OCP Prep Guide**	Nazar Abdul	Rs. 295.00	474
8170088658	**Oracle 11i—The Complete Reference**	Rashmi Anandi	Rs. 495.00	975
8131800067	**Toxonomy of Database Management System**	Aditya Kumar Gupta	Rs. 75.00	146
8131800385	**Introduction to SQL and PL/SQL**	Sharad Maheshwari, Ruchin Jain	Rs. 200.00	389

ISBN	TITLE	AUTHOR	PRICE	PAGES
	DOEACC 'O' LEVEL			
8170088089	**DOEACC 'O' Level Model Test Papers**	Ramesh Bangia	Rs. 175.00	296
8170089115	**DOEACC 'O' & 'A' Level Programming & Problem Solving Through 'C' Language (Model Test Paper with Solutions)**	Mukesh Sharma	Rs. 95.00	213
8170089069	**DOEACC 'O' & 'A' Level Business Systems (Model Test Paper with Solutions)**	Mukesh Sharma	Rs. 100.00	252
8170085640	**Programming and Problem Solving Through "C" Language**	Harsha Priya, R. Ranjeet	Rs. 95.00	306
8170084474	**IT Tools and Applications**	Ramesh Bangia	Rs. 145.00	370
8170085594	**Business Systems**	Ramesh Bangia	Rs. 175.00	452
8170089514	**Internet & Web Design**	Ramesh Bangia	Rs. 150.00	300
	ELECTRONIC COMMERCE			
8170085497	**Electronic Commerce**	Pete Loshin, John Vacca	Rs. 295.00	472
817008119X	**E-Commerce**	Mamta Bhusry	Rs. 95.00	215
8170083524	**Marketing in the Cyber Age**	Kurt Rohner	Rs. 295.00	223
	HARDWARE/EMBEDDED SYSTEMS			
8170087473	**Essential Electronics for PC Technicians**	John W. Farber	Rs. 295.00	546
8170086264	**Grid Computing: A Practical Guide to Technology and Applications**	Ahmar Abbas	Rs. 295.00	408
8170088186	**CD Cracking Uncovered Protection Against Unsanctioned CD Copy**	Kris Kaspersky	Rs. 295.00	422
8170083435	**Practical Linux Programming: Device Drivers, Embedded Systems and the Internet**	Ashfaq A. Khan	Rs. 295.00	420
8170083575	**TCP/IP Application Layer Protocols for Embedded Systems**	M. Tim Jones	Rs. 295.00	460
8131800520	**PC Repair and Maintenance : A Practical Guide**	Joel Rosenthal, Kevin Irwin	Rs. 195.00	362

ISBN	TITLE	AUTHOR	PRICE	PAGES
8131800768	**The A+ Certification and PC Repair Handbook**	Christopher A Crayton, Joel Z. Rosenthal	Rs. 495.00	888

INTERNET & WEB TECHNOLOGY

ISBN	TITLE	AUTHOR	PRICE	PAGES
8170083206	**The Internet Handbook for Writers, Students and Teachers**	Mary McGuire, Linda Stilborne	Rs. 195.00	276
8170084776	**Way in-Internet Getting Started**	Elizabeth Bramire	Rs. 95.00	165
8170088976	**Web Technology**	Ramesh Bangia	Rs. 250.00	560
8170087163	**Web Design with Macromedia Studio MX 2004**	Eric Hunley	Rs. 295.00	558
8170083400	**Professional Web Design (Techniques and Templates)**	Clint Eccher	Rs. 295.00	425
8170088046	**HTML, XHTML, CSS and XML**	Teodoru Gugoiu	Rs. 195.00	355
8170083583	**FrontPage 2000 for Visual Learners**	Chris Charuhas	Rs. 95.00	200
8170083591	**HTML & Java Script for Visual Learners**	Chris Charuhas	Rs. 95.00	200
8170083605	**The Visual Learners Guide to Managing Web Projects**	Chris Charuhas	Rs. 95.00	130
8170083613	**Dreamweaver 4 for Visual Learners**	Chris Charuhas	Rs. 95.00	200
8170084768	**IT Resource-Implementing XML: Managing and Formatting Data**	Johhny Brochard	Rs. 125.00	279
8170089476	**Design Your Web World**	Sunil Jalota	Rs. 75.00	146

KEEPING AHEAD SERIES

ISBN	TITLE	AUTHOR	PRICE	PAGES
8170084652	**Keeping Ahead-Exchange 2000 Server**	Philippe Levesque	Rs. 145.00	285
8170084660	**Keeping Ahead-Windows 2000 Professional**	Jose Dardoigne	Rs. 175.00	388
8170084679	**Keeping Ahead-Windows 2000 Server**	Philippe Mathon	Rs. 175.00	360
8170084687	**Keeping Ahead-Linux Administration Kernel Version 2.0 to 2.2**	Bruno Guèrin	Rs. 125.00	240

ISBN	TITLE	AUTHOR	PRICE	PAGES
8170084695	**Keeping Ahead-Using Linux Kernel Version 2.0 to 2.2**	Bruno Gùerin	Rs. 125.00	258
8170084709	**Keeping Ahead-Java 2**	Benjamin Aumaille	Rs. 145.00	284
8170084717	**Keeping Ahead-SQL Server 7**	Joelle Mosset	Rs. 145.00	329
8170084725	**Keeping Ahead-JavaScript and VBScript**	Benjamin Aumaille	Rs. 145.00	313
8170084733	**Keeping Ahead-C++ Programming Language**	Bruno Dubois	Rs. 125.00	234
8170084741	**Keeping Ahead-TCP/IP in the NT Environment**	Bruno Ferec	Rs. 125.00	230

MCSE

ISBN	TITLE	AUTHOR	PRICE	PAGES
817008489X	**MCSE-Administering SQL Server 7.0**	Jerome Gabillaud	Rs. 295.00	580
8170084903	**MCSE-Networking Essentials**	Jose Dordoigne	Rs. 245.00	453
8170084911	**MCSE-Windows 2000 Professional**	Jose Dordoigne	Rs. 325.00	665
817008492X	**MCSE-Windows 2000 Server**	Phillippe Mathon	Rs. 345.00	712

MULTIMEDIA AND ANIMATION

ISBN	TITLE	AUTHOR	PRICE	PAGES
8170088208	**3DS Max 6 Animation with Character Studio 4 and Plug-Ins**	Boris Kulagin, Dmitry Morozov	Rs. 175.00	216
8170088216	**Adobe Audition: Soundtracks for Digital Video**	Roman Petelin, Yury Petelin	Rs. 195.00	278
8170086205	**Building A Digital Human**	Ken Brilliant	Rs. 295.00	380
8170086213	**Making Digital Videos**	Ben Long	R/s. 295.00	284
8170087171	**Illustrating with Macromedia Flash ™ MX2004**	Robert Firbaugh	Rs. 245.00	366
8170082439	**Multimedia Basics-Technology (Vol. I)**	Andreas Holzinger	Rs. 195.00	312
8170082447	**Multimedia Basics-Learning (Vol. II)**	Andreas Holzinger	Rs. 195.00	326
8170082455	**Multimedia Basics-Design (Vol. III)**	Andreas Holzinger	Rs. 195.00	280
8170083532	**Maya Feature Creature Creations**	Todd Palamar	Rs. 295.00	376

Please write for a free color Firewall Media Catalog for details on the above books.

ISBN	TITLE	AUTHOR	PRICE	PAGES
8170083540	**Sound Forge Power**	Scott R. Garrigus	Rs. 195.00	344
8131800288	**Multimedia and Web Technology**	Ramesh Bangia	Rs. 395.00	878
813180044X	**Photoshop CS**	Shruti Lal	Rs. 195.00	434

NETWORKING

ISBN	TITLE	AUTHOR	PRICE	PAGES
817008721X	**Networking Essentials**	Jose Dordoigne	Rs. 195.00	453
8170089328	**TCP/IP Distributed System**	Vivek Acharya	Rs. 250.00	474
8170087023	**Computer Networks**	Ajit Kumar Singh	Rs. 95.00	181
8131800148	**The Real—world Network Troubleshooting Manual**	Alan Sugano	Rs. 295.00	396
817008203X	**Telecom & Networking Glossary**	Robert Mastin	Rs. 300.00	250
8170082048	**Data Networking Made Easy**	Karen Patten	Rs. 360.00	350
8170082056	**Digital Convergence**	Andy Covell	Rs. 300.00	234

OFFICE AUTOMATION

ISBN	TITLE	AUTHOR	PRICE	PAGES
8170089891	**Desk Top Publishing**	Dinesh Maidasani	Rs. 150.00	311
8170087805	**Learning Computer Fundamentals, MS Office and Internet & Web Technology**	Dinesh Maidasani	Rs. 95.00	301
8170087686	**MS-Word 2000 Thumb-Rules and Details**	Snigdha Banerjee	Rs. 175.00	390
8170089239	**Computer Accounting with Tally 7.2**	Firewall Media	Rs. 195.00	330

ON YOUR SIDE SERIES

ISBN	TITLE	AUTHOR	PRICE	PAGES
8170084830	**On your Side-Powerpoint 2002**	Andrew Blackburn	Rs. 145.00	282
8170084849	**On your Side-Excel 2002**	Adrienne Tommy	Rs. 125.00	275
8170084857	**On your Side-Word 2002**	Adrienne Tommy	Rs. 125.00	289
8170084865	**On your Side-Access 2002**	Adrienne Tommy	Rs. 125.00	303
8170084873	**On your Side-Frontpage 2002**	Andrew Blackburn	Rs. 95.00	245
8170084881	**On your Side-Windows XP**	Adrienne Tommy	Rs. 125.00	310

Please write for a free color Firewall Media Catalog for details on the above books.

ISBN	TITLE	AUTHOR	PRICE	PAGES
	OPERATING SYSTEMS			
8170087236	**Linux—A Practical Approach**	B. Mohamed Ibrahim	Rs. 95.00	187
8170088623	**Red Hat Linux Study Guide**	Vijay Shekhar	Rs. 350.00	635
8170088631	**Red Hat Linux-The Complete Bible**	Vijay Shekhar	Rs. 545.00	1176
8170089581	**Unix and Shell Programming**	Archana Verma	Rs. 80.00	137
8170089131	**Operating System Concepts**	P.S. Gill	Rs. 95.00	181
8170083427	**The MS-Windows XP Professional Handbook**	Louis Columbus	Rs. 295.00	330
8170084784	**Way in-Windows XP Home Edition**	Andrew Blackburn	Rs. 95.00	183
8170086221	**Cyber Rookies—Operating System Fundamentals**	D. Irtegov	Rs. 295.00	498
	PROGRAMMING			
8170087791	**The Art of Programming Through Flowcharts & Algorithms**	Anil Bikas Chaudhuri	Rs. 95.00	160
8170086248	**Preventative Programming Techniques: Avoid and Correct Common Mistakes**	Brian Hawkins	Rs. 295.00	322
8170083443	**Learning Computer Programming : It's not about Languages**	Mary Farrell	Rs. 295.00	375
8170086256	**Object-Oriented Programming: From Problem Solving to Java**	José M. Garrido	Rs. 295.00	360
817008931X	**Object-Oriented Programming-Concept and Implementation**	A. Rajesh	Rs. 95.00	182
8170089107	**Java: J2SE-5 A Practical Approach**	B. Mohammad Ibrahim	Rs. 175.00	332
8170089409	**Advance Java**	Gajendra Gupta	Rs. 175.00	305
8170088038	**Assembly Language Programming for Intel Processors Family**	Vasile Lungu	Rs. 295.00	577
8170088178	**The Assembly Programming Master Book**	Vlad Pirogov	Rs. 395.00	726
813180075X	**Java Messaging**	Eric Bruno	Rs. 295.00	480

ISBN	TITLE	AUTHOR	PRICE	PAGES
	PROGRAMMING - C#, C, C++			
8170083702	**The Power of C#**	Rajiv Parida	Rs. 295.00	576
8170085632	**Mastering Graphics Programming in 'C'**	Sudhir Dawra	Rs. 145.00	286
8170088879	**Programming in C and Numerical Analysis**	J.B. Dixit	Rs. 350.00	355
8170087074	**Mastering C Programs**	J.B. Dixit	Rs. 195.00	434
8170081262	**Programming in C**	J.B. Dixit	Rs. 295.00	506
8170087619	**Unix and C Programming**	Ashok Arora, Shefali Bansal	Rs. 295.00	606
817008878X	**C Interview Questions and Answers**	J. Rajaram	Rs. 75.00	139
8170089034	**Pragmatic C**	R.K. Jangda	Rs. 150.00	258
8170086140	**Data Structure for 'C' Programming**	Ajay Kumar	Rs. 145.00	290
8170081270	**Programming in C++**	J.B. Dixit	Rs. 260.00	602
8170088194	**Hackish C++ Pranks & Tricks**	Michael Flenov	Rs. 245.00	326
8170082889	**Basics of C++ Programming**	Nishant Kundalia	Rs. 95.00	168
8170083648	**Mastering C++ Programs**	J.B. Dixit	Rs. 295.00	598
817008623X	**Cyber Rookies—C++ Programming Fundamentals**	Chuck Easttom	Rs. 295.00	417
8131800202	**Data Structure using C++**	N. Jayalakshmi	Rs. 65.00	126
8170089123	**C++ Made Easy**	T.D. Malhotra	Rs. 250.00	449
8131800393	**C++ & Introduction to C#**	T.D. Malhotra, Rajeev A. Parida, A. Rajesh	Rs. 200.00	440
8131800350	**OOPS with C++**	M. Jaya Prasad	Rs. 150.00	317
	SECURITY			
8170083419	**Computer Forensics : Computer Crime Scene Investigation**	John Vacca	Rs. 445.00	731
8131800156	**Computer Evidence (Collection and Preservation)**	Christopher L.T. Brown	Rs. 295.00	394
8170083494	**Firewall Architecture for the Enterprise**	Norbert Pohlmann, Tim Crothers	Rs. 295.00	480
8170086272	**Net Spies**	Andrew Gauntlett	Rs. 195.00	210
3826607546	**Firewall Systems**	Norbert Pohlmann	Rs. 1630.00	544
8131800504	**Homeland Security Techniques and Technologies**	Jesus Mena	Rs. 295.00	346

ISBN	TITLE	AUTHOR	PRICE	PAGES

ENGINEERING AND TECHNOLOGY

ISBN	TITLE	AUTHOR	PRICE	PAGES
817008718X	**Human Aspects of Software Engineering**	James E. Tomayko, Orit Hazzan	Rs. 195.00	338
8131800032	**Management Information Systems**	Avdhesh Gupta, Anurag Malik	Rs. 195.00	400
8170087953	**Human Computer Interaction**	Rajendra Ranjan Kumar	Rs. 95.00	210
8170088097	**Structured System Analysis and Design**	Preeti Gupta	Rs. 125.00	192
817008802X	**Autocad 2005 for Engineers**	Ionel Simion	Rs. 175.00	271
8170088054	**Digital Signal Processing Fundamentals**	Ashfaq A. Khan	Rs. 295.00	391
8131800164	**Digital Communication System Using System VUE**	Dennis Silage	Rs. 295.00	365
8170089719	**Foundations of Computer Science**	Ashok Arora	Rs. 250.00	386
817008363X	**Practical Project Management**	Ivan Bayross	Rs. 195.00	342
8131800806	**Digital Signal Processing using MATLAB and Wavelets**	Michael Weeks	Rs. 350.00	452
8131800792	**Classical Electrodynamics**	Hans C. Dhanian	Rs. 395.00	620
8131800512	**The Software Vulnerability Guide**	Herbert H. Thompson, Scott G. Chase	Rs. 195.00	368
8131800776	**Robot Modelling and Kinematics**	Rachid Manseur	Rs. 295.00	380
8131800369	**System Software**	M. Joseph	Rs. 95.00	185

STRAIGHT TO THE POINT SERIES

ISBN	TITLE	AUTHOR	PRICE	PAGES
8170084601	**STTP : Word 2002**	Corinne Hervo	Rs. 45.00	154
817008461X	**STTP : Excel 2002**	Corinne Hervo	Rs. 45.00	153
8170084628	**STTP : Dreamweaver 4**	Corinne Hervo	Rs. 45.00	135
8170084636	**STTP : Flash 5**	Corinne Hervo	Rs. 45.00	183
8170084644	**STTP : Photoshop 6**	Corinne Hervo	Rs. 45.00	152
817008881X	**STTP : MS Office 2000**	Dinesh Maidasani	Rs. 125.00	290
8170086100	**STTP : MS Office 2003**	Dinesh Maidasani	Rs. 145.00	288
8170087651	**STTP : MS Word 2003**	Firewall Media	Rs. 60.00	150
8170088011	**STTP : Photoshop CS**	Firewall Media	Rs. 60.00	150
8170088143	**STTP : MS Excel 2003**	Firewall Media	Rs. 60.00	150
8170088151	**STTP : CorelDraw 12**	Firewall Media	Rs. 60.00	150
8131800105	**STTP : 3ds MAX 7**	Dinesh Maidasani	Rs. 95.00	182

ISBN	TITLE	AUTHOR	PRICE	PAGES
8131800083	**STTP : Auto CAD 2006**	Dinesh Maidasani	Rs. 95.00	190
8131800245	**STTP : CorelDraw X3**	Dinesh Maidasani	Rs. 75.00	188
8131800253	**STTP : Dreamweaver 8**	Dinesh Maidasani	Rs. 75.00	148
8131800237	**STTP : Photoshop CS2**	Dinesh Maidasani	Rs. 75.00	172
8170088380	**STTP : Tally 7.2**	Firewall Media	Rs. 175.00	322
8131800091	**STTP : Flash 8**	Dinesh Maidasani	Rs. 95.00	180
8131800407	**STTP : My SQL 5.0**	Dinesh Maidasani	Rs. 85.00	166
8131800458	**STTP : Microsoft Power Point 2003**	Dinesh Maidasani	Rs. 75.00	142

STUDIO FACTORY

ISBN	TITLE	AUTHOR	PRICE	PAGES
8170084792	**Studio Factory—Photoshop 6**	Christophe Aubry	Rs. 175.00	364
8170084806	**Studio Factory—Flash 5**	Sami Ben Yahiya	Rs. 145.00	314
8170084814	**Studio Factory—Dreamweaver Ultradev 4**	Phillippe Chatellier	Rs. 95.00	240
8170084822	**Studio Factory—Dreamweaver 4**	Christophe Aubry	Rs. 175.00	373
8170087643	**Studio Factory—Dreamweaver MX**	Christophe Aubry	Rs. 195.00	407
8170087627	**Studio Factory—Flash MX**	Arnaud Blanche	Rs. 145.00	337
817008766X	**Studio Factory—Photoshop 7**	Cyril Guerin	Rs. 195.00	420

LAXMI PUBLICATIONS (P) LTD

113, Golden House, Daryaganj, New Delhi-110002

Phone : **011 - 43 53 25 00**

Fax : **011 - 43 53 25 28**

EMAIL : info@laxmipublications.com

Website : www.laxmipublications.com

BRANCHES

- 129/1, IIIrd Main Road, IX Cross, Chamrajpet, **Bangalore** (*Phone* : 080-26 61 15 61)
- 26, Damodaran Street, T. Nagar, **Chennai** (*Phone* : 044-24 34 47 26)
- 43/1394D, St. Benedict's Road, Ernakulam North, **Cochin** (*Phone* : 0484-239 70 04)
- Pan Bazar, Rani Bari, **Guwahati** (*Phones* : 0361-254 36 69, 251 38 81)
- 4-2-453, Ist Floor, Ramkote, **Hyderabad** (*Phone* : 040-24 75 02 47)
- Adda Tanda Chowk, N.D. 365, **Jalandhar City** (*Phone* : 0181-222 12 72)
- 106/A, Ist Floor, S.N. Banerjee Road, **Kolkata** (*Phones* : 033-22 27 37 73, 22 27 52 47)
- 18, Madan Mohan Malviya Marg, **Lucknow** (*Phone* : 0522-220 95 78)
- 142-C, Victor House, Ground Floor, N.M. Joshi Marg, Lower Parel (W), **Mumbai** (*Phones* : 022-24 91 54 15, 24 92 78 69)
- Radha Govind Street, Tharpagna, **Ranchi** (*Phone* : 0651-230 77 64)